The Metaphysics of Meaning

Representation and Mind
Hilary Putnam and Ned Block, editors

Representation and Reality
Hilary Putnam

Explaining Behavior: Reasons in a World of Causes
Fred Dretske

The Metaphysics of Meaning
Jerrold J. Katz

The Metaphysics of Meaning

Jerrold J. Katz

A Bradford Book
The MIT Press
Cambridge, Massachusetts
London, England

This book was set in Palatino
by Compset, Inc., Beverly, Massachusetts
and printed and bound in the United States of America.

Library of Congress Cataloging-in-Publication Data

Katz, Jerrold J.
    The metaphysics of meaning / Jerrold J. Katz.
        p.   cm.
    "A Bradford book."
    Includes bibliographical references.
    ISBN 0-262-11151-9
    1. Languages—Philosophy.   I. Title.
P106.K2995   1990
149'.94—dc20   90-34173
                                                                      CIP

Contents

Preface   vii

Acknowledgments   xiii

1
Introduction   1

2
Wittgenstein's Critique of Theories of Meaning   21

3
Wittgenstein on Rule Following   135

4
Kripke on Rule Following   163

5
Quine's Arguments against Intensionalist Semantics   175
Appendix: Quine's Replies   199

6
The Domino Theory   203

7
The Naturalistic Fallacy   235
Appendix: On Ethics   281

8
Conclusion: The Problems of Philosophy   291

Notes   321

Index   353

This book is dedicated to Rose H. and Bernard E. Sherman

Preface

In the following passage, Kripke expresses a tension felt by many philosophers:

> . . . I find myself torn between two conflicting feelings—a 'Chomskyan' feeling that deep regularities in natural language must be discoverable by an appropriate combination of formal, empirical, and intuitive techniques, and a contrary (late) 'Wittgensteinian' feeling that many of the 'deep structures', 'logical forms', 'underlying semantics' and 'ontological commitments', etc., which philosophers have claimed to discover by such techniques are *Luftgebäude*.[1]

When we consider what is sacrificed in resolving this conflict either way, we can see that Kripke is posing a dilemma of the utmost significance for contemporary philosophy.

Chomsky appeals to our scientific side. As citizens of this century, we can hardly doubt that natural languages are a fit subject of scientific study, and nowadays the Chomskyan approach, in broad outline, is virtually "synonymous" with scientific linguistics.[2] This approach holds out the prospect of theories that reveal deep principles about the structure of particular natural languages and of language in general, the precision of formalization that has been of such importance to the development of logic and mathematics, the security of having scientific methodology available to us in the study of language, and, finally, interdisciplinary connections that promise new insights into logical form and into some of the higher cognitive functions of the human mind.

The late Wittgenstein appeals to our philosophical side. As philosophers in this century, we can hardly think that empirical science will solve the philosophical problems with which Frege, Russell, Wittgenstein, and their descendants have struggled, and the Wittgensteinian approach seems to provide the only account of why empirical discoveries in psychology and the brain sciences do not come to grips with those problems. Moreover, when Chomskyan linguistics itself is looked at philosophically, as it has been from time to time, it seems clear that those problems remain despite the considerable scientific progress that has been made in linguistics proper. It is even quite plausible to think that the problems become worse for being obscured by philosophically unilluminating formalisms and technicalities. Furthermore, linguistic theories, with "deep structures," "logical forms," "underlying semantics," and all the other paraphernalia of the Chomskyan approach, in major respects seem to be refurbishments of Frege's semantics and Wittgenstein's early philosophy which, despite the technical sophistication, embody their central metaphysical assumptions. The Chomskyan approach thus seems to reflect a failure to have learned the lessons of the Wittgensteinian critique of metaphysics in *Philosophical Investigations*. In contrast, the late Wittgenstein, whether or not he succeeded in dissolving philosophical problems or was even on the right track, at least engages them in a deep enough way to make it clear that philosophical progress requires subsequent philosophers to work through his investigations of them.

Philosophers, faced with the choice between the two sides of their nature, behave in very different ways. Some find it easy to make the choice, but they do not, I believe, fully appreciate the sacrifice they are making, or perhaps they mistakenly think that some rapprochement can be found between the Chomskyan and the (late) Wittgensteinian approaches. Many philosophers feel themselves torn, and vacillate. Most choose either the Chomskyan approach or the (late) Wittgensteinian, but feel they have lost something, and continue to recognize advantages in the other approach.

In another context, Frank Ramsey once wrote:

> Evidently, however, none of these arguments are really decisive, and the position is extremely unsatisfactory to anyone with real curiosity about such a fundamental question. In such cases it is a heuristic maxim that the truth lies not in one of the two disputed views but in some third possibility which has not yet been thought of, which we can only discover by rejecting something assumed as obvious by both the disputants.[3]

I believe that Ramsey's maxim is sound in the present context, too. In this book, I argue that the truth lies not in either the Chomskyan or the Wittgensteinian view but in a "third possibility" that emerges only when "something assumed as obvious by both the disputants" is rejected. Thus, I argue that the dilemma is a false one: it is unnecessary to sacrifice either an appropriately scientific approach to natural language or an appropriately philosophical approach to the problems of philosophy. The unsatisfactory alternatives to which the dilemma limits us seem to be the only alternatives we have because of an assumption which restricts our options. This assumption, which seems obvious to Chomskyans and (late) Wittgensteinians, as well as to most of contemporary Anglo-American philosophy, and which, for this reason, goes largely unnoticed, is that the proper approach to natural language is naturalistic.

Later, particularly in chapter 7, I shall say more precisely what I think naturalism is. Here I need only say that, as I am using the term, naturalism covers a wide variety of views all of which, in one way or another, claim that natural history, broadly construed to include our natural history, contains all the facts there are. In standard philosophical terminology, naturalism is a monism which claims that everything that exists in the world is a natural phenomenon in the sense of having a place in the causal nexus of spatio-temporal objects and events. Chomsky has frequently expressed this naturalistic outlook with respect to language; for example, he writes: ". . . mentally represented grammar and UG [universal grammar] are real objects, part of the physical world. . . . Statements about particular grammars or about UG are true or false statements about steady states attained or the initial state (assumed fixed for the species), each of which is a definite real-world object, situated in space-time and entering into causal relations."[4] Wittgenstein expresses his naturalistic outlook in various places, for example, in his claim that what we should say about mathematical proof is that "this is simply what we *do*. This is use and custom among us, or a fact of our natural history."[5]

Questioning naturalism opens up the possibility of going between the horns of the dilemma. In the course of this book I shall argue that we should give up a naturalistic conception of language. I try to show that this is not as hard as it might at first seem nowadays, because the arguments for a naturalistic conception of language turn out not to hold up, and, independently, there are good reasons against adopting such a conception. I shall also present a non-naturalistic account of language which provides a way out of the dilemma, enabling us to enjoy both the scientific advantages of the Chomskyan approach and the philosophical relevance of the (late) Wittgensteinian approach.

The issues here go deeper than the study of language. With the linguistic focus of philosophy in this century, the naturalistic conception of language led straightforwardly to a naturalistic conception of philosophy itself. The fundamental issue with which the present work is concerned is the metaphilosophical question of the adequacy of the naturalistic picture of language and of philosophy which emerged in the course of the so-called linguistic turn.

Wittgenstein, Chomsky, Quine, Goodman, Davidson, Putnam, and their followers have made naturalism the dominant philosophy of our time. Though one certainly sees, here and there, philosophers who have broken ranks, or perhaps were never in ranks, that is, philosophers who take a genuinely non-naturalist—i.e., realist—view of properties and relations, even those philosophers adopt such a view of properties and relations in the context of work on particular problems in the philosophy of language, logic, and mathematics. There has not yet been a comprehensive philosophical examination of the reemergence of naturalism in the twentieth century and the special forms it has taken. What is lacking is a rationale, suitable for the present philosophical situation, which can provide the foundations for appeals to non-natural objects in philosophy.

The current influence of naturalism is so strong that it is worthwhile reminding ourselves that naturalism was not always as widely accepted in this century as it is today. Earlier, the philosophy of logic and mathematics, under Frege's influence, and ethics, under G. E. Moore's, had a distinctively non-naturalistic cast. The subsequent success of naturalism in these areas depended on particular arguments about meaning and language, given primarily by Wittgenstein and Quine. Their arguments led twentieth-century Anglo-American philosophy into naturalism, and, accordingly, only a successful critique of those arguments can permit us to find a way out.

In this book I have tried to give such a critique. The critique is a two-part affair. In the first part I concentrate on the architects of contemporary naturalism, Wittgenstein and Quine, examining their arguments in a detailed, systematic, and comprehensive manner. I believe I have shown that their arguments are inadequate to support naturalism. In the second part of the critique I try to identify the underlying problem in the naturalist position. On my account, the problem arises from the paradoxical use of philosophical means to establish a position on which such means would not exist. However, I do not claim to have accomplished everything necessary in order to establish non-naturalism. Indeed, the present book is only a prolegomenon to a future non-naturalism: its aims are limited to vindication and exploration.

I have already said enough about vindication: success here should be measured by the effectiveness of the critique of the Chomskyan, late Wittgensteinian, and Quinean approaches, together with the formulation of arguments for an alternative non-naturalist approach that sacrifices neither the advantages of scientific investigation into language nor such things as Wittgenstein's insights into the problems with Frege's, Russell's, and his own early position. The book's exploratory aim concerns the metaphilosophical question of the scope of naturalism and non-naturalism. That naturalism does not extend to sciences like linguistics, logic, and mathematics will, I hope, be clear from the main line of argument.

But what can be said about areas like ethics and metaphysics, where things are more obscure than they are in the formal sciences? Gödel, apparently, was prepared to take realism even as far as theology.[6] However, to make a philosophically convincing case, one has to carry out an investigation to determine whether, for unclear cases like ethics and metaphysics, there actually is a route from a non-naturalistic treatment of logic and mathematics to such a treatment of those other disciplines. The question of how far the realist view in logic and mathematics can be extended—that is, how general a conception of realism we can have—is answered satisfactorily only by painstakingly charting the philosophical terrain.

From this perspective, the present book's concern with language puts it in an ideal position to begin charting the terrain. Linguistics has many strong similarities to logic and mathematics; for example, linguistics seems to be a formal science, to have necessary truths (i.e., truths expressed in analytic sentences) in its domain, and to justify its laws on the basis of intuition. Furthermore, a formulation of the realist position for linguistics already exists.[7] Thus, the question of whether the realist view can be extended to areas like ethics should become easier to deal with if we already have an example of how the view can be extended to an area *prima facie* closer to logic and mathematics, but not too close. The example can tell us what relations must obtain if realism is to be taken to cover this area despite the respects in which the area differs from logic and mathematics, e.g., the fact that proof plays a much smaller role. It may even enable us to infer the conditions for extension to another area, even though it may be very hard to determine whether those conditions are met in particular cases.

Acknowledgments

I want to thank the students in my courses at the CUNY Graduate Center over the last several years for making examination of the issues dealt with in this book a stimulating and enjoyable experience. Also, I want to express my gratitude to a number of people with whom I have had helpful discussion or communication in the course of the writing. It is a pleasure to thank Rogers Albritton, Jawad Azzouni, George Bealer, Alan Berger, Ned Block, Martin Brown, William Fisk, Paul Horwich, Mark Johnston, Peter Lupu, Sidney Morgenbesser, Yuji Nishiyama, Gary Ostertag, Charles Parsons, David Pitt, Paul Postal, David Rosenthal, Stephen Schiffer, Robert Tragesser, Peter Unger, Virginia Valian, Hao Wang, Stephen Yalowitz, and Palle Yourgrau.

Special thanks go to Leigh Cauman and David Pitt. My debt to them is great. Leigh did an excellent job of copy editing. She also contributed to the clarity of the exposition and made an inherently tedious and worrisome stage of production pleasant and free of care. David helped me prepare the manuscript for submission, checked proofs with me, and compiled the index. David not only performed these duties skillfully, but his suggestions and questions led to many improvements in both style and content. The intelligence and good humor of both Leigh and David made my production tasks tolerable and, quite often, fun. I hope they know how fortunate I feel to have had their assistance.

Finally, thanks to the people at the MIT Press—Betty Stanton, Helen Osborne, Joanna Poole, Brooke Stevens, and Sandra Minkkinen—for their efficiency and cheerfulness throughout.

The Metaphysics of Meaning

1
Introduction

More than any other philosopher of the century, Wittgenstein was responsible for its celebrated linguistic turn. In his hands the linguistic turn became a powerful new form of critical philosophy which sought to eliminate metaphysics rather than reconstruct it. Unlike Kant's reformist critical philosophy, which aimed as much to provide a solid foundation for large parts of traditional metaphysics as to expose improperly formulated metaphysical questions, Wittgenstein's radical critical philosophy aimed at exposing all metaphysical questions as improperly formulated. Kant is like the liberal who is trying to improve the political system from within; Wittgenstein is like the revolutionary who is trying to bring it down.

Frege provided many of the essential ideas for the linguistic turn, particularly in its earliest phases. He introduced—or provided influential formulations of—such ideas as that certain philosophical problems are pseudo-problems arising from imperfections of natural language, that such problems can be solved by constructing an ideal language to replace natural language for the purpose of precise reasoning, and that the construction of the ideal language can be based on technical notions from within logic. Frege supplied something of a blueprint for an ideal language in his *Begriffsschrift*, as well as many of its technical notions, including that of a logical function, quantifiers, the functional calculus, the sense/reference distinction, and the grammatical form/logical form distinction.

But at heart Frege was a traditional philosopher, highly sympathetic to Kant's metaphysics and a staunch Platonist in the philosophy of logic and mathematics. Frege would have been the last person to use his ideas to launch a critique of metaphysics designed to refute its claim to provide genuine knowledge of the most abstract aspects of reality. Like Leibniz before him, Frege saw his logico-linguistic ideas as in the service of the metaphysical enterprise, as helping it to make good on some of its traditional claims.

The early Wittgenstein saw Frege's ideas in a quite different light. Wittgenstein saw Frege's work, together with the work of Whitehead and Russell, as the logico-linguistic basis for a throughgoing critique that would expose the pretensions of metaphysical philosophy to a knowledge of reality not obtainable from the study of nature.[1] This critique of metaphysics would use such logico-linguistic ideas to show that metaphysical language as a whole is without meaning. Nothing in his early philosophy better sums up all the essential elements in this critique—its linguistic form, its implacable hostility to metaphysics, and its underlying naturalistic perspective—than Wittgenstein's penultimate comment on one of the *Tractatus*'s principal theses: "The right method of philosophy would be this: To say nothing except what can be said, i.e., the propositions of natural science, i.e., something that has nothing to do with philosophy: and then always, when someone else wished to say something metaphysical, to demonstrate to him that he had given no meaning to certain signs in his propositions."[2]

This quotation comments on the thesis that the general form of a proposition is a truth function of elementary propositions. This thesis derives from the theory of propositional structure in Frege's *Begriffsschrift* and Whitehead and Russell's *Principia Mathematica*.[3] That theory provided Wittgenstein with a basis for working out "the right method of philosophy," that is, for charting the limits of meaningful language and showing that metaphysical sentences are literally nonsense because they go beyond those limits. Applying Frege's and Russell's conception of the conditions for factual assertion to sentences of natural language, Wittgenstein sought in the *Tractatus* to specify the principles in accord with which factual sentences of natural science and everyday life receive a meaning while metaphysical sentences do not. Applying Frege's grammatical form/logical form distinction, he tried to explain how, in virtue of resembling factual sentences in overt grammatical form, metaphysical sentences can mislead us into thinking that they too inform us about how things are. But metaphysical sentences only give the appearance of making assertions; they do not actually do so, because they do not picture reality. Once we appreciate how metaphysical sentences differ from factual sentences with respect to logical form, we will recognize the boundary within which we can speak sensibly, beyond which we must remain silent.

The transition from the *Tractatus* with its "right method of philosophy" to the *Philosophical Investigations* with its denial of a single right method and its insistence on many methods ("like different therapies") was brought about by profound changes in Wittgenstein's thinking, many of them rejections of Fregean elements in his early philosophy.[4] Wittgenstein abandoned Frege's theory of meaning with senses as objective presentations of reality and its truth-functional conception of the form of propositions, Frege's idea of logical form as something hidden beneath the grammatical surface of sentences, together with its associated idea of analysis as revealing underlying logical form, and, finally, Frege's conception of a logically perfect language as a calculus with fixed rules, embodying the logician's ideal of complete precision.

[handwritten margin note: w. abandoned this]

But two of the principal ideas of Wittgenstein's early philosophy survive to become principal ideas of his late philosophy. One is the leading idea of the early critical philosophy, the thesis that metaphysical sentences are nonsense because they transcend the limits of language. As a consequence of Wittgenstein's abandoning of the *Tractatus*, which provided the framework within which it has been originally formulated, the thesis had to be drastically reformulated. But, reformulated in the newly created framework, it becomes the leading idea of the late critical philosophy. The key notions of the thesis: 'meaning', 'limits of language', and 'transcend', are fleshed out in a very different way. Languages are conceived of as gamelike activities in which participants use signs in accordance with rules, analogous to rules of chess and other social practices, themselves part of more general "forms of life." Meaning, on this approach, is not something to be sought beneath the surface grammar of signs—in, as it were, the logical microstructure of sentences—but is out in the open, in the public use of signs. Techniques of applying words in everyday affairs, based on a mastery of their use in the community, replace the formal rules of a Fregean calculus as the determiners of meaning. Everyday language, contrary to Frege, is perfectly all right as it is (PI: 120–124). Accordingly, its everyday functioning sets the limits of language. Transcending the limits is now a matter of departing from ordinary use in ways that outstrip our practices and thereby go beyond the possibilities for meaningful application contained in the rules (PI: 116–119). Thus, in spite of all the differences between the *Philosophical Investigations* and the *Tractatus*, the sentences of metaphysics are still simply "one or another piece of plain nonsense," and the work of philosophy is still to prevent "bumps that the understanding has got by running its head up against the limits of language" (PI: 119).

The other principal idea to survive from Wittgenstein's early philosophy is the idea that "what can be said" are "the propositions of natural science," although this idea, too, undergoes reformulation, specifically by using the notion of natural science in conjunction with the broader notion of natural history and by adding the therapeutic device of imagining possible natural histories. Wittgenstein writes: "What we are supplying are really remarks on the natural history of human beings; we are not contributing curiosities however, but observations which no one has doubted, but which have escaped remark only because they are always before our eyes." (PI: 415) This idea that significant expression concerns the natural world is, of course, connected with the idea that metaphysical sentences are non-sense. The former idea makes it possible to identify metaphysical claims about a reality beyond the natural world, e.g., about abstract objects and essences, as what cannot be said. Thus, the Tractatus's equation of the contrast between sense and nonsense with the contrast between the natural and the transcendent remains in the Philosophical Investigations. Wittgenstein's point is still that there are no non-natural, metaphysical facts. He writes:

> Why shouldn't I apply words in ways that conflict with their original usage? Doesn't Freud, for example, do this when he calls even an anxiety dream a wish-fulfilment dream? Where is the difference? In a scientific perspective a new use is justified by a *theory*. And if this theory is false, the new extended use has to be given up. But in philosophy the extended use does not rest on true or false beliefs about natural processes. No fact justifies it. None can give it any support. (C&V: p. 44e)

The Tractatus's use of natural science and the Philosophical Investigations's use of natural history are supplemented in the context of the latter book's therapeutic orientation. In part II, section xii, Wittgenstein explains why his philosophical investigations are not simply natural science or natural history. If the focus of the investigations were exclusively on the "causes of the formation of concepts," they would be, but the focus is also on the invention of "fictitious natural history for our purposes" (PI: xii). The purposes are therapeutic, namely, to show people in the grip of a metaphysical concept of how things must be that "certain very general facts of nature" might be different and, thereby, to show them that other concepts of how those things are are "intelligible" (PI: xii). This explanation in no way undercuts the naturalistic outlook common to the Tractatus and the Philosophical Investigations.

From the perspective of the Philosophical Investigations, the Tractatus stands accused of many of the sins of which it accuses metaphysics. The old critical philosophy is seen as deeply incoherent because the Tractatus expresses the claim that metaphysics sins against language metaphysically, and, consequently, it is subject to its own charge of being nonsense. The Tractatus goes beyond the limits of language (in the new sense) because it employs Frege's and Russell's theoretical conception of meaning and language, and much of the metaphysics that goes with it. The *Tractatus* assumes that the possibilities of meaning lie hidden in the essence of language, in the general form of its propositions. Propositions are senses, logical bodies of sentences lying beneath and disguised by their grammatical clothing. Given that it is thus necessary to penetrate beneath words to the meanings they disguise, the *Tractatus* is deeply committed to a logical theory that pictures the hidden meanings and unifies the elements of the picture into a conception of the general form of language. Such a theory, not being a piece of natural science, must be a piece of metaphysics.

The role of logical theory in philosophy is thus seen, in some significant respects, as like that of theory in science: it takes us to places that observation cannot reach and provides us with the understanding essential to solving—or, in this case, dissolving—problems. On the new critical philosophy, however, theories are no longer an essential part of the solution; they are rather an essential part of the problem. Philosophical theories, especially those dealing with the essence of language, such as Frege's and Russell's, put us in the grip of a picture of how things must be: "'But *this* is how it is —' I say to myself over and over again. I feel as though, if only I could fix my gaze absolutely sharply on this fact, get it in focus, I must grasp the essence of the matter." (PI: 113) We are entrapped in philosophical problems because the pictures that our theories present keep us from seeing how things actually are: "One thinks that one is tracing the outline of the thing's nature over and over again, and one is merely tracing round the frame through which we look at it." (PI: 114)

The first part of *Philosophical Investigations* is a sustained critique of philosophical theories of meaning. It is designed to expose the role of theories in philosophical perplexities about language and to replace the picture they present of meanings as objects with a conception of meaning in terms of use (PI: 120). This critique is the means by which Wittgenstein replaces the traditional view of philosophy as a search for abstract essences with his new view of philosophy as dissolving philosophical problems by showing how they arise as the result of misuses which get us lost in the maze of our own rules (PI: 123). As Wittgenstein puts it at one place, "The fundamental fact here is that we lay down rules, a technique, for a game, and that then when we follow the rules, things do not turn out as we had assumed. That we are therefore as it were entangled in our own rules." (PI: 125) The crux of the new critical philosophy is that proper methods of philosophy enable us to see such entanglements clearly enough to extricate ourselves from them: "Philosophy simply puts everything before us, and neither explains nor deduces anything.—Since everything lies open to view there is nothing to explain. For what is hidden, for example, is of no interest to us." (PI: 126) The new critical philosophy thus leaves no room for metaphysics. Philosophical method is entirely therapeutic (PI: 133). The critical philosophy of the *Tractatus* had left room for metaphysics in its various Fregean and Russellian doctrines about propositions, logic, and language. Such philosophical doctrines themselves go beyond the propositions of natural science and natural history, and, for this reason, are, at bottom, paradoxical. The late philosophy thus achieves a consistent formulation of Wittgenstein's critical thesis that the sentences of metaphysics, which assert nothing about the natural realm, have no meaning.

Wittgenstein's new critical philosophy expresses the most radical challenge to metaphysics in the history of Western philosophy. It calls into question the basic conception of philosophy in the Western tradition from Socrates to Frege, Russell, Moore, and Husserl. On this challenge, philosophers are mistaken to think they can grasp essences, or understand the most abstract aspects of reality, or discover the general foundations of the sciences, or provide a metaphysical explanation of how we can have the knowledge we suppose ourselves to have. If Wittgenstein is correct, metaphysics must disappear completely. Compared to this critical challenge, Kant's critical philosophy, which sought merely to restrict metaphysics to matters within its reach, is simply business as usual.

2

Wittgenstein's critique of theories of meaning plays the same pivotal role in his later philosophy that Descartes's proof of the *Sum* played in his new epistemological foundations.[5] If successful, Wittgenstein's critique would provide a fixed point that enables him to move the philosophical world away from its traditional concern with trying to answer metaphysical questions to a therapeutic concern with trying to cure us of asking them. Instead of seeking to discover the most abstract aspects of reality in an attempt to solve philosophical problems, philosophers would seek "*complete* clarity" in an attempt to make "philosophical problems . . . *completely* disappear" (PI: 133). For Descartes to be successful in laying his new epistemological foundations, he had to show how to eliminate *all* doubts about his own existence. For Wittgenstein to be successful in his radical critical purpose, he has to show how to eliminate *all* theories of meaning on which metaphysical questions are meaningful.

The initial question I shall examine in this book is: Does Wittgenstein succeed? Do his arguments in the *Philosophical Investigations* sweep the boards clear of every theory of meaning that gives the traditional conception of philosophy a semantic foothold? This is the primary question about Wittgenstein's late philosophy. The reason is clear: Wittgenstein's arguments against theories of meaning in the first part of *Philosophical Investigations* pave the way for everything he says about philosophy, mind, logic, and mathematics in later parts of the book and in other places like *Remarks on the Foundations of Mathematics*. His doctrines about philosophy, mind, logic, and mathematics are largely applications of the account of meaning with which he replaces theories of meaning.

Yet, despite all the attention paid to his late philosophy, so far there has been no sustained, systematic examination of Wittgenstein's arguments against theories of meaning which, on the one hand, interprets them carefully and responsibly, and on the other, judges them by a sufficiently high standard of evaluation.[6] By this I mean that, just as Descartes's arguments had to overcome *every* doubt about his existence, so Wittgenstein's have to refute *every* theory of meaning that could block his challenge to traditional philosophy. Chapters 2 and 3 of this book and, in a certain sense, chapter 4, examine Wittgenstein's critique of theoretical conceptions of meaning using this standard. I have based this examination on a careful reading of the text and have tried to be informed by the best contemporary scholarship and to put the question of adequate interpretation first. Still, my examination proceeds from a commitment to a theory of meaning and a conception of philosophy diametrically opposed to Wittgenstein's. But, given the need to impose a sufficiently high standard of evaluation, this is an advantage. A partisan examination is uniquely suited to subjecting Wittgenstein's arguments to the severest test. As noted above, Wittgenstein's own philosophical aims require us to judge his arguments by whether they refute *all* theories of meaning. In this respect, the theory of meaning to which I am committed is ideally suited for the job of evaluation. First, the theory defines the limits of language in a way that allows metaphysical sentences to be meaningful; hence, it provides semantic grounds for metaphysics. Second, the theory differs, in important ways, from the theories Wittgenstein explicitly considered when he fashioned his critique of theories of meaning; hence, it optimizes the chances of revealing any limitation in the scope of his arguments.

Chapter 2 argues that there are such limitations. They have not come to light before because Wittgenstein's arguments work so well against the theories for which Wittgenstein designed them. But Wittgenstein's way of structuring his overall critique of theories of meaning mistakenly supposes that the range of the theories encompassed in the critique includes all those which must, considering his ultimate philosophical aims, be included. Wittgenstein supposed, not without some justification, that Frege's theory, Russell's theory, his own *Tractatus* theory, and certain similar theories—"Begriffsschrift theories," as I shall call them—are fully representative of the theories of meaning that could be put forth to ground traditional metaphysics.[7] On this supposition, he designed his arguments to undercut such theories at fundamental points. Since his arguments are, for the most part, effective in this, once this supposition is granted, the overall critique of theories of meaning is fully convincing. But there is no need to grant this supposition. Unlike other criticisms of Wittgenstein's arguments which try to defend Frege's theory or one of the other theories that Wittgenstein was explicitly addressing, my criticism calls this supposition into question and tries to prove it false by exhibiting a significant restriction of the range of theories for which the critique works.

My examination of Wittgenstein's critique reaches four principal conclusions:

I. Wittgenstein's circumscription of theories of meaning is too narrow; hence, his critique of theories of meaning, though successful in the particular cases of the theories against which he directs his arguments in the *Philosophical Investigations,* is unsuccessful in the general case. The critique does not eliminate all theoretical conceptions of meaning. We can exhibit the type of theory against which it fails.

II. Wittgenstein's paradox about rule following, which is an extension of his earlier arguments against semantic theorists, depends upon the general success of his critique of theories of meaning.

III. The paradox about rule following can be shown not to arise in connection with the type of theory that was shown, in connection with conclusion I, to survive the earlier arguments. Hence, it can be resolved without adopting Wittgenstein's account of meaning and rule following.

IV. Wittgenstein does not succeed in making his case against the traditional metaphysical view of philosophy and in favor of his own therapeutic view.

In formulating my argument for conclusion I, I have adopted the following strategy. I simultaneously pursue two lines of development, one starting at the beginning of *Philosophical Investigations* and running through each of its arguments against theories of meaning, the other starting with certain familiar and intuitively clear facts about the meaning of expressions in natural language and, step by step, working from them to a theory of meaning substantially different from Begriffsschrift theories. The idea behind the strategy is this. I focus on the points where these two lines of development intersect, that is, where one of Wittgenstein's arguments challenges a step in the construction of the theory. I try to show, at every such point, either that the argument at that point is inapplicable, say, because of some significant difference between the theory in question and Begriffsschrift theories, or that the argument is inadequate, say, because of some inherent difficulty. If the second line of development is not blocked at any point, the theory that emerges from it escapes Wittgenstein's critique.

My argument for conclusion II shows how Wittgenstein's arguments against theories of meaning prior to his statement of the paradox about rule following enter essentially into the paradox. The argument for conclusion III shows how the failure of the prior arguments blocks the paradox. It proceeds in two stages, the first directed to Wittgenstein's own discussion of the paradox and the second to Kripke's. In the first, I explain why the theory of meaning previously shown to survive Wittgenstein's critique resolves Wittgenstein's version of the paradox, and, in the second, I explain why that theory also resolves Kripke's version. By proceeding in this way, I steer clear of taking a position on the controversial (and, in the present context, tangential) issue of whether Kripke's Wittgenstein is Wittgenstein.[8] In the course of both these stages, I hope to explain how the theory enables us to formulate an un-Wittgensteinian but nonetheless unparadoxical account of following a rule.

My argument for conclusion IV derives from my arguments for conclusions I–III. Wittgenstein's argument for his therapeutic view of philosophy involves three major steps: eliminating theoretical conceptions of meaning, putting his notion of use in their place, and, on the basis of that notion, showing that metaphysical sentences are a form of nonsense which arises when words are taken too far from their "original home" in everyday use (PI: 116). If Wittgenstein has not succeeded in putting his own notion of use in the place of theoretical conceptions of meaning because one of these conceptions survives his criticisms, then there is a theoretical basis on which metaphysical sentences can be meaningful, and he has not made a case for his therapeutic view of philosophy.

3

In this and the next section, I want to indicate how this line of argument against Wittgenstein fits into the broader anti-naturalist line of argument in the book as a whole.

Wittgenstein's critique of theories of meaning has been and still is a significant force behind the revival of naturalism in Anglo-American philosophy during this century. America, of course, had its own naturalist philosophers. Although they contributed importantly to the tradition of naturalism in American philosophy, they did so more by way of entrenching and articulating the naturalist position than by way of providing major arguments that, like many of Wittgenstein's, significantly strengthen the contemporary naturalist's arsenal. Thus the arguments of American naturalists today, e.g., those of Quine, Goodman, and Putnam, are, in general, of a linguistic cast and, even in some matters of detail, are more like Wittgenstein's arguments than like those of Santayana, Woodbridge, Dewey, and Ernest Nagel. This, I think, is no accident. We can trace a line of development from Wittgenstein to philosophers like Schlick and Carnap and from them to philosophers like Quine and from them and Quine to philosophers like Goodman and Putnam.

As we have seen, the *Tractatus* took the naturalistic view that what can be said can be said in the propositions of natural science. Logical Positivists like Schlick were deeply influenced by both the naturalistic outlook and the logico-linguistic form of Wittgenstein's early thought. They opposed the claims of philosophers that there are things outside the causal nexus which are, as a consequence, beyond the reach of the empirical methods of natural science.[9] Such Logical Positivists made use of Wittgenstein's ideas to argue against the claims of philosophers like Husserl that our logical, mathematical, and metaphysical knowledge is about non-natural objects and rests on a faculty of intuition. The aim of Logical Positivism can, in large part, be seen as a use of Frege's, Russell's, and Wittgenstein's contributions to logic and the philosophy of logic to modernize Hume's naturalism and empiricism. Hume's vague remarks about relations of ideas were to be explicated on the basis of such logical and philosophical contributions. His equally vague characterization of matters of fact was to be explicated on the basis of the criterion of empirical significance which the Positivists set themselves the task of framing with the new technical apparatus from logic.[10]

As later Logical Positivism became more Fregean in the hands of Frege's student Carnap, e.g., in becoming more accommodating to rationalist doctrines about abstract entities and necessary truth, Wittgenstein began to move away from the early position that had been so influential with the Vienna Circle and began to rid his thinking of all Fregean elements. In certain respects Wittgenstein's thinking was becoming more naturalistic in a sense akin to Hume,[11] but, more significantly, it was taking the very novel linguistic direction already described. Around the same time, Quine's thinking, initially much stimulated by the ideas of Carnap and other Logical Positivists, was becoming critical of certain of those ideas, especially of meanings as abstract entities and analytically necessary truth. Quine, too, began to move in the direction of Humean Empiricism and to rid his thinking of all Fregean elements. As early as 1951, Quine wrote:

> Once the theory of meaning is sharply separated from the theory of reference, it is a short step to recognizing as the business of the theory of meaning simply the synonymy of expressions, the meaningfulness of expressions, and the analyticity or entailment of statements; meanings themselves, as obscure intermediate entities may well be abandoned. This is the step that Frege did not take . . . there is great difficulty in tying this well-knit group of concepts down to terms that we really understand. The theory of meaning, even with the elimination of the mysterious meant entities, strikes me as in a comparable state to theology.[12]

Wittgenstein and Quine faced much the same problem of removing the vestiges of non-naturalist metaphysics from earlier philosophical thinking. They solved it in different ways. Their different solutions provide the two different forms of naturalism in contemporary philosophy.

Logical Empiricists like Carnap allow non-natural semantic entities and logical knowledge irreducible to experience. They even allow the metaphysical principle that significant truths divide exhaustively into those expressing relations of ideas and those expressing matters of empirical fact, a principle which is itself semantically questionable in that it expresses neither a relation of ideas nor an empirical matter of fact. Frege, of course, insisted on semantic realism and synthetic *a priori* knowledge. Wittgenstein's rejection of non-natural entities and non-natural knowledge was accomplished by a reformulation of his radical critical philosophy in terms of a new conception of language and meaning which provides an uncompromising treatment of metaphysical sentences as nonsense.

Quine, unlike Wittgenstein, is not a critical philosopher. His rejection of such entities and such logical knowledge was accomplished by fashioning a naturalism on the model of the uncompromising empiricism of J. S. Mill, upgraded with the addition of a conception of the structure of knowledge which seemed to Quine to account better for the certainty of logic and mathematics. Quine treats philosophical investigation not as therapy but as naturalized epistemology, as natural science reflecting on itself. For Quine, a metaphysical principle is not *ipso facto* nonsense; it may be either a scientifically efficacious myth like the posit of physical objects or a scientifically impotent myth like that of Homer's gods.[13]

The tenor of Quine's naturalism is very well conveyed in this passage:

> . . . we see all of science—physics, biology, economics, mathematics, logic, and the rest—as a single sprawling system, loosely connected in some portions but disconnected nowhere. Parts of it—logic, arithmetic, game theory, theoretical parts of physics—are farther from the observational or experimental edge than other parts. But the overall system, with all its parts, derives its aggregate empirical content from that edge; and the theoretical parts are good only as they contribute in their varying degrees of indirectness to the systematizing of that content.
>
> In principle, therefore, I see no higher or more austere necessity than natural necessity; and in natural necessity, or our attributions of it, I see only Hume's regularities, culminating here and there in what passes for an explanatory trait or the promise of it.[14]

All knowledge is continuous with the paradigmatic natural sciences of physics, chemistry, and biology. The truths of logic and mathematics have a greater degree of certainty than those of other disciplines not because, as the non-naturalist thinks, they are about objects outside the causal nexus and known in a different way, but because logic and mathematics occupy a more central position in our overall system of beliefs. The revision of logical or mathematical statements disturbs the system as a whole far more than revision of statements in physics, chemistry, or biology, which lie closer to its observational or experimental edge. The greater support that the former statements give to and receive from other statements—in virtue of their central position in the system—accounts for their greater certainty.

In some respects, Quine's naturalistic message is similar to Wittgenstein's. Quine's target, too, is the intensionalist tradition in the philosophy of logic and language stemming from Frege. Quine's concern with Carnap was largely a concern with certain of Frege's views which survive in Carnap's semantic doctrines. In particular, Quine's criticisms of Carnap were directed against Carnap's use of analyticity to fashion an empiricism that compromises with rationalism by conceding a place to a priori knowledge. Quine's motivation here, like Wittgenstein's in some places, is to avoid what he takes to be the philosophical confusion that results from countenancing "mysterious"—i.e., non-natural—entities, particularly Fregean senses and propositions.

Furthermore, Quine and Wittgenstein see language as the philosopher's basic concern, and, accordingly, both have an extremely broad view of the linguistic. Its sphere is sufficiently broad for language to encompass all the areas of philosophical concern. Quine and Wittgenstein both conceive of language as a social art. Quine is sympathetic to Wittgenstein's injunction that philosophers should confine themselves to what lies open to public view. To be sure, Quine does not share Wittgenstein's aversion to theories, but sees the injunction as stemming from the desirability of objective or behavioristic constraints on them. Both think there are no language-independent meanings. Quine takes meaningfulness as relative to a language system and its cultural matrix just as Wittgenstein takes it as relative to a system of linguistic techniques and practices and its supporting form of life. Finally, both are foes of absolute necessity. Quine, too, eschews any hope of truths "given once and for all; and independently of any future experience" (PI: 92). Even truths of logic and mathematics are open to revision in the light of future experience.[15]

But in other respects Quine differs sharply from the late Wittgenstein. Although Quine shares Wittgenstein's antipathy for Frege's philosophy, he does not share Wittgenstein's antipathy for Russell's. Russell's logical approach to philosophy can be seen as model for Quine's.[16] Whereas the Wittgensteinian form of naturalism abandons the ideal of an logically perfect language with the character of a Begriffsschrift, the Quinean form remains faithful to that ideal. Furthermore, Quine shares Russell's scientific orientation to philosophy. Quine goes a step further in seeing the philosopher's constructive task as continuous with the scientist's. For Quine, philosophy differs from the special sciences "only in breadth of categories"; that is, the philosopher's questions are more general than the physicist's, but their answers are ultimately given on the same empirical basis.[17] Thus, contrary to Wittgenstein (PI: 109), Quine sees philosophers as scientific theorists of a more general sort.[18]

Wittgenstein's and Quine's forms of naturalism, broadly construed, represent the only options open to the aspiring naturalist with the general linguistic orientation of twentieth-century philosophy and with a sensitivity to the shortcomings of earlier forms of naturalism.[19] Unlike Wittgenstein's critical naturalism, which claims that metaphysics makes no sense, Quine's scientific naturalism claims that good metaphysics makes good scientific sense and bad metaphysics makes bad scientific sense. Quine expresses the difference between these two forms of naturalism as follows:

> . . . the Vienna Circle had already pressed the term "metaphysics" into pejorative use, as connoting meaninglessness; and the term "epistemology" was next. Wittgenstein and his followers, mainly at Oxford, found a residual philosophical vocation in therapy: in curing philosophers of the delusion that there were epistemological problems.
>
> But I think that at this point it may be more useful to say rather that epistemology still goes on, though in a new setting and a clarified status. Epistemology, or something like it, simply falls into place as a chapter of psychology and hence of natural science.[20]

Quine moved a large segment of Anglo-American philosophy in a naturalistic direction on a wide range of philosophical topics—language, logic, mathematics, epistemology, and metaphilosophy. To appreciate the debt that the revival of naturalism owes to Quine, it suffices to look briefly at the role his arguments against intensionalism have played in recent American philosophy. The arrival of Carnap and Logical Empiricism on the American scene brought a sharp analytic/synthetic distinction which, being developed within sophisticated systems of formal semantics, seemed to vindicate Kant's metaphysical conception of philosophy as an attempt to explain synthetic *a priori* knowledge.[21] Carnap's work in particular seemed to put the full authority of current logical philosophy behind a rapprochement between rationalism and empiricism.[22] Logical Empiricism in its modern form thus compromised with empiricism and naturalism in the areas of language, logic, and mathematics by giving abstract objects sanctuary on the analytic side of the distinction and advocating the existence of necessary truths. In recognizing knowledge that cannot be accounted for with the empirical methods of natural science, Logical Empiricism seemed to present a formidable barrier to naturalism.

This barrier was seen to come crashing down with Quine's criticism of the analytic/synthetic distinction in "Two Dogmas of Empiricism."[23] This criticism was widely seen as practically eliminating intensionalist approaches from the philosophical landscape. Extensional approaches of various sorts, all of which owe an enormous debt to Quine, came to dominate the landscape. For example, Quine's criticisms of intensionalism paved the way for Davidson's program; without those criticisms, few philosophers would have had sufficient "fear of being enmeshed in the intensional" to go along with Davidson's proposal to switch from the traditional "*s*" *means that p* paradigm of analysis to the extensionalist "*s*" *is true if, and only if, p* paradigm.[24] Also, the claim of extensionalist theories of possible-worlds semantics that there is no finer-grained notion of proposition than the one defined in terms of extensions in possible worlds would seem arbitrary and counterintuitive without Quine's criticisms of meaning.[25] With the collapse of the analytic/synthetic distinction and the eclipse of Carnap's logical empiricism, the way was open for a neo-Millian naturalism in which all truths are contingent (in the sense of being revisable on the basis of observation of nature), all objects are natural objects, and all knowledge is acquired on the basis of the empirical methods of the natural sciences.[26]

Wittgenstein and Quine are, then, the makers of contemporary naturalism. Their arguments provide the necessary criticisms of Fregean intensionalism, the bulwark against the forces of Millian naturalism in the nineteenth century, and hence, the basic rationale for the recent revival of naturalism. Their versions of naturalism, linguistic therapy and naturalized epistemology, provide the two forms of naturalism now available. Therefore, if conclusions I–IV can be established, it remains to show only that Quine's arguments against intensionalism fail to rebut contemporary naturalism in every form. Accordingly, I will couple the arguments for conclusions I–IV with arguments that show, first, that Quine's criticisms of intensionalism are inadequate and, second, that without them the other major anti-intensionalist arguments, e.g., Davidson's and Putnam's, do not work. Accordingly, it will be a further conclusion of the present book that:

V. Contemporary naturalism is based on Wittgenstein's and Quine's arguments against intensionalist theories of meaning, and, since Quine's arguments also fail, there are no good arguments in support of contemporary naturalism.

4

In the context of philosophy today, V is a strong conclusion, but I think we can do better. Moreover, I think that an even stronger anti-naturalist claim is required. If we were to stop with conclusions I–V, we would not address the logically next question of whether there is, as traditional non-naturalists have frequently insisted, beyond mere want of support, some inherent fallacy in programs to naturalize disciplines like logic, mathematics, language, and epistemology. If we did not address this question, we would forfeit the chance to strengthen significantly our case against naturalism. Therefore, I shall try to establish the further conclusion that there is some fallacy in the program to naturalize these disciplines. In the rest of this chapter, I will say a bit more about the form in which this question will be discussed.

Given Frege's role in stemming the tide of nineteenth-century naturalism, it is easy to see why intensional objects and traditional theories of meaning were the focus in Wittgenstein's and Quine's attempts to revive naturalism. Fregean senses create islands which challenge the naturalist claim that all branches of science form an epistemologically seamless web of belief about an ontologically uniform world. Hence, the naturalist response to Fregean non-naturalism has been to reject the theory of meaning in order to reject objects which bifurcate the ontological realm and which make knowledge of language and logic depend on a faculty of intuition over and above sense perception.

Although naturalists have generally felt that the price of doing without a theory of meaning is well worth paying, they would certainly find it preferable not to have to pay any price. It is in this connection that Chomsky's work assumes its special importance for the naturalism/non-naturalism controversy. Chomsky offers naturalists the prospect of a naturalism that is, in this one respect at least, preferable to Wittgenstein's and Quine's. Chomsky's theory of language suggests a way of splitting the ontological issue of a commitment to non-natural objects off from the scientific issue of the value of a theory of meaning in the study of natural language. It seems to offer the possibility of resuscitating the traditional theory of meaning without abandoning naturalism. That is, it seems to provide a framework within which we can do justice to the linguistic facts about synonymy, ambiguity, analyticity, etc. without committing ourselves to non-natural intensions.

Chomskyan linguistics seems to offer this possibility because it conceives the object of study in linguistics to be grammatical competence, i.e., the ideal speaker's knowledge of the language.[27] This enabled linguists to take the object of study in the theory of meaning to be a component of grammatical competence, namely, semantic competence, i.e., the ideal speaker's knowledge of the language's synonymy relations, ambiguities, analyticities, etc. Within Chomsky's theory of grammatical competence, the notion of sense is a psychological, or biological construct; so, the theory of meaning, like the theory of semantic competence, is a theory in the natural sciences.

Indeed, it was just this prospect of developing traditional semantics within linguistics viewed as a natural science that first interested me in Chomsky's work. The aim of much of my early work was to formulate intensional semantics within the framework of Chomsky's theory of generative grammar.[28] At the time I began to work in linguistics, *Syntactic Structures* was the *Das Kapital* of the Chomskyan revolution. Since it contained no theory of the semantic component of a generative grammar, I undertook, together with Jerry Fodor and Paul Postal, to try to develop a theory of the semantic component and its place in a generative grammar.[29] I had various philosophical reasons for trying to show that a version of traditional semantics could be constructed within empirical linguistics. I wanted to find an alternative to the then current approaches in the philosophy of language. Carnap's artificial-language approach seemed to me to fail to provide a clear relation between semantic principles and the facts of natural language, and the ordinary-language approach seemed to me to concentrate too narrowly on facts of usage to the exclusion of any theory of the grammar of sentences. I wished to show that traditional semantics could be made responsive to facts of usage in a straightforward scientific way[30] and, thereby, restore to that theory the respectability it lost as a result of Quine's criticism.[31]

I thought that the theory of meaning could be given materialist foundations.[32] My explicit goal was a naturalistic version of the theory of meaning within generative grammar understood as an empirical theory about the biology of human beings. Giving the traditional theory of meaning a place in the theory of generative grammar would resuscitate that theory without posing a threat to naturalism, because Chomsky had shown how to interpret the entire theory of generative grammar psychologically and, hence, naturalistically.[33]

It is just such a viewpoint which, in the present context, suggests that naturalism does not have to turn its back on the facts about synonymy, ambiguity, analyticity, etc. with which the traditional theory of meaning was concerned, and hence, pay some price in antecedent plausibility. Chomsky's work thus raises the issue over naturalism in a new form. His psychological interpretation of formal theories of sentence structure becomes the focus of interest in the question of whether linguistic naturalism involves some sort of fallacy.

Chomsky's psychological interpretation of grammars is one interpretation of them, but not the only one. Before Chomsky, linguistics was dominated by a school of thought on which the objects of grammatical study are physical sounds. The Chomskyan revolution changed the conception of grammar from that of a taxonomic analysis of speech sounds to that of a theory of the ideal speaker's grammatical competence, thus making it possible to treat sense as part of the grammatical structure of sentences even though it lacks any acoustic realization. Logically speaking, it is clear that this physicalistic interpretation is not the only alternative to Chomsky's psychological interpretation. Formal theories of grammatical structure could be interpreted as theories of abstract objects, like formal theories in logic or mathematics. Generative grammars could be understood as theories of the structure of sentences in the sense in which a realist about mathematics understands arithmetic as a theory of the structure of numbers. This alternative presents a new way to pose the issue over naturalism in linguistics, namely, as the question of whether imposing a psychological interpretation of theories in linguistics—as Chomsky does and as any naturalist who wished to avoid paying the price of jettisoning the traditional theory of meaning would—is correct.

Posing the issue in this way immediately suggests an extension of our argument against naturalism. Recall G. E. Moore's thought that naturalistic interpretations of moral theories lead to a fallacy in the definition of moral concepts.[34] Moore's naturalistic-fallacy argument has, to be sure, been subjected to extensive criticism, but, perhaps, despite mistakes in his formulation, Moore was on to something. I think he was right that naturalistic interpretation of ethical theory involves a fallacy of definition. Moreover, I think the fallacy is more general, arising also when theories in logic, mathematics, and certain other areas are interpreted naturalistically. In particular, I think a fallacy arises when theories of natural language are understood in psychological or biological terms. Hence, if we can reconstruct Moore's notion of a naturalistic fallacy and show that, in the reconstructed sense, such a fallacy does arise with respect to language, we will significantly strengthen our case against naturalism. Accordingly, the final conclusion I will argue for in this book is the following:

VI. The philosophical claim that theories of natural language should be interpreted naturalistically commits a fallacy.

Here is a brief overview of my argument in this book. It begins with a comprehensive examination of Wittgenstein's critique of theories of meaning. The aim of this examination is to establish conclusions I–IV. I then turn to Quine's criticisms of theories of meaning, the other pillar of contemporary naturalism. I try to show that these criticisms, despite their wide influence, are inadequate. I next consider the anti-intensionalist criticisms of philosophers like Davidson, Putnam, Burge, etc. which have generally been seen as independent, at least to some extent, of Quine. I try to show that these criticisms depend completely on Quine's arguments. This completes the argument for conclusion V. After this, I present an argument for conclusion VI which, though in the spirit of traditional non-naturalism, is based on a novel conception of the naturalistic fallacy. I conclude with a chapter on the implications of these specific results and of the non-naturalism they support for how philosophical problems should be understood.

2
Wittgenstein's Critique of Theories of Meaning

1

This chapter begins my examination of Wittgenstein's critique of theories of meaning. The aim here is to show that the arguments prior to the paradox about following a rule do not succeed in eliminating all theoretical conceptions of meaning. Chapters 3 and 4 complete the examination by showing that the theory that escapes those arguments also escapes the paradox.

I will use the following plan to achieve the aim of this chapter. I will set out, alongside each other, two lines of argument. One is Wittgenstein's line of argument against theories of meaning as it unfolds from the very beginning of the *Philosophical Investigations* up to the paradox about following a rule. The other is a line of argument that I will develop for a particular theory of meaning. At each point where these two lines of argument intersect, I will look to see whether development of the theory is blocked by the arguments at that point in the first line of argument. If it is not blocked, I will go on to the next point of intersection, continuing this process as far as necessary. If Wittgenstein's case against theories of meaning is airtight, the second line of development will be blocked at some point before it can reach its goal of a theory of meaning. If it is not blocked at any point, there is nothing in Wittgenstein's line of argument to refute the theory of meaning in question, and consequently, this phase of Wittgenstein's critique of theories of meaning fails.

The direction of the second line of argument is the resolution of two vectors. One is a commitment to constructing a theory of meaning that explains a set of semantic facts. Thus, like Wittgenstein's, my line of argument begins with a set of familiar semantic facts relating to natural language, but it proceeds in an opposite direction, toward semantic explanation. The other vector is a commitment to maximizing the differences between the theory under construction and the theories against which Wittgenstein explicitly directed his arguments. This vector is designed to provide a stronger test of Wittgenstein's critique than it has had thus far. By and large, Wittgenstein's arguments work well against the theories of Frege, Russell, and the *Tractatus*, and, because those have been generally assumed to be the only theories that need be considered, the flaws in his arguments have not yet come to light. My working hypothesis is that Wittgenstein's arguments fail against theories of meaning in general, but that their flaws emerge only when the arguments are applied to theories that are maximally different from those to which he himself applied them in framing his critique.

If I am right, the basic problem with Wittgenstein's overall argument against theories of meaning is, ironically, the same type of mistake he pointed out in Augustine's account of meaning. Wittgenstein, quite rightly, accuses Augustine of reaching his conception of meaning by generalizing beyond the cases that the conception fits. My objection to Wittgenstein's critique will be that its negative conclusion is a generalization beyond the cases that his arguments refute. To establish this objection, I will show that the theory that comes out of the second line of argument is sufficiently different from those considered in the critique to escape it entirely. Starting with quite ordinary and familiar facts about meaning in natural language, I will try to show that we can proceed to a semantic theory in a step-by-step fashion, where no step—in particular, not the step from factual description to theoretical explanation—runs afoul of any of Wittgenstein's arguments. If this can be shown, it follows that, in devising those arguments, Wittgenstein did not pay sufficient attention to differences among kinds of theories. He thought primarily of theories like those of Frege, Russell, and his early philosophical self, and of certain similar theories in the history of philosophy; the remaining kinds of theory he regarded "as something that would take care of itself."

Although Wittgenstein was wrong about theories of meaning generally, he was right, and deeply so, about theories in the Fregean tradition. It is a subtheme of this chapter and of the book as a whole that Frege's semantics has, in various ways, misdirected intensionalist thinking. The unfortunate fate of intensionalism in the middle of the twentieth century is due, I believe, to a widespread, but false, identification of intensionalist semantics with Fregean semantics. I will try to show that, once an intensional semantics alternative to Frege's is developed, Wittgenstein's criticism of Fregean views of meaning, language, and theory construction become part of the case for this alternative. Most importantly, Wittgenstein's arguments in this connection help to explain how theory construction within the

Fregean tradition mishandled the critical transition from pretheoretical semantic observations to a theory of meaning.

2

Wittgenstein's critique of theories of meaning begins at the very beginning of the *Philosophical Investigations* with a quotation from Augustine. The strategy of beginning with this passage, which seems to consist entirely of obvious truths about languages and the way they are learned, encourages readers to see their own views—or views they would find it plausible to accept—in the positions expressed by Wittgenstein's interlocutor and thereby eases those readers into identifying with the interlocutor and taking the interlocutor to speak for them. This beginning can seem a bit peculiar to the professional philosopher, since it appears to facilitate contact with readers at the expense of going directly to the doctrines about language of Frege, Russell, and the early Wittgenstein with which the early sections of the book are centrally concerned. For Augustine's truisms, although related to those highly complex and recondite doctrines, cannot be identified with them in any straightforward way.

But this way of beginning highlights something common to Augustine, Frege, Russell, and the early Wittgenstein which is of more immediate concern to Wittgenstein than a direct confrontation with their specific doctrines. This is the idea that linguistic understanding comes via discovery of a hidden semantic reality on the basis of inferences from something public. Augustine says that learning a language is a process of inferring private mental states of speakers from their public use of the words. Frege, Russell, and the early Wittgenstein conceive of linguistic understanding as a matter of inferring the hidden logical form of sentences beneath their surface grammatical form. These philosophers take linguistic understanding to be, in a sense, like the scientific understanding derived from theories that penetrate the surface of things to reveal secrets of nature. The child's and the philosopher's feat is analogous to the scientist's theoretical inference which pictures a discrete physical reality underlying the uniform appearance of matter. The child's and the philosopher's acquisition, respectively, of language and, of significant truths about language, requires something tantamount to a theoretical inference in order to picture the semantic reality underlying the misleading appearance of sentences.[1]

Although the Augustine quotation that begins the *Philosophical Investigations* expresses essentially the same theoretical conception of linguistic understanding as the highly technical theories of Frege, Russell, and early Wittgenstein, it expresses this conception in so common-sensical a form that its various theses strike most readers as obvious truths. But it is Wittgenstein's point that the very fact that these theses strike readers as obvious truths is a clear sign of their having already embraced a rudimentary form of the scientific conception of linguistic understanding, and, in a certain sense, already embarked on a course of philosophizing of the sort mapped out by Frege, Russell, or the early Wittgenstein. Augustine's common-sense conception of linguistic understanding is one starting point in a process of theory construction whose final point might well be a theory of the language taking a form something like a Begriffsschrift theory.

Once we see Wittgenstein's idea, the seeming peculiarity of the beginning of the *Philosophical Investigations* disappears. We can appreciate, first, how crucial a role Wittgenstein thinks such first steps play in "the bewitchment of our intelligence by means of language" (PI: 129) and, second, how unaware are those who think of Augustine's reflections on linguistic understanding as innocent truisms, of the deep waters they are in. Wittgenstein's first remarks are intended to jolt his readers out of this complacency and make them realize how much philosophy they have, in fact, already bought into.[2] Wittgenstein is here making the initial moves in his attempt to show his reader how important a role seemingly innocent beliefs about a hidden semantic reality can play in trapping us in a philosophical problem. Seen retrospectively, these moves begin a line of investigation whose purpose is to show that the course charted by philosophers leads not to the answers to philosophical questions, but to endless "torment . . . by questions which bring [philosophy] *itself* into question" (PI: 133).

This way of beginning the book has the further advantage of making it possible for Wittgenstein to confront our theorizing about the nature of language without its already having the protection of a philosophically and technically sophisticated metaphysical position. Focusing on common-sense theories like Augustine's enables Wittgenstein to investigate embryonic theories before they grow into dogmatically held metaphysical pictures of what reality must be (PI: 131). Another advantage for Wittgenstein in this way of beginning is that, to some extent, he can recreate the process by which philosophers end up with such pictures, enabling him to enter that process, not only at the initial stage where the impulse to theorize begins to work, but also at subsequent stages where it has produced metaphysical pictures. Their production can be examined at various steps in the process from fresh viewpoints informed by criticism of earlier steps.

Wittgenstein's focus in this examination is to exhibit the special role that theoretical conceptions of linguistic understanding play in the etiology of philosophical problems. On such conceptions, what is philosophically significant, "the *essence* of language, of propositions, of thought," is "something that lies *beneath* the surface. Something that lies within, which we see when we look *into* the thing, and which an analysis digs out. *'The essence is hidden from us'*: this is the form our problem now assumes." (PI: 92) With such a conception, we fabricate simulacra of scientific theories, containing technical vocabulary and exact formulations like theories in science. Such simulacra involve metaphysical ways of speaking, since there is nothing in the natural world corresponding to what they picture: ". . . our forms of expression prevent us in all sorts of ways from seeing that nothing out of the ordinary is involved, by sending us in pursuit of *chimeras*" (PI: 94). Theoretical conceptions of linguistic understanding seduce us into looking beyond the ordinary naturalistic facts of language in search of explanatory semantic atoms, but in so doing we become "entangled in our own rules" (PI: 125). Metaphysical ways of speaking outstrip the power of the rules of our language to confer sense on its signs.

From the very start, Wittgenstein's criticisms do double duty. In addition to being criticisms of philosophy as it is done, they are illustrations of a quite different idea of how philosophy should be done. Wittgenstein says that "the work of the philosopher consists in assembling reminders for a particular purpose" (PI: 127). Indeed, the very first criticism of the *Philosophical Investigations* is the reminder that there are different kinds of words (PI: 1). Its purpose is to show us that Augustine's seemingly innocent truisms about language rest on an unnoticed and unwarranted generalization from the presence of a property in a narrow range of cases to a conclusion about its presence in a different, quite wider range. These truisms harbor the idea that typical features of the semantics of ordinary nouns are a reliable basis from which to extrapolate to features of the semantics of all parts of speech. Wittgenstein's reminder about "names of actions and properties" is intended to separate relatively harmless thoughts, such as that "table" names an object, from dangerous thoughts, such as that "five" denotes an object. Separating them enables one to evaluate the dangerous thoughts outside the context of the generalization that represents them as part of the discovery of a deep regularity. The idea is that, when a thought such as that "five" denotes an object, stands by itself, its queerness can be revealed by simply comparing the use of "five" with the use of ordinary nouns like "table."

Reminders, e.g., about how the word "five" is used, help us to see that a certain case included under the generalization is not sufficiently like the plausible cases from which the generalization was made for that case to count as fitting the generalization. Before such reminders, the philosopher can't get a clear view of the linguistic facts. The generalization, seen as capturing a deep regularity about meaning, obscures the fact that there are cases that do not fit (PI: 5). Behind such generalizations, then, is the lure of discovering the underlying semantic essence of words, which leads philosophers to impose a metaphysical interpretation on recalcitrant cases, under which those cases appear to fit perfectly. Thus, in making number words fit the generalization that the meaning of a word is the object for which it stands, philosophers, being unable to say that such words name natural objects, say that they name non-natural objects, viz., abstract objects. In this way philosophers, misled by the parallel with scientific explanation, come to think that they have discovered a deep philosophical truth about reality.

As Wittgenstein sees it, instead of discovering a deep truth, such philosophers have only succeeded in creating an intractable problem, since now they must explain how we have knowledge of objects with which we can have no causal contact. Wittgenstein says: "One thinks that one is tracing the outline of the thing's nature over and over again, and one is merely tracing round the frame through which we look at it." (PI: 114) Wittgenstein's reminder that there are differences between the use of number words and that of words like "table" is designed to free us from such epistemological problems by getting us to see that such a route to Platonism is based on a false generalization. Thus, Wittgenstein's reminders are often accompanied by a gloss to clarify the point. Accordingly, he next explains that the overlooked differences between kinds of words are a matter of use. He presents an example to show that attention to the details of the use of words in ordinary circumstances can raise doubts about what might otherwise seem a direct route to metaphysical revelation The shopping example is designed to raise such doubts. Wittgenstein's gloss: "No such thing [as the meaning of the word "five"] was in question here, only how the word "five" was used." (PI: 1)

This remark exemplifies the basic aim of Wittgenstein's therapeutic practice: to make philosophers see that there are only descriptive truths about the use of words, not metaphysical truths about a theoretical meaning, and thereby to extricate them from intractable problems that result from the mistaken belief that philosophy, like science, seeks to uncover truths about reality. As Wittgenstein at one point expressed himself,

> . . . our considerations could not be scientific ones. . . . And we may not advance any kind of theory. There must not be anything hypothetical in our considerations. We must do away with all *explanation*, and description alone must take its place. And description gets its light, that is to say its purpose, from philosophical problems. These are, of course, not empirical problems; they are solved, rather, by looking into the workings of our language, and that in such a way as to make us recognize those workings: *in spite of* an urge to misunderstand them. The problems are solved, not by giving new information, but by arranging what we have always known. (PI: 109)

Such arrangings are valuable in spite of the fact that they seem to destroy "everything interesting," for the explanations destroyed are "nothing but houses of cards" (PI: 118). Their destruction is "the real discovery . . . that gives philosophy peace" (PI: 133).

3

The line of theoretical development I will initiate is in the sharpest possible conflict with Wittgenstein's position that a philosophically promising approach to language "could not be scientific." My diagnosis of the difficulties with the theories of language of Frege, Russell, and the early Wittgenstein is not that those theories were too scientific but that they were not scientific enough. In this line of development, I want to provide a theory of meaning which is scientific in being an explanatory theory in linguistics concerned with the semantic phenomena of natural language and which is also of philosophical significance in contributing to our understanding of philosophical problems in the traditional metaphysical sense. It is hard to see how there could be an approach more opposed to Wittgenstein's position. This is, of course, as it should be, since our aim is to provide the strongest possible test of Wittgenstein's arguments against theories of meaning in the *Philosophical Investigations*.

On one point my theoretical approach is in full agreement with Wittgenstein's anti-theoretical approach, namely, that the study of natural language involves a primary and undischargeable responsibility to be faithful to the facts of natural languages. If one undertakes to develop a theory of natural language from a scientific standpoint, there is no less an obligation to do justice to the linguistic facts than there is in the case of someone who undertakes to describe the language with the therapeutic aim of "bring[ing] words back from their metaphysical to their everyday use" (PI: 116). But agreement on this responsibility still leaves room for disagreement about the nature and significance of various linguistic facts. Linguistic facts, like other kinds of facts, often do not wear their true nature on their sleeves. That linguistic facts can require some interpretation if we are to see them in a revealing light is not a controversial point. Wittgenstein uses analogies with tools and games to get us to see certain linguistic facts in the right light.

The linguistic facts with which my line of development begins are those to which speakers refer in certain judgments about the language. Speakers use their language to talk about ships, shoes, and sealing wax, but they also use it to talk about the language itself. Speakers have always had a lively interest in matters of language. The record of that interest is found in the rich metalinguistic vocabulary of the language, for example, words like "noun", "verb", "rhyme", "alliteration", "nonsense", "ambiguity", "pun", "palindrome", "antilogy", "acronym", "synonym", "antonym", "eponym", and even "anonym". Just as Eskimo has a large number of words referring to different kinds of snow, so English has a large number referring to different kinds of linguistic phenomena.

Now among the facts to which such terms refer, we make a distinction between those which concern the application of expressions, for example, the fact that "ship" refers to ships and "Santa Claus" refers to no one, and those which concern grammatical structure, such as that "Santa Claus" is a noun like "ship", that "ship" rhymes with "blip", and that "open" and "closed" are antonyms. And among the grammatical facts, we make a distinction between those which concern facts of pronunciation or syntax and those which concern facts about meaning. Among the latter, some arouse our interest as semantic curiosities. Consider the following:

(i) Although "soluble" and "insoluble" are antonyms, "flammable" and "inflammable" are synonyms.
(ii) "Valuable" and "invaluable" are neither antonyms nor synonyms.
(iii) "Pocket watch" is similar in meaning to "pocket comb," but the similarity does not extend to "pocket battleship."
(iv) The expressions "free gift" and "true fact" are redundant.
(v) "Bank" and "dust" are ambiguous, but only the latter is an antilogy, i.e., a word with antonymous senses.
(vi) "Flammable integer" and "the color of contradiction" are not

(fully) meaningful.

(vii) All the senses of the individual words in expressions like "Kick the bucket", "The fat's in the fire", and "Cat got your tongue?" occur in their non-idiomatic senses, but not all the senses of the individual words occur in their idiomatic senses.

(viii) The sentences "A sister is a sibling" and "A square is a rectangle" are analytic, i.e., have pleonastic predicates.

I have chosen (i)–(viii) as illustrations of semantic facts for which I will try to develop a theory because, as curiosities, they cry out for explanation. On first encounter, we wonder how the members of the second pair of words in (i) can be the same in meaning when the members of the first are opposed in meaning. We wonder what the point of expressions like those in (iv) can be when the sense of the noun already tells us what is contributed by the sense of its modifier. In the other cases, we at least find the constructions intriguing. Such cases sometimes lead to linguistic discussions and sometimes to speculations about what is going on. But, typically, such discussions are abandoned before they really get very far, since their participants are ordinary people, with more pressing concerns, indulging their curiosity, rather than linguists working in their discipline.

Nonetheless, such parlor semantics, like other intelligent amateur concerns, must be based on some general knowledge of the subject matter. Discussions of facts (i)–(viii) presuppose something like the following principles: some expressions have a sense, though some do not; some expressions have the same sense, some different senses; some have only different senses, some different and opposed senses; some expressions have more than one sense; there is similarity among expressions both in number and in content of sense; senses of expressions appear as parts of the senses of other expressions; syntactically complex expressions can have both senses that contain the senses of their component words and senses that do not.

I will refer collectively to such principles as "folk semantics." In saying that our everyday discussions of semantic facts like those in (i)–(viii) presuppose folk semantics, I mean nothing more than that such discussions are couched in terms of senses and of the relations among senses expressed in the above principles. Thus, for example, it makes no sense to talk about ambiguous, synonymous, or antonymous expressions if, in no sense of "sense", are there senses that may be multiple, the same, or opposed. I want to make clear that I take nothing in such talk to specify what we are talking about when we talk about senses. Since nothing is assumed about the nature of senses, nothing of philosophical significance follows just from the fact that we talk in these ways about semantic phenomena.

Facts like (i)–(viii) involve, on the one hand, a linguistic form or forms (in the case of these particular examples, particular English expressions), and on the other, a certain semantic property or relation, e.g., synonymy, antonymy, ambiguity, redundancy, similarity in meaning, meaningfulness, and meaninglessness (less than full meaningfulness). These properties and relations are exhibited by the form or forms in virtue of their sense. Folk semantics therefore contains a common-sense notion of meaning or sense, namely, *whatever it is that is the same in synonymous linguistic forms, that is opposed in antonymous linguistic forms, that there is more than one of in ambiguous linguistic forms, that is duplicated in redundant linguistic forms, and so on.* Like everyday semantic discussions and the folk semantics involved in them, this common-sense notion doesn't tell us what senses are, that is, what is the same in the case of synonymous expressions or what sameness is, what is opposed in the case of antonymous expressions or what opposition is, etc. The notion only connects talk about sense (and meaning) with talk about those properties and relations. We may express these connections as follows:

(1) Virtually all the words, phrases, and sentences of a natural language have meaning. Their meaning consists in senses, which are what ambiguous expressions have more than one of, what meaningless expressions have none of, and what synonymous expressions have in common (in virtue of which they are so related). Senses can be more or less alike, as well as opposed. The senses of the syntactic constituents of non-idiomatic expressions *seem* to occur in the senses of the expressions, whereas the senses of the syntactic constituents of idiomatic expressions *seem* not to occur in them. The senses of expressions and sentences can make them redundant.[3]

Since folk semantics takes no position on the nature of senses, philosophers and linguists are free to speculate about what its talk of synonymy, ambiguity, and so on is really about—intensional objects, extensions, inner psychological objects, behavior, the use of words, or inscriptions. Thus, folk semantics can be taken as a jumping-off point for our line of argument to provide a theory of meaning. Starting in this way makes no assumption that the attempt to construct such an argument will be successful. Whether or not the argument constructed leads to a scientific semantics with the proper philosophical import is a matter of what the subsequent steps of the argument are. Hence, assuming facts like (i)–(viii) and the principles of folk semantics is not something with which Wittgenstein would quarrel. His criticisms do not target our ordinary talk about sense and meaning. He has no objection to saying that a word has a meaning or that two sentences have the same sense. He, too, thinks that such talk is one thing and what we try to make of it another.

Of course, a quarrel must eventually come, since at some point my line of argument must try to understand facts like (i)–(viii) in terms of intensional objects. Wittgenstein's objection will come on behalf of his very different idea of what such facts and vocabulary are about. His most explicit statement of this idea is his remark that "for a *large* class of cases—though not for all—in which we employ the word 'meaning' it can be defined thus: the meaning of a word is its use in the language" (PI: 43). Wittgenstein is not here putting forth a general statement about meaning or a standard definition of the term—indeed, it would be inconsistent of him to do so. But he is expressing a view about what semantic talk is predominately about, and I believe he is expressing the view that, in the cases that figure significantly in the issues facing us, reference to the meanings of words is reference to their use in the language.

4

Some Wittgensteinians will object to taking folk semantics as a jumping-off point for the construction of a scientific theory of meaning with philosophical significance. They think there is no appropriate relation between our ordinary and philosophical talk of semantic properties and relations and the technical notions that would reconstruct them in such a theory. On this basis, they would attempt to rule out the possibility of such a theory in advance. This section considers such an attempt.

J. V. Canfield claims that our ordinary disputes about sameness and difference of meaning are one thing, and disputes in linguistics which also seem to be about sameness and differences of meaning are quite another.[4] Canfield thinks that theories in linguistics set their own requirements on what counts as sameness and difference of meaning, whereas the participants in an ordinary dispute make "substantive claims, whose content requires that we take seriously and literally the idea of 'meaning change'"; hence, he thinks that the linguist, in large part, stipulates the requirements on such semantic relations, so that linguistic accounts of them perforce contain a large arbitrary element, guaranteeing, at best, only a "rough extensional equivalence" between the ordinary notions and their theoretical correlations.[5]

But Canfield supplies no reason for thinking that there have to be limits on theories in linguistics which prevent them from making "substantive claims." Canfield says nothing to show that linguists cannot take the notion of meaning in "ordinary dispute[s]" as their object of study. This is precisely what I propose to do in taking the beliefs in (1), extracted from ordinary facts such as (i)–(viii), as the starting point in developing a theory of meaning suitable for linguistics. If sciences like mathematics and physics can develop out of common-sense reflections on number and the behavior of matter without turning out not to be about the objects of such reflection, why can't scientific semantics, assuming there is such a thing, develop out of folk semantics without a change of subject matter? In advance of having a scientific semantics whose character we may examine, how could there be reasons for ruling out the possibility of scientific theories that specify the actual conditions under which sentences and their constituents are synonymous or non-synonymous?[6]

It seems to me that Canfield and others who take the same view of the limits of science in relation to natural language have too narrow a conception of theories in linguistics. I suspect that they have in mind either a Begriffsschrift theory of Frege's sort or its Carnapian offspring. Such theories, having been invented as ideal languages, are the theories that fit Canfield's account of theories out of touch with ordinary language. The fit is especially good in the case of Carnap's conception of language construction, with its "principle of tolerance."[7] In allowing enormous latitude to depart from ordinary language, Carnap precludes the possibility of making "substantive claims" about meaning in ordinary discourse.

But the Begriffsschrift model is neither the only model nor the natural model for a linguist to use in constructing a semantic theory of natural language. The linguist can try to construct a theory of meaning along the lines of scientific theories, in the way theories of phonology and syntax have been constructed in linguistics. Instead of the principle of tolerance, the linguist would be guided by the familiar principle of faithfulness to the facts, in this case the semantic facts of natural languages such as (i)–(viii). Clearly, nothing prevents us from setting our sights on a scientific theory that is literally concerned with the semantic notions in ordinary talk about meaning and change of meaning. Of course, we may be setting our sights too high, and we may be in for no end of philosophical trouble, just as Wittgenstein warned. Still, if we succeed in constructing such a theory, its characterization of meaning and meaning change in natural language would go beyond "rough extensional equivalence." Those who hold Canfield's view simply overlook the option of trying to construct a scientific theory of meaning for a natural language, probably because their only models for such a theory are Carnapian ideal languages.

5

We have embarked upon the program of showing that the common-sense notion of meaning, based on (1), leads by an acceptable route from folk semantics to scientific semantics. Acceptability requires two things. First, the route must terminate in a theory that explains semantic facts like (i)–(viii) in terms of the hypothesis that senses are underlying intensional objects. Second, at no point can the development of the theory run afoul of any substantial argument in the *Philosophical Investigations*.

With respect to the very tiny part of that book that we have looked at so far, we are off on the right foot. For it is clear that none of its arguments against Augustinian theories that take the meanings of expressions to be extensional objects, are, at least as they stand, arguments against a theory that takes the meaning of expressions to be intensional objects. Thus, Wittgenstein's arguments at the very beginning of the *Philosophical Investigations*, as well as those later in the book which continue the argument against extensional theories of meaning, are inapplicable to the theory I will be developing. Similarly, my theory avoids the familiar objections to conceptions of meaning like the one Russell held early in the century, e.g., the objection that co-referential expressions like "creature with a heart" and "creature with a kidney" are not synonymous or the objection that an expression like "the largest integer" is not meaningless.[8] Such objections are restricted to theories that take the beliefs in (1) to be about the referents of linguistic expressions.[9]

Though our program rejects the identification of sense with reference, it certainly does not deny that sense is somehow related to reference. But I assume, as seems reasonable, that the folk semantics with which we have begun says nothing about the nature of the relation between them, and it will be wise for us at this early stage to say nothing positive about it, since, in fact, this will turn out to be an extremely complex question whose answer depends on general features of the intensional theory at which we will arrive. Thus, in working out a position on the relation between sense and reference, we will not assume any commitment to any doctrine about it, even, and especially, any commitment to traditional doctrines like Frege's.[10] Accordingly, we add the weak principle (1'):

(1') Sense and reference are different, but related somehow to each other.

6

In addition to criticizing meaning as extension, Wittgenstein's discussion in section 5 fashions a technique for criticizing other general notions of meaning. In this respect his most portentous remark in the first five sections is his response to the interlocutor's protest that the meaning of the word "five" has been left out in treating the shopping example. Wittgenstein responds: "No such thing was in question here, only how the word 'five' was used." (PI: 1) This response gives the example a cast on which it reflects one of the central themes of the *Philosophical Investigations*. The example becomes an illustration of the general point that the significant semantic facts of language are examples of the use of language and, in themselves, do not involve philosophical concepts of meaning, which are introduced into our thinking under the impulse to explain but which serve only to obscure facts about use. We can maintain a clear view of those facts only if we keep in mind that the significant semantic facts are facts about the use of words, as they are in the shopping example.

The discussion in section 5 is thus illustrative of how a general concept of meaning can begin life as an oversimplification and, under the impulse to explain, end as a purported metaphysical truth. Under pressure to explain, a descriptive generalization, first based on a restricted set of cases, is extended to cover the full range. The restrictions are lost sight of with the promotion of the generalization to the status of explanation. Cases that do not fit the generalization are then construed, from the higher perspective of the explanation, as conforming to it in ways that reveal a deeper truth about those cases. Thus, the oversimplification is protected against counterexample. As a result, the oversimplification—now celebrated for its insights into the essence of language—becomes the lens through which the language is seen and, hence, blocks a clear view of linguistic facts.

Wittgenstein has such a process in mind when he says that Augustine's notion of meaning "surrounds the workings of language with a haze which makes clear vision impossible" (PI: 5). Thus, the first order of business is to find a way to provide the reader, whose vision can be presumed to be obscured to some extent, with a clear view of the language. Wittgenstein's approach is to return to philosophical basics: the validity of a generalization about meaning (or anything else) must be judged, first and foremost, by how well it fits all the facts. Wittgenstein thinks that, if philosophers can be kept descriptively honest, explanatory generalizations purporting to reveal something about the essence of language can be exposed as the false descriptions they are. They can be shown to be descriptively mistaken about many of the cases to which they apply. At a later point, Wittgenstein will explain why such generalizations have to be false. He will say that it is in the nature of the case that linguistic generalizations will fail to be comprehensive: such generalizations, properly seen, express only resemblances; there are no essences for them to capture (PI: 65–67).

Here, however, Wittgenstein's particular interest is in finding a way of overcoming the effects of an explanatory approach to language and focusing the reader's attention on the linguistic facts long enough for them to be given their due. How to do this when the reader may have already gone beyond linguistic description and already have an obscured view of the linguistic facts? Wittgenstein comes up with an ingenious solution. He observes that there is an equivalence between "a primitive idea of the way language functions" and "the idea of a language more primitive than ours" (PI: 2). Thus, someone's overly simplified generalization about our language, such as Augustine's conception of meaning, can be put in the form of an entirely appropriate generalization about a language that is overly simple in comparison to ours. Putting oversimplifications in this way provides readers with a new perspective on the language from which their view of the linguistic facts is no longer obscured by a cherished theory. It thus confronts readers with a clear picture of what they are taking the language to be in adopting an explanatory conception of meaning. The contrast between their language and the more primitive language presented to them in this picture forces them to recognize the distortions that arise when a generalization fitting a restricted range of cases is taken as an account of the whole language. There is a good chance that, once they recognize that they have been representing the whole language as something that is so obviously just a fragment of it, they will see that, under the impulse to theorize, they have failed to give the linguistic facts their due.

Wittgenstein's example of a builder's language in section 2 implements this solution. It is intended to show how much of the workings of language are overlooked in Augustine's conception of meaning. The example is, moreover, the first appearance of Wittgenstein's "language-games." From here on, such examples are a principal means for exhibiting aspects of the use of language obscured by a general concept of meaning.

In the course of criticizing Augustine's account of meaning, Wittgenstein introduces the idea that *use* is the critical aspect of language in evaluating such accounts. In sections 2–10 Wittgenstein's criticisms of Augustine's account of meaning are based on showing that the account overlooks one or another feature of the use of signs. From the beginning (PI: 1, 5–9) Wittgenstein takes it as somehow given that the only facts relevant for evaluating claims about meaning or for developing proper ways of talking about meaning, are facts about use. Thus, he sums up by saying: "But assimilating the description of uses of words in this way cannot make the uses themselves any more like one another." (PI: 10)

The move to present semantic facts as facts about use is taken further in the next section, where Wittgenstein encourages the reader to think of words on analogy with tools. This section presents the "function" or "application" of words as the semantically significant thing about them. The phraseology Wittgenstein uses when he says that use is what dispels the confusion caused by "the uniform appearance of words" strongly suggests that use is now being accorded the place of honor once held by Fregean senses in the discussion of how the surface grammar of a sentence can mislead us concerning its logical powers. By the time we reach sections 11 and 12, we have been subtly led to think that the analogies with tools and artifacts reveal what is semantically significant about words.

Partly by virtue of the unobtrusive way in which use has been brought into the criticism of Augustine's conception of meaning—a conception which is so clearly mistaken that the reader feels no inclination to take up its defense—and partly by virtue of the fact that use works well enough for this purpose, we are eased into thinking of meaning as primarily a matter of use. The seemingly innocent way in which this happens keeps us from pausing at any point to ask whether perhaps things haven't gone a bit too fast. We do not ask the question that needs to be asked about what happens in the course of sections 1–12, namely, whether there might be competition for Wittgenstein's view that semantic facts are facts about use. When, in retrospect, we see how much of the subsequent argument in the *Philosophical Investigations* hangs on securing this view in these early sections, we should recall Wittgenstein's own words: "The decisive movement of the conjuring trick has been made, and it is the very one that we thought quite innocent." (PI: 308)

In making this criticism, I am not saying that Wittgenstein doesn't eventually consider competing views of meaning which could also explain what is wrong with Augustine's generalization that the meaning of a word is the object for which it stands. Rather, I am saying that, in proceeding as he does at the outset, he gains an unearned advantage for his own view of meaning and for his arguments against theories of meaning. By giving no hint of other possible semantic facts and by making it seem as if use were the true source of the facts that expose wrongheaded conceptions like Augustine's, Wittgenstein conditions his readers from the very start to rely on use in evaluating semantic claims. This conditioning facilitates getting his readers to shift from thinking of language in terms of general concepts of meaning to thinking of it in terms of how speakers employ verbal artifacts and, hence, to judging claims about linguistic meaning in these terms. Accordingly, when Wittgenstein later does criticize intensionalist views like those of Frege and Moore, the criticisms receive a more sympathetic reception than they actually deserve.

Wittgenstein's only explicit motivation for introducing use at the end of section 1 is the fact that it provides a basis for criticizing Augustine's theory. Although he makes no attempt to show that nothing else would work as well in exposing the defects of that theory, it is fairly obvious that, for *this* purpose, use is dispensable. As we have seen, Frege presents us with an equally good basis for exposing the defects of extensionalist theories. Fregean arguments— such as that if the meaning of an expression were the object for which it stands, then expressions that stand for the same object, say, "the morning star" and "the evening star", would be the same in meaning, or that an expression standing for no object, say, "the largest integer", would be meaningless—do not invoke use. These arguments make no reference to what someone does with an utterance. Rather, their conclusions are based on a direct recognition that the expressions "the morning star" and "the evening star" are nonsynomyous and that the expression "the largest integer" is meaningful. Such recognition suffices to show that the sense properties and relations of these expressions do not correspond to their referential properties and relations, as required. Of course, it would be possible to claim that facts about synonymy, meaningfulness, and the other sense properties and relations are somehow facts about use, but this would have to be argued, and my criticism of Wittgenstein at this point is only that this is something he does not do.

The issue here is one to which I will be devoting a great deal of attention. I mention the prospect of an alternative view of the nature of semantic facts now because bringing it out into the open as early as possible helps to put the argument for Wittgenstein's view in perspective. I think that Wittgenstein's view reflects the naturalist's desire to understand sense in terms of the linguistic behavior of speakers within a language community with a particular history. But one could as well think that the order goes the other way around. That is, one could think that reference to use is *inter alia* reference to sense. Behind this thought is the non-naturalist desire to understand linguistic behavior as the exercise of a speaker's knowledge of autonomous semantic structures. Knowledge that "the morning star" and "the evening star" are nonsynonymous is simply knowledge that their senses are not identical.

I submit that Wittgenstein is up to much more in the beginning of the *Philosophical Investigations* than just arguing that an obviously inadequate account of meaning is obviously inadequate. He is laying the groundwork for a broad attack on theories of meaning generally, which, if successful, would leave non-naturalistic approaches with no semantic leg to stand on. Therefore, his attempt to gain acceptance for the idea that use is the proper basis for evaluating accounts of meaning is anything but innocuous. If the idea is left unchallenged, Wittgenstein himself gets to determine the kind of fact to which a description of a language must be faithful. This would certainly concede too much, since his argument that there is no legitimate way to proceed from a description of linguistic facts to a general concept of meaning depends, in part, on linguistic facts' being taken to be facts about the use of signs. On the other hand, the existence of an independent body of linguistic facts having to do with the senses of expressions would offer the possibility of proceeding from a description of linguistic facts to a general concept of meaning.

I have left it open whether the facts concerning sense properties and relations such as those in (i)–(viii) are properly interpreted as facts about use or as facts about a *sui generis* sense structure, conceived of as an aspect of grammatical structure along with syntactic and phonological structure. The fact that Wittgenstein presents no argument in sections 1–12 to rule out the latter interpretation is enough justification for us to take that interpretation as a starting point for developing a theory of meaning. If we can start from the assumption that facts about sense properties and relations are facts about such *sui generis* sense, and then, in the sense indicated, safely reach a theory of meaning, it would not matter whether Wittgenstein succeeds in arguing that a theory of meaning cannot be reached starting with facts about use. His argument would be a demonstration that such facts are the wrong starting point.

Let us now look a bit further into the distinction between facts about sense and facts manifestly about use. My aim in doing this is not actually to draw the distinction, but to clarify somewhat the difference between the two interpretations of facts like (i)–(viii) and, to a certain extent, motivate the grammatical interpretation of facts about sense. To begin, note that, *prima facie* at least, we can conceptually distinguish between facts like (i)–(viii) and facts about use such as Wittgenstein employs to criticize Augustine's theory. Facts of the latter kind are about what someone does with an utterance in speech; for example, a builder requests a thickly cut stone by calling out "slab". Facts of the former kind, in contrast, do not, as they stand, involve either speakers or utterances. The fact that the senses of "creature with a heart" and "creature with a kidney" are different from each other is a fact about two English expressions, to wit, that they do not bear the synonymy relation to each other. The fact that "the largest integer" has a sense is a fact about an English expression, to wit, that it has the property of being meaningful. On their face, facts about sense involve no reference to speakers, utterances, or inscriptions.

There is a reason for this difference. Facts about the sense of expressions of a language are facts about linguistic *types*, whereas facts about use, being facts about what people do with their articulatory organs or hands at a particular time and place, are facts about linguistic *tokens*. Charles Sanders Peirce drew the distinction between types and tokens in this way:

> There will ordinarily be about twenty "the"s on a page, and of course they count as twenty words. In another sense of the word "word", however, there is but one "the" in the English language; . . . it is impossible that this word should lie visibly on a page or be heard in any voice.[11]

Given the type/token difference, the interpretation of facts about sense on which they are really about use will have to say that facts about types are just facts about tokens under some appropriate resemblance relation. On the other hand, the interpretation on which they are facts about a *sui generis* grammatical structure will say that facts about types are autonomous, that is, not reducible to facts about their tokens. On this latter interpretation, types provide the principal component of a conformity relation which imposes categorical structure on linguistic tokens. On the former interpretation, something else, logically prior to types, is required to provide the relation of resemblance that imposes appropriate structure on linguistic tokens. As we shall see below, the latter interpretation leads to a "top-down" approach to semantic phenomena in which the structure of concrete tokens is an exemplification of the structure of abstract types, while the former leads to a "bottom-up" approach in which such abstract structure, or what passes for it, is only a generalization of similarities among tokens.

7

In sections 1–15 Wittgenstein equates facts about meaning with facts about use, ignoring the question of whether facts about use are the only facts or the privileged facts for evaluating alternative views of meaning. I have raised the possibility that facts like (i)–(viii) might not be facts about use, but are instead facts about autonomous senses, and that, in some way, as yet not spelled out, facts about use might reflect facts about senses. In this section I want to motivate this possibility in order to explain why it should be taken seriously. To do this, I will present some reason for thinking that equating facts like those in (i)–(viii) with facts about use involves difficulties that do not arise when such facts are equated with facts about autonomous senses.

One such reason is that social conventions on the part of speakers and the connotations of words conspire to make speakers use words with the same sense differently. For example, the juvenile connotation of "pee-pee", the vulgar connotation of "piss", and the absence of those connotations in the case of "urine" result in speakers' using those words in quite different ways despite the fact that they have the same sense. A biomedical scientist reporting to colleagues at a conference will use not the word "piss" or "pee-pee" but the word "urine". But Tennessee Williams, choosing between these synonyms in writing dialogue for the loutish Stanley Kowalski in *Streetcar Named Desire*, will select "piss" over the others. Middle-class parents are likely to use "pee-pee" in socializing their young children. There are many other sets of words that raise this problem, e.g., "rabbit" and "bunny", and also other connotations, e.g., pejorative connotations of words referring to members of races or religions. Such problems are like the problems posed by the existence of conflicting dispositions for attempts to define mental concepts in terms of dispositions to respond: the responsive behavior is under the influence of concerns that are quite extraneous to the concepts in question.

Of course, those who wish to interpret facts like those in (i)–(viii) as facts about use need not cave in in the face of such problems. One line of defense, taken by a number of philosophers, is to replace the ordinary notion of use with a technical notion that idealizes away from unwanted aspects of use such as connotation. This line is taken by Anglo-American philosophers of language like Austin, Alston, Searle, and Strawson. They see the ordinary notion of use as too undiscriminating, and so they advocate a theoretically constructed notion that is less inclusive. Such a theoretical notion would identify linguistic meaning with some special set of uses. Austin's classification of locutionary acts into illocutionary and perlocutionary made it possible to formulate a technical notion of use in terms of the potential of expressions and sentences to perform one or another type of speech act.[12] Followers of Austin like Searle take the type to be illocutionary acts; followers of Grice take the type to be a special class of perlocutionary acts in which the speaker intends to bring about a certain belief in his or her hearers in virtue of their recognition of his or her intention.[13] However, this line, insofar as it involves theory and technical construction, is, of course, not open to Wittgenstein. He can hardly abandon the ordinary notion of use in favor of a theoretical one (PI: 109–127).

Another line of defense is to argue that connotation *is* part of sense. On this line, words like "pee-pee", "piss", and "urine" are not the same in meaning because connotation is as much a part of their meaning as the concept of liquid. It is hard to deny that the English word "meaning" is elastic enough to cover connotation. After all, it covers reference, as, for example, in the sign "Trespassers will be prosecuted, and that means you!". But, as this example suggests, the scope of the English word "meaning" is not a deciding factor. The issue is whether there is a kind of meaning covered by the English word which corresponds to the intuitive notion of sense in (i)–(viii) and which is distinguishable from such things as connotation in the way that reference—which also happens to be covered by the inclusive English word "meaning"—is distinguishable from sense. Are there considerations like those which Frege uses to distinguish sense from reference which can be used to distinguish a notion of sense from the notion of connotation?

Various considerations come to mind. For one thing, connotation does not support valid implication. Sentences like "There is urine (piss, pee-pee) on the floor" entail the sentence "There is a liquid on the floor"; but the sentence "There is pee-pee on the floor" does not entail sentences such as "A child pee-peed on the floor", "A child is speaking", or "A child is being spoken to". The truth of sentences identifying the speaker or addressee as a child is no doubt pragmatically suggested, but that is clearly a different matter. For another thing, there are certain contexts that distinguish cognitive content from connotation. Witnesses in a court of law testifying under oath who use "piss" instead of "urine" or use "flatfoot" instead of "police officer" are not guilty of perjury, though they may be in contempt of court.[14]

Other reasons for thinking that it might be wrong to equate facts like those in (i)–(viii) with facts about use have to do the role of sentence size and complexity in determining sentence use. Ordinary people often observe that there seems to be no longest sentence of English, because any sentence can be turned into a longer one in a number of ways. Children often catch on to the trick with the primitive device of adding another occurrence of an intensifying adjective or adverb, e.g., "I want one", "I want a big one", "I want a big big one", . . . or "They are mean", "They are very mean", "They are very very mean". . . . There are more sophisticated devices for starting with an English sentence of length n, i.e., with n words, and forming another sentence of length $n + k$. For instance, "Mary is one year old or (and) Mary is two years old or (and) Mary is three years old . . ." and "I thought about myself thinking about myself thinking about myself . . .". Linguists who have studied such things have come to the same conclusion: English sentences get longer and longer without limit.[15]

But even if one does not accept the view that there is no longest English sentence, it seems obvious enough that syntactic mechanisms of sentence formation produce sentences that, given reasonable assumptions about the biological and physical constraints on behavior, are too long ever to occur in speech or writing. It also seems obvious that indefinitely many such megasentences, as I shall call them, are fully meaningful. If S_n is a meaningful sentence, then the sentence that results from conjoining S_n with a meaningful sentence S_m of the same type is meaningful. The meaning of the sentence "S_n and S_m" is just the joint assertion of S_n and S_m, and the meaning of "S_n or S_m" is the assertion of the truth of at least one. Thus, there are meaningful English megasentences; hence, having a meaning does not correspond with having a use.[16]

Some will not find such considerations compelling because they reject the idea that there are infinitely many English sentences, and even the idea that there are megasentences. The linguistic counterparts of extreme constructivists in mathematics will think that, with increases in the length of the to-be-conjoined sentences, and no other changes, there eventually comes a point at which the next sentence is no longer grammatically well-formed. They think this because they think that human constructivity is the basis of sentencehood, just as the mathematical constructivists think that it is the basis of numberhood. We will return to the constructivist position in chapter 7. Here it should be pointed out that it is just such facts about sentence size that, in the minds of the ideologically uncommitted, cast doubt on such constructivist views.

But the argument for a divergence between meaning and use can be made without challenging constructivism. We can construct well-formed meaningful sentences that cannot be used.[17] The sentence

"The man who the boy who the students recognized pointed out is a friend of mine" involves the embedding of one clausal structure within another of the same syntactic type, as, for instance in this case, embedding the clause "who the students recognized" within the clause "who the boy pointed out". As this example shows, even two self-embeddings make a sentence difficult to produce or understand. Sentences with, say, ten or twenty self-embeddings, although not of mega length, are clearly unprocessable, and hence, beyond the range of human use. Nonetheless, given our knowledge of their grammatical construction, it is relatively easy to see that such multiple-self-embedded sentences are meaningful. Their embeddings can be undone in a way that provides a synonymous sentence that is clearly meaningful. For instance, Chomsky's example can be transformed into the comprehensible sentence "The man is a friend of mine and the boy pointed out the man and the students recognized the boy". Pairs consisting of an unusable self-embedded sentence and its easily usable transform provide an example of synonymous sentences that are different in use, and the first member of the pair provides an example of a sentence that is meaningful but not usable. These examples illustrate the divergence between meaning and use in a particularly clean form. In this case, there is no issue of whether the feature that produces the difference in use is part of meaning, as in the case of connotation, and there is no complaint that the critical examples cannot be constructed, as in the case of megasentences.[18]

I will not pursue these matters further. I am not trying to establish an autonomous grammatical interpretation for facts about sense, but only to build credibility for such an interpretation by exhibiting certain difficulties with Wittgenstein's introduction of use as the basis for evaluating claims about meaning.

8

The last two sections of this chapter took the first step from (1) in the direction of a theory of meaning. Their aim was to establish the possibility of a route to such a theory whose starting point is recognition of facts about sense like (i)–(viii) and whose termination is a theoretical explanation of these facts in terms of the postulate that autonomous senses are part of the grammatical structure of sentences. We now take the next step of pulling together the various strands of our discussion of facts about sense, subjecting them to autonomous grammatical interpretation, and identifying the common-sense notion of meaning with an aspect of the grammatical structure of linguistic types. To do this, we explicitly adopt a distinction between sense and use parallel to the distinction between sense and references. Thus:

(2) The domains of meaning and use are different. Meaning is an inherent aspect of the grammatical structure of expression and sentence types (like their syntactic form). Thus, facts about sense properties and relations such as synonymy, meaningfulness, etc. are also inherent aspects of the grammatical structure of linguistic types. In contrast, use cannot be an aspect of types: it is something speakers do with utterances and inscriptions, something forming part of the causal nexus.

(2′) Meaning is related to use, but the relation is one on which the meaning of expression and sentence tokens is derivative from the meaning of linguistic types.

Putting (1), (1′), (2), and (2′) together, we get a first approximation to a linguistic/extralinguistic distinction for semantics. The general idea is that the linguistic is concerned with those phonological, syntactic, and semantic properties and relations which depend upon the structure of sentence types, whereas the extralinguistic, although it may in part depend on sentence structure, depends also on things falling beyond it. For example, rhyme is linguistic, but being a tongue twister is extralinguistic. Since it interprets facts like (i)–(viii) as facts about the structure of sentence types in the sense in which facts about rhyme are facts about the structure of sentence types, thesis (1) states that sense properties and relations such as synonymy, meaningfulness, ambiguity, redundancy, antonymy, etc. depend on the semantic part of the structure of sentences. Thesis (2) states that use, as such, falls outside the structure of sentence types—as do tongue twisters. Use is partly a product of extralinguistic factors like connotation, socialization, etc.—just as being a tongue twister is partly a product of peculiarities of the articulatory mechanism.

These considerations lead directly to a principle for deciding what belongs to the semantics of sentence types and what belongs outside it. The principle is this: information is semantic just in case it directly determines sense properties and relations, that is, just in case the information is the basis of sentences having synonymy relations, ambiguities, redundancies, etc. If the sense properties and relations of sentences can be determined without assuming that certain information is part of their grammatical structure, parsimony tells us it is nonsemantic.[19] We can illustrate the principle in connection with what Grice has called a "generalized conversational implicature."[20] One of his examples of such implicatures is the inference from "John is meeting a woman" to the conclusion that the woman in question is not his wife. Was Grice right in thinking that this inference is not given by the meaning of the sentence? That is, is the inference extralinguistic rather than linguistic? Applying our principle, we can easily see that, as Grice thought, it is extralinguistic. The premise is not synonymous with "John is meeting a woman who is not his wife", and furthermore the clause "who is not his wife" in this latter sentence does not occur redundantly in the way "who is naked" occurs redundantly in "nude who is naked". Also, "John is meeting a woman who is his wife" is not contradictory in the manner of "John is meeting a woman who is male". Since the information about the woman in the Gricean conclusion is not part of the premise, Grice was correct to think that an account of the inference would have to go beyond considerations of sentence meaning.

I have developed this linguistic/extralinguistic distinction in order to bring my line of development into its first direct conflict with Wittgenstein's line of development in the *Philosophical Investigations*. In section 16, Wittgenstein claims that "it is most natural, and causes least confusion" to count such things as color samples among the words of the language. The case of color samples may seem *prima facie* to be trivial, but it is the thin edge of the wedge. If color samples count as linguistic, on a par with actual words, it is hard to see how all sorts of other things can be prevented from counting as linguistic. Since almost anything can be a sample, there could be no sharp linguistic/extralinguistic distinction at all.

If Wittgenstein has a good argument for counting color samples as part of the language, our line of development will be blocked after its first step. His argument is the following:

> . . . when I say to someone: "Pronounce the word 'the'," you will count the second 'the' as part of the sentence. Yet it has a role just like that of the colour-sample in the language-game (8); that is, it is a sample of what the other is meant to say. (PI: 16)

The word "sentence" has the type/token ambiguity Peirce describes. We can understand the word in the sense of 'sentence type', as when a linguist says that the sentence "John loves Mary" is a declarative sentence of English, or in the sense of 'sentence token', as when a master of ceremonies says, "The words of the next sentence you hear will be those of our esteemed president".[21] To be sure, in the case of Wittgenstein's request to pronounce the word "the", the word "sentence" has the token sense and refers to Wittgenstein's utterance on the occasion.[22] But it does not follow from "the"'s being part of the sentence in this sense of "sentence" that it is "part of the *language*", unless, of course, the notion of language itself is to be understood exclusively in a token sense. In the present context, however, such an understanding cannot be taken for granted, because there is a notion of language in the type sense. Given the above linguistic/extralinguistic distinction, we have a notion of language on which languages are collections of sentence types.

With the possibility of this type notion of language, it is clear that Wittgenstein's argument does not go through. There is no way to validly move from the premise that something is part of an utterance of sentential form to a conclusion that it is part of a sentence in the type sense and, hence, part of a language in the type sense. With respect to the type-notion of language, being part of a sentence (type) automatically means being part of a language, but, surely, being part of a sentence token does not mean being part of a language. We don't count all parts of a speaker's utterance as parts of the sentence that the utterance is a token of. We discount the soft sweet voice, the flattering tone, the alcoholic slur, the repeated words, the false starts and stops, the "uhs" and "ahs", the belches and burps. These come out of the speaker's mouth, and some are even utterances, but they are not part of his or her *sentence* in the sense of that term which we use in referring to sentences of English.

We can identify a category of utterance components, which excludes vocal quality, repeated words, etc., such that when an utterance belonging to that category occurs in an utterance of sentential form, there is a constituent of a sentence type of which the component is a token. When we see what that category is, it will be clear why such things as color samples do not belong to it, nor to sentences, nor, therefore, to the language.

Since Frege's distinction between mention and use, philosophers have been sensitive to the differences between quoting, and other ways of presenting signs in order to talk about them, on the one hand, and, on the other, the employment of signs to talk about their referents. In the present context, the significant thing about mention is its permissiveness. Grammatical devices for mentioning accommodate nearly anything that the mouth or hand can produce, including obscene noises, hiccups, animal imitations, elaborate pictures, doodles, words of foreign tongues, musical compositions, and so on. They are not restricted to the standard signs of the language, and, accordingly, the occurrence of something in a "mention" context is no grounds for thinking that it belongs to the stock of English words. In contrast, contexts of use are so restricted, and, accordingly, the occurrence of something in a context of use, other things being equal, authorizes us to take it to be part of English. For example, words like

"Wiener schnitzel" and "kibitz" now seem to be part of English, since presumably it is English to say "I like Wiener schnitzel, but not ice cream" or "Don't keep kibitzing". But "sagen" cannot claim the same status, since it is not English to say "We sagen that life is a bowl of cherries."

Occurrence in contexts of use is the real test of whether an item is part of the vocabulary of English. This test identifies the category of utterance components which token genuine vocabulary items and, thereby, enables us to see why Wittgenstein's argument does not go through. In the utterance that his example concerns, the component "the" to which color samples are compared is mentioned, not used. Thus, the argument employs the wrong context to establish that something is part of the language. The inclination that readers have to suppose that the mention context in Wittgenstein's example confers the status of English vocabulary on an item occurring in it is due, not to the context's being a reasonable test for this status, but to the fact that the context seems to be such because it is initially employed to authenticate the word "the" which is antecedently known to be an English word.

The argument of PI section 16 which we have been examining is an important element in Wittgenstein's overall critique of theories of meaning. It is intended not only to challenge the legitimacy of theoretically drawn sharp boundaries for languages, but also to prepare the way for the next stage of the critique where the related idea of a complete language is explicitly challenged. Theories of meaning, especially those in the *Begriffsschrift* tradition, assume an in-principle completeness of language. Hence, if section 16 had succeeded in showing that there is nothing to bar such things as color samples from the language, it would, in effect, have shown that languages are open-ended and subject to continuous accretion. This in itself would undercut the idea of a complete language. Section 18 explicitly raises the issue of the completeness of a natural language, and sections 19 and 20 address it directly.

Wittgenstein introduces the issue by urging us not to be troubled by the fact that the languages of sections 2 and 8 consist entirely of orders, saying: "If you want to say that this shews them to be incomplete, ask yourself whether our language is complete." (PI: 18). He suggests that our language was not complete "before the symbolism of chemistry and the notation of the infinitesimal calculus were incorporated in it" (PI: 18). The implication is, of course, that the march of science will continually extend our language and, consequently, that it is as foolish to think that it is or will someday be complete as it is to think that scientific progress will someday stop. At this point,

Wittgenstein presents his urban metaphor of the history of language. That metaphor expresses his alternative conception of a natural language as susceptible to limitless development in directions dictated by unpredictable scientific and cultural events. On this conception, it makes no sense to speak of absolute completeness. One must speak comparatively. It makes sense to speak of greater "completeness" only relative to other stages of the language or to comparable stages of other languages. In such comparisons, our judgment is like describing the language game in section 2 as "a language more primitive than ours."

Wittgenstein's striking metaphor is not accompanied by an argument against the notion of absolute completeness for a language. He presumably thinks we have only to be reminded of something we know about language and linguistic change for us to see that the notion of absolute completeness is confused or mistaken. But such a reminder is not enough when there exists a conception of language and language change for which the notion of absolute completeness makes sense and is not obviously wrong. The Fregean tradition provides such a notion, and what Wittgenstein says here about the dependency of linguistic development on scientific and cultural development is relevant only to the different notion of completeness that he thinks proper. Frege talked about how "with a few syllables [language] can express an incalculable number of thoughts, so that even a thought grasped by a human being for the very first time can be put into a form of words which will be understood by someone to whom the thought is entirely new."[23] Tarski once said that "a characteristic feature of colloquial language" is that whatever we can speak meaningfully about "we can speak meaningfully about . . . in colloquial language."[24] The notion of completeness in these discussions is *expressive completeness*. Wittgenstein's remarks seem to concern only a notion of *notational completeness*. Expressive completeness does not require that the stock of signs of a language contain every sign that can or will enter it at some point in its history, but requires only that the notational and semantic resources of the language suffice for full expressibility—roughly, the relation between sentences and senses in a language such that, for any thought, there is at least one sentence of the language with a sense which is that thought. My claim is not that the notion of expressive completeness is without its problems—Frege himself was aware of some of them—but only that we have a different notion of completeness which might well be suitably explicated.

Wittgenstein is doubtless right that the stock of signs of a natural language grows without limit and, hence, that there is no such thing as a notationally complete natural language. But notational incompleteness does not entail expressive incompleteness. A natural language without a particular specialized vocabulary may express the same thoughts as a natural language with the highly specialized vocabulary. This is because grammatical devices compensate for the absence of special signs. For example, English contains no word corresponding to "starve" which means 'die from lack of water', but the compositional meaning of the expression "die from lack of water" plugs the lexical gap for purely expressive purposes. Even lack of a scientific notation can be got around if we are prepared to accept high levels of prolixity in synonymous forms. Thus, a language does not have to have the symbol π to express geometrical truths, since these can be expressed using "the ratio of the circumference of a circle to its diameter". No doubt verbiage can reach enormous proportions, but prolixity is irrelevant in the present discussion because it concerns only the stylistic side effects of expressing information one way rather than another.

The possibility for expressive completeness in the face of notational incompleteness is provided both by the potential of syntactic principles of natural languages for forming infinitely many sentences from a modest finite vocabulary of lexical items and by the potential of semantic principles for forming senses out of senses and relating them to syntactic structures. Together these principles constitute a theory of compositional meaning, that is, a theory of how the meaning of syntactically complex expressions is a function of the meanings of their constituents and their syntax.[25]

Of course, Wittgenstein has arguments against compositional meaning. Therefore, we cannot assume that his failure to consider the alternative notion of expressive completeness here is of philosophical significance. It may be a tactical matter, and his argument thus far may look ahead to those arguments against compositional meaning. Nonetheless, we can claim that there is nothing up to this point in Wittgenstein's critique of theories of meaning to show that natural languages are more than notationally incomplete. We can thus provisionally assume that there might be principles of compositional meaning which compensate for the absence of vocabulary and which provide natural languages with full expressive power.

9

From a naturalistic viewpoint, languages evolve, by causal processes, from less to more complex forms. The learning of a language is seen in a similar way. This viewpoint does not actually dictate a conception of semantic facts about expression types on which they reflect conditions of the use of expression tokens, but it does lead quite naturally to such a conception. As Wittgenstein recognized, from this viewpoint, the very idea of absolute completeness seems foolishly confused. Consider something that is, indisputably, a product of evolutionary development, say, Western civilization. It *is* analogous to a city with its ancient and modern parts; it wasn't complete before Einstein, Freud, and Darwin, and it isn't complete now.

But, whereas there is no other perspective to take on Western civilization, there is another perspective that can be taken on language. One can look at the domain of language in something like the way that a realist in mathematics looks at the domain of sets, understanding languages, as suggested above, as collections of sentence-types. From this viewpoint, abstract grammatical structure constrains the evolution of linguistic forms in the way that mathematical structure constrains the evolution of natural forms. The directions that linguistic evolution and linguistic acquisition can take are set by the range of possibilities in the grammatical structure of language.[26]

On this perspective, evolutionary and developmental processes do not bring languages into existence. They only produce competence in them on the part of communities and individuals. Causal processes only bring it about that people come to have knowledge of a natural language, that is, psychological representations of abstract grammatical structures. This perspective also reverses the naturalist's picture of the order of things in the use of language. The relation between a language and its use is now seen as a complex relation involving, first, a relation between knowledge and the language that is known, and, second, the exercise of such knowledge in speech. Accordingly, the use of language is a "top-down" affair in which the categorical structure of linguistic tokens derives from their subsumption under linguistic types in the exercise of a knowledge of the system of types.

Although some "top-down" direction is possible within the naturalistic perspective on language, no naturalistic approach can be fully "top-down"; in particular, none can, as it were, start at the top. In comparing his approach of generative grammar to the inductive approach of taxonomic grammarians, Chomsky describes his as "top-down."[27] Taxonomic grammarians took the facts of language to be facts about the distributional relations among utterances in speech. The phonological and syntactic categorical structure of those utterances was thought to be inherent in the co-occurrence patterns of segments of utterances. Explicit grammatical statements of such structure were taken to be "bottom-up" inductive generalizations from such co-occurrence patterns. Chomsky began linguistics as a taxonomic grammarian, his first major descriptive project being to write a taxonomic grammar of Hebrew. He describes the turning point in his thinking as coming when he realized that the attempt to inductively project Hebrew phonological and syntactic categories from distributional regularities could not succeed and that the only alternative was to proceed the other way around by imposing categories from above.

Chomsky's idea was that phonological and syntactic categories could be specified directly in generative grammars, set out in the manner of logical calculi, and that such grammars could then be related to linguistic phenomena. To relate them, Chomsky interpreted generative grammars as psychological theories of the speaker's linguistic knowledge.[28] An account of the categorical structure of speech is then an account of how speech is produced in the exercise of the speaker's linguistic knowledge. The grammatical categories are thus part of the psychological makeup of speakers, and the assignment of linguistic tokens to particular grammatical types is supposed to come via relations established in the exercise of linguistic knowledge.

Thus, for Chomsky, the category structure of language has its reality in the mind, naturalistically conceived. The approach is Kantian—that is, it regards category structure as imposed on phenomena by the mind—in contrast to inductive approaches, which take experience to write category structure on the *tabula rasa* of the mind. However, this degree of "top-down" direction does not amount to a full "top-down" assignment of linguistic tokens to linguistic *types*. Generative grammars, on Chomsky's view, are theories dealing with concrete psychological or neurological systems in the mind/brains of speakers. Since such systems are concrete things, located in particular places, at particular times, and involved in causal interactions with other concrete things, there are no types in them, since types, by definition, have no temporal, spatial, or causal properties. Therefore, if there is a full "top-down" path to linguistic phenomena, the psychological route from competence to performance that Chomsky describes is surely not it.

Apart from the Wittgensteinian issues of concern here, the posit of a full "top-down" approach can be motivated on the same sort of grounds that motivated Chomsky to posit his quasi–"top-down" approach. Just as Chomsky found in earlier taxonomic theory a problem of how the inductivist methodology applied to the concrete material of speech could deliver phonological and syntactic categories, we shall find a problem in his theory of how these can be delivered by the theories of the concrete stuff of the mind/brain. Since such categories, e.g., 'noun', are second-order types, that is, types that encompass particular sentences and their constituents, how could they, any more than first-order types, have the temporal, spatial, and causal properties required for existence in mind/brains? In chapters 3, 4, and 7, we shall see that attempts to solve this problem with a dose of psychology are as hopeless as are attempts to solve the parallel problem for taxonomic theory with a dose of inductive methodology. Here, however, I want only to make two points: the "top-down" approach I have introduced is different from what Chomsky calls a "top-down" approach; his approach is, in a perfectly straightforward sense, not really *top*-down.

Given that neither taxonomic grammarians nor Chomskyan grammarians can explain how linguistic tokens are assigned to linguistic types and how linguistic types are assigned to higher-order linguistic types, and given further that linguistics is the study of sentences in the type sense, there is a rationale for a "top-down" approach to language within linguistics. The best alternative approach to language available to naturalists is, then, Wittgenstein's deflationary approach. The strength of this approach lies in the fact that it does not face the problem found in taxonomic theory and in Chomsky's theory. It denies the legitimacy of the notions of universal language and of the essence of language on which the problem depends. Hence, in adopting a "top-down" approach, I am sharpening the opposition between my attempt to vindicate a theoretical conception of language and meaning and Wittgenstein's attempt to resist such conceptions of them. On my approach, a language, being a collection of sentence types which are ineliminable and irreducible, cannot evolve historically, by causal processes, from less to more complex forms—though, of course, the speaker's knowledge of it can so evolve. Facts of language, unlike facts of fluency, have nothing to do with developmental processes. The notion that a natural language is complete makes perfectly good sense.

10

Sections 19 and 20 of the *Philosophical Investigations*, which we shall consider when we return to Wittgenstein, are extremely important for the issue of whether the notion of meaning in (1) and (2') can be developed into a theory of meaning. Those sections initiate his argument against construing ellipsis as a sign of the existence of underlying grammatical structure. Since the aim of theory, as the term is understood here, is to reveal underlying structure, and since sense structure, as I understand it, must be grammatical structure, a theory of meaning must be a theory of underlying grammatical structure. Now, there is a long tradition in linguistics of using ellipsis and related phenomena to justify theoretical inference to underlying grammatical structure—a tradition going back at least to the *Port-Royal Grammar* and to Santius's *Minerva*.[29] In my critical step beyond the description of observable sentence structure to the explanation of unobservable underlying semantic structure, my justification will be an extension of this tradition's use of ellipsis. I depart from the tradition only in the novel application of such a rationale to the case of sense structure. Thus, Wittgenstein's arguments in those sections will directly oppose our line of development.

It has been noted that the reasoning of grammarians trying to justify underlying syntactic structure on the basis of the insufficiency of surface syntax to account for the properties of ellipsis seems parallel to the reasoning of early physicists trying to justify molecular structure on the basis of the insufficiency of observable features of matter to account for its properties. In both cases, the posit of underlying structure is justified on the grounds that it makes otherwise incomprehensible properties comprehensible. "Democritean" grammarians claim that a full description of the surface syntactic structure of an elliptical construction fails to account for certain of its syntactic properties and relations. For example, the surface syntax of an imperative like "Clean yourself!" does not account for the well-formedness of this sentence or for related facts such as that "Clean yourselves!" is well formed, but "Clean itself!", "Clean themselves!", and "Clean herself!" are not. Such grammarians argue that, if imperative sentences had an underlying structure with a second-person subject, somehow not realized in surface syntax, such patterns of well-formedness and ill-formedness would be immediately comprehensible on the basis of the otherwise well-established rule of English grammar that reflexive direct objects agree with their subjects.

There is, of course, a corresponding "Democritean" tradition in modern logic which advocates posits of underlying logical structure to overcome the insufficiency of surface grammar to account for certain logical inferences. Recall Frege's view that surface similarities and differences among sentences can be misleading concerning their logical powers and also his view that precise reasoning requires a "conceptual notation" in which conceptual content is perfectly reflected in the syntax of formulas.[30] Many Anglo-American philosophers consider Russell's treatment of sentences with definite descriptions as a paradigm of logical analysis.[31]

Before taking up Wittgenstein's arguments in sections 19 and 20, I have to spell out how my use of ellipsis and related phenomena to justify underlying sense structure differs from their use in the Democritean traditions within linguistics and logic. My main purpose in doing this is to make very clear how my use of ellipsis and related phenomena differs from the use of them by Wittgenstein's interlocutor. It will be my contention that the interlocutor's use of ellipsis and related phenomena does not exploit their full potential for justifying theoretical inference. Once this difference is explained, I will turn immediately to sections 19 and 20 and try to show how my justification of theoretical inference escapes Wittgenstein's arguments. My claim will be that his arguments are not general enough to block an inference to underlying structure which exploits the full potential of the phenomena and the full resources of theoretical inference in linguistics.

From the standpoint of the present work, the Democritean traditions in linguistics and logic each suffer from a shortcoming that prevents them from providing a satisfactory justification for underlying sense structure. The shortcoming of the tradition in linguistics is that the idea of inference to underlying grammatical structure, although now a secure explanatory paradigm in the study of phonological and syntactic structure, has not become sufficiently entrenched in the study of sense structure to provide anything like an explanatory paradigm there. There are various reasons. The most influential of them is Quinean and other forms of skepticism about intensional semantics. These will be dealt with in chapters 5 and 6. Apart from such skepticism, the principal reason is that semantic posits are seen as different in kind from phonological and syntactic posits. The latter seem to have a conservative character in virtue of the fact that the underlying structures posited are of the same sort as the surface structures on the basis of which they are posited. For example, the inference to an underlying second-person subject in imperative sentences may extend grammatical structure beyond surface structure, but the posit itself, a second-person-pronoun subject, is something we already encounter in surface structure. In contrast, inferences to sense structure seem to introduce structure not to be found in surface grammatical form, i.e., in the observable sound or sign configurations of the language. So semantic inferences are seen as enlarging the domain of grammatical structure. It is possible to argue that, since there is no prior need to acknowledge the existence of sense structure, there is a comparatively heavy burden on the theoretical inference to underlying sense structure: it must justify both an underlying grammatical level *and* a new grammatical kind.

The shortcoming of the Democritean tradition in logic is that it provides no clear position on the relation of formulas in a conceptual notation to sentences of a natural language. Indeed, much of the philosophy of language and the philosophy of logic seem to be about the question to what degree such formulas capture, or should capture, the logical powers of sentences in natural language. On the one hand, one of Frege's basic claims, echoed by everyone in this tradition, was that, since natural languages are logically imperfect, one task of a conceptual notation is to perfect them and, if possible, to provide us with an ideal logical language. On the other hand, neither Frege nor, presumably, anyone else in this tradition thinks that the construction of a conceptual notation can completely ignore natural language. Almost everyone in the tradition thinks that sentences of natural languages have logical powers and that the formulas of an ideal logical language to some extent represent the logical forms from which those powers derive. But, at this point, things become murky. There is no well-established doctrine to reconcile the many issues that arise in practice when faithfulness to grammatical features of the natural language comes into conflict with the freedom to improve logical calculi.

The main figures in this tradition have contributed little to solving this problem.[32] Carnap's proposal of explication is vague just where the problem requires precision. In a typical passage, speaking about "the various interpretations of descriptions by Frege, Russell, and others," he writes:

> [they] may be regarded as so many different explications for phrases of the form 'the so-and-so'; each of these explications consists in laying down rules for the use of corresponding expressions in language systems to be constructed. The interpretation which we shall adopt following a suggestion of Frege . . . deviates deliberately from the meaning of descriptions in ordinary language. Generally speaking, it is not required that the explicatum have, as nearly as possible, the same meaning as the explicandum; it should, however, correspond to the explicandum in such a way that it can be used instead of the latter.[33]

How close to the meaning of the explicandum should the meaning of the explicatum be? It is mind-boggling to contemplate the semantic range in explicata that can replace the explicandum.

Or consider Quine's pronouncement on the issue:

> [the job of paraphrasing ordinary language into the theory] will usually present little difficulty to one familiar with the canonical notation. For normally he himself is the one who has uttered, as

part of some present job, the sentence of ordinary language concerned; and he can then judge outright whether his ends are
served by the paraphrase.[34]

In this passage Quine sounds remarkably like the Carnap of the principle of tolerance. Both seem to be saying that the only issue is the
practical one of whether a chosen explication (paraphrase) does the
job the philosopher wants it to do, as if the explication (paraphrase)
were a personal choice like picking a tie. It is hard to believe that
Quine would maintain this attitude of tolerance if a philosopher tried
to vindicate the analytic/synthetic distinction on the grounds of its
serving certain of his or her ends.[35]

Since my attempt to develop a theory of meaning draws on both
Democritean traditions, the first order of business is to show how
their shortcomings are overcome. Recall that, apart from skepticism
about intensional semantics, the reason that the tradition in linguistics lacks a well-worked-out inferential paradigm for underlying
sense structure is that, unlike phonology and syntax, theoretical inference in semantics seems to have to justify a new grammatical kind
over and above a new underlying grammatical level. I want to show
that, properly understood, theoretical inference in semantics does
this.

First, the step beyond surface grammatical structure to a level of
underlying grammatical structure is already justified by the theoretical inferences in phonology and syntax. The critical step from the
observable to the unobservable has already been taken. Whatever objections there are to introducing underlying grammatical structure
have presumably been met, if they have been, by the arguments for
the theoretical inferences in phonology and syntax. That they are met
can be seen by looking at those arguments.

Second, once the option of underlying grammatical structure is secured, there is no problem of justifying a new kind of underlying
grammatical structure beyond showing that it is required to account
for grammatical facts. The idea that there is a further problem, because the new kind of grammatical structure is not exhibited in the
surface form of sentences, is just a holdover from the "bottom-up"
approach of taxonomic theory. Since, on that approach, categories are
established by working up inductively from surface grammatical
structure, whatever is not part of the sounds or signs of surface grammatical structure is not part of grammatical structure. This is why
semantic structure was never part of grammatical structure at the
time when the taxonomic theory dominated linguistics. But, as
Chomsky recognized in his criticism of that theory, the phonological

and syntactic facts with which inferences to underlying grammatical structure properly begin go well beyond what is found in surface structure, and the inferences themselves require no more justification than the fact that they account for grammatical facts that cannot be accounted for otherwise. This is well illustrated in Chomsky's famous example of the sentences "John is easy to please" and "John is eager to please". Here the syntactic facts are that "John" is the object of the verb "please" in the former sentence but its subject in the latter. The facts are evident to fluent speakers of the language despite there being nothing in the surface structure of the sentences which reflects them. Posits of underlying syntactic structure which successfully account for the syntactic relations speakers recognize require no further substantiation.[36]

Third, an appropriate paradigm of theoretical inference in semantics can be obtained by modeling it on theoretical inference in syntax. I will first show how the theoretical inference in syntax works and then construct theoretical inference in semantics to work the same way. In formulating a paradigm of inference to underlying sense structure, sense properties and relations play the role that syntactic properties and relations play in inferences to underlying syntactic structure, namely, the role of providing the facts for posits of underlying grammatical structure to explain. Inferences to underlying sense structure in sentences are based on properties and relations like meaningfulness, ambiguity, synonymy, redundancy, antonymy, etc. in a way that is exactly parallel to the way in which inferences to underlying structure in syntax are based on such properties and relations as well-formedness, subject and direct-object relations, and agreement.

The two basic features of this formulation will be, first, an explanation of why a posit of semantic structure is required over and above posits of syntactic structure and, second, an explanation of why description by itself is inadequate to account for the facts about semantic properties and relations, so that appeal must be made to underlying sense structure to account for them. With both of these explanations in place, the justification of underlying sense structure is a special case of a justificatory paradigm used elsewhere in linguistics, which, in turn, is a special case of justificatory paradigms elsewhere in science.

The shortcoming of the Democritean tradition in logic was that there is no clear position on the relation of formulas in a conceptual notation to sentences of a natural language. I will avoid this shortcoming by agreeing with Wittgenstein that natural languages are in no need of improving, reforming, or perfecting. My inquiry into the grammatical locus of the inferential potential of sentences aims at nothing more than discovering what it is. Indeed, this modest policy seems to be demanded by a commitment to developing a theory of meaning within the science of linguistics, since the aim of a science is to reveal the nature of the phenomena it studies, not to improve, reform, or perfect them. Linguists have no more business being dissatisfied with ambiguity and other features of natural languages which have been called "limitations" or "imperfections" than physicists have being dissatisfied with the speed of light as the limiting velocity in nature. Moreover, such a "hands off" policy has the significant advantage for my argument in this chapter of deflecting Wittgenstein's acute criticisms of theories that try to improve, reform, or perfect language.

My aim is to construct a theory in the sense of a set of statements about the nonobservable structure of objects from which we can derive facts about their intrinsic properties and relations. This aim ensures that the line of development I am pursuing is on a collision course with Wittgenstein's line of argument in the *Philosophical Investigations*. As I understand the term, a *theory* explains why objects in its domain have certain properties and relations—which are unexplained on the basis of their observable structure—by picturing a hidden structure that is such that any objects having that structure would have those properties and relations. In the present case, I will understand an observable aspect of objects to be a perceivable aspect of the configuration of signs that constitutes those objects. (For example, a grammarian's claim that "Clean yourself!" has a second-person subject is a claim about a nonobservable structure insofar as the configuration of signs out of which this imperative is formed does not contain the sign "you" in subject position.) Further, I use the qualification "intrinsic" to restrict attention to properties and relations that reflect something about the nature of the objects. For example, being ambiguous is an instrinsic property of sentences, just as being prime is an intrinsic property of numbers, but being the subject of Jespersen's meditations on English is not an intrinsic property of an English sentence.

Thesis (1) provides an initial set of intrinsic properties and relations for the senses of linguistic forms in natural language. Thus, an inquiry into the semantics of natural language in our sense will try to say what it is in virtue of which expressions are meaningful or meaningless, ambiguous or univocal, synonymous with certain expressions and not others, redundant, and so on. Of course, such an inquiry does not begin by assuming that it will have to resort to theory in order to account for such properties and relations. If it does resort to theory, it must have already exhausted what observation can tell us without having learned what it needs to know about the properties and relations. That is, the step from semantic description to semantic explanation is legitimate only if the attempt to account for intrinsic properties and relations cannot be carried to a successful conclusion on the basis of observational evidence, and then only if the postulated structure actually offers sufficient basis on which to account for the properties and relations in the language.

To model the step from semantic description to semantic explanation on the step from syntactic description to syntactic explanation, we require an example of the latter. I have chosen what is perhaps the best known example of such a step in the literature, namely, Chomsky's cases "John is easy to please" and "John is eager to please".[37] Chomsky argued that description of the observable syntactic structure in those sentences does not provide a sufficient basis on which to account for the syntactic fact that "John" is the direct object of the verb in the former sentence, but the subject of the verb in the latter. The observable structure in the sentences gives no clue to this difference in intrinsic grammatical relations, since in both sentences the noun phrase "John" is followed by the copula, then a predicate, and then the infinitive "to please". That is, the single lexical difference, that the predicate is "easy" in one case and "eager" in the other, does not suffice to account for the dramatic grammatical difference in the way that "John" relates to the verb in the two sentences. Accordingly, on the basis of what we know about subject and direct-object relations in sentences like "John loves Mary", Chomsky hypothesized appropriately different underlying syntactic structures. In the underlying structure for "John is easy to please", "John" is related to the verb "please" in the same way that "Mary" is related to "love" in "John loves Mary". In the underlying structure for "John is eager to please", "John" is related to the verb "please" in the same way that "John" is related to "love" in "John loves Mary". Using the notation of phrase markers, the hypotheses are, respectively,

$$((\text{someone})_{NP} ((\text{please})_V (\text{John})_{NP})_{VP})_S$$

and

$$((\text{John})_{NP} ((\text{please})_V (\text{someone})_{NP})_{VP})_S.$$

The main feature of these phrase markers is that the former places "John" within the verb phrase, but the latter places it outside the verb phrase, respectively, the canonical positions for the direct object and subject in constituent structure.

Let me pause to reassure the reader that I am aware that Wittgenstein's discussion of ellipsis contains objections even to posits of underlying syntactic structure such as Chomsky's. Those objections will not be ignored. I am now simply formulating the position that will subsequently be confronted with those objections. Thus, we can provisionally accept Chomsky's syntactic explanation in order to ask how a parallel semantic explanation might be modeled on it.

In semantic description, the domain is the same as in syntactic description, namely, sentences of the language, but sense properties and relations like those in (i)–(viii) take the place of the syntactic properties and relations. Corresponding to the aim of syntactic description, the aim of semantic description is to account for the fact that sentences have the sense properties and relations they do have. The correctness of a semantic account is a matter of whether what the account says about the sense properties and relations of sentences is true of them, and the completeness of an account is a matter of whether it says everything that is true about their sense properties and relations.

Since the only difference between semantics and syntax is the set of properties and relations to be accounted for, semantic description, too, ought to give way to semantic explanation when sticking to description prevents us from obtaining a complete and correct account of the relevant properties and relations and when moving from one level of grammatical structure to another makes it possible to do so. Hence, the critical question here is whether there is a point at which progress toward a complete and correct account of sense properties and relations forces us to abandon sheer description and resort to explanation on the basis of hypotheses about underlying sense structure.

To see why a posit of semantic structure is required, it suffices to show why semantic explanation cannot simply piggyback on Chomsky's transition from surface to underlying syntactic structure. One might suppose that it is possible to account for sense properties and relations on the basis of the underlying syntactic structure already introduced to account for syntactic properties and relations. But, for such a "free ride" approach to work, sense structure would have to be reducible to underlying syntactic structure. The semantic facts strongly suggest that this is not the case. For one thing, sameness and difference of syntactic representation do not coincide with sameness and difference of semantic representation. The syntactic representations of "bachelor" and "adult human male who has not married" differ far more than the syntactic representations of "bachelor" and "spinster". Also, nothing in syntax distinguishes the meaningless expression "slippery number" from the meaningful expression "slippery worm". Furthermore, the parallel syntactic structure of expressions like "free gift" and "free dish" offers no hope of accounting for the redundancy of the former and the nonredundancy of the latter. Finally, syntactic structure fails in both directions as a basis for accounting for sense ambiguity, since an ambiguous word like "bank" does not have multiple syntactic structures, and an unambiguous expression like "It was done with an automated processing device" does, viz., ((automated processing) (device)) or ((automated) (processing device)).[38]

Semantic facts like these show that sense structure cannot be reduced to syntactic structure. We are thus forced to suppose that sentences have senses over and above their syntactic form, and, as our knowledge of facts like (i)–(viii) shows, that we are somehow acquainted with the senses of words, phrases, and sentences in our acquaintance with language. Hence, if we are to successfully make the transition from semantic description to semantic explanation, there must be a point at which we can legitimately move from "surface semantics" to "deep semantics." To determine that point, we can see how far it is possible to push the null hypothesis: the hypothesis that description of surface semantics suffices for a complete and correct account of sense properties and relations. I will call this the Fregean view.[39] The view involves the following theses:

(a) The existence of senses, as well as their identity and difference, can be determined on the basis of synonymy, analyticity, analytic entailment, etc. (e.g., in connection with identity sentences like "Hesperus is Hesperus" and "Hesperus is Phosphorus" or substitution into opaque contexts).

(b) The sense of each meaningful syntactic simple (i.e., morpheme) is itself simple.

(c) The simple senses are just the semantic elements necessary for the meaning of all nonidiomatic syntactically complex expressions and sentences of a language to be compositional.

Now if we can show that the Fregean view is wrong, i.e., that surface semantics (in the sense of that view) is insufficient for an account of sense properties and relations whereas deep semantics in an appropriate sense is sufficient, then we have an argument for semantic explanation. To be sure, the argument still has to be tested against Wittgenstein's objections, but at this point we are merely formulating the position that will be put to the test. The claim so far is only that such an argument is on a par with Chomsky-style arguments for underlying syntactic structure—a claim with which Wittgenstein would no doubt agree.

To explain the insufficiency of the Fregean view, consider the following partial formalization. The primitive vocabulary for the semantic notation contains a list of atomic symbols representing the senses of the syntactic simples of the language (i.e., the morphemes). The signs for this vocabulary might be the numerals "1", "2", . . . , "n" (it might be other signs, since it doesn't matter from a formal viewpoint). The full notation, which includes non-atomic symbols for representing compositionally formed senses, would take the form of constructions out of such a numeral vocabulary (i.e., complex numeral configurations). And representations of meaning might be sets of such simple or complex numeral configurations. Given such a notation, a number of sense properties and relations can be defined. We can define a meaningless expression (e.g., "slippery number") as an expression whose representation is the null set of numeral configurations, a meaningful expression (e.g., "slippery worm") as one whose representation is a set containing at least one numeral configuration, an ambiguous expression (e.g., "bank") as one whose representation is a set of numeral configurations, and expressions synonymous on a sense (e.g., "dough" and "money") as ones whose representations are sets with a common numeral configuration.

The Fregean view will be inadequate in case such a notation fails, in principle, to provide a complete and correct account of the semantic properties and relations in natural language. No doubt, the numeral notation works well enough over a certain range of sense properties and relations; the notation enables us to define 'meaningless', 'meaningful', 'ambiguous', and 'synonymous'. But what about sense properties and relations outside that range? In Chomsky's argument for deep syntactic structure, we saw that the relations of 'subject of the verb' and 'direct object of the verb' could be defined in terms of surface syntactic structure over a certain range of sentences (e.g., "John loves Mary"), but that those relations could not be defined in terms of surface grammatical structure for all sentences, because syntactic relations are not always faithfully preserved in such structure. Our question is whether semantic representation on the Fregean view fails in a similar way.

To identify a set of parallel cases, we have to find cases where the semantic structure required to define sense properties and relations is not reflected in syntactic structure even at underlying levels. There are two kinds of sense properties and relations. We will call them "expressional" and "nonexpressional." Expressional properties and relations hold of expressions themselves, rather than senses, in virtue of the senses they express. It makes no sense to apply an expressional property or relation to a sense. Thus, 'being meaningful' and 'being ambiguous' are expressional sense properties because it makes no sense to apply them to the sense of a sentence, whereas it makes perfectly good sense to apply them to sentences, e.g., to say that "I met you at the bank" is meaningful and ambiguous. This is because meaningfulness and ambiguity are properties that an expression has in virtue of the number of senses it has. On the other hand, saying that a sense itself is meaningful or ambiguous is nonsense (tantamount to saying that a sense has at least one sense or has two or more senses). Expressional properties and relations are, as it were, counts of the senses of expressions.

Nonexpressional properties and relations, like 'being redundant', 'being analytic', 'being a superordinate of', 'being antonymous with', and 'being contradictory', hold directly and absolutely of senses, and only indirectly and relatively of expressions. Nonexpressionality can be illustrated by a sentence that is analytic on one of its senses but contradictory on another. We can say that one of the senses of "Dusting a surface is removing dust from it" is analytic (and the other contradictory) or, what amounts to the same thing, that the sentence is analytic *on one of its senses* (and contradictory on the other), but we cannot say, directly and without relativization, that the *sentence* is analytic. Rather than simply presenting a count, nonexpressional properties and relations say something about the structure of individual senses. Attributing analyticity to a sense of a sentence says something about how parts of the sense are related—in an example like "Bachelors are unmarried", the attribution says that the sense of the subject includes the sense of the predicate.

The Fregean view works well enough for expressional properties and relations, but fails for nonexpressional properties and relations. It fails for the latter because they must be defined in terms of the structure of senses, and, in a wide range of cases, sense structure does not coincide with syntactic structure at any level. To see how the numeral notation fails in such cases, consider the nonexpressional property of redundancy. The numeral notation can capture redundancy in a case like "a woman who is a woman" because the inclusion of the sense of the modifier in the sense of the head is reflected in the syntactic structure of the expression. (We could define an expression as redundant when the numeral representing the sense of the modifier is the same as the numeral representing the sense of the head.) But the notation cannot capture redundancy in cases of redundant expressions like "a woman who is a female", "a sister who is a sibling", and "a free gift". In such expressions, the redundancy is not reflected in syntactic structure, and, as a consequence, the numeral notation will represent the sense of the modifier and the sense of the head as distinct numerals. Accordingly, the Fregean view treats such redundant expressions in the same manner that it treats nonredundant expressions like "a woman who is frail", "a sister who is a hireling", and "an expensive gift".

The Fregean view prevents us from giving a full account of sense properties and relations in natural language. As long as we hold on to that view, our notation for describing sense structure will be restricted to a vocabulary in which the symbols representing semantic simples stand for senses of syntactic simples. In this case, we will be unable to account for the redundancy of expressions like "a woman who is female". These expressions are redundant in an intuitively obvious sense; viz., the meaning of their modifier is already part of the meaning of their head. But the complex sense structure that involves the containment of the meaning of "female" in the meaning of "woman" is masked by the syntactically simple form of the morpheme "woman", making it impossible to exploit that structure to account for the redundancy of the expressions. Expressions like "woman who is female", "sister who is a sibling", and "free gift" present a new type of ellipsis which frustrates the surface-semantics hypothesis every bit as effectively as the syntactic ellipsis in "John is easy to please" and "John is eager to please" frustrates the surface-syntax hypothesis.

But once we abandon the surface-semantics hypothesis, we can construct a notation to represent the semantically complex senses of syntactic simples.[40] In this notation, atomic symbols are replaced with symbol complexes whose parts represent the sense components and relations in complex senses of syntactic simples. We can then account for cases like "a woman who is female". We postulate that the sense of the syntactic simple "woman" is complex, consisting of the sense of "human", the sense of "adult", and the sense of "female". On this postulation of a decompositional sense structure for "woman", the redundancy of "a woman who is female" is immediately accounted for with the same intuitively obvious notion of redundancy that accounts for the redundancy of expressions like "a woman who is a woman".

This case is exactly parallel to that in which Chomsky postulated an underlying syntactic structure in order to extend the account of subject and direct-object relations in sentences like "John loves Mary" to sentences like "John is easy to please" and "John is eager to please". By parity of reasoning, we postulate an underlying semantic structure in order to extend the account of redundancy in expressions like "woman who is a woman" to expressions like "woman who is female". Decompositional postulations require a grammatical locus for the unobservable complex senses they postulate; so we are led to taking the step of positing that grammatical structure contains an underlying level of sense structure.

Like Chomsky's postulation of underlying syntactic structure, our postulation of underlying sense structure accounts for a wide range of grammatical properties and relations. Consider the nonexpressional relation of superordination. With this postulation, we can suppose that a syntactic simple like "house" has a complex sense, and, hence, we can account for the superordination relation between "dwelling" and "house" on the decompositional hypothesis that the sense of "house" contains two components, one identical with the sense of the superordinate "dwelling" and the other specifying what it is about dwellings and dwellers that distinguishes "house" from "prison", "barracks", etc. Semantic properties and relations like analyticity and analytic entailment, which also depend on sense containment, can be accounted for on the same decompositional hypotheses used to account for redundancy and superordination.

The postulation of underlying sense structure is also required for a full account of synonymy and antonymy. That this is so can be seen from cases like the synonymy of "sister" and "female sibling" and the antonymy of "open" and "closed". A numeral notation fails in the former case because these synonymous expressions will not be assigned the same numeral representation; it fails in the latter case because, although the antonymous expressions will be assigned distinct numeral representations, such representations will not be relevantly different from the distinct representations assigned to the merely non-synonymous expressions "open" and "destroy".

To account for their antonymy, the senses of "open" and "closed" must be represented as complex, containing, among the sense components in each, concepts expressing mutually exclusive positions. For instance, we might represent the senses of "open" and "closed" as, respectively, the concepts 'positioned to allow passage from one side of a contained space to the other' and 'positioned other than to allow passage from one side of a contained space to the other'. Here the concepts themselves have a built-in notion of negation taking the form of an 'other than' relation that represents exclusive positions on some dimension (such as spatial disposition, color, and age). Each concept representing a point on the dimension is incompatible with every other such concept. Thus, when a grammatically negative element occurs, as in "not open" or "not closed", it is not the external, truth-functional operator of logical negation, but what is sometimes distinguished from it as "internal negation." Rather than an operator on propositions, it is an operator on concepts, turning a concept in its scope into a concept specifying another position on the dimension. With negation available from the sense structure of syntactic simples, the contradictoriness of "The open door is closed" can be accounted for in terms of the occurrence of more than one concept from the same antonymy dimension within its predicate structure.[41]

We have now formulated the core of our inference to underlying sense structure. The rationale for the inference is that it is the only way to discharge the obligation to account for the semantic facts. Only by postulating underlying sense structure and constructing a decompositional semantics can we obtain the set of natural generalizations about sense properties and relations which enables us to account for the nonexpressional sense properties and relations in the case of sentences with syntactic simples. We will call the formulation we have thus far the "proto-theory"—to emphasize that it is only a first approximation to a full theory of decompositional sense structure.

Moreover, as our discussion makes clear, the inference to complex underlying sense structure in the case of syntactic simples is parallel to the syntactician's inference to underlying syntactic complexity. Hence, we can claim that our semantic inference to deep sense structure is on a par with the syntactician's inference to deep syntactic structure and that both of them are on a par with explanatory inferences in other sciences.

Thus, we may introduce the following:

(3) The senses of syntactic simples in natural language can have complex structure, i.e., have component senses, and an account of the semantics of natural languages must represent such *decompositional* sense structure, as well as representing compositional sense structure. Since decompositional sense structure is, by definition, underlying sense structure, an account of senses in a natural language must be a theory.

11

The appropriateness of the proto-theory for linguistics may be accepted without accepting its appropriateness for philosophy. Especially since the formulation here is so sketchy, it is easy to anticipate the question of how it is relevant to the philosophical issues with which Frege, Russell, and Wittgenstein were concerned. In this section I want to show that the proto-theory is directly relevant to those issues. I want to do this by exhibiting the power of the theory to deal with problems that Wittgenstein encountered in the *Tractatus* when he tried to use Frege's and Russell's logical ideas to treat the logical form of sentences in natural language. The unavailability of a solution to those problems within their logical theories was an important factor in Wittgenstein's change from the positive attitude he had toward theory in the *Tractatus* to the negative attitude he has toward it in the *Philosophical Investigations*. The availability of a solution within the proto-theory would establish at least its relevance to the issues in question.

In the *Tractatus*, Wittgenstein tried to fashion an account of the semantics of a language on the basis of the ideas in the *Begriffsschrift* and in *Principia Mathematica*. Of special importance was the idea that the grammatical form of sentences disguises their logical form, so that theory is necessary to reveal the hidden aspects of logical form and state them with precision. Frege's was what we might call a "prosthetic" conception of the relation between grammatical form in natural language and logical form as expressed in a conceptual notation. Just as a prosthetic device artificially compensates for the deficiencies of a natural organ, so a conceptual notation artificially compensates for the imperfections of natural languages.[42] But this analogy, even together with the other things Frege says about the relation between conceptual notation and natural language, leaves the relation unclear in much the same ways in which, as we indicated above, the relation is still unclear in the work of Carnap and Quine.

Now, in the *Tractatus*, Wittgenstein needed to be very clear about the relation between formulas of a logical calculus and sentences of a natural language because he was trying to exploit logical semantics to show that metaphysical sentences are literally nonsense. If one is trying to establish that the sentences of some class have no sense according to the rules of the language, then it is necessary to show how those sentences differ from sentences that are meaningful but whose meaning is hidden or disguised. Thus, Wittgenstein's project requires that there be a way to infer the hidden senses of sentences on the basis of aspects of them that are open to inspection. But how could he exhibit a way of making such inferences, of distinguishing the sentences which really lack a sense from those which merely have theirs deeply hidden, when the relation between a calculus and a language is itself unclear? Wittgenstein struggled with the problem, ultimately concluding that there simply is no way to infer them:

> Language disguises thought. So much so, that from the outward form of the clothing it is impossible to infer the form of the thought beneath it, because the outward form of the clothing is

not designed to reveal the form of the body, but for entirely different reasons.[43]

Let us look at one of the most important aspects of this problem. In the case of negation, the logical powers expressed in formulas of calculi developed on the basis of Frege's or Russell's work diverge significantly from intuitively clear logical powers of the sentences that are their obvious counterparts. Because the *Tractatus* employs logical notation in a semantics for language, the occurrence of negative elements in sentences are represented by the truth-functional operator $\sim$: the proposition $\sim p$ is true just in case the proposition p is false.[44] Formulas employing this negation operator are appropriate as representations of the logical powers of compound sentences containing an external or propositional negation operating on a sentence. But, as Wittgenstein saw, such formulas cause trouble when taken as representations of simple sentences like "The spot is blue", "The spot is red", and "The spot is green". Wittgenstein wrote:

> One could say, the denial is already related to the logical place determined by the proposition that is denied.
> The denying proposition determines a logical place *other* than does the proposition denied.
> The denying proposition determines this logical place, with the help of the logical place of the proposition denied, saying that it lies outside the latter place.[45]

On this account, there is a form of incompatibility in sentences which seems to go beyond the representational capacities of external negation, i.e., the incompatibility found in sentences like "The spot is completely blue at every time" and "The spot is not completely blue at every time". Such incompatibility seems to depend on an unformalized negation in color concepts. This negation might be something like the negation in the simple sentence "The spot is non-blue," meaning that the sentence is synonymous with "The spot is some color other than blue". But such an account, however intuitively plausible, conflicts with the doctrines about logical necessity and logical possibility to which Wittgenstein commits himself in adopting Frege-Russell logic in a semantics for the language. Wittgenstein writes:

> As there is only a *logical* necessity, so there is only a *logical* impossibility.
> For two colors, e.g., to be at one place in the visual field, is impossible, logically impossible, for it is excluded by the logical structure of color.

Let us consider how this contradiction presents itself in physics. Somewhat as follows: That a particle cannot at the same time
have two velocities, i.e., that at the time it cannot be in two
places, i.e., that particles in different places at the same time cannot be identical.

(It is clear that the logical product of two elementary propositions can neither be a tautology nor a contradiction. The assertion
that a point in the visual field has two different colors at the same
time, is a contradiction.)[46]

If the only impossibility is logical impossibility and if, therefore, two
elementary propositions cannot contradict each other, then how can
the logical product of two elementary sentences, one asserting that a
point has one color and the other asserting that the point has another
color, be a contradiction?

Wittgenstein returns to this difficulty in the only paper he pub-
lished, remarking that "Atomic propositions, though they cannot
contradict, may exclude each other."[47] This doesn't help, since in the
logical framework within which he was still working, there is no content to the notion of a relation of exclusion which is not logical incompatibility. And, in the *Philosophical Remarks,* Wittgenstein concedes
that not all necessary propositions can be accounted for as tautologies
and denials of tautologies.[48] Thus, at this point, he seems to abandon
the fundamental thesis of the *Tractatus's* logical framework that
atomic propositions are logically independent and to accept the view
that certain words belonging to the extralogical apparatus of a language give rise, in virtue of intrinsic aspects of their sense, to genuine
logical properties and relations like contradiction.

Wittgenstein came to regard the fact that such logical properties
and relations in sentences of natural language cannot be represented
in formulas of logical calculi as a challenge to the basic assumptions
of his early philosophy. He saw, quite rightly, that the difficulty that
had surfaced in connection with logical relations between atomic
propositions was a clear sign that there is something fundamentally
wrong with trying to use logic in a comprehensive semantics for natural language. But what? And what is to be done? Answers to these
questions had to be found if Wittgenstein was still to carry through
his critical project of showing that metaphysical sentences have no
sense.

Wittgenstein's way out of this impasse was to abandon the entire
Tractatus approach to meaning—with its calculus model, hidden
senses, and ideal of a logically perfect language—in favor of the use-
oriented approach in the *Philosophical Investigations.* This choice made

it possible for Wittgenstein to give a uniform treatment of the logical powers of sentences like "The spot is simultaneously red all over and blue all over" and sentences like "The spot is red and it is not the case that the spot is red" in terms of linguistic practices for the use of so-called logical and extralogical words. Much of Wittgenstein's late philosophy can be seen as having its genesis in this solution to the impasse to which his early philosophy had come.

There are, however, *two* other ways out of the impasse. One of them is to hold on to the Frege-Russell framework but abandon Frege's notion of sense. This way out denies Frege's claim that sense is a genuine logical concept, required for a complete statement of laws of logic. This way out is taken by Quine and his followers.[49] It is motivated by the fear that making use of Frege's concept of sense to extend logical properties and relations to the extralogical vocabulary opens up a Pandora's box of ontological ills. Quine's skeptical arguments against analyticity and synonymy make it possible to pursue this way out by purporting to show that no objective scientific sense can be made of the concept of sense. If senses are on all fours with Homer's gods, then the concept of sense is unacceptable scientifically, and if, as Quine would have it, extralogical words have only stimulus meaning, then extralogical words cannot give rise to necessary truths and necessary falsehoods.

The Wittgensteinian and the Quinean directions have been the standard ways out of the impasse. The choice between them is, in effect, the choice that Kripke talks about in the quotation with which this book began—the Chomskyan approach being simply a more linguistically sophisticated version of the Quinean (see chapter 8 of this book for further discussion).

The third way out is to preserve a notion of sense something like Frege's and his conception of logical structure, but separate them. This way rests on a different diagnosis of the impasse. On this diagnosis, there is nothing wrong about the application of a logic like Frege's to natural language, except insofar as the application is supposed to play a role in perfecting the language, and there is nothing wrong with Frege's introduction of senses, except insofar as they are supposed to be defined in terms of reference. Rather, what is wrong is Frege's unification of logic and the semantics of natural language in his definition of analyticity.

Frege joined semantics and logic in the course of reconstructing Kant's account of analyticity. Kant had given two definitions of analyticity: a semantic definition, namely that analytic propositions are those whose predicate concept is contained in their subject concept, and a logical definition, namely that analytic propositions are those whose denials are logical contradictions.[50] Frege combined these definitions. He defined analytic truths as "truths deducible from general laws of logic and definitions without assumptions taken from the sphere of a special science."[51] On this definition, the analytic sentence "All bachelors are unmarried men" is a definitional variant of the analytic sentence "All unmarried men are unmarried men", and, in virtue of this, both sentences are treated as instances of the logical truth "For anything there is, if it is F and G, then it is F and G". But in order to treat them in this way and, thereby, bring both types of sentence under a single concept of analyticity, it is necessary to assume that there is no semantic difference between the grammatically simple and the grammatically complex sentence. Therefore, in order to initiate the third way out, we require some basis for denying that the simple sentence "All bachelors are unmarried men" is an instance of "For anything there is, if it is both unmarried and a man, then it is both unmarried and a man".[52]

The third way out dissolves Frege's union of logic and semantics. The possibility of resolving the impasse this way is rarely considered because, I think, of Frege's enormous prestige. But there is nothing necessary about the connection between semantics and logic. If we cut that connection, necessary truths and falsehoods in language can be distinguished from necessary truths and falsehoods in logic, and each type of truth and falsehood can be explained as arising from a different kind of structure. If there is a different basis for each type, it would be no surprise that even Wittgenstein could not assimilate necessarily false propositions like "The spot is simultaneously red all over and blue all over" to necessarily false propositions like "The spot is red and it is not the case that the spot is red".

The key idea underlying the first way out is Wittgenstein's idea that facts about the use of language are the fundamental facts about meaning in natural language. The key idea underlying the second way out is Quine's idea that the concepts of the theory of meaning are not proper scientific concepts: we cannot make objective sense of them on the basis of any of the methods for clarifying logico-linguistic concepts in the sciences. The key idea underlying the third way out is the independence of sense structure from logical structure.

The proto-theory of the last section is the necessary linguistic means of implementing the third way out. The principal claim of the proto-theory is that the senses of syntactically simple words generally have a semantically complex, decompositional structure. That is, their senses decompose into simpler senses or concepts. This idea is inherent in the Kantian definition of analyticity which says that analytic judgments are those which add "nothing through the predicate to the concept of the subject, but merely break . . . it up into those constituent concepts that have all along been thought in it."[53] This definition needs only to be separated from Kant's logical definition of analyticity and translated into a systematic linguistic doctrine about lexical meaning, in order to locate the source of the analyticity of sentences like "Bachelors are unmarried men" and "A red spot is not blue" in the decompositional sense structure of the words "bachelor", "unmarried", "man", "red", and "blue" and to distinguish such truths from those arising from the logical structure of complex sentences.

The case of antonymy is, of course, of special interest in connection with the impasse Wittgenstein reached in connection with elementary sentences. "The spot is red" and "The spot is blue" contradict each other; yet cannot do so within the semantics of the *Tractatus*, since, being elementary, they contain no logical operators, and their nonlogical vocabulary cannot contribute a form of negation. The problem is intractable as long as we try to solve it within a semantics derived from logic, where, as Wittgenstein said, "the *application* of logic decides what elementary propositions there are"—and what propositional structure is related to necessary incompatibility.[54] There is simply no negative element to account for the incompatibility of the sentences.

But once we separate semantics from logic and adopt the proto-theory's decompositional view of sense structure, there is an appropriate negative element. Now logic is not the only conception of propositional structure which provides us with a notion of an elementary proposition. Logic gives us the notion of a *logically* elementary proposition, and linguistics, in the form of the proto-theory, gives us a notion of a *semantically* elementary proposition. And, as we have seen, the semantically elementary propositions do not coincide with the logically elementary ones, since some logically elementary propositions are semantically complex. As a consequence, the existence of a negative element needed to account for the incompatibility relations among logically elementary propositions can be located in the complex sense structure of the syntactically simple predicates in such (logically) elementary propositions.

The third way out has important advantages over the others.[55] Although all three offer the promise of an escape from the difficulties that Wittgenstein believed had brought the Fregean approach to an impasse, only the third offers an escape which, on the one hand, does not sacrifice the full-blooded notion of necessity and the use of formal methods in the study of natural language—as Wittgenstein's later philosophy does—and, on the other hand, does not rely on what prove to be fallacious skeptical arguments against meaning—and for all that, still faces Wittgenstein's problem in a somewhat different form.[56] We shall have a good deal more to say about this in the course of the book.

12

I want to return briefly to the argument in the *Tractatus* against the possibility of inferring "the form of the thought" from "the outward form of the clothing." In the next section, I will turn to Wittgenstein's arguments concerning ellipsis, starting with those in PI sections 19 and 20. Section 13 will initiate a direct confrontation between the proto-theory and Wittgenstein's arguments in the *Philosophical Investigations*.

From the present perspective, Wittgenstein's remark that "the outward form of the clothing is not designed to reveal the form of the body" (*Tractatus*: 4.002) suggests that he thinks that the syntactic simplicity of words like "red" and "blue"—which presumably obtains for reasons of communication—is what makes it impossible to infer the complex logical anatomy responsible for their necessary incompatibility. If so, it is easy to see why he came to think that inferences to underlying sense structure are bogus. He thinks that such inferences do not give us full value for our money. We are paying for a solution to the mystery that sentences have logical powers that cannot be understood on the basis of what appears on the surface to be their grammar. We pay the price of countenancing underlying senses, and, in exchange, the mystery is supposed to be dissolved. But the deal is phoney: paying the price, as Wittgenstein had in the *Tractatus*, doesn't buy us demystification. The mystery about the source of the logical powers of sentences is simply replaced by another mystery, namely, the mystery about the nature of the underlying logical forms. The "disguise" works so effectively that we are prevented from discovering the features of the senses of elementary propositions responsible for their logical relations.

Thus, it is not the impulse to demystify itself that is bad, but indulging it under conditions where, in the end, it still goes unsatisfied. Wittgenstein's solution, as we have seen, was to introduce a new way to demystify. He radically changed his conception of what it is in virtue of which sentences have inferential powers, taking them to have such powers in virtue of their use in the language. This brings the source of those powers into open view and, as a consequence, does not leave us with a mystery.

Seeing the way he himself had got entangled in the metaphysics of Fregean meaning became a paradigm for Wittgenstein of how philosophers get caught in metaphysical problems. Wittgenstein uses the paradigm to turn the traditional idea of the relation of philosophical theory to philosophical problems on its head. Philosophical theory is no longer the solution of philosophical problems; it is their source. Philosophers are misled by the parallel with science, which encourages them to engage in theory construction, and, when they do not find the objects they seek in what is observable, they think the objects must be unobservable. Thus, they erect theories to picture hidden meanings, but this creates only the illusion of understanding, since nothing in nature corresponds to such pictures. Philosophers take themselves to be "tracing the outline of a thing's nature . . . and [they are] merely tracing round the frame through which we look at it" (PI: 114).

My way out of the impasse in the *Tractatus* accounts for how sentences have inferential powers without abandoning a scientific approach or leaving us with the mystery. My way out rejects the assumption that semantic theorizing at its best takes place within the Fregean conception of the general form of propositions. Indeed, it denies that theorizing based on that conception is *semantic* theorizing at all. It takes the crux of the problem to be that, within the Fregean framework, the inferential powers of sentences are seen through the prism of logical structure, and hence, elementary propositions are seen as having no inferential relations to one another. Such relations, being logical, arise only from the compounding of elementary propositions by logical operators. As a consequence, there can be no inference to the "form of the body" which pictures the relations responsible for elementary propositions as excluding or entailing one another. But once we abandon Frege's assimilation of linguistic meaning to logical structure, we need no longer be stymied in our desire to understand the inferential powers of elementary sentences. We can provide a purely semantic account of their grammatical source by locating it within the sense structure of signs which are left as unanalyzed grammatical wholes within the *Tractatus* framework. We can thus explicate relations of sense opposition and sense containment on the basis of representations of decompositional structure.

On the proto-theory, the mystery about the source of inferential powers that cannot be attributed to surface grammar is solved in a way which leaves no mystery about how our knowledge of underlying senses can be legitimately inferred. Posits about the underlying sense structure of logically elementary sentences are guided by a clear factual requirement to account for the semantic facts and the same methodological constraints which constrain theoretical inferences in science. As we saw, we stuck to semantic description as long as possible, departing from it only when continuing to stick to it would prevent us from accounting for facts about sense properties and relations. Thus we can claim that this way of taking the step from semantic description to semantic explanation, unlike the way Wittgenstein took in the *Tractatus* and like his solution in the *Philosophical Investigations*, leaves no mystery.[57]

13

We have used a form of ellipsis to justify the view that meaning is "hidden from us" because it is "something that lies *beneath* the surface . . . which we see when we look into the thing, and which analysis digs out," and this view is what Wittgenstein is perhaps at most pains to refute in the *Philosophical Investigations* (PI: 92). Wittgenstein's view that the structure and function of language is "something that already lies open to view and that becomes surveyable by a rearrangement" is central to his therapeutic conception of philosophy (PI: 92; 109). Therefore, the issue about ellipsis may well be the most important issue raised in deciding whether our line of argument can establish (I) or is blocked virtually at the outset.

The issue about ellipsis is whether it supports inferences to underlying linguistic structure. The assumption about ellipsis which supports these inferences is that the unelliptical form is semantically more fundamental than the elliptical because it spells out what is missing in the elliptical form. On this "directionality assumption," we infer that what is missing in the surface grammar of the elliptical form must be present in its underlying grammar since the elliptical and the unelliptical forms have the same meaning. This is the pattern of my inference to underlying semantic structure. I argued that what is missing in a syntactic form like "sister," which has the same meaning as the more fundamental, unelliptical "female sibling," must be present in the underlying semantics of the word. Wittgenstein wants to show that such inferences go wrong in assuming that the unelliptical form is more fundamental.

Wittgenstein's interlocutor, assuming that elliptical forms omit information that is present in their unelliptical counterparts, feels there is a problem about the status of "Slab!" in PI section 2. The interlocutor believes that understanding this "shortened form" requires us to recognize its sense as the sense of the full sentence "Bring me a slab." But the language in section 2 contains no such sentence to which "Slab!" can be related as its elliptical form and from which it can, in virtue of the relation, obtain complete sense as a builder's order to bring a slab. So the interlocutor thinks there is a problem about how "Slab!" can mean what it does mean in the imagined language of section 2. In contrast, Wittgenstein thinks that the interlocutor's inability to see how "Slab!" could be appropriately understood without the senses of the missing words "bring", "me", and "a" is due to the interlocutor's being in the grip of the picture of compositional meaning on which the meaning of the sentence must be put together from the meanings of its component words. Since "Slab!" is supposed to mean "Bring me a slab", the components of its meaning for which words are missing must somehow be supplied on the basis of its relation to the complete sentence.[58] Wittgenstein's aim is to loosen the grip of this picture by showing that the directionality assumption on which such an understanding of "Slab!" rests is problematic. To show this, he employs a symmetry argument: "But why should I not on the contrary have called the sentence 'Bring me a slab' a *lengthening* of the sentence 'Slab!'?"(PI: 19) By pressing this argument, he intends to show that no deep truths about language are to be discovered from ellipsis because elliptical expressions and their unelliptical counterparts are simply expressions with similar uses, one of which is shorter than the other (PI: 20).

Let us begin our examination of Wittgenstein's argument by setting out some standard cases of ellipsis. Webster's example of ellipsis is "virtues I admire" instead of "virtues which I admire". Other examples are "Helen eats at home and in fancy restaurants" instead of "Helen eats at home and Helen eats in fancy restaurants", and "Natasha plays chess better than Boris" instead of "Natasha plays chess better than Boris plays chess". Comparing such cases of ellipsis with the cases in Wittgenstein's discussion produces the surprising conclusion that Wittgenstein's example of "Slab!" and "Bring me a slab" is not a case of ellipsis at all. In genuine ellipsis, the elliptical form is synonymous with the unelliptical one. Indeed, without the synonymy of the two forms, it makes little sense to try to use ellipsis to ground inferences to underlying sense structure, since the inferences would depend on interpreting the longer form as explicitly presenting the sense that the two forms have in common. But "Slab!" is not synonymous with "Bring me a slab". No doubt, the former sentence can be used to make the same request (to bring a slab) as the latter, but the meaning of "Slab!" is less specific; so it can with equal naturalness be used to make requests that "Bring me a slab!" cannot make. For example, "Slab!" can be used to warn or alert. "Slab!" is as close in meaning to "Watch out, a slab!" or "Lo, a slab" as it is to "Bring me a slab", although "Bring me a slab" is quite different in meaning from "Watch out, a slab" or "Lo, a slab". This contrasts dramatically with the example from Webster and the other examples of ellipsis.

What encourages the reader to take "Slab!" to be the elliptical form of "Bring me a slab!" is the focus in Wittgenstein's discussion on its use in the context of the building activities in PI section 2. Within this context, semantic equivalence between *sentences* is not distinguished from pragmatic equivalence between their *utterances*. The illocutionary equivalence of the utterances "Slab!" and "Bring me a slab!" in this context, together with the similarity in meaning of the sentences, makes the semantic relation between the sentences—if we think at all about the contrast between the sentences and their utterances—seem stronger than it is. Note that, as this diagnosis predicts, if we change the context, the illusion of sentential synonymy disappears. For example, in a context in which A and B are ducking falling stones, "Slab!" would more naturally be matched up with something like "Watch out, a slab!", or perhaps, "Watch out for the falling slab!" In a context where A and B are building a tall building with a notoriously clumsy co-worker, utterances of "Slab!" would be equivocal.

It is instructive to compare Wittgenstein's case with the imperative cases presented earlier. There is an obvious reason why "Slab!" exhibits the semantic slack that we just noted, but the imperatives "Dress!", "Salute!", and "Attack!" do not. The words "dress", "salute", and "attack" are verbs as well as nouns, and can, as a consequence, give rise to imperatives, but the word "slab" is just a noun and, hence, cannot give rise to an imperative.[59] Further, since "slab" is a noun, the word type has a semantics which leaves open what activity it is that is going on in connection with the slabs to which the tokens refer. The activity may be bringing them to the speaker, watching out for them, noticing them, etc. Insofar as the semantics of the type specifies nothing in this connection, the speech context carries the full burden of supplying the information that specifies the activity in question. This is why, as we just saw, the activity changes with changes in the context. In contrast, insofar as the word "dress" is a verb in the imperative form "Dress!" the activity in question is specified by the semantics of the word as that of putting on clothes. In standard uses of "Dress!" addressees do not have to figure out from the context what activity the speaker has requested of them. In such uses, the context does not carry the burden of supplying information that will specify the desired activity, but may carry an opposite burden. The burden may be to supply information that cancels the activity specified in the meaning of the type, e.g., in a context where soldiers know to stay put when their captain shouts "Attack!" so as to make the enemy reveal their position.

Given these considerations, Wittgenstein's symmetry argument is seen to be based on an ill-chosen example. Even without further examination, it is clear that any arguments based on the example of "Slab!" and "Bring me a slab" can be dismissed as raising no serious objection to the use of genuine cases of ellipsis as a basis for inferring underlying grammatical structure.

But perhaps Wittgenstein's example is dispensable. To determine whether his arguments will work without the example, we should examine them on the basis of genuine short imperatives in place of "Slab!" We want to know whether there are reasons to think that the directionality assumption is true, or whether the assumption is arbitrary, as Wittgenstein claims. Are there solid reasons for saying that imperatives are reductions of longer forms, or can one say just as well that the longer forms are expansions of the shorter? (PI: 19)

As we saw above, there are reasons for taking short imperatives like "Clean yourself!" and "Dress!" to be reduced forms of an underlying sentential structure that contains a second-person subject. For example, unless we take such imperatives in this way, we cannot account for a wide range of syntactic facts about agreement, such as that "You dress!" and "Dress yourself (yourselves)!" are well-formed sentences, whereas "It (he, she) dress!" and "Dress itself (himself, herself, themselves)!" are not. If we suppose that the imperatives have an underlying syntactic structure something like

$$((you)_{NP} ((dress)_V (you + self)_{NP})_{VP})_S$$

these facts about agreement follow immediately from the rule that a reflexive direct object agrees with the subject of its verb in number, gender, and case. The rule is independently required to distinguish syntactically well-formed sentences like "She dresses herself" and "She dresses herself all by herself" from syntactically ill-formed strings like "She dresses itself" and "She dresses herself all by itself". Further, the posit of an underlying structure with a second-person subject accounts for the existence of imperative forms like "You dress!" and their synonymy with forms like "Dress!". Still further, the posit accounts for the synonymy of sentences like "Dress, you naughty child!", "You dress, you naughty child!", and "You dress, you naughty child, you!", and also for the ill-formedness of corresponding cases where agreement is absent. Thus, besides accounting for these particular facts, the posited underlying structure for short imperatives makes possible a full statement of the rule for English pronominal agreement.

Wittgenstein's symmetry argument is misleadingly formulated in another respect: it makes it seem as if the issue were adequately stated in terms of a single case like "Slab!". In fact, an adequate formulation requires that the issue be stated in terms of an infinite or open class of cases. If there were just a single item, or even a (small enough) closed class, it would be plausible to suppose that our use of it is simply a matter of the sort of training that Wittgenstein has in mind, say, as we may presume our use of the greeting "Hi!" is. My criticism is not that "slab" is syntactically simple. Certain syntactically complex signs, viz., idioms, might be understood on the basis of training which connects them directly with appropriate uses. My criticism is rather that genuine ellipsis occurs productively within an infinite or open class of cases. Instances of a particular case of ellipsis are found in the members of such a class of sentences. For example, our earlier example "Natasha plays chess better than Boris" and "Natasha plays chess better than Boris plays chess" is only one among an infinite or open class of pairs of sentences of the form 'NP$_1$ VP Aer than NP$_2$' and 'NP$_1$ VP Aer than NP$_2$ VP'. The problem is to account for the relation between the members of the pairs over the entire class. Thus, the problem is structural and, hence, sufficiently abstract to make the Wittgensteinian formulation misleading. An account of the speaker's mastery of the syntax and semantics of the pairs in such a class is an account of a mastery which permits the speaker to recognize the synonymy of any pair in the class, in particular, pairs he or she has never encountered before. Wittgenstein's formulation leaves this problem out of the picture.

There is a sense in which Wittgenstein is right to say there is no more reason to think that the short form is a shortening of the long than to say the long form is a lengthening of the short. Formal rules for ellipsis could be written relating short and long forms either by deletion operations that shorten long forms or by addition operations that lengthen short ones. But these formal options do not settle the substantive issue about directionality. There are two issues concerning directionality which are conflated in Wittgenstein's symmetry argument. One, which we have conceded, is the question of the direction in which the syntactic rules work, and the other, which is independent, is the question of the direction in which the semantic analysis goes. Although there may be symmetry as far as how the rules are written, we still can, and indeed must, say that certain of the syntactic and semantic features of the short form can be analyzed as being those of the long. That is, the short form must have an underlying structure in which the syntactic and semantic features are part of its grammar. Since they are not part of its surface structure, if we don't say this, there will be nothing in the grammatical analysis of the short form to account for syntactic facts like agreement and semantic facts like synonymy. If, for example, there were no second-person subject in the grammar of "Dress!", it would be a mystery why the reflexive direct object is "yourself" or "yourselves" rather than "itself", "myself", or "themselves". Similarly, it would be a mystery why "Dress!" is synonymous with "You dress!" or why "Natasha plays chess better than Boris" is synonymous with "Natasha plays chess better than Boris plays chess" rather than, say, "Natasha plays chess better than Boris sings folk songs". The issue of whether the long form explicitly marks the semantically significant structure of both forms does not depend on whether surface elliptical expressions are thought of as the beginning of a process of lengthening or the end of a process of shortening.

14

Given that Wittgenstein's interlocutor is saddled with a spurious example of ellipsis and a spurious commitment to defending the wrong directionality claim, it is no wonder the poor soul is driven to psychology. Once it appears clear that no case for process directionality can be made on the basis of similarity of sense and difference of length, psychology comes to seem the only recourse. When Wittgenstein presses his symmetry argument, the interlocutor replies, "Because if you shout 'Slab!' you really mean: 'Bring me a slab'". At this point, the interlocutor is in real trouble. Wittgenstein easily shows that this appeal to psychology cannot justify the directionality claim either because the appeal presupposes the intended directionality or else because it raises considerations that are merely epiphenomenal. Wittgenstein asks:

> But how do you do this: how do you *mean that* while you *say* "Slab!" Do you say the unshortened sentence to yourself? And why should I translate the call "Slab!" into a different expression in order to say what someone means by it? And if they mean the same thing—why should I not say: "When he says 'Slab!', he means 'Slab!'"? (PI: 19)

Since one does not introspect a saying of the longer sentence as part of the mental preparation for uttering the shorter sentence, either no such internal saying occurs or it occurs unconsciously. But neither of these alternatives can justify the claim that the speaker means the longer sentence in uttering the shorter one. The interlocutor's claim thus comes down to nothing more than that we use the longer form to say what someone means by the shorter. Wittgenstein delivers the devastating response: ". . . if they mean the same thing—why should I not say: "When he says 'Slab!', he means 'Slab!'?" (PI: 19) Hence, the appeal to psychology has come full circle, and the interlocutor is back at the original point where justification was called for. But, not having learned the lesson that the mental does not provide the needed justification, the interlocutor continues with more psychology: ". . . when I call 'Slab!', then what I want is, *that he should bring me a slab!*" (PI: 19). This, of course, fares no better than previous appeals to psychology. Wittgenstein replies: "Certainly, but does 'wanting this' consist in thinking in some form or other a different sentence from the one you utter?" (PI: 19)

Having shown that the proto-theory can rest on facts about ellipsis without being vulnerable to Wittgenstein's arguments here, we do not at this point need to take the plunge into psychologism along with the interlocutor. I will continue to defend the proto-theory without appealing to the mental. I agree with Wittgenstein that turning to the subjective to try to answer objective grammatical questions is hopeless because mental phenomena (e.g., images) are conceptually distinct from grammatical phenomena; hence, once there is a shift to the mental, accounts of the grammatical are no longer about the grammatical. In this respect, both our positions echo Frege's antipsychologism in logic, though, of course, they diverge on the question of what ought to replace appeals to the mental.

Siding with Wittgenstein against psychologism has the same advantage for my line of argument as siding with him against programs to perfect natural languages, namely, it guides the proto-theory safely around some of the most forceful arguments in his critique of theories of meaning and, hence, takes my line of argument in this chapter a step closer to showing that there is a theory of meaning that escapes all Wittgenstein's criticisms. Accordingly, I add (4) as a further thesis of the proto-theory:

> (4) Questions about a language are about the grammatical structure of sentences, nothing more. Grammatical structure is neither constructed out of nor dependent upon mental states or mental events, conscious or unconscious, actual or idealized. Grammar is autonomous: grammars are not about speakers; they are simply about grammar.

Thesis 4 doesn't say what languages and sentences are. In later chapters, I will develop a realist position on which a language is a collection of sentences and sentences are abstract objects.[60] But I want to make clear at this point that neither (4) nor any of my replies to Wittgenstein's criticisms of theories of meaning depends on linguistic realism. The overall argument of this book proceeds the other way around. It tries to vindicate a theory of meaning without prejudging its ontological interpretation and then tries to support linguistic realism as the best interpretation for the theory. Therefore, it is necessary for there to be no assertion of linguistic realism until the arguments to vindicate the proto-theory are complete. And for Wittgenstein the parallel obligation is clear: to keep his linguistic naturalism out of the picture until the arguments for his account of meaning are complete. For one of his prime objectives in criticizing theories of meaning is to motivate a conception of meaning that will serve as a basis for attacking realism in the philosophy of logic and mathematics.[61]

15

At the beginning of PI section 20, Wittgenstein raises the possibility that someone might use "Bring me a slab" as a one-word command. He proposes that we mean it as a four-word sentence when we contrast it with other sentences like "*Hand* me a slab", "Bring *him* a slab", and "Bring *two* slabs". Having taken the plunge into psychologism, the interlocutor is likely to explain what it is to use a sentence in contrast with others by saying that "the others . . . hover before one's mind." Continuing his criticism of the interlocutor's psychologism, Wittgenstein challenges this explanation, rejecting the idea that such introspectable objects are present and making the comparison between our understanding of "Bring me a slab" and a foreigner's to show that its status as a four-word sentence depends on the fact that "*our language* contains the possibility of those other sentences." We can agree: it is linguistic possibility rather than psychological possibility that counts.

On our "top-down" approach, such contrastive use is use of tokens of sentences in accord with the grammatical structure of types in the language. The speaker's understanding of the meaning of sentence types is based on a knowledge of the meanings of their component words and of how those meanings combine with one another in relation to the syntax of the expressions. On the "top-down" approach, then, contrasts like those in the examples come from the potential for variation in the compositional process, that is, its potential to produce, with the change of a word, the different meanings of "Hand me a slab", "Bring him a slab", "Bring two slabs", and "Bring me a slab". Indeed, the fact that the differences in meaning among the members of such sets of sentences are solely a function of the differences in the meaning of the contrastive words is typical of the evidence adduced for the claim that the meaning of a sentence is a compositional function of the meanings of its syntactic parts.

Two theses about compositionality can be distinguished. One is a psychological thesis about the understanding of sentences, and the other is a nonpsychological thesis about sentences themselves. The former says, in effect, that the subjective processes whereby the mind calculates, or in some fashion determines, an inner representation of the meaning of a sentence are processes that work compositionally on inner representations of the meanings of its constituents. The latter, in contrast, says that the meaning of a sentence is a function of the meaning of its constituents and their syntactic relations. The former is about people—in particular, the psychological conditions for their understanding utterances or inscriptions in a language—whereas the latter is about languages—in particular, the grammatical structure of their sentence types. Conflation of these theses can make it seem as if some of Wittgenstein's arguments tell against compositionality *per se*, when, in fact, they tell only against a use of the understandability thesis.

Wittgenstein is surely right to deny that a *sentence* is elliptical "because it leaves out something that we think when we utter it" (PI: 20). Again, I side with Wittgenstein against psychologism. On the proto-theory, a sentence is elliptical in virtue of its grammatical structure, and this structure is a matter of both syntactic form and compositional meaning.

Wittgenstein anticipates the objection that it will be granted that elliptical and unelliptical forms have the same sense. If this were granted, it would then be granted that the former "leaves out" something that is verbally expressed in the latter. But Wittgenstein does not grant that the two forms are the same in sense. He reminds us that sameness of sense consists in sameness of use, leaving it for the reader to see that elliptical and unelliptical forms do not have the same use. Whatever one thinks of this reply with respect to the position Wittgenstein takes himself to be rebutting, it does not rebut the position on sense expressed in the proto-theory, because nothing up to this juncture in the *Philosophical Investigations* provides an argument against (2) and (2') and for Wittgenstein's position that sameness of sense consists in sameness of use.

16

This section digresses from the examination of Wittgenstein's critique of theories of meaning to defend the distinction between questions of grammar and questions of understanding against Michael Dummett's highly influential criticisms. These criticisms need to be addressed because, as the result of them, there is a tendency to think that it is pointless to distinguish the two types of questions because no theory of meaning that is not at the same time a theory understanding can be acceptable. Dummett writes:

> . . . we may substitute for an enquiry into the nature of meaning one into the nature of significance (meaningfulness) or of synonymy (sameness of meaning). Neither type of enquiry is, however, likely to lead to a satisfactory account of meaning as we intuitively apprehend this notion. Rather, the complex phrase on which attention needs to be concentrated is 'knowing the meaning of . . .': a theory of meaning is a theory of *understanding*.[62]

Before looking at Dummett's development of this line of thinking, it is important to reveal the straw-man character of the position Dummett sets up as the rival position. It is set up by the use of two tactics. The first is what might be called a "divide and conquer" tactic. Dummett divides inquiry into the nature of meaning into an inquiry into meaningfulness on the one hand and, on the other, an inquiry into sameness of meaning, proceeding then to judge them independently. To appreciate the peculiarity of the division, we have only to contemplate essentially the same division in other areas, for example, dividing inquiry into the nature of logical implication into an inquiry into logical significance (having logical consequences) and an inquiry into logical equivalence (sameness of logical consequences), or dividing inquiry into the nature of pronunciation into an inquiry into pronounceability and an inquiry into sameness of pronunciation. It clearly makes no sense to separate the natural parts of logical and phonological inquiry and judge the success of the artificially separated parts independently. Why then think that it makes sense to separate the natural parts of semantic inquiry and judge them separately?

The tactic of separating inquiry into 'having a meaning' and 'having the same meaning' works in tandem with another less explicit tactic for promoting the view that semantic inquiry unbolstered by being made part of an inquiry into understanding does not shed much light on our intuitive notion of meaning. The second tactic is to focus on 'having a meaning' and 'having the same meaning' to the exclusion of all other aspects of the notion of meaning, such as 'having multiple meanings', 'having redundant meaning', 'having opposed meanings', 'having superordinate meaning', 'having analytic meaning', and so on. This exclusion makes the inquiry Dummett is criticizing appear far too narrow and inconsequential ever to give a satisfactory account of our intuitive notion of meaning. But what inquiry wouldn't look unsatisfactory after having been fragmented and narrowed in such a way?

It is interesting to note that the approach this chapter takes to developing a theory of meaning is the very reverse of Dummett's two tactics. The chapter tries to collect all the aspects of the notion of meaning together in order to obtain a comprehensive picture of the aims of inquiry into an autonomous notion of meaning. The result is the notion of meaning in (1)–(4). An inquiry with the aims specified in (1)–(4) is clearly not so narrow and inconsequential that it can be dismissed out of hand as not "likely to lead to a satisfactory account of meaning as we intuitively apprehend this notion." Only by formulating the aims of inquiry into an autonomous notion of meaning in a way that incompletely comprehends those aims is Dummett able to make the inquiry seem unlikely to provide "a satisfactory account of the notion of meaning that we intuitively apprehend."

Since it no longer appears obvious that such an inquiry cannot explicate our intuitive notion of meaning, Dummett owes us a reason for thinking that an account of grammatical meaning independent of an account of the knowledge required for understanding meaning is unacceptable. In a more recent publication, he tries to provide such a reason:

> . . . if it were possible to give an account of, for example, when two expressions have the same meaning, which did not overtly rely on an account of what it was to know the meaning of an expression, then it would not be possible to derive an account of knowledge of meaning from it. There is, indeed, good reason to suppose it impossible to give an account of synonymy save via an account of understanding, since it is a requirement on the former that whoever knows the meanings of two synonymous expressions must also know that they are synonymous: but I am saying merely that, if such an account of synonymy were possible, there would be no route from it to an account of understanding.[63]

This is hardly better than no reason at all. The first sentence is virtually a tautology. Further, the "good reason" with which we are presented is irrelevant to the issue of whether an account of synonymy can be given save via an account of understanding. The requirement is, and is explicitly presented as, a requirement on a theory of sentence understanding. No reason is given to think that a requirement on a theory of sentence understanding is or implies a requirement on a theory of sentence meaning. Hence, to claim, as Dummett does, that the requirement is a requirement on an account of synonymy is merely to reassert, this time in the idiom of requirements, the original claim that a theory of meaning is a theory of understanding.

It is, of course, quite true, as Dummett says, that, if an account of synonymy were to be formulated apart from an account of understanding, "there would be no route from it to an account of understanding." But so what? This is exactly what we should expect on the view that grammar is autonomous. After all, there is no route from an account of syntax to an account of the understanding of syntax, or from an account of the calculus to an account of the understanding of the calculus. True enough, we are also curious about what our understanding of meaning consists in. But Dummett gives no reason to think that the route to satisfying that curiosity is what he thinks it is instead of proceeding on the basis of an already developed independent account of autonomous meaning. Many approaches to an account of understanding syntactic structure proceed on the basis of an already developed independent account of autonomous syntax.[64]

Once we entertain the possibility of a "top-down" approach, we can conceive of an order of things in which we first develop a theory of the syntactic or semantic structure of sentence types and then develop a theory of the production and understanding of their tokens on the basis of the first theory. At this point, it is clear that an argument against autonomous theories of meaning cannot succeed if it fails to consider the possibility of a "top-down" approach. It is even plausible that this is the natural order of things, since it is plausible to think that we have to discover what is understood before we can discover how it is understood.

17

At the beginning of PI section 21, Wittgenstein raises the question "Now what is the difference between the report or statement 'Five slabs' and the order 'Five slabs!'?" In raising this question, he sets out to criticize positions on sentence meaning which explain the differences between such sentences in terms of contrasting assertive, requestive, etc. elements in the underlying semantic content of the sentences. The immediate target of this criticism seems to be the position Frege expresses in this passage:

> An interrogative sentence and an indicative one contain the same thought; but the indicative contains something else as well, namely, the assertion. The interrogative sentence contains something more, too, namely, a request. Therefore, two things must be distinguished in an indicative sentence, the content, which it has in common with the corresponding sentence-question, and the assertion.[65]

The opposition is between Frege's claim that the difference between such sentences has to do with components of their senses and Wittgenstein's claim that the difference is a matter of "the part which uttering these words plays in the language-game" (PI: 21). In section 21 and subsequent sections, Wittgenstein develops a criticism of Frege's position on sentence meaning which parallels his criticism of Augustine's position on word meaning. Just as Augustine is criticized for ignoring differences in kinds of words, so Frege is criticized for ignoring differences among "countless" kinds of sentences. Wittgenstein thinks that the Fregean position cannot, in principle, do justice to the limitless variety among the different things speakers use language to do (PI: 23). This is an important criticism in the *Philosophical Investigations.* It continues the attack on hidden sense, questions the calculus model of language, and constitutes a major step toward developing an alternative to Frege's conception of sentence meaning.

Although the notion of sense in the proto-theory differs considerably from Frege's, the proto-theory also claims that sentence meaning contains an illocutionary component. Indeed, the theory is committed to such a claim. As indicated, the proto-theory has to acknowledge sense components whenever they are required for an account of sense properties and relations. Given the differences in sense among sentences like "Enough wine will be bought for the party", "Will enough wine be bought for the party?", and "Buy enough wine for the party!", the proto-theory is committed to their senses' containing the appropriately different illocutionary sense components required to account for their nonsynonymy. Therefore, we are obliged to show that Wittgenstein's criticisms do not work against the proto-theory's conception of sentence meaning.

Wittgenstein first observes that intonational and similar features do not distinguish reports and statements from orders and commands. He then points out that we use "Isn't the weather glorious today?" with interrogative intonation to make a statement about how glorious the weather is (PI: 21). This is supposed to show that differences in application correlate with differences in meaning and, hence, that application of signs, rather than alleged senses, is what counts semantically. Now this sort of argument may have force against Frege's position on sentence meaning, as formulated within his overall semantics, but it doesn't work against the proto-theory. To appreciate the reason, it is important to see that issues between one "top-down" approach and another "top-down" approach can sometimes be as significant for philosophical questions as those between such approaches and "bottom-up" approaches. Before evaluating the arguments in PI section 21, I want to look at some of the differences between Frege's approach and the approach I have taken.

In ordinary parlance, we talk about senses of types and about senses of tokens—though we may not talk about them in just those terms. For example, we refer to a sense of a type when we explain what such-and-such an English sentence means, and we refer to a sense of a token when we explain what so-and-so's remark means. The question thus arises whether we are referring to different things which both happen to go under the name "sense" or to the same thing which happens to be associated with different linguistic objects. The unattractiveness of the former dualism makes it attractive to say that senses are just one kind of thing—associated in the one case with types and in the other with tokens. So, suppose we choose this monism. The next thing that has to be decided is which kind of thing senses are, something abstract like types or something concrete like tokens, that is, which association of senses with objects is basic and which derivative. The options are a "bottom-up" approach, which takes the assignment to go from senses of tokens to senses of types, and a "top-down" approach, which takes it the other way around, that is, from senses of types to senses of tokens.

Empiricists prefer the "bottom-up" approach, rationalists the "top-down" approach (see chapter 8). Because rationalists see no way of understanding senses and sentence types as arising from the context of linguistic tokens, they understand senses and sentence types to be *sui generis* and understand the use of sentence tokens to derive from the speaker's knowledge of sentence structure. Frege's semantics and ours, being rationalist, thus have this much in common, but they begin to diverge once their rationalism no longer dictates their position on semantic issues. The first question within a "top-down" approach is how to explain the way linguistic tokens come to have the senses of linguistic types. Frege's answer is that sense determines reference: information in the sense of an expression identifies its referent(s).[66] If we couple this view with Frege's view that the elements of assertion and request are part of the sense of sentences, then he seems committed to claiming not only that "wine" refers to wine and "the party" refers to the party, but also that "Enough wine will be bought for the party" makes a statement and "Will enough wine be bought for the party?" makes a request. But, then, Wittgenstein's example of the sentence "Isn't the weather glorious today?"—which can be used and, in fact, standardly is used, to make a statement—is a counter-example to Frege's semantics.

But this sound criticism of Fregean intensionalism does not apply to all intensionalist theories taking a "top-down" approach. This is because the Fregean answer to the question of how linguistic tokens come to have the senses of linguistic types is not the only answer available within a "top-down" approach. "Top-down" implies that tokens obtain their syntactic character from syntactic types and their semantic character from senses of syntactic types; it does not imply that the relation under which they do so has to be as strong as deter-mination. Intensionalists can formulate their "top-down" approach in terms of a weaker relation between the sense of types and the sense and reference of their tokens. Once this fact is recognized, it is clear that the difficulty that Wittgenstein's criticism raises is not a difficulty for the view that the sense of a sentence contains an illocutionary component, but is a difficulty only for "top-down" approaches that adopt too strong a relation between the sense and reference of tokens and the sense of types.

A number of philosophers mistakenly equated intensionalism with Fregean intensionalism, and, as a consequence, we have seen many "refutations" of intensionalism based on arguments like Wittgen-stein's. I will examine some of them in chapter 6. Here I want to probe further by asking why the equation has seemed so straightforward, why the possibility of relations weaker than determination is never considered. I believe it is because Frege's notion of sense, which en-tails determination, is seen as the only notion that intensionalists have available to them.

Frege defined the sense of an expression as that which contains the mode of determination of its reference.[67] Senses thus provide identi-fying information necessary to fix their extension. This is not the only definition of sense open to intensionalists. There is at least the alter-native definition on which the proto-theory is based, namely that sense is that aspect of the grammatical structure of an expression in virtue of which it has properties and relations like synonymy, antony-my, ambiguity, meaningfulness, meaninglessness, and redundancy. The critical difference between these definitions is that Frege's spec-ifies sense in terms of reference, thereby making sense a deriv-ative notion whose entire *raison d'être* is that it is the source of reference-fixing information. In contrast, our definition specifies sense in terms of an aspect of the grammatical structure of sentences, thereby making sense independent of reference and purely internal to the language. Therefore, on our definition, it is possible to have a weaker relation between sense and reference than Frege's without undercutting the *raison d'être* for the notion of sense.[68]

I will sketch a weaker relation than Frege's determination, which I will call "mediation."[69] Then I will explain how a "top-down" approach based on the idea that sense mediates reference can maintain that the meaning of sentences contains an illocutionary component and yet not be subject to criticisms like Wittgenstein's criticism in PI section 21.

The effect of abandoning the strong relation of determination, while retaining the monism that holds that senses of utterances are not some new things over and above the senses of sentences, is simply to rule out the invariable identification of the meaning of a linguistic token with the meaning of the linguistic type of which it is a token. It allows for cases in which the meaning of an utterance departs, even perhaps radically, from the meaning of its type. But abandoning determination does not abandon the "top-down" approach, because the meaning of an utterance in such cases can be identified with the meaning of a linguistic type other than that of which the utterance is a token. Of course, in such cases, the identification cannot be based solely on the information in the sense structure of the linguistic type—but making room for extragrammatical information is one of the aims of abandoning determination. Thus it is open to us to give an explanation of why the meaning of an utterance of the sentence "Everybody is coming to our party" is the meaning of a sentence type like "Everybody in our circle of friends is coming to our party", which is different from the explanation we give of why the meaning of an utterance of "Two plus two equals four" is just the meaning of the sentence type of which it is an utterance.

The move from determination to mediation gives us the option of saying that the sense of an utterance or inscription is the sense of some sentence other than that of which it is a token, providing we change the explanation from a purely grammatical one to one that involves extragrammatical information. To put the point another way, the *grammatical principles* that correlate senses with sentence types in the language do not also correlate senses with sentence tokens in language use; therefore, there seems to be another set of principles that correlate utterances and inscriptions with senses. For obvious reasons, I will call these *pragmatic principles*. The "top-down" approach is, then, a conception of pragmatic principles which assumes that grammatical principles play a mediating role in correlating senses with utterances and inscriptions. The proto-theory and the "top-down" approach thus belong to different domains.

Some philosophers have argued that the linguist's notion of sense cannot be identified with the divergent contextual senses associated with uses of indexical words such as "today" and "yesterday". If this were so, we could not construct a theory of meaning within linguistics with substantial philosophical implications for the issues raised in the *Philosophical Investigations*. Tyler Burge, for example, sees an incommensurability between the linguist's meanings, which are "each governed by a single linguistic rule and have a single context-free dictionary entry," and Frege's idea that the "sense expressed in an indexical utterance *can* be the same as that expressed in another utterance with a different meaning. Thus, 'yesterday' and 'today', used in appropriately different contexts, can be employed to express the same sense. Here sense remains constant while meaning shifts."[70] Given a non-Fregean "top-down" approach, it is clear that such shifts can be accommodated as well by assigning meanings of sentence types to sentence tokens on the basis of pragmatic principles as by separating linguistic meaning from utterance meaning. Surely "John got toys today" said on Christmas Day and "John got toys yesterday" said the day after can both have the sense of the sentence "John got toys on Christmas Day". Burge's argument for the incommensurability between linguistic meaning and utterance meaning overlooks the conceptions of grammar and pragmatics which a non-Fregean "top-down" approach makes available.

One final point. In addition to explaining the basis on which meanings of linguistic types are assigned to linguistic tokens in contexts, pragmatic principles must specify the basis on which reference is assigned to utterances in contexts. They must account for how, beyond grammar, the reference of utterances depends on extralinguistic factors, such as the beliefs of speakers, information from the context, etc. Such factors are responsible for the departure of the sense and reference of tokens from the sense and reference of types; hence, they are what prevent sense from determining reference. Our "top-down" approach claims that *sense mediates reference*, meaning by this that the senses of expression types are necessary, in a way to be explained, to determine the senses and reference of their tokens.[71]

Let us return to Wittgenstein's example "Isn't the weather glorious today?". We have to explain how, on our non-Fregean "top-down" approach, the sentence itself can be a question, while utterances of it, as Wittgenstein rightly says, can be statements. The explanation has to be sufficiently general to apply to other examples, such as

Wittgenstein's case of "You will do this" which functions sometimes as a prophecy and sometimes as a command (PI: 21).

The following six things may be distinguished:

(i) the illocutionary act of making a statement, making a request, etc.
(ii) the statement, request, etc. made in the act
(iii) the utterance, inscription, etc. used to make the statement, request, etc.
(iv) the sentence of the language of which the utterance is a token
(v) the sense of the sentence of the language
(vi) the sense of the utterance in the context.

Since from our perspective (i)–(iii) and (vi) are matters of pragmatics, whereas (iv) and (v) are matters of grammar, different sorts of considerations are involved in determining the character of the English sentence "Isn't the weather glorious today?" and in determining the character of its utterances and what they are used to do. Considerations that enter into categorizing the sentence as an interrogative or question are grammatical features such as the inversion of subject and auxiliary and the contour indicated by the question mark. Considerations that enter into categorizing utterances of it as making the statement that the weather is glorious are pragmatic features such as that, in the context, the weather is so obviously glorious that no one with normal vision could need to be told. Similarly, considerations that enter into categorizing "You will do this" as a declarative sentence expressing something about the addressee's future behavior are the absence of inversion, the presence of the future modal, and a verb phrase appropriate to indicating an action, whereas considerations that enter into categorizing utterances of it as a prophecy or command are such things as whether they come out of the mouth of a fortune-teller or a master sergeant.

Thus, from our perspective, the proper answer to Wittgenstein's question of what makes someone's *utterance* of "You will do this" a prophecy or a command is, as Wittgenstein implies, the use. But this answer is completely compatible with the claim that the sentence itself has a sense, part of which is an assertion and part of which is a content expressing what is asserted as a future act of an unspecified kind. The sense of the sentence does not have to contain a command for us to account for the fact that an utterance of it is a command. In the mouth of the master sergeant, the utterance of the assertive proposition is understood by the soldiers as conveying the message that the prediction about their future behavior is one they had better make true. Indeed, it is the fact that the sentence is simply an assertion that helps to give this use its peculiar force of an order backed up by higher authority.

The sentence "Isn't the weather glorious today?" is an interrogative with a sense containing both a requestive element and a component that specifies what is requested as an answer to the query about the weather. It is not necessary for the sense of the interrogative to actually contain an assertive element for its utterances to make the statements it makes. The utterances can be pragmatically correlated with the sense of an assertive sentence like "The weather is certainly glorious today!". To make the correlation, all that is necessary beyond knowledge of the meaning of the sentences is knowledge of the context of the utterance of the interrogative. Presumably, the members of the audience know that the speaker who has said "Isn't the weather glorious today?" can see perfectly well that the weather is truly glorious, and can see that they see it is, and hence, they have the choice of taking him or her to be asking a pointless question or to be stating that the weather is glorious in a way that expresses evident pleasure in that fact. Because there is no reason to impose an unflattering interpretation and because they know that the speaker can reasonably be taken to have anticipated their working out his or her intention to express pleasure in the day, the members of the audience recognize the speaker's intent to use the utterance with the sense of a sentence like "The weather is certainly glorious today!".[72]

Whether or not this explanation is right (nothing hangs on it in particular being correct), the explanation has to be pragmatic, since some utterances of "Isn't the weather glorious today?" have the erotetic sense that this sentence has in the language. A blind person, after being told a lot about how glorious the weather is, then hears something suggesting the opposite, and asks "Isn't the weather glorious today?" to confirm or disconfirm what he or she has been told.

Wittgenstein is right in saying that use is what determines the sense of an utterance, but this, as we may now conclude, does not show that it is wrong to claim that the meaning of sentences contains an illocutionary element. There is no implication about how the senses of sentences should be understood, because not all "top-down" approaches restrict the meaning of an utterance to the meaning of the type of which it is a token. Those approaches based on a mediation relation allow selection from the entire range of grammatically determined sentence meanings.[73]

18

In section 22, Wittgenstein explicitly criticizes Frege's conception of the meaning of an assertive sentence as containing an assertion in addition to a content. Denying that an assertive sentence contains an assertive element and an assumption, Wittgenstein writes:

> Frege's idea . . . really rests on the possibility found in our language of writing every statement in the form: "It is asserted that such-and-such is the case."—But "that such-and-such is the case" is *not* a sentence in our language—so far it is not a *move* in the language-game. And if I write, not "It is asserted that . . .", but "It is asserted: such-and-such is the case", the words "It is asserted" simply become superfluous.
>
> We might very well also write every statement in the form of a question followed by a "Yes" . . .
>
> Of course, we have a right to use an assertion sign in contrast to a question-mark . . . It is only a mistake if one thinks that the assertion consists of two actions, entertaining and asserting . . . , and that in performing these actions we are following the propositional sign roughly as we sing from the musical score. (PI: 22)

There are three arguments here. The first attempts to show that a Fregean conception of the sense of assertive sentences is either incoherent or superfluous. If the verbal expression of the assumption is just a clause, how can it play the independent inferential role that this conception would have it play? But if it is a full sentence, doesn't the original assertive element become superfluous? Frege might deny that his conception rests on the possibility of expressing *Begriffsschrift* analyses in suitable natural-language paraphrases, arguing that the absence of an appropriate paraphrase is just the sort of imperfection that makes construction of an ideal language necessary. There is no point in taking a position here.[74] Even if the reply blocks this argument, it is unavailable to us because we have forsworn Frege's view concerning natural and ideal languages.

Our position must be that the assertive element of indicative sentences like "Snow is white" is part of their underlying grammatical structure, an element which does not appear in their surface structure in virtue of one of the two kinds of ellipsis, either the syntactic kind in which an underlying syntactic form containing a particular constituent has a surface form not containing it or the semantic kind in which a syntactically simple form masks a semantically complex one.[75] On the assumption that there is some form of ellipsis that conceals the assertive element, Wittgenstein is correct to say that spelling out the underlying assertive element produces a sentence in which the constituent expressing the underlying assertive element is super-fluous. But why should its superfluousness bother us? It can be taken as showing nothing more than that the missing constituent in some cases of ellipsis cannot itself be realized in surface structure—in the way the second-person subject of "Help them!" can be realized in "You help them!"—so that, when the content of the underlying struc-ture is independently inserted in surface structure, there is semantic duplication.

Rather than an argument against the presence of an underlying assertive element, the superfluousness of "It is asserted that" in the rewritten form in Wittgenstein's example is evidence *for* the presence of an underlying assertive element. "Superfluousness" is just another name for redundancy, which, as we have seen, is one of the sense properties and relations that provide evidence for sense structure. Wittgenstein's case is no different from that of rewriting "John is a bachelor" in the form "John is a bachelor: he is an unmarried man", where the redundancy of the latter, spelled-out form is evidence for the existence of the concepts 'unmarried' and 'man' in the decom-positional structure of the sense of "bachelor". The redundancy of the rewritten forms shows them to have the same meaning as their corresponding unrewritten forms; hence, this feature testifies to the existence of the missing element in the unrewritten forms. Since the superfluousness of sentence tokens in the rewritten sentences sup-ports the view that there is an assertive element in the underlying sense structure of assertive sentence types, Wittgenstein's first argu-ment backfires.[76]

The second of Wittgenstein's arguments in the above quotation is an adaptation of his earlier symmetry argument, deployed here to provide a *reductio* of the Fregean view of sentence meaning. Wittgenstein asks whether the fact that we can write the statement "It is raining" in the form "Is it raining? Yes!" shows that the state-ment contains a question. Our answer is No. The sentence "Natasha plays chess better than Boris" has an underlying form containing the structure "Boris plays chess" because the sentence has the same sense as "Natasha plays chess better than Boris plays chess". But the rewritten form of "Is it raining? Yes!" does not have the same sense as "It is raining". True enough, "Is it raining? Yes!" gives us the same information as "It is raining", in some sense of 'information', but the interrogative form isn't synonymous with "It is raining". The sen-tence "If the tree were five feet taller, it would be ten feet tall" is informationally equivalent to "The tree is five feet tall", but it is not synonymous with it. The grammatical structure of neither spelled-out form is a basis for inferring the grammatical structure of its informationally equivalent form. "Is it raining? Yes!" is not a basis for inferring that the sentence "It is raining" contains an interrogative component expressing a question, any more than "If the tree were five feet taller, it would be ten feet tall" is a basis for inferring that "The tree is five feet tall" contains a subjunctive component expressing a counterfactual. (Note also that the properties of the two forms differ; e.g., the simple indicative sentence cannot give rise to the response that the speaker has answered his or her own question.) Since synonymy, but not informational equivalence, justifies us in saying that everything that is part of the sense of one sentence is part of the sense of the other, Wittgenstein's second argument doesn't work.

The third argument is irrelevant to the proto-theory's Fregean view of the sense structure of assertive sentences, because the proto-theory, being a theory about sentence types, concerns only (iv) and (v). It takes no stand on whether asserting consists of two actions or one, or on whether, in asserting, we follow a concept notation in the way we sing from a score. Of course, the broader framework of the "top-down" approach concerns (i)–(iii) and (vi), and must at some point address itself to the nature of illocutionary acts themselves. But it is hard to see that this approach makes any "mistake." The approach has a large range of options open to it, not all of which are modeled on singing from a musical score. Moreover, it is not completely clear what the specific mistake is. If it is one of the "mistakes" that the two previous arguments concern, they have been dealt with. If the "mistake" is something else, more needs to be said to see what it is. Perhaps it is the mistake in psychologized accounts of following a rule. If so, it will be discussed at length in the next chapter.

19

In section 23, Wittgenstein follows up with considerations which are intended to show that Frege's proposal about assertive, erotetic, and requestive elements in sentence meaning cannot be carried through in the systematic way required to do justice to the full range of facts about the use of sentences. He writes:

> But how many different kinds of sentence are there? Say assertion, question, and command?—There are *countless* kinds: countless different kinds of use of what we call "symbols", "words", "sentences". And this multiplicity is not something fixed, given once and for all; but new types of language, new language-

games, as we may say, come into existence, and others become obsolete and get forgotten. (PI: 23)

From the standpoint of the confrontation I am orchestrating between Wittgenstein's critique of theories of meaning and the proto-theory, this argument fallaciously slides from "kinds of sentence" to "kinds of use." If it were being used as an argument against a notion of kinds of sentence based on a "bottom-up" approach or, what amounts to the same thing, if Wittgenstein had already shown that there is no locus for semantic categories within the grammatical structure of sentences types, there would be nothing wrong with the slide from kinds of sentence to kinds of use. Then the variety of kinds found among sentences would be determined by the variety of uses found among utterances. But this step in the argument is not legitimate when applied to the proto-theory, in which kinds of sentence are determined autonomously, and the "top-down" approach, which, as we have seen, maps sentence kinds one-many onto kinds of use.

We may concede Wittgenstein's claim that there is no possibility of exhaustively enumerating the "countless different kinds of use" (of "sentences" in the token sense in which Wittgenstein employs the term) without thereby causing any trouble for our claim that, in principle, an exhaustive enumeration of the kinds of sentence (in the type sense of the term) can be given. From the perspective of our "top-down" approach, what holds for classifying utterances, which are, in part, the product of pragmatic factors that go far beyond the structure of sentences, does not hold in general for classifying sentences of a language. Thus, the "countless different kinds of use" to which Wittgenstein refers arise from extragrammatical features of contexts, such as the aims, purposes, and intentions of speaker and audience. These introduce a taxonomy for use whose categories go well beyond those found in the grammatical taxonomy for sentences of the language.

Furthermore, I do not dispute the claim that "the *speaking* of a language is part of an activity, or a form of life" (PI: 23). Speaking surely is an activity, and it can reasonably be said to take place within a form of life, but the speaking is not the language spoken. My approach distinguishes sharply between the speaking of a language and the language that is spoken, e.g., speaking English vs. English. It even goes further, distinguishing, contra Chomsky, between the knowledge that speakers exercise in speaking a language and the language that the knowledge is knowledge of, e.g., English competence vs. English.[77]

I am also not disputing Wittgenstein's claim that speech is creative in a way that outstrips efforts to catalogue its *"countless* kinds" (PI: 23). Once we distinguish language from speech, we are led directly to distinguishing the creativity in language from the creativity in speech, as, respectively, a creativity that is rule-governed and a creativity that is not. Once we make this distinction, we can see that conceding Wittgenstein's claim about the open-endedness of speech does not impugn our claim about a fixed catalogue of grammatical types and subtypes in the language.

The creativity of language is said to lie in the fact that the sentences of a language are so structured that, with finite linguistic knowledge, speakers can, in principle, produce or understand infinitely many of them and, hence, can, in principle, produce and understand sentences they encounter for the first time.[78] Such creativity is rule-governed: the sentences we encounter for the first time belong to the set of sentences whose structure is specified by the grammatical rules of the language. The creativity of language allows for a fixed catalogue of kinds because sentence and constituent types are given in terms of the abstract categories that appear in the construction of the rules. These kinds limit variety among sentences to what the rules countenance. In contrast, the creativity in speech, as Wittgenstein supposes, is not rule-governed. There are no rules for generating uses of language, speech acts, and language-games, and, hence, no fixed catalogue of types that limits the variety of what we can do with utterances and inscriptions. But acknowledging this creativity in speech does not undermine the claim that the creativity in language is strictly rule-governed.

In the preceding quotation, Wittgenstein speaks of assertion, question, and command as "different kinds of sentence." In the type sense, these are not kinds of sentence. Declarative, interrogative, imperative, hortative, etc. are kinds of sentence. The sentences "I see nothing", "I hereby promise to help", "I request you let me see them", and "I thank you for it" are all declaratives. Moreover, sentences of different syntactic kinds can have senses of the same kind, as do, for example, "I request that you let me see them" and "Let me see them". Accordingly, it seems plausible to say further that Wittgenstein's open-endedness claim, in virtue of being about uses of utterances, speech acts, and the like is *twice* removed from what the Fregean proposal in question is about, namely, kinds of senses of sentence types.

In PI section 23, Wittgenstein reviews a number of different kinds of uses of "symbols," "words," and "sentences." His examples show that the distinctions he is drawing are, for the most part, independent of a classification of kinds of sentence types. For instance, he cites describing an appearance, giving something's measurements, reporting an event, etc. These are cases of use typically involving sentences of the same propositional type which differ in content: one might talk about a silver-blue color, another about a height of six feet, and still another about an explosion. The differences we recognize in the acts performed are a function not of the semantic kind of the sentence, but of differences in the descriptive content of the sentences and differences in the circumstances in which their utterances occur, e.g., indications that the speaker intends to impress us with the new car he or she has just ordered. To the extent that Wittgenstein's distinctions here turn on such factors—and by and large they do—they are independent of specifications of syntactic or semantic categories of sentence types; hence, the plethora to which the factors give rise cannot count against the proto-theory's fixed system of categories.

Wittgenstein remarks that "new types of language, new language games . . . come into existence, and others get forgotten" (PI: 23). It is easy to see how such novelty can occur without the addition of new sentence types or new senses. The familiar case of indirect speech acts is one illustration of this. In this case, a sentence with a sense of one kind is used to perform a speech act of another, as, for example, when a speaker makes the request to close the window by saying "The window is open" in circumstances where everyone will grasp the intention on the basis of seeing the pointlessness of the utterance on its literal sense. Here the utterance of "The window is open" receives the sense of the sentence "Close the window"; and so no sentence types or senses beyond those already in the language are required. Our "top-down" approach quite naturally accommodates accounts of the pragmatic reasoning in indirect speech acts.

A new vocabulary item can make performing certain kinds of speech act more convenient, but it is not required for their performance. Suppose that by the twenty-first century manners have declined to the point that people typically express formal disapproval for harms done to them in a manner parallel to the way we now thank people for benefits to us. Let us suppose the term "chank" has come into English as a performative verb on a par with "thank". It is not necessary that "chank" be in the language in order for the new language game of chanking to take place. Just as one can thank someone without the performative verb "thank", so one can chank someone without the performative verb "chank". Suppose that someone in the twenty-first century reads in a newspaper from today about a hostess saying to a departing guest, "I disapprove of your disgusting behavior at my dinner party". It would be accurate for the newspaper reader to comment that that guest had been soundly chanked. Indeed, such cases of performing an illocutionary act without a specialized performative verb for the act are no different from making a statement using a constructed expression to compensate for an ordinary lexical gap. As noted, English today has no word meaning 'to die from lack of water' parallel to "starve", but no increase in the lexicon is required to express the fact that someone died from lack of water. Syntactic and semantic compositionality overcome lexical gaps in the language—though, of course, they may do so in a rather unwieldy way.[79]

The vocabulary of a natural language is inevitably incomplete. Despite the fact that each year hundreds of new words enter English, there is no way for its finite lexicon to mark morphologically the infinitely many senses that syntactic and semantic compositionality produce. But the existence of a word to express a sense is only an accidental feature of a language. English does not stop being English when forms disappear or when new forms appear. What is essential is not the presence or absence of vocabulary, but the syntactic and semantic categories and the relations among them. Wittgenstein says nothing here to show that such structures come and go in the way lexical items do.

20

We now come to another example of how successfully blocking Wittgenstein's criticisms up to one point strengthens our hand against his criticisms at a later point. In PI section 24, Wittgenstein takes himself to be in a position to argue against asking questions like "What is a question?" He bases the argument on "the multiplicity of language-games" which he has just illustrated and on the foolishness of answers like "I wish you would tell me such-and-such." Both of these points can be granted, but, since he has not established his claims relating to sense and use, Wittgenstein cannot draw the conclusion that it is a mistake to ask a question like "What is a question?"

Consider the first point. We can take "What is a question?" in the way Wittgenstein is taking it, as asking for a general definition that picks out the class of utterances that count as activities of questioning. Or we can take it as asking for a general definition that picks out the erotetic senses of sentences. If we take it in the first way, "the multiplicity of language-games" gives us formidable reasons for thinking the question may be wrongheaded. But, if we take in the second way, those reasons, as we have seen, have no such relevance. Hence, as yet, there are no reasons for saying that the question on the construal appropriate to the proto-theory is wrongheaded.

Wittgenstein's second point, too, can be granted. No doubt, construing questions on the basis of such solipsistic glosses as "I wish you would tell me such-and-such" is foolish, but, on the proto-theory, there is no necessity to so construe them and no motivation to do so either, since the proto-theory is not a psychological theory.

21

Wittgenstein's overall critique of theories of meaning is an elaborate fabric of interconnecting arguments which support one another to give great strength to the fabric as a whole. But the weave of the fabric is such that certain connecting threads, such as the claims relating sense and use, are critical. If the responses I have made to Wittgenstein's arguments are correct, those connecting threads have not been knotted properly, and, as a consequence, the threads supported by them come loose, and the entire fabric unravels.

22

In PI section 26, Wittgenstein initiates a devastating critique of the account of names and related matters in the Augustinian picture of language, Russell's early philosophy, and his own *Tractatus*. To some extent, the critique continues earlier lines of criticism, particularly of the generalization that words are names of objects, but it introduces various new criticisms of assumptions of that account. This critique need not concern us, since the proto-theory rejects the Augustinian picture of language and language learning, the account of names and naming in question, and the appeals to psychology that Wittgenstein considers. The criticisms themselves are often ones a proponent of the proto-theory would naturally make. For example, consider Wittgenstein's criticism in section 39 of the thinking behind the view that names ought to denote simples, viz., that it uses "meaning" in a way which confuses "the meaning of a name with the *bearer* of the name" (PI: 40). This criticism is one that a proponent of the proto-theory could easily use against identifying the sense of a name with its reference.[80] It is not until the critique runs its course in section 45 that we come to arguments that apply to the proto-theory. The only section among these sections that conflicts with the proto-theory is section 43, but this contains no arguments.

Wittgenstein launches his attack on analysis and logical atomism in section 46. The target is analysis as practiced by Frege, the author of the *Tractatus*, Russell, and Moore. But Wittgenstein's opposition to analysis is a facet of his broader opposition to philosophical theories purporting to reveal hidden truths about language: analysis is the technique for revealing such truths. Therefore, Wittgenstein's criticisms can be expected to apply to the proto-theory's decompositional analysis—which is akin to Moore's form of linguistic analysis.[81]

Wittgenstein's criticisms begin with the notions of simplicity and complexity basic to analysis in any form. He observes, quite rightly, that it makes no sense to speak of something as simple or complex absolutely. He writes:

> To the *philosophical* question: "Is the visual image of this tree composite, and what are its component parts?" The correct answer is, "That depends on what you understand by 'composite'." (And that is of course not an answer but a rejection of the question.) (PI: 47)

To make sensible use of these notions, we must specify the aspect of the object with respect to which we intend to set up a division into parts. Wittgenstein is also right to observe that almost anything can be a whole or a part, depending on the aspect chosen in relativizing simplicity and complexity for the case at hand. Further, Wittgenstein is correct to claim that the words "composite" and "simple" are used "in an enormous number of different and differently related ways" (PI: 47). Different ways of using these notions typically provide different divisions into parts, each resulting from the choice of an aspect with respect to which the operation is relativized, and each recommendable as a means of achieving the purpose dictating the choice.

The proto-theory obviously assumes notions of simplicity and complexity. But the theory does not assume them in the absolute form that Wittgenstein criticizes. The proto-theory employs notions of syntactic and semantic structure which depend only on relativized notions of simplicity and complexity. To obtain the appropriate relativization, the proto-theory takes its cue from the treatment of structure in the physical and mathematical sciences. This approach is possible because the proto-theory is a theory within linguistics.

Consider the case of physics. Since Wittgenstein's reasons for thinking there are no absolute notions of simplicity and complexity are logical reasons, they apply to the physicist's use of these notions, and the physicist's statements about the structure of matter must be relativized. But not all relativizations are epistemologically equal. In physics, the notions of simplicity and complexity are relativized with respect to the purpose of discovering the complete truth about nature, and, hence, statements in physics about the structure of matter enjoy a privileged status with respect to statements about matter that might be made on the basis of other relativizations. This is clear from the absurdity of saying, "Well, matter may be taken as composed of molecules and atoms relative to discovering the truth about nature, but it isn't composite at all relative to other aims".

Like the scientific study of matter, the scientific study of language has the purpose of discovering the complete truth about its subject. Hence, linguistics relativizes its notions of simplicity and complexity to the aim of discovering the complete truth about the structure of sentences, and, accordingly, it gains the same privileged status for its statements about sentence structure as physics gains for its statements about matter. Thus, in adopting a vericentric standpoint, linguistics, too, avoids equalitarianism among claims about sentence structure based on different relativizations. Therefore, as with the use of notions like 'simple' and 'complex' in physical analysis, we can drop explicit mention of the relativization to truth in talking about grammatical analysis. We can straightforwardly pose questions like "Do syntactically simple expressions have complex senses?", "What are their sense components?", and "How do the components form a complex sense?"

Section 60 initiates the arguments that are at the heart of Wittgenstein's criticisms of analysis. These arguments concern the goal of linguistic analysis, namely, revealing the sense structure of expressions alleged to be hidden by grammatical form and, ultimately, revealing the fundamental elements in the semantic structure of the language. Wittgenstein imagines a language game (a) in which composite things have names and another language game (b) in which only parts have names. He asks: "In what sense is an order in the second game an analyzed form of an order in the first? Does the former lie concealed in the latter, and is it now brought out by analysis?—True, the broom is taken to pieces when one separates broomstick and brush; but does it follow that the order to bring the broom also consists of corresponding parts?" (PI: 60) Wittgenstein answers these questions, respectively, "none", "no", and "no". He takes it that, having established these answers with respect to (a) and (b), he has undermined analysis.

This, however, is not true. Having established these answers with respect to (a) and (b), he has indeed undermined analysis in the case of one type of language, but not in the cases of other kinds. (a) and (b) are language games in which words are names and names are mere labels. In a language with just two labels for a broom, one a simple label for the whole broom and the other a compound label consisting of a label for the stick and a label for the brush, there is nothing concealed. But the negative answers to the questions are correct only because, words being understood in this restricted way, analysis has to take a vulnerable form with respect to those languages, and, accordingly, Wittgenstein's criticisms apply. The criticisms are good objections to the early Wittgenstein's view and to Russell's view.

The criticisms are not good objections to Moore's view or to the proto-theory's because, on those views, analysis does not apply to words that are mere labels. On those views, a common noun like "broom" has a sense independent of its referents, and, consequently, there is something concealed for analysis to make known. So Wittgenstein's criticisms of analysis based on the language games (a) and (b) do not carry over to versions of analysis within an intensionalist conception of the semantics of words.

That Wittgenstein's criticisms do not carry over to such versions can be seen from the fact that, on an intensionalist conception of the semantics of words, all the answers to his questions are affirmative. Let us reconsider Wittgenstein's three questions, replacing (a) and (b) with language games (a') and (b') where the analysanda are common nouns with a sense. The first of these questions, "In what sense is an order in (b') an analyzed form of an order in (a')?", no longer requires the answer "none". This question can be taken as referring either to (v) or (vi) or to (i) or (ii). We can assume reference to (v) or (vi), since analysis in the sense now in question applies only to such linguistic objects. In this case, however, we can say that the order in question *is* an analysis in that the surface structure of the analysans expresses explicitly the components of the meaning of the analysandum which its surface structure conceals. Therefore, the answer to the first question is "In the sense that the analysans reveals senses hidden beneath the syntactic simplicity of the analysandum". The fact that the answer "none" was required in the case of (a) and (b) reflects nothing more than the fact that the words in those language-games, being mere labels, are not fit objects for decompositional analysis because there are no senses hidden beneath the syntactic simplicity of the analysanda.

Of course, the analysis is not very deep in the present case, but that is another matter, since the issue here is only whether analysis is revealing of anything. It is worth pointing out, however, that the proto-theory provides us with a plausible notion of the depth of an analysis. The depth of an analysis is a function of three variables: the complexity of the sense structure of the analysandum, the degree to which this structure is hidden, and the degree to which the structure is revealed by the syntax of the analysans. The more complex, the more hidden, and the more revealed, the deeper the analysis.

"Does [an order in the second game] lie concealed in [an order in the first], and is it now brought out by analysis?" Now the answer can be "yes". We *can* say that the orders "Kiss someone unmarried" and "Kiss a man" lie concealed in the order "Kiss a bachelor". In addition, there does not seem to be more than a verbal basis for objecting to someone who says that the order issued in a standard use of "Kiss a bachelor" includes the orders to kiss someone single and to kiss someone male and that analysis brings out the inclusion.[82] But, of course, we may not wish to speak this way.

"True, the broom is taken to pieces when one separates broomstick and brush; but does it follow that the order to bring the broom also consists of corresponding parts?" It does not follow from the fact that broomsticks have a brush part and a stick part that the word "broomstick" has a sense which decomposes into a sense of "brush" and a sense of "stick". Rather, such an analysis would follow only from the fact that there are sense properties and relations of expressions containing "broomstick", whose explanation requires the hypothesis that the sense of "broomstick" contains the sense of "brush" and the sense of "stick". What encourages the conclusion in the versions of analysis that Wittgenstein had in mind is the assumption that language ought to be isomorphic with reality. But, as stated above, the proto-theory, being part of linguistics, is committed to describing natural languages as they are, and cannot prescribe how they ought to be. Our program is to construct an ideal theory of natural language, not a theory of an ideal language. Thus, we agree with Wittgenstein that "every sentence in our language 'is in order as it is'. That is to say, we are not *striving after* an ideal, as if . . . a perfect language awaited construction by us." (PI: 98) Therefore, the proto-theory would include a hypothesis expressing an isomorphism between language and reality if, and only if, facts about the meanings of words forced such a hypothesis upon us. But they don't. To account for sense properties and relations stemming from the word "trolley-car", we do not have to say that its sense has parts corresponding to the parts of trolley-cars, that is, concepts for gears, panes of glass, screws, seats, lights, wheels, bushings, handstraps, and all the other thousands of parts in a trolley-car.[83]

Finally, we agree with Wittgenstein that someone who says that the broom is in the corner does not mean to speak of the stick or brush in particular:

> Suppose that, instead of saying, "Bring me the broom", you said "Bring me the broomstick and the brush which is fitted on to it."!—Isn't the answer: "Do you want the broom? Why do you put it so oddly?"—Is he going to understand the further analyzed sentence better?—This sentence, one might say, achieves the same as the ordinary one, but in a more roundabout way. (PI: 60)

This is surely right, but it hardly counts against sense analysis. The analysans in a decompositional analysis, even in the case of Moore's paraphrastic analysans, is intended to describe sense structure, but there is no obligation to do so in a form that can be used in all the ways that the analysandum itself can be used. In this respect, sense analysis is like arithmetical analysis. $(10 \times 3) + 7$ remains an arithmetical analysis of 37 in spite of the fact that an order for "$(10 \times 3) + 7$ pencils" might so annoy a stationery store owner that the order would not be filled. Just as such differences in use do not count against $(10 \times 3) + 7$'s being an arithmetical analysis of 37, so the differences in use that Wittgenstein imagines do not count against the claim that "Bring me the broomstick and the brush that is fitted on to it" is a semantic analysis of "Bring me the broom". Wittgenstein seems to think that analysis must provide us with another tool with the same uses as the analysandum. But sense analyses are judged not by how good they are as surrogates but by how successfully they explicate sense.

In section 63, Wittgenstein argues that analysis cannot, in principle, give the full meaning of an analysandum because the analysans must miss aspects of its meaning. He writes: "To say, however, that a sentence . . . is an 'analyzed' form of [another] readily seduces us into thinking that the former is the more fundamental form; that it alone shews what is meant by the other, and so on. For example, we think: If you have only the unanalyzed form you miss the analysis; but if you know the analyzed form that gives you everything.—But can I not say that an aspect of the meaning is lost on you in the latter case as well as the former?" (PI: 63) Here the fabric of Wittgenstein's argument continues to unravel. The expected affirmative answer follows if meaning and use are related as Wittgenstein claims, but a negative answer follows if they are related as suggested in section 7 of this chapter. Since Wittgenstein hasn't established his claims about the relation between meaning and use, he is in no position to assume that an aspect of the meaning of "Bring me the broom" is lost in "Bring me the broomstick and the brush that is fitted on to it". It can be said just as well that the only things lost are non-semantic features of syntactic form such as length. Hence, Wittgenstein's interlocutor sticks his neck out too far in saying "the analyzed form . . . gives you everything". This is too ambitious a conception of analysis, since "everything" means everything about the use of the analysandum. Wittgenstein easily refutes the conception, but the refutation doesn't carry over to the conception of analysis in Moore or in the proto-theory. Being considerably more modest, i.e., promising only the prospect of exposing everything about the sense structure of the an-alysandum, these conceptions are not refuted.

Although such conceptions are modest in comparison to the con-ception which Wittgenstein puts in the mouth of his interlocutor, it is ambitious enough when one considers what is involved in decom-positional analysis. The enterprise of specifying everything that makes for sameness and difference in sense is on a par with the enterprise of specifying everything that makes for sameness and dif-ference in syntax or inference. This may be appreciated from the proto-theory's conception of what full analyses of senses consist in when the primitive senses of a language are reached. A full analysis of a sense is one that exposes all its structure. We know that all sense structure has been exposed when the analysans marks every com-ponent sense and every relation among component senses necessary to account for the relevant sense properties and relations of the analysandum. When some sense structure is unmarked in the analy-sans, the analysis continues, typically by extending the apparatus of semantic representation to make finer discriminations. Such changes continue until the making of such finer discriminations reaches a ter-minus. This is the point at which all the semantic properties and re-lations of the analysandum are accounted for and further changes would only complicate the analysans. Given a full analysis of each lexical item in the language, the primitive senses of the language can presumably be factored out.[84]

23

The *leitmotiv* of Wittgenstein's early thought is that philosophical sen-tences, unlike the sentences of natural science, do not represent real-ity, that philosophical sentences are meaningless because they transcend the limits of language, and that the proper task for philos-ophy is, therefore, not to provide us with new truths but to provide clarification, in particular, by showing what cannot be said. These ideas, as I see it, took Frege's thinking on propositions in a novel direction. Frege's idea of a sense as a mode of presentation of a referent is transformed in the *Tractatus* into the idea of a proposition as a representation of reality (TLP: 4.01), and then used, together with the general theory of propositions deriving from Frege's and Russell's work in logic and the philosophy of logic, to show that logical words and philosophical sentences are those which have no representative semantic function (TLP: 4.0312).

The *leitmotiv* of Wittgenstein's early philosophy continues as the *leitmotiv* of his late philosophy. The late philosophy results from a shift in assumptions about language and meaning and an accompanying inversion of the *Tractatus*'s traditional conception of the relation between theory and problem, making theory the source of philosophical problems rather than their solution. Thus, Wittgenstein's denial that there is a *"general form of propositions* and of language" (PI: 65) has the special status in the late philosophy of rejecting the very theory on which the whole of the early philosophy rests (PI: 116). This special status explains why Wittgenstein refers to the question of what is common to all linguistic phenomena in virtue of which they are linguistic as "the great question which lies behind all these considerations" (PI: 65).[85]

The answer to "the great question" of the *Philosophical Investigations* is parallel in importance to the "fundamental idea" of the *Tractatus* that logical words have no representative semantic function (TLP: 4.0312). And Wittgenstein's answer that the things to which we apply a word have nothing in common in virtue of which it applies to them all is, in effect, the same deflationary doctrine as the early deflationary doctrine deriving from this "fundamental idea": philosophical sentences, which purport to reveal the concepts underlying the application of philosophical words, have no sense.

To underscore the importance of the question and to emphasize how radical a break with traditional philosophy is in the works, Wittgenstein has his interlocutor at first fail to see that what is at stake is the very presupposition of the "great question" and, hence, the presupposition of virtually all traditional Western philosophy. So the interlocutor complains that Wittgenstein is ducking the really hard question of what the essence of language is. Wittgenstein concedes that he has not provided "something common to all that we call language," but *that* is the point: "these phenomena have no one thing in common which makes us use the same word for all" (PI: 65). Wittgenstein's intentions are far more radical than the reader might at first think: he is not out to reform traditional philosophy, so that it may return to business as usual, but to sweep it away.

Wittgenstein thus rejects "the great question." This move is like the earlier rejection of the question "Is the visual image of this tree composite, and what are its component parts?" (PI: 47). In both cases, the question falsely presupposes that it makes sense to speak in absolute terms. The question of the general form of propositions and of language falsely presupposes that it makes sense to speak in absolute terms about the use of words. It does not make sense because words have no inherent semantic essence. As a consequence, to speak sensibly, we have to speak of the use of words relative to our linguistic training, the linguistic practices within a form of life, and the peculiar features of the situations where we use them.

In this connection, it is interesting to recall Frege's view that

> for all the multiplicity of languages, mankind has a common stock of thoughts. If all transformation of the expression were forbidden on the plea that this would alter the content as well, logic would simply be crippled; for the task of logic can hardly be performed without trying to recognize the thought in its manifold guises. Moreover, all definition would then have to be rejected as false.[86]

Wittgenstein agrees with Frege's reasoning, but welcomes the conclusion that Frege raises as a specter for logic. Wittgenstein's argument that analysis can offer nothing more fundamental than the analysandum itself and that the analysans always loses some aspect of the matter, was designed precisely to show that there is no notion of content invariant over the transformation of expressions. Logic in Frege's sense *is* "crippled," and, as a consequence, all definition in Frege's sense *has* to be rejected as false. But, for Wittgenstein, these conclusions are not the end of "all that is great and important" (PI: 118), but the beginning of proper philosophy (PI: 126–133).

Wittgenstein thinks he has already said enough to discredit essentialist doctrines concerning propositions and language like Frege's. Thus, he sees his task in section 66 and those immediately following as to explain how we do apply words, including the word "language" itself, without relying on traditional definitions. He wants to answer the question "How do we use a word to group together things that are alike, without a definition to tell us what their common feature is?" He tries to answer it by showing us what is really the case in the application of words and by formulating an alternative to the definitional view which is truer to the facts of how words are applied. His strategy is to "focus on the details of what goes on; . . . look at them *from close to*" (PI: 51).

The famous discussion of the use of the word "game" is an instance of this strategy. The discussion is intended to show, contrary to the definitional view, that there is nothing common to everything we call "games", but only "a complicated network of similarities overlapping and criss-crossing: sometimes overall similarities, sometimes similarities of detail" (PI: 66). Thus, the discussion of "game" explains why Wittgenstein rejects the question about the essence of language: the question presupposes that there is something common to the things grouped together in the applications of a word, when, in fact, there is only a "family resemblance" among them. (The discussion serves as a paradigm of the kind of descriptive examination that Wittgenstein thinks ought to replace analysis.)

Now, it seems safe to say that this discussion is widely taken to present a powerful (albeit controversial) argument that the semantics of general terms is based on family resemblance rather than on definition in any of its essentialist forms. However, I think there is no such argument here. I do not doubt the correctness of Wittgenstein's finding that there is nothing more than family resemblance in cases like the application of "game", but this finding is far from a general argument against essentialist definition. The supposition that the finding provides such an argument rests on the notion that a definitional account of the semantics of general terms is incompatible with family resemblance in the application of words like "game." But, in the case of at least one definitional account—the proto-theory and the "top-down" approach—family resemblance is exactly what is predicted!

It is plausible to think that a definitional account implies the opposite of family resemblance if what one has in mind is the traditional Fregean account on which we proceed from an ideal language to the referents of expression tokens via the Fregean relation of determination. The Fregean essentialist is stuck with the prediction that there is more than a family resemblance among the things to which "game" applies. But essentialists do not have to adopt the Fregean account, and essentialists who instead adopt the proto-theory and the "top-down" approach are not stuck with the Fregean prediction. The critical differences are, first, that the "top-down" approach proceeds from a natural language, not an ideal language, and, second, that it proceeds to the reference of tokens via the relation of mediation rather than the stronger relation of determination. The result is that we can expect exactly the family resemblance among the things to which "game" applies which Wittgenstein finds.

Let me explain why. On the "top-down" approach, a speaker starts with knowledge of the grammatical structure of *expression types*, that is, syntactic structure in some appropriate sense and semantic structure in the sense of the proto-theory. Wittgenstein's finding that there is only a family resemblance among the things to which we apply "game" concerns *expression tokens*. Now, the expression types of a natural language, as opposed to a Fregean ideal language, exhibit ambiguity, homonymy, etc. Moreover, the mediation relation allows the influence of extralinguistic factors in the process of assigning senses of linguistic types to linguistic tokens and in fixing the reference of linguistic tokens. These two factors are more than enough to show that we should expect the proto-theory and the "top-down" approach to present a picture of overlappings and criss-crossings of similarities at the utterance level.

To make this clear, consider the application of the English word "game" on the proto-theory and the "top-down" approach. As a convenience, I will ignore much of the ambiguity and homonymity of the word. This is legitimate because the effect of including the full ambiguity and homonymity would be only to strengthen my point by increasing the pragmatic scatter. Thus, I will suppose that the initial point in the "top-down" process is knowledge of just two of the senses that *Webster's* gives for the word "game", namely:

(A) a contest conducted according to rules governing the play of its participant(s),
(B) an amusement.[87]

(A) is the sense of "game" in "I'd rather win at games than at raffles or auctions". (B) is the sense on which "game" is antonymous with "serious", as, for instance, in "It is serious to you, but it's just a game to her" or in "Spying was a game for Mata Hari, but not for Sorge".[88]

The terminal point of the "top-down" process is the set of activities to which reference is made when English speakers use their knowledge of (A) and (B) in the use of "game". Supposing that, over a wide range of cases, speakers apply "game" to whatever they recognize as falling under one or the other of those senses, we will find the word applied not only to baseball, chess, bridge, solitaire, tick-tack-toe, tennis, go-fish, go, jacks, etc. but also to activities like ring-a-ring-a-roses and throwing a ball against a wall. Thus, we find exactly the family resemblance among the activities to which "game" is applied that Wittgenstein himself found. Features which, in the language, are kept separate by the boundaries of a sense are, in the domain of the language, collected together in the extension of "game". Hence, baseball, chess, etc. are members of this extension on a par with ring-a-ring-a-roses and tossing a ball against a wall; accordingly, the feature of contest, i.e., winning and losing, which is present in many members, is absent in others. These diverse activities are on all fours extensionally because they are simply activities to which "game" refers.

Of course, these activities are collected together as members of the extension of the *word*, not as members of the extension of a *sense of a word* or as members of the extension of a *word on a sense*. But, whatever the usefulness of the latter two notions, they are not involved in Wittgenstein's examination of the application of "game", and, as far as the point here is concerned, nothing would change if the notions were introduced, since introducing them would allow us to identify something common with respect to the divisions imposed by them within the extension of the word.[89]

PI section 67 considers the attempt, by brute disjunction, to frame a single concept of game out of the various features in the family resemblance. Wittgenstein rightly criticizes this move as "only playing with words," saying, "One might as well say: 'Something runs through the whole thread—namely, the continuous overlapping of fibers'" (PI: 67). His point is that a disjunction of family features is not a common property, not literally a property that runs through the whole class of cases. The move based upon a disjunction of family features does not use the notions 'common' and 'runs through' in their ordinary sense. To see this, contrast the manufactured sense of "runs through" with the sense in which a disjunctive property really does run through a class of cases *in the ordinary sense*, e.g., in the case of the class of *a priori* outcomes in tosses of a coin. Thus, although it is true on the manufactured senses that a disjunctive property "runs through" such a class, this is consistent with, and hence irrelevant to, Wittgenstein's claim that there is no common property in the ordinary sense.

Given that this is Wittgenstein's argument in section 67, the argument has no bearing on our explanation, since we agree with Wittgenstein that there is no common property for the class of things we call "games" except perhaps the trivial property of being an activity. On our explanation, it makes no sense to speak of common properties with respect to English and other languages where specific properties and relations are grammatically correlated with specific syntactic forms. As indicated, common properties can be found in the extensional melting pot, once the extension of a word is filtered to obtain the members that belong to the extension of the word on a particular sense, but this is not something that any of Wittgenstein's arguments at this point deal with. If he has a relevant argument, it will have to be his argument about following rules, which I consider in the next chapter.

Sections 68, 69, and 77 criticize the claim that a word like "game" has an exact extensional boundary. But this claim, too, is no part of our explanation. As we have already made clear in the discussion of rule-governed creativity of language and non-rule-governed creativity of language use, we agree with Wittgenstein that the boundaries of the class of things we call "games" have not been drawn. As he says, the use of "game" is "not everywhere circumscribed by rules" (PI: 68). This is also the consequence of the fact that, on our "top-down" approach, extralinguistic factors influence the extension of a word. Even in connection with the uses of a word on a particular fixed sense, extension may not be sharply circumscribed, because, for example, of the various extralinguistic beliefs on which the uses are based. Thus speakers may use a word with a particular sense, yet their utterances may not refer to anything in the extension of the word, as with Cotton Mather's use of "witch".

There is considerable flexibility in the way that the "top-down" approach handles the different sorts of cases Wittgenstein brings up. The way in which we handled the fact that competition is absent in some activities to which "game" applies is by no means a general paradigm. We do not handle all the "disappearing features" Wittgenstein mentions in section 66 in that way. He says that the feature of "play on a board" drops out when we pass from games like chess to games like bridge and that the feature of skill is different in chess and tennis, and nonexistent in ring-a-ring-a-roses. In such cases we can argue that absence of the feature in question is really a matter of its presence not being semantically mandated by sense. (A) and (B) leave open the question of the surface on which play takes place—allowing mental chess—and the question of skill.

The fact that the appearance in games of such features results not from anything in the meaning of "game" but from the absence of something in the meaning of "game" is straightforwardly explained on the proto-theory. "Game" is a superordinate of subordinate expressions such as "board game" and "card game". As will be explained more fully below, a subordinate like "bachelor" contains the sense of the superordinate "man" but also contains the sense of "unmarried", which qualifies the superordinate sense component to make the sense of the subordinate "bachelor" more precise than that of the superordinate "man". Hence, because "game" is a superordinate of "bc..rd game", "card game", etc., the former is not synonymous with any of the latter, but their senses include its sense. Thus, the sense of the superordinate "game" is sufficiently more abstract for its extension to encompass the extensions of "board game", "card game", etc., and not to be encompassed by their extensions.

Because the sense of "game" imposes no constraint concerning kind of skill or even the presence of skill, games of chess and tennis are equally games despite the difference in kind of skill involved, and ring-a-ring-a-roses is a game even though no skill at all is required to play it. Skill makes for more enjoyable or interesting games, but even people who have yet to develop any skill at chess or tennis may still manage to play. Skill is a matter of how well a game is played. Chess does, of course, belong to the category 'game of skill', contrasting with a game like roulette which belongs to the category of 'game of luck'. These, however, are further divisions of games in the sense (A), along with division in terms of what they are played on or what they are played with. In the sense (B), games do not divide into games of skill and games of chance because that sense does not contain the concept of a contest which is the superordinate of 'game of skill' and 'game of luck'.

Just before he explicitly poses the "great question," Wittgenstein claims that "one may say of certain objects that they have this or that purpose. The essential thing is that this is a *lamp*, that it serves to give light;—that it is an ornament to the room, fills an empty space, etc. is not essential. But there is not always a sharp distinction between essential and inessential." (PI: 62) There is no reason to argue about this claim so long as it is understood to be about the objects themselves, i.e., your Tiffany lamp or the ugly monstrosity Uncle Harry gave me. In this case, your lamp may serve the purpose of ornamentation and mine the purpose of keeping peace in the family, even though neither is good at giving light. Here it is true to say that what is essential shifts with the interests that determine the purpose to which we put the object, and hence, no general distinction between the essential and the inessential seems possible. But none of this counts against there being a distinction between the essential and the inessential when we move from the objects to the language. None of these considerations about interest prevent us from saying that, from the standpoint of literal English, for something to be what is called a "lamp", it is essential that it be an artifact whose function is to give artificial light. Whether the concept 'artifact whose function is to give artifical light' is part to the sense of the word "lamp" in English depends on the nature of the sense properties and relations of sentences containing the word "lamp".

This brings us to Wittgenstein's famous example of the disappearing chair. About such an object, he asks, rhetorically: "Have you rules ready for such cases—rules saying whether one may use the word 'chair' to include this kind of thing?" (PI: 80) Wittgenstein takes a negative answer for granted. But the answer can be affirmative. We obtain the rule covering the sense of a word by working out the simplest statement of its decompositional structure which accounts for the sense properties and relations of sentences in which the word occurs. Let us suppose that the statement we have worked out for the sense of "chair" is 'physical object which is a piece of furniture having a back and a seat, having the function of being a seat for one'. (The component sense 'having a back', for example, explains why "chair" is antonymous with "stool", and the component sense 'being a seat for one' explains why it is antonymous with "couch".) On this semantic rule, one may use the word "chair" to include disappearing chairs. Chairs have to be physical objects, but nothing in the rule requires them to be constantly appearing physical objects. The meaning of "chair" leaves open the possibility that chairs might have the physical property of being here one minute and gone the next—just as (A) leaves open the possibility that games involve intellectual skill or are played with marked cards. Whether chairs or any other physical objects can disappear and reappear is a question for physics.[90] There is nothing linguistically deviant in the supposition that at some future time we may have disappearing chairs designed specially for playing musical chairs.

The upshot of these reflections is that two forms of definition are compatible with what Wittgenstein says about family resemblance in the sections up through 67. One of them is explicative paraphrase, the form that Moore employed, and the other is decompositional and compositional semantic representation, the form the proto-theory employs. I think enough has been said to show that both are compatible with the kind of extensional facts that Wittgenstein calls to our attention in his answer to "the great question."

24

Section 68 of *Philosophical Investigations* initiates a set of arguments against Frege's position on exact concepts. Given Frege's conception of sense as mode of referential determination and given the desirability of an ideal language for purposes of rational inquiry, it is easy to see why Frege thought it an imperfection of natural languages that an expression's sense frequently does not determine which, if any, objects belong to its extension. Thinking that such features of natural languages make it a poor instrument for reasoning, Frege thought that an ideal language should be constructed to compensate for inexactnesses and other imperfections of natural language. He saw the situation as directly parallel to the construction of special optical instruments to compensate for the limitations of the human eye.[91]

Wittgenstein thought this view involves a fundamental misunderstanding:

> . . . logic does not treat of language . . . in the sense in which a natural science treats of a natural phenomenon, and the most that can be said is that we *construct* ideal languages. But here the word "ideal" is liable to mislead, for it sounds as if these languages were better, more perfect, than our everyday language. (PI: 81)

Expanding on this point, he says:

> "Inexact" is really a reproach, and "exact" is praise. And that is to say that what is inexact attains its goal less perfectly than what is more exact. Thus the point here is what we call "the goal". (PI: 88)

The goal, as Wittgenstein sees it, is given in the use we make of signs, by the interests and the purposes being served (PI: 88). Again, misunderstanding arises from using words, in this case "exact" and "inexact", as absolute terms. Suitably relativized to a goal, those terms would not encourage philosophers to reproach natural language for having inexact expressions and would lead them to recognize that inexactness is "often exactly what we need" (PI: 71). In an attempt to inject a sense of reality into the discussion, Wittgenstein writes, "But is it senseless to say: 'Stand roughly there'?" (PI: 70).

My anti-prescriptivist position, which has been made amply clear, is in full agreement with Wittgenstein's claims that "every sentence in our language 'is in order as it is'" and that the proper task is to understand our language, not to perfect it. Wittgenstein's position and mine both treat a sentence as meaningful just in case it has a sense. Accordingly, an inexact sentence like "Stand roughly here," being fully meaningful, unlike a sentence such as "The square root of 25 likes vanilla ice cream", has a sense every bit as much as an exact sentence like "The square root of 25 is 5". Further, without taking a stand on the question of his treatment of Frege, I can also agree with Wittgenstein's claim that the degree of exactness required of speakers is relative to their goals in the circumstances, to the constraints of the conversation. Thus, the proto-theory has no arguments to answer in connection with Wittgenstein's criticisms of Frege's views concerning exact concepts and ideal languages.

The differences between Wittgenstein's position and mine concern what meaningfulness and senselessness consist in. The proto-theory's conception of a meaningful sentence is that of a sentence in which the senses of its constituents compositionally combine as they must for the sentence as a whole to have a sense. Its conception of a senseless sentence is of a sentence in which some of the combinations of senses necessary to form a compositional meaning cannot take place because one or another sense does not meet a restriction governing a necessary combination. The difference between "Stand roughly here" and "The square root of 25 likes vanilla ice cream" is that, although all the necessary sense combinations can take place in the former, there is at least one in the latter that cannot take place.

Senselessness, as I am using the term, is a property of an expression or sentence type. It is the property of not having a sense in the language. Thus, one cannot infer just from the senselessness of an expression or sentence that some arbitary constituent of the expression or sentence is senseless, nor can one infer that a token of the expression or sentence is senseless. Moreover, senselessness is the limiting case of a process of blocking combinations of senses which, at various stages short of the limiting case, restrict the number of senses of expressions and sentences and hence, their degree of ambiguity. For example, in the sentence "Squares like TV quiz programs" a potential sense combination is blocked because the sense of a predicate expressing an attitude cannot apply to a subject that expresses a geometrical form, but the other sense of "square" can combine with such predicates; hence, the sentence is not senseless but only unambiguous. An unambiguous sentence can be thought of as a one-way ambiguous sentence, and a senseless sentence as a zero-ways ambiguous sentence.

In some respects, the proto-theory's position on exactness and inexactness complements Wittgenstein's. Many of Wittgenstein's remarks make the point that an inexact term often serves the speaker's interests better than an exact one (PI: 71). Such remarks seem to me to presuppose that words of the language are themselves inherently more or less exact relative to one another. How else would speakers have a choice of an inexact term to use in better serving their interests? The proto-theory enables us to characterize such inherent, or grammatical, differences in the exactness of words.[92]

Consider Wittgenstein's example "The ground is quite covered with plants" (PI: 70). Sentences employing expressions more exact than "plants" provide greater relative precision, for example, "The ground is covered with bushes", "The ground is covered with rose bushes", "The ground is covered with climbing tea-rose bushes", "The ground is covered with climbing tea-rose bushes in full bloom", and so on. With each successive sentence, more information is provided about the ground cover. To take another example, which stresses the decompositional route to a more specific sense, consider the transition "Pile some objects against the door", "Pile some furniture against the door", "Pile some chairs against the door", "Pile some rockers against the door." In both examples, the greater exactness of one sentence relative to another can be thought of as a matter of the meaning of the more exact expression closing options which the meaning of the less exact expression leaves open. As the examples show, the options can be closed either by the addition of modifiers like "rose" to a noun like "bushes" or by exploiting decompositional structure, e.g., replacing a noun like "furniture" with a noun like "chairs".

On the proto-theory, greater precision is achieved in virtue of the grammatical fact that, in the more exact of a pair of senses, one component sense qualifies another component sense to make the entire sense more specific (along some dimension). The relation between the sense qualified and the sense resulting from the qualification is the superordinate/subordinate relation referred to above. For example, the sense of "dwelling" is superordinate to the senses of "house", "barracks", and "prison". These subordinate senses are formed from the superordinate sense by means of qualifications concerning who dwells there and for what purpose. In the case of "house" the dwellers may be anyone, but the dwelling is their residence; in the case of "barracks" the dwellers are primarily soldiers, and the dwelling is a place for rest, recreation, and sleep; in the case of "prison" the dwellers are those convicted of crimes, and the purpose of the dwelling is incarceration.

To give an account of relative precision or specificity, we shall have to say more about the superordination/subordination relation, particularly, its role in word meaning. Thus far, we have spoken about the decompositional structure of word meaning principally in terms of factoring the sense of a word into its component senses. We mentioned that the component senses have to be related to one another to form the sense of a word, but said next to nothing about what those relations might be. Now, as the examples we have just given make clear, one such relation is superordination. Hence, the very notion of word meaning itself requires an account of superordination.

I now want to give a brief account of how degree of specificity can be given in a decompositional formalization of word meaning. Recall that, whereas the numeral notation discussed above uses a single semantic symbol to represent the sense of a syntactic simple, the proto-theory uses a number of semantic symbols to represent the component senses in the senses of a syntactic simple. These semantic symbols are connected by formal relations that represent qualifications of superordinate concepts which turn them into subordinate concepts. For example, we might represent the component senses of the sense of "chair", i.e., 'being an object', 'being physical', 'being an artifact', 'being furniture', 'having a back', etc., with, respectively, the symbols (M_1), (M_2), . . . , (M_n). We can represent the qualification of one such component sense by another in terms of a branch connecting the symbol representing the former to that of the latter. We can represent the entire sense as a tree structure with nodes labeled with such symbols and with branches connecting nodes representing qualifications of concepts by other concepts, the concepts resulting from qualification, and their relations to other concepts resulting from qualification. Such trees can be described schematically as in the figure below. This whole marker represents the complex sense c^* as being built up out of the component concepts c_1, c_2, . . . , c_n. Given our interpretations of the symbols c_1, c_2, . . . , c_n labeling nodes, this marker represents the complex sense of "chair". c_1 represents the component sense 'being an object', the branch connecting (M_1) to (M_2) represents qualification with the component sense 'being physical', and so on. The superordinate/subordinate relations would be that c_1 is superordinate to c_2, c_2 superordinate to c_3, and so on. In general, superordinate/subordinate relations can be defined in terms of the condition that the marker of the subordinate be a same-rooted subtree of the marker for the superordinate.

The synonymy of a syntactically complex expression like "a physical object which is a piece of furniture with a back and seat, serving as a seat for one" and a syntactically simple expression like "chair" shows that the sense relations involved in compositional meanings are the same as those within decompositional structure. The results of sense combinations in the compositional process simply recapitulate and extend the superordination structures in the senses of syntactic simples. This makes it possible to develop the proto-theory as a recursive procedure for sense combination. The principles specifying how senses of modifiers combine with senses of their heads can be formulated in terms of rules which form a new branch in the tree

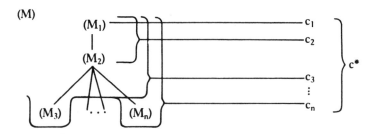

representing the head, off of which the tree representing the modifier is hung, thereby producing a new semantic representation which still has the form (M).[93]

I said above that meaningless sentences like "The square root of 25 likes vanilla ice cream" are the result of the fact that every set of sense combinations that could provide a meaning for the sentence is blocked at some point in the compositional process because the restriction at that point is not met. I can now explain what such restrictions are and what blocking consists in. We have seen that compositional senses have the same superordinate/subordinate structure as decompositional senses. Hence, to form a compositional sense from the sense of a modifier and the sense of its head, the sense of the modifier must be a subordinate of some concept in the sense of the head. The restriction on such combinations is, then, that the sense of the modifier must belong to the highest semantic category to which some concept in the sense of the head belongs. If the sense of the modifier belongs to no highest category of any concept in the sense of the head, there is no way to form a derived sense for the whole modifier-head construction. "The square root of 25 likes vanilla ice cream" is meaningless because the sense of "likes vanilla ice cream" cannot become a subordinate of the concept of a square root, whose semantic category is Abstract.[94]

To sum up: Frege's doctrines about exactness derived from his conception of sense as a self-sufficient mode of referential determination. Since senses are to provide all the information needed to fix reference, inexactness on the side of sense translates immediately into problems of determination on the side of reference, and such problems, in turn, are problems for relating sentences in natural language to propositions in logic. Hence, Frege is led to the construction of a logically perfect language with exact senses. Wittgenstein criticizes Frege's doctrines about exactness on the grounds that imprecise sentences, e.g. "Stand roughly here" or "The ground is covered with plants", do not ordinarily cause referential problems. We agree with the substance of Wittgenstein's observations. Indeed, our account of decompositional and compositional sense structure complements his observations by explaining the source of the essentially unlimited range of expressions of varying degrees of precision on which speakers can draw.

Since on the proto-theory and the "top-down" approach sense is only one ingredient in the recipe for language use, inexactness of sense does not automatically lead to problems of referential determination. Hence, there is none of the pressure for us to have a language with exact expressions that there is for Frege. For us, the language

makes available an essentially unlimited range of expressions of varying degrees of exactness, and its speakers make a selection on the
basis of pragmatic factors which often allow them to use relatively
inexact expressions in context. Thus, on my view as much as on
Wittgenstein's, it is the user of the language who bears the responsibility for problems that result from choosing an expression that is less
precise (or more precise) than required in the circumstances.

It should be noted that the proto-theory's formal representations
serve only to describe explicitly the sense structure of the language.
Formal precision here does not have the purpose of producing an
ideal language, but aims only to produce a more explicit theory of the
sense structure of natural languages. Explicitness is desirable since it
makes it easier to see what the claims of the theory are, how to verify
or refute them, and whether they can be developed and broadened
consistently.

There is nothing in Wittgenstein's criticisms of Frege's doctrines
about exactness that threatens the development of the proto-theory—
rather, there is much in the development of the proto-theory which
complements Wittgenstein's observations about exactness in language and use. Furthermore, there are no other arguments in the
sections from 68 through 80 that might pose a threat. Consider, for
example, Wittgenstein's claims in section 73 about our knowledge of
"what a game is"—that is, of our "concept of a game." On the proto-
theory and the "top-down" approach, there are two types of concept.
In an earlier work, I have referred to concepts of one type as *narrow
concepts* and concepts of the other type as *broad concepts*.[95] Narrow
concepts are senses of words in the language, and broad concepts
are conceptions of what a word's referent is. I will have more to say
about these notions in chapter 7. Here it suffices to say that we can
easily agree with Wittgenstein's claims, since they explicitly concern
broad concepts, and the proto-theory concerns only narrow concepts.

To take one more example, consider Wittgenstein's arguments in
section 79. Insofar as they are intended to show that the use of a name
does not depend on its having a *"fixed* meaning" that equips speakers
"with rules for every possible application of it" (PI: 79, 80), the arguments do not apply to the proto-theory and the "top-down" approach, which are not committed to such rules. Insofar as the
arguments are intended to show that names have no *"fixed* meaning"
of any sort, we could accept them if we subscribed to J. S. Mill's version of the theory. Strictly speaking, the proto-theory does not even
claim that names have meaning; it claims only that, *if* the words belonging to some class exhibit properties and relations like meaningfulness, ambiguity, synonymy, redundancy, antonymy, etc., *then*

they have meaning. Thus, only the proto-theory together with observations about the sense properties and relations of sentences could entail that a proper noun or any other kind of word has a meaning. Wittgenstein's arguments, in themselves, cannot refute intensionalism, though they might restrict its scope to common nouns and other parts of speech.[96]

25

We come now to section 81, where Wittgenstein raises the topic of normativity. This topic is important for the question of whether the proto-theory escapes Wittgenstein's critique of theories of meaning. My procedure will again be to find areas of agreement where I can, and where I cannot, try to show that Wittgenstein's arguments are ineffective against the proto-theory.

Wittgenstein says that F. P. Ramsey's remark about logic's being a normative science suggested to him that there is something gamelike about the use of language. Wittgenstein is anxious that this insight not be misunderstood through thinking of logic in terms of a Fregean ideal language. The misunderstanding that concerns Wittgenstein is that we might think of our language on the model of idealization in physical science, taking our use of language to involve "operating a calculus" and the idealization to express the laws of its operation in abstraction from empirical conditions (PI: 81).

I agree that logic and language involve a normative element which expresses, in some sense, what ought to be rather than what is. I also agree that the model of an idealization in physical science cannot deliver this normative element, and in chapter 7 I will have something of my own to say about why this is so. Further, I think that Wittgenstein's warning is at least as timely now as it was when the *Philosophical Investigations* was written. For the use of this model has become even more influential in Anglo-American philosophy since then, as the result of Chomsky's approach to language, in which the very definition of linguistics is based on the model. Recall that Chomsky takes the object of linguistic study to be the competence of an ideal speaker-hearer, presenting this view as an explicit analogue to idealizations in physics.[97] Hence, for Chomsky, the study of language is the study of an empirically presented natural phenomenon, namely, the linguistic knowledge of speakers and the language-learning capacities of children, both under suitable idealization. Thus, the questions about "the rule by which he proceeds" which Wittgenstein raises in section 82 apply directly to Chomsky's notion of competence as internalized linguistic rules.

If, as Chomsky thinks, the study of language is properly conducted as an idealization of an empirical phenomenon within a natural science like psychology or biology, then a normative element could no more come into the linguistic behavior of speakers than a normative element could come into the mechanical behavior of billard balls. We couldn't talk, as we do, about how English ought to be, rather than is, used—about grammatical correctness and mistakes—any more than we can talk about how billiard balls ought to, rather than do, move. If language were merely a natural phenomenon in the sense of the idealization model, what would be the normative force of saying that "She overestimates itself" is incorrect English or that it is a grammatical mistake to say that "pocket battleship" means 'battleship of a size to fit into the pocket'. For it is nonsense to say that a ball rolling on a plane is in error, or making a physical mistake, when its behavior diverges significantly from that of an ideal ball rolling on a frictionless, perfectly smooth plane.

The problem with the model of idealization in linguistics (or in logic) is that it conflates *conflict with a norm* with *divergence from an ideal*. The essential point is that an ideal is not a norm. As will be explained more fully in chapter 7, an ideal is a construct expressing a kind's perfection. Chomsky's ideal speaker is the perfection of the kind 'human speaker of a natural language'; that is, it is the construct of a human speaker without the performance limitations of actual speakers. The construct of an ideal speaker (or an ideal reasoner) is only the notion of an actual speaker (or reasoner) expressed in a form unadulterated by memory limitations, mortality, etc. Thus, the divergence of actual speakers from the ideal speaker is a case of greater or lesser degree of adulteration, not a case of something's failing to be what it ought to be. The ideal involves no notion of what ought to be, but only of what something perfect of its kind is.

In framing an idealization like Chomsky's, we start with the empirical phenomena of behavior in which there is nothing normative. We proceed to a speaker (or reasoner) whose behavior perfectly exemplifies certain psychological laws via a process of abstracting away from factors that complicate the statement of such laws. There is no point in the process where norms enter the picture, and, hence, utterances (or inferences) can be described as diverging from the behavior of the ideal speaker (or ideal reasoner), but not as "errors", "incorrect", "mistakes", "not as they ought to be"—as conflicting with a norm.

For such reasons, which I will amplify in chapter 7, I agree with Wittgenstein that the normative in language cannot be captured on the model of an empirical idealization. My disagreement with him is over how it can be captured. Wittgenstein thinks that he has to deny that the investigation of language and meaning can be scientific in order to capture linguistic normativity. He thought this because he believed that it is a mistake to think that "logic . . . treat[s] of language—or of thought—in the sense in which a natural science treats of a natural phenomenon" (PI: 81). He also wrote: "Philosophers very often talk about investigating, analyzing, the meaning of words. But let's not forget that a word hasn't got a meaning given to it, as it were, by a power independent of us, so that there could be a kind of scientific investigation into what the word *really* means." (BB: 27) But Wittgenstein's claim that the investigation of language and meaning cannot be scientific is an unwarranted conclusion from the premise that their investigation cannot be a matter of natural science. He mistakenly equates the sense in which science treats phenomena with the sense in which natural science treats phenomena, thus overlooking the possibility that mathematical sciences treat them in a way that is relevantly different from how the empirical sciences treat them. In virtue of this possibility, the analogy between language and mathematics provides an alternative to Wittgenstein's analogy between language and games as a way of accounting for the normative in language (PI: 83).

I think linguistic normativity can be captured within a scientific investigation of language and meaning which is like the mathematical sciences rather than the natural sciences. Construing the investigation as an *a priori* investigation along the lines of the realist conception of mathematical investigation, we can try to explain the normative element in linguistics on the model of that conception's understanding of the normative element in mathematical investigation. Such an explanation equates evaluations in mathematics like "this is correct calculation" or "this is the conclusion that ought to be drawn" with evaluations in linguistics like "this is correct English" or "this is English as it ought to be spoken". The force behind such normative mathematical evaluations is the assertion that the case in question conforms to the mathematical or logical facts. Since such facts are necessary, no other alternatives in those cases are possible. Taking a similar model of the normative in language enables us to entertain a similar account of the force behind linguistic evaluations.[98]

Looking at the normative element in language in this way is essentially looking at it the way Frege looked at the normative element in logic. This connects with my earlier suggestion that the sentences of a natural language can be looked at as abstract objects in the mathematical realist's sense. On this viewpoint, the grammatical types of the language constitute the norms for the linguistic correctness of utterances or inscriptions of its speakers. Frege, of course, did not extend his realism to language, but viewed language conceptualistically.[99] However, nothing prevents us from extending realism to language, since Frege's reasons for thinking of natural languages conceptualistically were tied up with his doctrine about their imperfections, which we have already rejected.

I wish neither to suggest that Frege's realism can be transferred without significant modifications nor to give the impression that it is an easy matter to work out a realistic view of language.[100] I am now only trying to indicate an alternative to Wittgenstein's way of saving the normative element. My aim in doing this is to meet the argument that, since considerations of the kind raised in section 81 show that scientific approaches to language and meaning cannot save linguistic normativity, the proto-theory, as a scientific approach, can be ruled out on the same basis as approaches like Chomsky's.

With this understanding, let me here set out the following points about a realistic view of natural languages. Sentences of natural languages are conceived of as abstract objects, as in the mathematical realist's conception of numbers. Such sentences and languages are independent of us: facts about them are *discovered,* not created. The syntactic and semantic structure described in truths about sentences are *in* those objective, non-natural objects. Such structured grammatical objects provide the linguistic norms. Just as it is in virtue of the structure of numbers that there is only one even prime and, hence, that it is a mistake to assert that there is more than one, so it is in virtue of the structure of English sentences that there is more than one kind of English interrogative sentence, and, hence, that it is a mistake to assert that there is only one kind. None of this implies that linguistics is like any particular branch of mathematics.

Our linguistic realism provides an alternative to Wittgenstein's view on either the "conventionalistic" interpretation or the "individualistic" interpretation of that view. The former is championed by philosophers like Winch and Kripke, and the latter by philosophers like Stroud and McGinn.[101] The issue, in a nutshell, is whether Wittgenstein thinks that linguistic norms have their locus in the community, so that correctness is a matter of conformity to the linguistic practices of the community, or in the linguistic dispositions of individuals—arising from the action of linguistic experience on human nature—so that correctness can, in principle, be assessed independently, apart from a community. We have no need to take a stand on the exegetical issue, since both interpretations portray Wittgenstein's late philosophy as grounding linguistic normativity in facts about the natural world, in particular, facts about human behavior. Our linguistic realism presents an alternative to the late philosophy on either the conventionalistic or the individualistic interpretion. On this realism, neither the philosopher nor the linguist is describing natural facts in describing the criteria for correctness in the use of a natural language.

26

We are now in a position to look at Wittgenstein's claim that the use of a word "is not everywhere circumscribed by rules" (PI: 68). The notion that it denies—that rules provide an *a priori* specification of the full application of words which takes all choice out of the hands of the speaker—is especially important in Wittgenstein's discussion of the paradox about rule following, to which we turn in the next chapter. That notion is one of the assumptions that give rise to the paradox.

It should be clear at this point that I agree with Wittgenstein's claim that rules do not completely determine application. The rejection of Frege's conception of the relation between sense and reference is the cornerstone of the intensionalism I have developed, and I have acknowledged the creativity in speech which prevents it from being rule-governed. The "top-down" approach sketched in this chapter does not attempt to strait-jacket the speaker's use of language in the manner of the theories Wittgenstein was criticizing. What I have said about the extensions of expressions is fully in accord with Wittgenstein's claim that we can use a word "so that the extension of the concept is *not* closed by a frontier" (PI: 68). But, as has been shown, the absence of a rule-determined boundary on the extensional side is quite compatible with a rule-determined boundary on the intensional side. We have shown how the *senses* of expression and sentence types can have fixed boundaries, can be circumscribed by rules everywhere in the language, without their tokens' having fixed boundaries or being circumscribed by rules everywhere in the domain of the language. For example, we showed how it can be open what activities count as a game in the sense of either concept (A) or (B), without its being open what the boundaries of those concepts are in English.

The possibility of divorcing meaning and use in this way did not occur to Wittgenstein. If he was ever in the grip of a picture, it was the picture of meaning and use wedded for life. During the entire time that Wittgenstein entertained the idea of a grammatical notion of meaning (see *Tractatus*: 4.002), it was inextricably bound up in his thinking with usage. Thus, in the Cambridge lectures of 1931–32, the last point at which he took seriously the idea that meaning has its locus in the underlying grammar of words, he says:

> The grammatical rules applying to it determine the meaning of a word. Its meaning is not something else, some object to which it corresponds or does not correspond. The word carries its meaning with it; it has a grammatical body behind it, so to speak. Its meaning cannot be something which may not be known. It does not carry its grammatical rules with it. *They describe its usage subsequently.*[102]

It is clear here that the meaning of a word is something descriptive of its future use. This is brought out even more clearly in his Cambridge lectures of 1932–35 where he finally sees the idea of a grammatical notion of meaning as a fundamental error. In rejecting the notion, he says:

> . . . we are tempted to think we can deduce the rules for the use of a word from its meaning, which we supposedly grasp as a whole when we pronounce the word. This is the error I would eradicate. The difficulty is that inasmuch as we grasp the meaning without grasping all the rules, it seems as if the rules *could* be *developed* from the meaning.[103]

Of course, I would also eradicate the error of thinking that the meaning of a word contains full instructions for its use. But, on my diagnosis, the source of the error is not the one Wittgenstein identifies: conceiving of meaning grammatically. It is, rather, conceiving of grammatical meaning as something which gives full instructions for the use of a word.

Not being able to think about meaning apart from use, Wittgenstein could eradicate the error only by rejecting the notion of grammatical meaning. Thus, he was obliged to develop a non-grammatical conception of meaning. The development of such a conception in the *Philosophical Investigations* constitutes what I described in section 11 of this chapter as Wittgenstein's way out of the impasse to which the *Tractatus*'s treatment of the logical powers of atomic sentences had led. The problem about such sentences is a special case of the more general problem about grammatical meaning discussed in the 1932–35 Cambridge lectures. The proto-theory's separation of grammatical meaning from reference and use constitutes the alternative way out that I recommended in section 11.

27

The arguments in PI sections 79, 80, and 82–87 have inspired some of the most influential anti-intensionalist arguments in the philosophy of language over the last two decades. Section 79 is particularly important in this connection. This short passage of approximately one page criticizing the view that proper nouns have a sense that functions as a reference-fixing description contains the germ of Kripke's criticisms of the description theory.[104] Furthermore, the more general criticism of intensionalism developed by Donnellan, Putnam, and Kripke can be seen as an implementation of Wittgenstein's suggestion in section 87 that his line of argument in connection with proper nouns can be extended to common nouns.[105]

In chapter 6 I will examine these extensions of Wittgenstein's thinking in sections 79, 80, and 82–87. Here I can only promise that I will show there that the arguments of Donnellan, Putnam, and Kripke do not succeed against my version of intensionalism built upon the proto-theory. My point will be that such arguments fail to be general arguments against intensionalism because, like many of Wittgenstein's own arguments, they conflate intensionalism with Frege's version of it. Although these arguments refute certain of Frege's assumptions about sense and reference, they do not thereby refute intensionalism, since the existence of the proto-theory's version of intensionalism leaves intensionalists free to abandon those assumptions.

In sections 89–133 Wittgenstein is principally concerned with describing philosophical investigation as he thinks it should be and comparing this with philosophical investigation as it is traditionally. For expository reasons, I presented my account of this material at the beginning of this book and at various later points. In any case, this material does not contain arguments to which we are required to respond.

Finally, the sections following 133 set the stage for and lead into Wittgenstein's paradox about following a rule, which is explicitly stated in section 201. That paradox is definitely something to which we have to respond, but, owing to its special character, the response requires a chapter to itself. Those sections are treated in the next chapter as part of my response to the paradox.

28

We can now claim that the line of argument we have been pursuing in this chapter establishes (I), viz., that Wittgenstein's critique of theories of meaning in the sections of the *Philosophical Investigations* leading up to the paradox does not eliminate all such theories. Our argument is a sort of existence proof. It exhibits a theory, the proto-theory, which survives every criticism of theories of meaning in those sections. This is, for the most part, because Wittgenstein's criticisms, although incisive, were designed to apply to significantly different theories of meaning. He conceived too narrowly the range of theories against which he had to argue, and, as a consequence, the difficulties that his arguments bring to light, typically quite genuine difficulties with the theories he targeted, can be overcome not by abandoning the enterprise of theorizing about meaning, but by abandoning theories of meaning with those difficulties.

Many of Wittgenstein's criticisms concern difficulties with referential theories of meaning. These criticisms support sense theories against referential theories. Where Wittgenstein's criticisms concern difficulties in sense theories, the difficulties are almost invariably idiosyncratic to Frege's theory, Wittgenstein's own theory in the *Tractatus*, or certain psychologized versions of these. The proto-theory differs from such sense theories in three fundamental ways. These differences deflect Wittgenstein's criticisms.

First, the proto-theory does not define sense derivatively in terms of reference or think of sense as containing rules of use. As a consequence, the theory does not lead to a "top-down" approach on which sense determines reference or make sense responsible for rules that specify use in advance. As we have seen, and will see again in chapter 6, Frege's definition of sense was a fatal blurring of what started out to be a sharp sense/reference distinction. As we shall see in chapter 3, thinking of meaning as something in which "all the steps are already taken" is one of the things that makes an intensionalism vulnerable to Wittgenstein's paradox about following rules.

Second, the proto-theory is not introduced as an ideal language intended to improve upon natural languages. Rather, it was introduced as a scientific theory of natural languages with only the standard scientific aim of discovering the truth. Thus it escapes the charge of pursuing the chimera of an ideal language more perfect than our natural languages (PI: 81). In introducing the proto-theory as scientific theory, I do not wish to suggest that Wittgenstein thinks that natural languages cannot be studied scientifically, but only to deny his claim that such a study can make no substantive contact with philosophy. I go along with Wittgenstein in thinking that there is a line between scientific linguistics and philosophy, but, as will be made clear in chapter 8, this is only the thin line dividing a science proper from its foundations. The proto-theory is a piece of science, but one which, if my argument in this book is right, makes substantive contact with philosophy, with important consequences for the direction of twentieth-century philosophical thinking.

Third, the scientific character of the proto-theory was construed along the lines of mathematical sciences understood Platonistically. Wittgenstein had argued that a philosophically acceptable approach to language could not be scientific because a scientific study of language, as he understood it, is an empirical study. But, again, the scope of his argument was too narrow. As a consequence, his criticisms of theories of meaning that are scientific fail against theories that are scientific but not in the empirical sense. Since the proto-theory does not concern unconscious knowledge, computational states of language users, the subjective experiences of speakers, or any other empirical phenomena, but, instead concerns the structure of sentences construed as abstract objects, it escapes Wittgenstein's criticisms of psychologically oriented theories of meaning, particularly, those criticisms which apply because the theories fail to account for the normative criteria in languages.

Because of these differences, much of the time, our development of a theory of meaning and Wittgenstein's critique of theories of meaning pass each other like ships in the night. But not always. In virtue of the features that the proto-theory shares with its intensionalist predecessors, some of Wittgenstein's arguments do apply to it, most importantly, his arguments against the use of ellipsis to motivate the postulation of underlying linguistic structure and against the possibility of analysis. But the applicable arguments have been shown, in all cases, to be inadequate against a decompositional theory. Showing those arguments to be mistaken was the crux of my case for a theoretical conception of meaning.

At one point, Wittgenstein characterizes the traditional conception of meaning as follows: "You say: the point isn't the word, but its meaning, and you think of the meaning as a thing of the same kind as the word, though also different from the word. Here the word, there the meaning." (PI: 120) As far as it goes, this characterization captures the proto-theory's conception of meaning. On this theory, the meaning of a word is similar to the word in being, like its morphological structure, part of its grammatical structure, but it is different in being sense structure rather than syntactic structure. Being part of sense structure, meaning will, of course, not be public features of sentences in the way the words in their surface syntax are. Rather, syntactically simple words, even in the deep syntactic structure of sentences, conceal complex meanings. Thus, we have been able to appeal to grammatical ellipsis for evidence to support the proto-theory's postulation of underlying decompositionally complex senses.

To meet Wittgenstein's criticisms of appeals to ellipsis, we argued that the criticisms involve a mistaken conception of the phenomenon. We showed that, on an adequate conception, the proto-theory's postulation of underlying sense structure can be justified on the grounds that such structure is the only aspect of grammatical structure that can account for pre-theoretically recognizable sense properties and relations of sentences, such as meaningfulness, ambiguity, synonymy, antonymy, redundancy, etc. The justification claims that the proto-theory accounts for sense properties and relations in exactly the same way that other theories of underlying grammatical structure account for their properties and relations, and further, that this way fits the standard pattern of scientific theory construction in which, to give a complete account of pre-theoretically recognized properties and relations of the objects in the domain of study, it is necessary to acknowledge structure with no surface realization.

It is important to stress that this postulate of underlying sense structure successfully accounts for the pre-theoretically recognizable semantic properties and relations. The proto-theory's postulation does not put us in the position that the postulation of grammatical meanings in the *Tractatus* put Wittgenstein in, namely, the position of resorting to underlying structure without thereby clearing up the mystery about the inferential powers of sentences. Since it was construed as logical form in the sense of Frege's *Begriffsschrift* and Whitehead and Russell's *Principia Mathematica*, Wittgenstein's underlying sense structure left him with a mystery, namely, the mystery of how atomic sentences like "The spot is red" and "The spot is blue" can be contradictory and how such sentences can imply sentences like "The spot is colored". But our postulate of underlying sense structure does not leave us with such unanswerable questions, because the proto-theory's underlying sense structures are construed not logically but linguistically, in particular, decompositionally.

On the proto-theory, those sentences, which are atomic from the viewpoint of logical form, are not atomic from the viewpoint of semantic form. Accordingly, although purely logical theories are unable to account for the inferential relations in question because the terms and predicates in these atomic sentences are syntactic simples—the semantics of such theories at best being something like the numeral notation considered earlier—the proto-theory can account for such relations, because the terms and predicates are not simples. The terms and predicates contain the structure necessary to ground the relations in question.

The proto-theory represents two kinds of sense structure below the level of syntactic simples. One is a superordination structure which interconnects the component senses in the sense of a word in a conceptual hierarchy. The other is an antonymy structure of opposed concepts subordinate to a common superordinate. For example, the senses 'red', 'green', 'blue', etc. are opposed subordinates of the concept 'color', and the senses 'husband' and 'wife' are opposed subordinates of the concept 'spouse'. Like superordination, antonymy can be formally represented as an aspect of the decompositional sense structure. With reference to these relations, the proto-theory can explain why "John is a husband" entails "John is a spouse" and why "This spot is blue" contradicts "This spot is red."[106]

29

The proto-theory and the approach of the *Philosophical Investigations* both offer a solution to the mystery of why sentences whose syntax classifies them as atomic nonetheless have inferential powers. Both solutions represent a significant advance over the logical framework of the *Tractatus*. But they are very different sorts of advances over it, with very different consequences. The proto-theory abandons Frege's notion of sense, too, but not the intensionalism underlying it, replacing Frege's referentially defined notion of sense with a notion defined solely in terms of sense properties and relations internal to the grammar of the language, a notion which carries Frege's original distinction between sense and reference through to its natural conclusion, namely, the full separation of sense structure and logical structure. Wittgenstein's approach abandons not only the Fregean notion of sense but every intensionalist notion on which a sense is "a thing of the same kind as the word, though also different," developing an entirely different conception of sense and leading to a unification of sense structure and logical structure.

With respect to resolving the mystery, both approaches work: each gets us out of the quandary. (This is also true of the Quinean resolution, which seeks to debunk the mystery on the grounds that the meanings necessary for logically atomic sentences to have genuine inferential powers do not exist.) But these resolutions are not equal in other respects. Wittgenstein's rejects "the great question"; my own resolution (and Quine's) do not. Wittgenstein's (and Quine's) reject traditional metaphysical philosophy; mine does not. Wittgenstein's (and Quine's) reject necessary truth; mine does not. Wittgenstein's (and Quine's) take a naturalistic standpoint; mine does not.

Nonetheless, the very fact that the proto-theory and the approach of the *Philosophical Investigations* both work proves the point I set out to make in the present chapter, namely, that the arguments that Wittgenstein deploys against intensionalist notions of meaning—prior to the argument based on his paradox about rule following—do not succeed in refuting all of them and in thus establishing his rival notion based on use. Whatever powerful criticism of intensionalist theories of meaning may be found in the discussion of rule following, there is no good criticism of these theories in the arguments leading up to that discussion.

3
Wittgenstein on Rule Following

1

In this chapter, I argue that Wittgenstein's paradox about rule following depends on his critique of theories of meaning and that, because
the critique is unsuccessful in the case of the proto-theory, that theory
is not subject to the paradox. With respect to the goals set out in
chapter 1, this is to say that, having established (I) in the last chapter,
the present chapter tries to establish (II) and (III).

Wittgenstein recapitulates his paradox as follows:

> This was our paradox: no course of action could be determined
> by a rule, because every course of action can be made out to ac-
> cord with the rule. The answer was: if everything can be made
> out to accord with the rule, then it can also be made out to con-
> flict with it. And so there would be neither accord nor conflict
> here. (PI: 201)

He goes on to explain:

> It can be seen that there is a misunderstanding here from the
> mere fact that in the course of our argument we give one inter-
> pretation after another; as if each one contented us at least for a
> moment, until we thought of yet another standing behind it.
> What this shews is that there is a way of grasping a rule which
> is *not* an *interpretation*, but is exhibited in what we call "obeying
> the rule" and "going against it" in actual cases. (PI: 201)

This paradox is directed against philosophers who think that there is
more to the meaning of signs than customary use and teaching
(PI: 190). These are the philosophers Wittgenstein has been criticizing
all along, those who think that grasping the meaning of a sign enables
one to determine its future application because the meaning captures
something essential about the objects to which the sign applies. I will
refer to such philosophers as "semantic essentialists."

The most famous semantic essentialist is, of course, Socrates. He sought definitions that capture the essence of a class of particulars, that is, the universal in virtue of which each of them is a thing of *that* kind. Thus, when Socrates's interlocutors answer one of his questions with an example, he explains to them that examples, since they exemplify many universals, are of little use in discovering the nature of the universal in question. Socrates does not want his interlocutors to look outside themselves for instances of justice or virtue, but rather to look within themselves for concepts of those universals. He believed that such concepts lie hidden in the soul and can be brought to light by *elenchus,* a method that digs them out through an examination of the consequences of proposed definitions.

It is interesting to compare Socrates, who saw the search for essences as the organon of philosophy, with Wittgenstein, who saw it as pursuing chimeras. First, whereas Socrates thought that only knowledge of essence can put us in a safe position for rational action (see, e.g., the *Euthyphro*), Wittgenstein thought that the attempt to acquire such knowledge traps us in pictures that obscure our view of language, and can frustrate rational action.

Second, a definition on the part of Wittgenstein's interlocutor is the counterpart of an example on the part of Socrates'. For Wittgenstein, the philosophical enterprise is not to discover the nature of universals, but to break the hold that this traditional picture has on us by bringing words back to their everyday use (PI: 113–116), and for this purpose examples serve as reminders of such use (PI: 122, 127). Wittgenstein wants us to see that the enterprise of definition reveals a failure to understand that our concepts express not universals, but only family resemblance. There are no concepts of universals which lie hidden in the mind, waiting to be brought to light by analysis (PI: 208).[1]

Third, both Socrates and Wittgenstein use paradoxes to make their point. Socrates uses Meno's paradox about how it can profit us to inquire. The paradox is that, if we already know the nature of something, inquiry is unnecessary, and if we do not, it is impossible, since, without knowledge, we are unable to recognize what we are looking for. But if concepts of universals are all along hidden in the soul, they can be both unknown in a sense sufficient for inquiry to have a point and known in a sense sufficient for recognition. Tacit knowledge of a concept is the basis on which we recognize it when we encounter it in *elenchus,* but such knowledge differs from the explicit knowledge provided by definitions whose consequences stand up to unrelenting examination.

Wittgenstein uses his paradox to show that our explicit knowledge cannot rest on tacit concepts of universals. Nonetheless, the point in Wittgenstein's paradox is, curiously, like Socrates's point that an example is useless in determining a specific universal because it exemplifies many universals. Wittgenstein's paradox turns Socrates's point upside down. Semantic essentialists think that grasping a rule determines all applications in advance, but Wittgenstein claims that such grasping is useless because different courses of action can always be made out to accord with their rule, and, hence, the very notion of a rule loses its meaning. Like the examples of Socrates's interlocutors, the rules of Wittgenstein's are useless because they radically underdetermine what is semantically significant.

2

The explicit formulation of Wittgenstein's paradox begins to take shape in his response to the challenge that the meaning of a word cannot be the use we make of it because meaning is grasped instantaneously whereas use is spread over time (PI: 138). Wittgenstein writes:

> When someone says the word "cube" to me, for example, I know what it means. But can the whole *use* of the word come before my mind when I *understand* it in this way?
> Well, but on the other hand isn't the meaning of the word also determined by this use? And can't these ways of determining meaning conflict? Can what we can grasp *in a flash* accord with a use, fit or fail to fit it? And how can what is present to us in an instant, what comes before our mind in an instant, fit a *use*?
> What really comes before our mind when we *understand* a word?—isn't it something like a picture? Can't it be a picture?
> Well, suppose that a picture does come before your mind when you hear the word "cube", say the drawing of a cube. In what sense can this picture fit or fail to fit a use of the word "cube"?—Perhaps you say: "It's quite simple;—if that picture occurs to me and I point to a triangular prism for instance, and say it is a cube, then this use of the word doesn't fit the picture."—But doesn't it fit? I have purposely so chosen the example that it is quite easy to imagine a *method of projection* according to which the picture does fit after all. (PI: 139)

The mental picture of a cube does not determine a particular application of "cube", because application depends on a method of projection from the picture to the world and there exist methods that connect the picture to noncubes. The thought that the picture before our mind somehow compels us to apply "cube" to cubes is due to a failure of imagination: "only one case [of projection] and no other occurred to us" (PI: 140). The result of the failure is a confusion of psychological with logical compulsion. "The picture of the cube did indeed *suggest* a certain use to us, but it was possible to use it differently" (PI: 139).[2]

One might be tempted to think that all that is needed to determine the proper application of "cube" is to bring the method of projection itself into the picture. To counter this thought, Wittgenstein shows that it changes nothing to imagine that the method of projection too comes before the mind. Now we simply have another picture—one more complexly structured, to be sure, but one that still leaves us in the situation of having a mental model that needs connecting to the proper objects in the world. Hence, such supplementations lead to more elaborate but not more effective interpretations: ". . . any interpretation still hangs in the air along with what it interprets, and cannot give it any support. Interpretations by themselves do not determine meaning." (PI: 198)

Wittgenstein's reason for thinking that no replacement of a simpler with a more complex mental picture can determine application (in the desired sense) derives from the recognition that mental pictures, however complex, are still formal objects like physical signs themselves. As Wittgenstein says, "it is absolutely inessential for the picture to exist in his imagination rather than as a drawing or model in front of him" (PI: 141). Thus, it is mistaken to think that, when the substance of the model is mental stuff, we are somehow in a better position to mobilize its formal structure on behalf of fixing reference than we are when the substance is physical stuff. Once we see that mental models are essentially just formal objects, we should see that, as with physical models, embellishment, i.e., introducing more formalism, leaves us exactly where we started. "Whenever we interpret a symbol in one way or another, the interpretation is a new symbol added to the old one" (BB: 33). Thus, it is futile to think that we make progress toward fixing an application by embellishing a mental model to form a more elaborate one which is supposed to contain "a rule determining the application of a rule." Such interpretations cannot "stop up all the cracks" (PI: 84).

The original problem about application remains no matter how we ramify the construction before our mind. But what exactly is the problem? What is it about the picture of a cube, either before the mind's eye or before the body's eye, which always allows a divergent referential projection like Wittgenstein's application of "cube" to a triangular prism?

It is the fact that the picture is a concrete object. The impotence of pictures and similar constructions to fix the application of a word stems from the fact that such pictures, being concrete objects, are configurations of substances of various shapes and sizes and colors with a particular location, and hence, in and of themselves, formal structures with no inherent meaning. Wittgenstein makes this point in sections 47 and 48 when he discusses the examples of a visual image of a tree, a visual image of a chair, and a chessboard. He observes that it makes no sense, without *appropriate* explanation, even to speak of the component shapes as simples or parts or wholes. He writes:

> If I tell someone without any further explanation: "What I see before me now is composite", he will have the right to ask: "What do you mean by 'composite'? For there are all sorts of things that that can mean!"—The question "Is what you see composite?" makes good sense if it is already established what kind of complexity—that is, which particular use of the word—is in question. (PI: 47)

Therefore, sensible talk about what I see before me depends on first establishing a way of understanding it as a composite thing with specific component parts, and different ways of understanding it will determine different meanings. Without establishing "which particular use of the word . . . is in question," there is nothing in the configuration before my mind that marks it as the image of one thing rather than another.

This is essentially the same point that Wittgenstein is making in section 139 when he shows that, without establishing a particular use of "cube", there is nothing about the picture that comes before my mind when I hear the word to fix an application of it to a cube rather than to a triangular prism. Different methods of projection correspond to different ways of understanding compositeness. Relative to one method, an application of "cube" to a triangular prism fits the picture of a cube, just as, relative to one way of understanding, a chess board is "composed of the colors black and white and the schema of squares" (PI: 47).

We can now see why Wittgenstein's argument works so smoothly. Recall that, in the preceding quotation, as at various other places prior to section 139, Wittgenstein equates the appropriate way of understanding a complex structure with a particular use. Further, recall that, in section 139, he faces semantic essentialists with a case in which this way of understanding conflicts with theirs. Accordingly, their account of the application of "cube" is cut off from what *ex hypothesi* is the only thing capable of establishing the kind of complexity involved, or indeed any kind of complexity. Accordingly, the complex formal structure of the visual image that comes before the mind with the word "cube" (like the visual image of the tree and chair) is open to being understood in indefinitely many different ways, on each of which the word "cube" is related to a different type of object in the world (a cube, a triangular prism, etc.). But the semantic essentialist has no basis for saying that one of the indefinitely many ways of relating the word "cube" to objects in the world is correct.

In contrast, Wittgenstein does have such a basis. He can say that the language user proceeds on the basis of his or her mastery of the techniques for the use of the word. Mastery is exhibited when the user applies words in accord with the customs and practices of the language-game in which he or she has been trained (PI: 206). Training within "the system of reference" of a language-game provides the normative element absent in the semantic essentialist's situation. The criterion of correctness, for "obeying the rule," is whether the user applies the word as he or she has been trained to. Since correct application derives from training in the use of the sign, there can be no problem in the application of the word so long as conditions stay reasonably stable (PI: 142). As long as they do, the customs and practices will serve as a basis for deciding whether a particular application of a sign obeys or goes against the rules of the language. Consequently, thinking one is obeying a rule will be different from actually obeying it: the former is private, the latter public, a matter of conforming to the customs and practices in the form of life in which the user and those judging the use participate (PI: 202).

Wittgenstein's argument works smoothly because the semantic essentialists against whom he directs it are those who psychologize meanings; for to psychologize meanings is to understand them as concrete objects. All the rest follows from this. In taking meanings to be something mental and thinking of understanding a language in terms of the operation of a calculus which brings pictures before the mind's eye (PI: 81), those philosophers sacrifice the possibility of making sense of correctness in the use of language. Hence, it ought to come as no surprise that, having gone the subjective route, they lack an objective criterion for judging a sign to be meant one way rather than another. It is thus to be expected that the "meanings" of psychologized semantic essentialism are powerless to do what meanings are supposed to do.[3]

But it is not enough for Wittgenstein's argument against semantic essentialism that the paradox refute psychologized versions of the position. It has to refute *all* versions of the position. In particular, it has to refute versions of semantic essentialism which do not psychologize meanings, which understand them as abstract, not concrete, objects. *Prima facie*, such versions differ relevantly from the psychologized versions, since, as we have seen, it is reliance on concrete psychological "meanings" which brings on the paradox.

It may be that Wittgenstein takes the paradox to suffice at this point as an argument against semantic essentialism because he thinks that his critique of theories of meaning up to this point has eliminated a realist version of the position. He *does* say that the criteria for a sign to mean one thing rather than another are just "on the one hand, the picture (of whatever kind) that at some time or other comes before the mind" and "on the other, the application which—in the course of time—[the language user] makes of what he imagines" (PI: 141). But as we saw in the last chapter, the critique is unsuccessful, and so semantic essentialists are not restricted to what comes before the mind as their criterion for a sign to mean one thing rather than another. And the paradox that seals the fate of psychologized semantic essentialism is not necessarily a paradox for semantic essentialism *per se.*

The proto-theory, which was shown in the last chapter to survive Wittgenstein's critique of theories of meaning, provides the possibility of a third criterion for a sign to mean one thing rather than another. That criterion is *the correlation of senses with expression and sentence types in the grammar of the language.* As Peirce put it, expression and sentence types cannot be seen on a page or be heard in any voice, but neither can they occur at any time and have temporal bounds like mental phenomena, or have causes and effects the way utterances can, or even be the possession of one person as a speaker's utterance is. Thus, expression and sentence types are, by the standard definition, abstract objects. Similarly, their senses, being properties, relations, and propositions, are also abstract objects. Therefore, since it bases the application of language on a criterion involving abstract instead of concrete objects, a non-psychologized version of semantic essentialism does not face the problem of trying to make a concrete object with no inherent meaning do the work of fixing the application of language in the way meaning does. That problem arose because a concrete object such as a mental picture is impotent to fix the application of a word such as "cube", since its structure is just natural reticulation which, like that of a cloud, takes on one meaning or another depending on how we see it. With this third criterion, abstract objects replace concrete objects.

Obviously, the fact that the criterion invokes abstract objects is not enough to ground an account of what it is for a sign to mean one thing rather than another, since it would not help if the criterion invoked numbers. The critical point is that the abstract objects invoked are, on the one hand, expression and sentence types and, on the other, the properties, relations, and propositions which are their senses. It is their structure and their correlation—which together comprise the grammar of the language—that make the abstract objects invoked in the criterion the proper kind of abstract objects. A realist version of semantic essentialism does not face the problem of trying to manufacture linguistic meanings out of entirely unsuitable raw materials, because, on this version, the materials with which application begins *are* linguistic meanings!

To show that, in making use of the third criterion, semantic essentialists escape the paradox as cleanly as Wittgenstein does himself, I have to explain how the meanings of linguistic types, so understood, provide an objective norm for questions about the meaning of linguistic tokens. Wittgenstein saw that the determination of the meaning of a sign must be based on a criterion that can confer appropriate linguistic status on signs, and that what comes before the mind cannot do that because it cannot prevent divergent semantic construals. In stressing the artifactual character of signs, he pressed for their use as the proper criterion of meaning. Just as stones sitting on the ground have no artifactual status until, with use, they become building blocks, weights, sculptures, missiles, etc., so vocal sounds have no semantic status until use confers linguistic meaning on them. Now, there is something obviously correct about claiming that use transforms natural objects such as vocal sounds into the artifacts of speech. Because of its evident rightness, the claim is perhaps the most persuasive feature of Wittgenstein's position. But it is no part of my explanation to deny that use plays this role. In fact, on the realist version of semantic essentialism that I will be presenting, it *is* use that confers linguistic meaning on utterances. My disagreement with Wittgenstein comes over the nature of use and how it is pragmatically effective.

On the "top-down" approach to the use of utterances set out in the last chapter, the speaker's knowledge of the grammatical structure of the expression and sentence types in the language is the basis on which he or she uses tokens of the types. Grammatical structure is a correlation of expression and sentence types with their senses in the language. Knowledge of the correlation enables the speaker of the language to assign linguistic tokens to expression and sentence types and thereby affiliate them with the senses correlated with expression and sentence types. Thus, on this approach, the power of use to confer linguistic status is derivative, like a power of attorney, relying on the authority of another. The real authority lies not in use, which is merely an agent in the transaction, but in the grammatical structure of the language, that is, in the relations among its phonological, syntactic, and semantic types. Hence, on this approach, since those relations are the proper criterion for determining meaning, not use *per se* or what comes before the mind, to the extent that Wittgenstein was right in thinking that use is effective in conferring linguistic status on signs, he was right, I want to argue, only because use brings to bear such grammatical relations in the language via the speaker's knowledge of them.

On the "top-down" approach, the problem facing the semantic essentialist is to explain how speakers use their knowledge of the grammatical correlation of expression and sentence types with meanings to relate those meanings to verbal and orthographic tokens. Such an explanation will show how the criterion of the language's correlation of expression and sentence types with senses functions normatively in the use of language, revealing what objective fact it is in virtue of which a speaker means one thing rather than another. In the rest of this chapter, I will sketch such an explanation. The burden of this explanation is to specify the fact in virtue of which a speaker means one thing rather than another. The fact that I will specify will, of course, be different from the fact about use in Wittgenstein's solution to his paradox; but, as I will argue, it is no less effective in solving the paradox. This is as far as I try to go in this chapter. My aim is not to show that Wittgenstein's account of following a rule is unsatisfactory as a solution to the paradox, but only to show that mine is a satisfactory solution to it within the framework of semantic essentialism.[4]

3

As with most semantic inquiries in this day and age, the present search for an appropriate fact about meaning begins with Frege and, in particular, with his conception of sense. On Frege's conception, sense answers the question of how reference is determined. Frege thought that the sense of an expression contained all the information necessary for fixing its reference. Had Frege been right in this, there would be a purely semantic or grammatical fact in virtue of which a speaker means one thing rather than another. But Frege was wrong. The sense of an expression in the language does not determine the reference of its tokens in the world. It was Wittgenstein who began the line of criticism which, as developed in the work of Donnellan, Putnam, and Kripke, established this (PI: 79, 87). In chapter 6 we shall look closely at this line of criticism, particularly, in the way Putnam developed it. It will be shown that his famous science-fiction examples about Twin Earth, which reveal undeniable possibilities in the domain of the language, demonstrate that Frege's claim that sense determines reference is inconsistent with the intensionalist commitment to synonymy as the condition for identity of sense. I shall show that the anti-intensionist conclusion that Putnam draws is too strong, and that the proper conclusion to draw is simply that sense does not determine reference, as Frege—but not every intensionalist—thinks. I shall assume this conclusion here in order to agree with Wittgenstein that the objective fact in virtue of which a speaker means one thing rather than another cannot be a purely semantic or grammatical fact.

Given the failure of psychologized semantic essentialism to cope with Wittgenstein's paradox, the fact in question cannot be a purely psychological fact, either. But this conclusion does not leave us with just the fact about use that Wittgenstein takes to determine what a speaker means.[5] We still have the possibility of a mixed fact, one compounded of a grammatical fact about the language and a psychological fact about its speakers.

Let us explore this possibility. Wittgenstein was right to point out that the application of a word is not everywhere bounded by rules and to call attention to a creative element in the use of language—most salient in word play, poetry, wit, irony, hyperbole, etc. (PI: 83, 84). Frege erred in pushing conformity to semantic rule too far. But Wittgenstein erred, too, though in the opposite direction. He overemphasized linguistic deviation to the point of failing to recognize the area in which the use of language conforms to grammatical rule. As I see it, the pendulum first swung too far in one direction, and then, in reaction, swung too far in the other. To avoid these extremes, we have to specify the area in which use conforms to grammatical rule and the area in which it does not.

The area of conformity is, I submit, the area of literal use. Literal use is, roughly speaking, use conforming to the letter of semantic law. The distinction between literal use and nonliteral use is quite familiar, and clear illustrations are readily at hand. Given that the English lexical law for "cat" is that it has the sense 'feline animal', the awakened sleeper who correctly identifies the source of the awful midnight noises by saying, "That's a cat" is using the word "cat" literally. Alternatively, the householder who says, "He's a cat", referring to a burglar who got in by walking a narrow pipe, is using the word nonliterally. Similarly, when a baseball coach says "good catch" about a spectacular save, the utterance is literal, whereas when the coach says "good catch" in reference to a flub of an easy fly ball, the utterance is nonliteral.

We can further distinguish between the literalness and nonliteralness of the *sense* of an utterance and the literalness and nonliteralness of its *reference*. The natural thought about the literalness of sense is that it is the case where the speaker uses an expression with the sense it has in the language. The condition for a sense to be literal is that the meaning of the token is precisely the meaning of the type of which it is a token. Thus, the awakened sleeper's use was literal in sense, whereas the householder's use of "cat" was nonliteral in sense (assuming the utterance to mean something like "He's as agile as a cat").

Literalness of reference is, then, calling a spade a spade. The awakened sleeper's use of "cat" was literal in reference; the householder's use was nonliteral in reference. Note that there can be uses that are literal in sense but nonliteral in reference. Cotton Mather's uses of "witch" to refer to women accused of witchcraft were literal in sense but not in reference. The meaning of "witch" in his utterances was 'woman with magic powers obtained from an evil spirit', but its referents were not witches. For obvious reasons, there will be no cases where the use is nonliteral in sense but literal in reference.

The thought that a literal use is one in which the speaker uses a token with the sense it has in the language captures the basic idea of literal use, but it requires some care in formulation. A speaker who says "She plays well" in a situation where the utterance means "She plays the piano well" is speaking literally, even though the meaning of the utterance has more content than the meaning of the type of which it is a token. The sense of the token might even be much richer than the sense of the type, as, for instance, with an utterance of "She sings it well" meaning 'She sings Brahms's *Der Tod, das ist die kühle Nacht* well'. On the other hand, the sense of the token in a literal use cannot have less content than the sense of the type. We can formulate a rule for the literal sense of an expression token as follows:

> (RLS) The senses of the constituent tokens within a linguistic token *T* must be the senses of their expression types, but the sense of *T* may contain information not in the sense of the linguistic type if the information only makes the sense of *T* more specific.[6]

RLS (rule for literal sense) and the rule for literal reference stated below are not presented as final formulations.[7]

Let us now consider literal and nonliteral reference of expression and sentence tokens. The awakened sleeper's reference is literal because the alley cat on his back fence is in the extension of the sense of "cat". Further, the person who said "She plays well" with the token sense that she plays the piano well refers literally to the piano, as well as referring literally to the female pianist, because the piano is in the extension of the indefinite sense 'things that can be played', which is plausibly part of the meaning of the sentence. The typical case of nonliteral reference of a token occurs when such reference is a function of a nonliteral sense. Examples are the nonliteral reference of the householder's use of "cat" to refer to the burglar and the baseball coach's use of "good catch" to refer to the flub of an easy fly ball. But there are also cases of nonliteral reference for tokens with a literal sense, as in the Cotton Mather example.[8] Given these considerations, the rule for the literal reference is:

(RLR) The reference of linguistic token T is literal just in case its sense is literal and the object(s) to which T refers are in the extension of its sense.

In stating the semantic facts of the language to which conformity is required for literal use, RLS and RLR spell out the way in which such facts function as norms in judging linguistic use. The function of semantic facts parallels the way in which logical and mathematical facts function as norms in reasoning and calculation. Conformity to the facts about implication is the condition under which we reason as we ought if we would reason in a logically correct manner. Conformity to the facts about mathematical relations is the condition under which we calculate as we ought if we would calculate in a mathematically correct manner. Similarly, conformity to the facts about the grammar of a language is the condition under which we speak as we ought if we would speak in a linguistically correct manner.

RLS and RLR say that literal use, for both the sense and the reference of linguistic tokens, is strict adherence to the norms of the language. Of course, no one is obliged to speak strictly in accord with the norms of the language, just as no one is obliged to reason strictly in accord with the norms of logic or calculate strictly in accord with the norms of mathematics. Very often departing from the norms serves a purpose which is not served, or not served as well, by strict adherence to them. For example, the baseball coach could not express his disdain for his player's performance nearly as well by saying straightforwardly "very bad fielding".

RLS and RLR provide a resolution of the famous controversy between Humpty Dumpty and Alice. They are both right. If we are going to speak literally, we have to speak in accord with the norms of the language. This is the sense in which Alice was right: the English word "glory" does not mean 'a nice knock-down argument'. But, since we are free not to use words literally when we like, Humpty Dumpty was also right: we, not the words, are master.

Nonetheless, there is a sense in which Alice was righter than Humpty Dumpty. The linguistic types of a language provide the conditions under which our noises and scribbles count as English utterances and inscriptions with phonological, syntactic, and semantic structure. Moreover, this structure does not derive from the sound waves and ink deposits themselves. Rather, on the "top-down" approach, their structure is just the grammatical structure of the sentence types seen, as it were, from below. Those conditions obtain even in nonliteral use. Thus, Humpty Dumpty cannot use "glory" with an unwarned audience of English speakers in order to communicate 'nice knock-down argument'. Indeed, those conditions have various special roles to play in nonliteral use—for example, to achieve sarcastic force, as in the case of the baseball coach's "good catch", where the hearers must recognize that the speaker intends them to understand the meaning of the remark by inverting the meaning of the type.

This completes my sketch of the grammatical part of the mixed fact I have to specify. I now turn to the psychological part. The psychological part concerns the way that speakers exploit their knowledge of the norms of the language to use linguistic tokens with a particular sense and reference. Since this is an enormously complex subject, I cannot attempt a serious treatment of it here. Nevertheless, I must say something about it in order to specify the component psychological fact. Fortunately, it suffices for this purpose to indicate one account of how fluent speakers of a language put their knowledge of grammatical types to use in communication.

I have chosen H. P. Grice's account.[9] Grice's basic idea is that the pragmatic reasoning by which a speaker means something by an utterance has a structure which is determined by particular internal and external constraints. The internal constraint reflects the speaker's intention to mean something, and the external constraint, the nature of communication as a cooperative enterprise. Grice analyzes the intention to mean something by an utterance as the intention to have the utterance cause a particular state of mind in members of the audience in virtue of their recognition of the intention. Grice analyzes cooperative enterprises as talk exchanges having a particular ends-means structure. The end is the achievement of the purpose of the conversation. The means are the contributions of the participants who are committed to cooperation in achieving the purpose. Cooperation is spelled out in terms of a set of principles that specify how contributions are best made if they are to advance the conversation toward its end. The principles, which include maxims like "Contributions should be as informative as required, no more" and "Contributions should be true and supported as well as is reasonable in the circumstances", constitute a kind of practical ethic for conversations.

Relative to such an account, I can state the mixed fact in virtue of which a speaker uses a token T with a literal meaning m. It is the fact that (i) m is the literal meaning of T in the sense of RLS and (ii) the speaker uses T with the intention of causing the members of the audience to understand T to mean m in virtue of their recognition of his or her intention that they do so on the basis of their knowledge of the common language and common pragmatic principles. We can also state the mixed fact in virtue of which a speaker uses a token T to refer literally to the objects in a set O. It is the fact that (i) the members of O are the literal referents of T in the sense of RLR and (ii) the speaker intends to cause the audience to understand T to refer to the objects in O in virtue of their recognition of his or her intention that they do so on the basis of their knowledge of the common language and common pragmatic principles.[10]

Given this conception of the mixed fact in virtue of which a speaker means one thing rather than another and refers to one thing rather than another, let us return to Wittgenstein's discussion of why a mental picture of a cube doesn't determine the application of utterances of "cube". It can now be shown that the paradox about following a rule, which refutes psychologized versions of semantic essentialism, does not arise for our semantic essentialist position. On the one hand, there is the autonomous grammatical fact that the English word "cube" has the sense 'regular solid of six equal square sides'. On the other hand, given this grammatical fact, there is the psychological fact about fluent speakers of English that, in virtue of knowing English and having the ability to reason pragmatically, they know that "cube" has this sense and know how to make use of this lexical knowledge to form appropriate communicative intentions and to realize them in communication. Hence, there is a semantic norm by which to judge linguistic behavior, and, accordingly, there is "obeying the rule" and "going against it" in actual communication.

Consider again Wittgenstein's initial question whether "the whole *use* of the word can come before my mind?" (PI: 139). It is, of course, quite absurd to suppose that the entire range of actual uses of "cube" can come before the speaker's mind, telescoped, as it were, into a single momentary apprehension. But it isn't at all absurd to suppose (ignoring ambiguity) that a speaker can grasp the essence of all future *literal* uses in one momentary apprehension. The fluent speaker knows that every literal use of a token of "cube" must have the sense of the type (though it may be more specific in certain respects), and also that every successful literal reference of a token of "cube" refers to something in the extension of that sense. So we can say that the literal uses of "cube" can come before our mind in the sense that, in advance of those uses, we grasp that each will have the meaning 'regular solid of six equal square sides' and that each will refer to a regular solid of six equal square sides.

Wittgenstein is surely right in claiming that it is "queer" to think that "the whole *use* of the word" is already there in our act of grasping its meaning (PI: 197). Such instantaneous apprehension of "the whole *use* of the word" would be a kind of precognition. The queerness of the thinking that Wittgenstein is criticizing derives from the fact that the act is supposed to include the *whole* use. That is, it is supposed to include, on the one hand, aspects of nonliteral application that depend on the empirical circumstances in speech contexts, and, hence, on what speakers generally cannot be taken to know *a priori*, and on the other aspects of literal application that go beyond grammar and, hence, on what speakers generally should not be taken to know *a priori*. But my account of the speaker's knowledge of literal sense and reference and its exploitation in speech does not suppose it to include any such things.

Let us look at these two cases more closely. In the case of nonliteral application, my account agrees with Wittgenstein that such application cannot be brought under linguistic rule in the strong sense required. (As we saw in the discussion of family resemblance in chapter 2, there is no concept expressing what is common to all the uses of a word, and so there is no possibility of an abstract grasp of them all.) The account claims no more than that speakers can grasp the conditions for literal sense and reference of a word in advance of its use. This is to claim only that speakers have a grasp of the grammar of their language and of the criteria for literal use in RLS and RLR. But this much is enough to enable semantic essentialism to explain what speakers know in advance that enables them to decide that references of tokens of "cube" to triangular prisms are not literal. In the present context, this is what counts.

In the case of literal application, what comes before our mind in the act of grasping a sense is nothing more than what, qua speakers of English, we can get from our knowledge of the grammar of the types in our language and from the principles for assigning tokens to types. Thus, extrasemantic features of the word "cube" cannot be supposed to come before the mind either as part of a representation of its literal sense or of its literal reference. This prohibition even extends to necessary properties. For example, a speaker qua speaker cannot be supposed to grasp that the referent of "cube" is a twelve-edged object. Speakers do not have this information in virtue of their linguistic competence, but have it only, if they do have it, because of extragrammatical geometrical competence.

Moreover, for the constructive work of semantic essentialism, it is in no way damaging to admit that speakers cannot either have the nonliteral applications of a word come before their mind or even have the literal applications come before it with all their properties and in their full specificity. The actual pragmatic correlation of linguistic tokens with senses and referents is unnecessary to explain the essence of language and the general form of propositions, because the grammatical correlation of linguistic types with senses and referents suffices. Recall from the last chapter that, on the "top-down" approach, senses of linguistic tokens are senses of linguistic types under a pragmatic rather than grammatical correlation. Given this, the senses that appear in the pragmatic correlation of senses with expression and sentence tokens already appear in the grammatical correlation of senses with expression and sentence types. Thus, the senses that occur as token meanings are already available for theoretical purposes, in the stock of senses of expression and sentence types. Although "the whole of the *use* of the word" is not available to speakers, semantic essentialists have the concepts they need to form generalizations about the essence of language and the form of propositions.

Wittgenstein next asks "Isn't the meaning of a word also determined by its use?" (PI: 139) This question is ambiguous. Taking the word "word" to mean 'word type', the answer is negative. The meaning of the word type "cube" is determined by the grammatical structure of the English language just as much as a cube's having twelve edges is determined by the geometrical structure of Euclidean space. On the other hand, taking the word "word" to mean 'word token', the answer is affirmative, contrary to Wittgenstein's expectation of a straightforward negative answer from semantic essentialists. But, as indicated earlier, my semantic essentialist agrees with Wittgenstein's claim that use determines token meaning. Of course, my semantic essentialist's reason for answering affirmatively differs from Wittgenstein's reason. My semantic essentialist employs a "top-down" approach on which, instead of being fundamental, use is determined, in part, by the meaning of linguistic types.

RLS and RLR make this clear in the case of literal uses of language. But, even in the case of nonliteral uses, where the meaning of a token diverges from the meaning of its type, the meaning of types still plays an indispensable role. Recall that the sarcastic force of the baseball coach's use of "good catch" was achieved in part because the audience starts with the meaning of the type "good catch". This example illustrates the general point that nonliteral use honors the norms of the language in the breach. The meaning of linguistic types is the starting point in nonliteral uses of language. There is good reason for this. Since the meaning that is communicated in such uses is a departure from the literal meaning of the speaker's utterance, the hearers must be able to use what they know together with the speaker's pragmatic directions to work out the nonliteral meaning of this utterance. Since the basic thing they can count on is the fact that they share a common language with the speaker, the audience must be able to assume that the meaning of the sentence of which the utterance is a token is their intended starting point and be able to carry out their pragmatic reasoning on the basis of their knowledge of this meaning.

Wittgenstein goes on to ask "can't these ways of determining meaning [mental apprehension and application] conflict?" (PI: 139) To be sure, there are cases where they do conflict, and, in such cases, application takes precedence, as Wittgenstein supposed. But this is of no significance for the present issue, because these cases involve semantic essentialists like Wittgenstein's interlocutor, who want to fix the correct use of "cube" exclusively on the basis of introspection of subjective states. Conflict arises in these cases because application provides a linguistic criterion of correctness independent of the speaker's subjective states. Application takes precedence because mental apprehension is epiphenomenal with respect to such a linguistic criterion. In contrast, mental apprehension and application cannot conflict in the case of our semantic essentialists, who fix the correct use on the basis of an objective grammatical criterion. On their "top-down" approach, apprehension provides application with its grammatical criterion of correctness. The normative force in application thus derives from the criterion that apprehension supplies it. Since there is no independent linguistic criterion, there is no conflict between apprehension and application.

There is no conflict even in cases of nonliteral application. A case of nonliteral meaning occurs when the meaning of the token is different from the meaning of the type of which it is a token. In such cases, there are two apprehended meanings. Consider the example of a speaker who, playing on the 'person of conventional taste' sense of "square", uses of a token of "cube" to mean 'person of extreme conventional taste'. In such a case, the apprehended meaning of one linguistic type is related, in the communicative intention, to the apprehended meaning of another linguistic type, thereby making it possible for a use of a token of the former type to bear the meaning of the latter. Such a nonliteral application cannot conflict with the apprehension of the sense of the token of "cube", that is, 'a person of extreme conventional taste', because the application conforms to that sense. The intended sense *is* the sense of the token. But nonliteral application also cannot conflict with the sense of the type "cube". That sense, like the sense of "square" on which the application plays, is *not* the intended sense of the token of "cube" but simply a stepping stone to it.[11]

Wittgenstein follows up his question about conflict by asking "Can what we grasp *in a flash* accord with a use, fit or fail to fit it?," and then asks "And how can what is present to us in an instant . . . fit a *use*?" (PI: 139). These questions are meant to turn the interlocutor's interesting objection at the beginning of section 138 against the Fregean notion of compositionality. The interlocutor, with something like this notion in mind, wants to say that the meanings of the words in a sentence fit together to form the meaning of the sentence. Against this, Wittgenstein argues that such fitting together "makes no sense" if the meaning of a word is the use we make of it, since use takes time, but meaning is grasped instaneously (PI: 138).

We can make the following responses to Wittgenstein. First, as we pointed out in the last chapter, the fabric of Wittgenstein's argument has unraveled. If his critique had secured his account of "the meaning [as] the *use* we make of the word", then he would have shown that the notion of fitting makes no sense, and he could turn the interlocutor's objection around to show that what flashes before the mind cannot be what the sense of a sentence consists in. But, with the failure of the critique, he has not shown this and is in no position to turn the objection around on those who accept compositionality.

Second, on our autonomous grammatical notion of meaning, fitting makes perfectly good sense. The fit between one meaning and another is a matter of their internal structure's being such as to allow them to form a compositional meaning. As we saw at the end of the last chapter, talking of fit can be seen as a metaphorical way of talking about one sense's satisfying the compositional restriction that it be a subordinate of some concept in the sense with which it is to combine. For example, the sense of "large" combines with the sense of "cube" to form a compositional sense for "large cube" because the sense of "cube" contains the concept of volume with which the sense of "large" can form a subordinate. In contrast, the sense of "suffering" cannot combine with the sense of "cube" to form a compositional sense of "suffering cube" because the sense of "cube" does not contain a concept for which the sense of "suffering" is a subordinate, that is, a concept that can be qualified in this way. Since we can say that fit is a matter of the presence of an appropriate superordinate concept and, hence, a matter of the internal structure of words rather than their use, we can say that "what we grasp *in a flash*" in grasping fit is different from what takes place in time, without thereby disqualifying what we grasp as meaning.

Third, our third criterion enables us to answer Wittgenstein's questions about the notion of fit between a use and what we grasp in a flash. In a case of literal use, the speaker grasps the meaning of an expression type and intends to get the audience to recognize his or her intention to have them assign that meaning (which, since it is objective, they can also grasp) to the token of the expression type that he or she has produced. In a case of nonliteral use, the speaker grasps two meanings: the meaning of the expression a token of which will be used in the communication, and the meaning to be communicated. These meanings are related by a sequence of pragmatic inferences on the basis of which the audience can start with the former meaning and come to recognize the speaker's intention to have them assign the latter meaning to the token. In both cases, we can say that the meaning to be communicated fits the use when the process goes smoothly and the token used has that meaning.

We may now briefly say why Wittgenstein's paradox does not arise for our semantic essentialist. Let us return to the example in section 139, but replace the interlocutor's psychologized semantic essentialism with our position. On our position, grasping the sense of "cube" is grasping the *sense* 'regular solid of six equal square sides'. But, since grasping is no longer introspecting, the object grasped is no longer a concrete mental content. It is an abstract grammatical object, the word type "cube" with its sense(s). In virtue of the fact that there are regular solids of six equal square sides in the domain of the language, the sense of "cube" has a nonempty extension. The application of a token of "cube" to something fits the sense just in case, in virtue of an appropriate communicative intention and its recognition, the token has the sense 'regular solid of equal square sides', and the thing to which the word is applied is in the extension of this sense, that is, is a regular solid of six equal square sides. Now, if, intending to speak literally, I apply "cube" to a triangular prism, I am as wrong as if I had applied "glory" to a nice knock-down argument. The referent does not fit the sense.

Wittgenstein had responded to his interlocutor's claim that application of "cube" to a triangular prism doesn't fit his picture: "But doesn't it fit? I have purposely so chosen the example that it is quite easy to imagine a *method of projection* according to which the picture does fit after all." (PI: 139) This response is blocked on our version of semantic essentialism. One might very well *imagine* a projection from what is before my mind when I grasp the sense of "cube" to a triangular prism that appears to be a cube from the angle at which I see it. But there is no fit because the target of the projection, not being a regular solid of six equal square sides, is not in the extension of the sense of "cube". If I apply "cube" to a triangular prism, I am calling a steam shovel a spade.

Wittgenstein is technically correct in saying "it was possible for me to use the word 'cube' differently" (PI: 139). I can speak nonliterally. If I do so, we can have a case in which an utterance of the word "cube" is applied to a triangular prism. But is this a case in which there is a fit between the sense "cube" and a triangular prism? Not at all. There is a fit between the *intended* sense of the token and a triangular prism, but the intended sense is not the sense of the word "cube". In a nonliteral use, the intended sense shifts from the meaning of the word type to a meaning of the speaker's own choosing—in this case from the meaning of "cube" to the meaning 'triangular prism'. So, adjusting for the shift, we still have a case in which the object referred to can be said to fit the meaning that the speaker intends—only that meaning is no longer the meaning of the word "cube".[12]

Wittgenstein's claim that "it was possible for me to use the word 'cube' differently" is true only for Humpty Dumpty's reason that we are masters. We are also masters in logic and mathematics. Their principles do not control us. We are free to infer or calculate invalidly. But invalid inferences and calculations, even done for the best of motives, are departures from the principles of logic and mathematics. Similarly, a use of "cube" in application to a triangular prism is a departure from the principles of the language: it doesn't fit the sense of the English word. Only literal applications unadulteratedly reflect the grammatical rules of a language, only such applications are instances of those rules.

Although Wittgenstein is right to think that making meaning a matter of subjective experience provides no criterion for correctness in the use of words, he is wrong to think that the only way to obtain such a criterion is to adopt *his* criterion of use. Wittgenstein's approach and ours represent two ways to account for objective semantic norms. He accounts for them by locating meanings in techniques for using language—arising in "the natural history of human beings" (PI: 415). We account for them by locating meanings in the realm of non-natural, i.e., abstract, objects, identifying them with the properties, relations, and propositions that are senses of linguistic types.

4

Is there any important philosophical difference between these two ways of obtaining objectivity in language? Perhaps the most important difference is that naturalistic accounts of the formal sciences must sacrifice the necessity of their truths, whereas non-naturalistic accounts can preserve it. As Kant observes in the *Critique of Pure Reason*, "Experience teaches us that a thing is so and so, but not that it cannot be otherwise." Non-naturalists take this sacrifice to be the Achilles heel of naturalism, since they think that a philosophy of logic and mathematics cannot do justice to these fields without recognizing their truths to be necessary. The two great naturalistic philosophers of this century, Wittgenstein and Quine, have explicitly denied this. They have argued that there is no sacrifice because there is no valid notion of absolute necessity. Both have therefore given a high priority to showing that we can do justice to logic and mathematics without the notion of necessity.

In this book, I focus on the basic arguments of Wittgenstein and Quine (see chapter 4) intended to show that there is no valid notion of necessary truth. My criticisms of those arguments try to explain why they fail in this. I make no attempt to show that the notion is required in order to do justice to logic and mathematics, or to criticize the view that logic and mathematics can be understood without it. It seems clear to me that the position of choice is one that recognizes these truths to be necessary truths and that philosophers back off from this position only under duress, that is, only when the position seems to them to have been undermined by philosophical doubts like those raised by Wittgenstein and Quine. Accordingly, once the arguments that raise those doubts are defused, this position should again become the position of choice.

If the semantic essentialist has not been refuted, none of Wittgenstein's examples in the *Remarks on the Foundations of Mathematics* of how inference, counting, and calculation might be done differently need be taken as counterexamples to accepting the notion of absolute necessity. Without the refutation, the examples need not count as *bona fide* instances of inference and calculation contrary to the laws of logic and mathematics. As in the case of applying the word "cube" to a triangular prism, the semantic essentialist can say that continuing the series "add two" by writing 1004 directly after 1000 is simply not using that expression in a way that is literally in accord with the principles of arithmetic. Wittgenstein's examples are intended, as Stroud claims, to show "that the inhabitants of earth might have engaged in [inferring, counting, calculating, etc.] with rules that are different from those we actually follow."[13] But, unless the paradox and the critique of theories of meaning are in place against all versions of semantic essentialism, not merely the psychologized version, such examples can be taken to be merely instances of inferring, counting, calculating, etc. with invalid rules.

Wittgenstein says that it is wrong to suppose that someone who does not write down 1002 after 1000 must either be irrational or have stupidly failed to grasp the meaning of the instruction "add two." He says this because he believes that it is entirely possible for that person to be "a rational person and yet not be playing our game" (RFM, I, 115). That may be so, of course, but, as should be clear at this point, our reply is that, if the person is not playing our game, then he or she isn't doing a *mathematical* sum or making a *logical* inference. Whatever the game these people are playing, it can't be described as "their mathematics" or "their logic", as if what they were doing were mathematics or logic, only different from ours. In a similar connection, Frege said, "we have here a hitherto unknown kind of madness."[14] His point is that there is no other mathematics and logic than what we know. This is *because* the truths in these fields are necessarily true, and so what conflicts with them is necessarily false. Thus, if someone who obtains 1004 by adding 2 to 1000 seriously insists that he or she has made an arithmetically valid calculation or if someone who infers q from p insists that he or she has drawn a logically valid conclusion, that person is, to say the least, mistaken. Either such results are not about the number system or the implication relation, in which case the game isn't mathematics or logic, or the results are about them, in which case the person is wrong.

Non-naturalists can explain the uniqueness of mathematics and logic in terms of their position that mathematical and logical truths are absolutely necessary. They can, moreover, give an account of how such truths can be absolutely necessary on the basis of their view that mathematics and logic are about abstract objects. Abstract objects exist necessarily and have their intrinsic properties and relations necessarily, and, hence, true statements about the intrinsic properties and relations of an abstract object in this world cannot be false of that object in any other.

If the Wittgensteinian and Quinean arguments that have cast doubt on the notion of absolute necessity can be defused, then the position of choice on logic and mathematics is one that recognizes their truths to be absolutely necessary. In that case, it is a strong recommendation for non-naturalism that it incorporates the position of choice on logic and mathematics, whereas naturalism can neither derive necessity from contingency nor undermine the traditional claim that those truths are necessary.

5

Our criterion of linguistic correctness is simply correspondence to the grammatical facts of the language, just as the logical criterion and the mathematical criterion are correspondence to the facts of implication, number, etc. The criterion for a language is given by the grammatical rules that define its sentences, senses, and the correlation between them. Syntactic rules give the well-formedness conditions for being a sentence of the language. Semantic rules give the well-formedness conditions for being a sense. The compositional function determines which sentences of the language are meaningful (i.e., have at least one sense) and what their senses are. Syntactic rules are analogous to the rules of a geometry. They are constitutive of the language's sentence space, as we might put it, in the way that geometrical principles are constitutive of a geometrical space: different sets of syntactic rules define different sentence spaces, i.e., different natural languages. Semantic rules are analogous to logical principles: they are constitutive of senses for all languages, in analog to the way that logical principles are constitutive of valid arguments.[15]

Just as there are no valid arguments that violate logical principles, there are no senses that violate semantic rules. In providing universal conditions for well-formed senses, semantic rules constrain speakers, no matter how they use the language, so long as they would speak sense rather than nonsense. The proper translation of nonsense in one language is nonsense in another. This is not to say that a *token* of a meaningless expression type like "itchy prime number" couldn't have a sense in context, but only that, if it does, the use would be nonliteral, and that the sense it has in the context would be the sense of some other (meaningful) expression type.

Thus, on our approach, too, there is a notion of the limits of language. These limits are given by the semantic rules. The rules define the limits by determining the senses available to natural languages and their properties and relations. The principal difference between our notion of the limits of language and Wittgenstein's is that, on our notion, the limits are fixed only by the constraints on sense combination within sentence structure. Everything that can be compositionally formed, whether logically inconsistent, mathematically impossible, factually absurd, or whatever, falls safely with the limits of the meaningful. The limits of language are so liberally drawn on our approach that it is even hard to think of a metaphysical sentence that transcends them.[16] Perhaps the legendary "Nothing nothings" succeeds in having no compositional meaning, but, if so, it is a rarity, by no means the paradigmatic case of a metaphysical sentence that Carnap and other logical empiricists took it to be. (The consequences of this are discussed in chapter 8.)

Given the option of our criterion of linguistic correctness, there can be logical compulsion. The application of "cube" to a triangular prism which the interlocutor fails to notice and which Wittgenstein uses to argue that there is nothing more than psychological compulsion, is, of course, a piece of possible behavior. But it is Humpty-Dumptyan, since our being master of our inferences and speech in this sense does not prevent them from being under the higher authority of logic or the language. In this sense, objective implication relations function normatively for reasoners, and objective grammatical relations function normatively for speakers. Just as one cannot validly infer q from p, one cannot literally mean 'triangular prism' by "cube". A speaker who uses the word "cube" literally *must* mean 'regular solid of six equal square sides': the modal has the force of logical compulsion.

6

Wittgenstein thought that his argument against mentalistic versions of semantic essentialism carried over to realistic versions. He saw Frege's conception of understanding as "something like seeing a picture from which all the rules followed, or a picture that makes them all clear" (PI: 40). He argued that "Frege does not seem to see that such a picture would itself be another sign, or a calculus to explain the written one to us" (PI: 40). Wittgenstein thinks that there is nothing at bottom to distinguish realists from mentalists because both take speakers to base their use of words on mental pictures.

It should be clear by now that not all realists are in the same boat with the mentalists, that some realists can provide norms for speech in the facts about grammatical correlations between linguistic types and senses, even though others have nothing to offer over and above the mind's own subjective states. Frege's view about the psychological or sociological character of natural languages muddies the issue of whether Wittgenstein's criticism of him is justified, but, this issue to one side, that criticism does not extend to our version of semantic essentialism. On our linguistic realism, a speaker's application of "cube" to a triangular prism would be incorrect as a literal use of the language, not because of some subjective fact about the speaker's mind, but because of the objective fact about English that its word "cube" means 'regular solid of six equal square sides'.

Such objective facts are presented in English speakers' intuitions of the grammatical properties and relations of sentence types, e.g., that the English sentence "Flying planes can be dangerous" is ambiguous. Thus, we are not restricted to the introspection of inner experiences of mental pictures or sign configurations, which are on a par with outer experiences of physical pictures or sign configurations. In both introspection and perception, speakers are presented with concrete objects, which, as such, have no status as tokens of linguistic types, and consequently, there is the problem that a concrete object can fit all sorts of things. But if we start with linguistic types, we have their grammatical structure as a basis for producing a concrete object (via speech or writing) *as* a token of a particular linguistic type. The problem of concrete mental pictures or sign configurations that fit all sorts of things never arises.

Wittgenstein sneers at intuition, calling it "an unnecessary shuffle" (PI: 213). However, he takes this attitude because he has a rather peculiar conception of intuition. He thinks of it as "an inner voice" which speaks to us, presumably in the words of our language, advising us on how to continue the series. Intuition, on such a view of it, is obviously of no help: an inner utterance is no better than an inner picture. It is simply another formal object and, hence, is no more potent to settle a question of how to go on than a mental picture is. But it is puzzling that Wittgenstein should have considered only this Jiminy Cricket conception of intuition, especially since he taught at the same institution as the Platonist mathematician G. H. Hardy and the genius of mathematical intuition Ramanujan. Besides the "inner voice" view, there are other conceptions of intuition, the best known of which is the classical conception of intuition, which take it to be something like perception wherein we are directly acquainted with the structure of abstract objects. Of course, this conception has the well-known epistemological problem raised by the impossibility of causal contact with abstract objects, and Wittgenstein might have tried to exploit this problem (e.g., by arguing that causal contact is necessary for knowledge). But, since he opted instead for a caricature, his remarks about mathematical intuition are not relevant to sophisticated conceptions of the faculty.[17]

Colin McGinn has given a sympathetic amplification of Wittgenstein's criticism of the Platonist on intuition. McGinn writes that grasping a sense is akin to those acts of 'mathematical intuition' by which Platonists conceive us to be cognitively related to numbers: a kind of mental act in which a certain sort of entity comes before the mind . . . so the Fregean conception does not differ in *this* respect from the empiricist conception—both locate understanding in the apprehension by consciousness of some 'intentional object'.

. . . it is hard to see how Frege's conception can be *au fond* anything other than a manifestation of the idea that understanding consists in an association of signs: for what is a sense but an 'interpretation' of the sign whose sense it is? Tacitly, we are being offered a 'rule for interpreting a rule'.[18]

Like Wittgenstein, McGinn may be right about Frege, but, like Wittgenstein, he is wrong to think that realist conceptions of understanding are vulnerable in the way they agree Frege's is.[19] Standard realisms, including the one I have sketched here, do not "locate understanding in the apprehension . . . of some 'intentional object'" (i.e., mental object), but locate it rather in the apprehension of some intensional object (i.e., abstract object). Intuition is, to be sure, a mental act, but its object is not, for that reason, something psychological. Perception is a mental act, but its objects are not mental. We do not consider astronomy a branch of psychology because it rests on perception, and we need not consider logic, mathematics, or linguistics to be branches of psychology because they rest on mental acts.

Realists do not have to conceive of understanding as association of signs and of a sense as an interpretation. Interpretations, on Wittgenstein's usage, are concrete things like projection diagrams which are naively invoked to block Wittgenstein's application of "cube" to a triangular prism. The sense of "cube", however, is nothing concrete, and it is not "a rule for interpreting a rule" but an abstract object.

A proper realist conception of understanding differs from "the empiricist conception," since, for the realist, "apprehension by consciousness" is intuition of abstract objective objects, whereas, for the empiricist, such apprehension is introspection of concrete subjective objects. Besides the difference that introspection and intuition inform us about different ontological kinds, there is the related difference that introspection gives only particular knowledge, whereas intuition gives general knowledge. Generality in introspection, as in perception, comes subsequently—by putting the experience together with similar experiences and making an inductive generalization. In contrast, generality in intuition comes simultaneously—in the intuition itself, without further steps. A single geometrical intuition about the type *cube* validates for us the general truth that all cubes have twelve edges, and a single linguistic intuition about the English sentence type "Cubes have equal square sides" validates for us the general truth that all its tokens that have a literal sense are analytic. Mathematical intuition could hardly be about a concrete cube without sacrificing its power to validate *general* mathematical judgments, and linguistic intuition could hardly be about a concrete sentence without sacrificing its power to validate *general* grammatical judgments.[20]

McGinn makes one final claim which seems to bring out something else in Wittgenstein's thinking about intuition. McGinn writes: "The real objection to 'ideas' as meanings is not their 'subjectivity' but their logical independence from use; but *this* objection seems to apply equally to 'objective senses'."[21] The objection has force against Wittgenstein's interlocutor because mental ideas of themselves are impotent to determine meaning. Logical independence from use is fatal to the ideas-as-meanings doctrine because it cuts one off from what "for a large class of cases" *is* meaning (PI: 43) and, hence, from what would provide an effective, because normative, semantic criterion (PI: 140). But the objection does not carry over to objective senses. On the proto-theory's conception of autonomous abstract meanings together with the "top-down" approach, senses are logically independent of use without that being fatal.[22] McGinn is right that there is an essential relation between sense and use, but the relation of dependency can go the other way. On the position I have set out, use depends on autonomous objective senses because it gets its normativity from them. It is unnecessary for objective senses to get normativity from anything, since they (in connection with expression and sentence types) *are* the semantic norms.

7

Jorge Luis Borges's story "The Garden of Forking Paths" contains this passage:

> I proposed several solutions—all unsatisfactory. We discussed them. Finally, Stephen Albert said to me:
> "In a riddle whose answer is chess, what is the only prohibited word?"
> I thought a moment and replied, "The word *chess*."
> "Precisely," said Albert.[23]

The missing word in Wittgenstein's riddle about following a rule is "meaning" in the realist's sense. On the supposition that autonomous abstract meanings have been eliminated in the critique of theories of meaning, the semantic essentialist is taken to be left with only mental ideas, and these, the riddle shows, lack the normative force to distinguish obeying rules from going against them. But once it is recognized that the critique fails, that is, once "meaning" in the realist's sense is no longer a prohibited word, the semantic essentialist, too, has a solution to Wittgenstein's riddle.

4

Kripke on Rule Following

This chapter is concerned with whether Saul Kripke's paradox about rule following in *Wittgenstein on Rules and Private Language* succeeds where Wittgenstein's paradox fails.[1] The chapter does not go beyond this question. It does not consider other aspects of Kripke's account of Wittgenstein or the problem of private language; in particular, it does not enter the controversy over whether Kripke's Wittgenstein is the real Wittgenstein. Although there is surely at least a family resemblance between the two, the fact that, nonetheless, they are very likely not exactly the same raises the question with which this chapter is concerned. I will argue that the paradox about following a rule presented by Kripke's Wittgenstein, like Wittgenstein's own paradox, does not constitute an objection to the conception of language and meaning in the present work.

Kripke says that a solution to the paradox about following a rule must satisfy two conditions:

> First, it must give an account of what fact it is (about my mental state) that constitutes my meaning plus, not quus. But, further, there is a condition that any putative candidate for such a fact must satisfy. It must, in some sense, show how I am justified in giving the answer '125' to '68 + 57'. The 'directions' . . . , that determine what I should do in each instance, must somehow be 'contained' in any candidate for the fact as to what I meant. Otherwise, the sceptic has not been answered when he holds that my present response is arbitrary. (WRPL, p. 11)

There are two ways to interpret Kripke's conception of the skeptic's challenge: one epistemological and the other metaphysical. On the former, the challenge is to justify our claim to know that our answer of 125 is correct with respect to our communicative intentions. Again, the skeptic wants us to explain how we know that we meant by "table" the sense *table*, say, (C), rather than *tabair*, (C'):

(C) a piece of furniture consisting of a flat surface, to serve as the locus of activities in the use of the artifact, and supports for holding the surface in a position for it to function as a locus for those activities.

(C') something that is a table not found at the base of the Eiffel Tower, or a chair found there. (ibid., p. 19)

At the end of the quotation, Kripke seems to suggest that this challenge is a special case of the challenge of the traditional philosophical skeptic. This challenge, however, would be too strong to be of concern in the present semantic context. Warren Goldfarb makes this point: ". . . a skeptical problem cannot be assumed to arise from the logical possibility of error. To take it that skepticism about meaning can so arise is to agree to a jejune global skepticism about all our knowledge and, perhaps, all our concepts. In any case, nothing has as yet been invoked that is special about ascriptions of meaning."[2] The skeptic's question, How do we know that we meant (C) rather than (C') by "table"?, must challenge ascriptions of meaning without challenging everything else.

On the metaphysical interpretation, the skeptic's challenge calls into question the existence of a semantic fact of the matter with respect to which we can settle issues about whether a speaker meant one thing or another. Goldfarb notes this challenge, referring to it as "ontological," but makes little of it. He says (pp. 474–475) that, insofar as Kripke formulates the second challenge in terms of a physicalistic factual realm supplemented by introspectively knowable sensations, it has no force against Frege's position. Frege's anti-psychologism criticizes attempts to identify semantic facts with aspects of sensations, and his realism argues that the realm of the physical does not exhaust the realm of the factual.

One might also think that the metaphysical challenge, even more than the epistemological challenge, shows that Kripke's reconstruction of Wittgenstein's paradox is far from the spirit of the original. For the reconstruction seems to suggest that Wittgenstein is presenting us with a new metaphysical puzzle, and we know that this cannot be so. Posing metaphysical puzzles is the last thing that Wittgenstein, modern philosophy's most throughgoing anti-metaphysical philosopher, would do. Were Wittgenstein propounding a new metaphysical problem, he would be encouraging us to provide a metaphysical solution, and he would thereby be contradicting a central critical thrust of the *Philosophical Investigations,* as expressed in sections 116–133.

Colin McGinn rejects both the idea that Wittgenstein is questioning the existence of semantic facts, viz., facts that fix meaning, and the idea that Wittgenstein's solution is, accordingly, a skeptical one which treats ascriptions of meaning as nonassertive.[3] McGinn makes an interesting case for the view that the point of Wittgenstein's paradox is that the supposition that understanding is an inner state or process gets the semantic facts wrong. The paradox, as McGinn sees it, is a *reductio* intended to show that "the *fact* that gives signs life is a fact about use, not a fact about inner states."[4] This is close to the way in which I took Wittgenstein's paradox in the last chapter. But I understood the notion of a semantic fact against which Wittgenstein was arguing in a broader way which includes facts about abstract linguistic objects.

Whether or not such criticisms of Kripke are correct, his metaphysical challenge is still significant for the present attempt to vindicate a theoretical conception of meaning. The challenge can be seen as introducing a skepticism especially targeted to such conceptions. Moreover, since Kripke's skeptic provides specific reasons for thinking that there may be no semantic fact of the matter of the sort presupposed in traditional intensionalist theories, it is not open to the reply of "jejune global skepticism" with which Goldfarb rightly dismisses the epistemological challenge resting merely on the "logical possibility of error." Kripke sometimes suggests his own reasons, arguing that the existence of deviant ascriptions of meaning casts doubt on whether even full knowledge of what there is would suffice to establish a fact of the matter about someone's meaning something. And he sometimes suggests reasons not his own, as when he compares the metaphysical challenge to Quine's use of his indeterminacy argument to show that there are no meanings for the intensionalist to be right or wrong about (WRPL, pp. 55–57). Clearly, we cannot ignore reasons purporting to establish such a conclusion.

The primary question facing us, then, is whether this metaphysical challenge is based on reasons that succeed in showing that there are no semantic facts of the kind on which intensionalist theories are based. I shall answer the question in two stages. In this chapter, I address the reasons that Kripke himself suggests. In the next chapter, I address the reasons of Quine's to which Kripke alludes. I acknowledge that, by this point, I have piled up a number of promissory notes, but I assure the reader that they will be paid in full in the next chapters.

The first of Kripke's conditions on a solution to the paradox is that it must specify what fact it is that constitutes the speaker's meaning one thing rather than another. I think we can say that this has already been done. The fact in question is the mixed grammatical/psychological fact described in the last chapter. In accord with the discussion there, we can say that a speaker's literal use of "table" means *table*, rather than, say, *tabair*, in virtue of the fact that "table" means (C) in English, not (C'), and that the speaker has the communicative intention to use the utterance of "table" literally in the sense of RLS. Furthermore, assuming in the case of the speaker's use of "table", in contrast to the case of Cotton Mather's uses of "witch", that the relevant beliefs about the world are true, his or her utterance refers to a table rather than, say, to a chair situated at the base of the Eiffel Tower, since, then, the reference of the utterance is literal in the sense of RLR.

The second of Kripke's conditions is that the solution must explain how we are justified in claiming to mean one thing rather than another. The explanation must refer to our following directions for application that ground our use in semantic fact, thus preventing us from being accused of arbitrariness. As we have already seen, the justification we are being asked for need not be such as to satisfy the philosophical skeptic who intends to rob us of everything not logically nailed down. This being so, I think we can show that the discussion in the previous chapter, with certain elaborations, provides an explanation that satisfies Kripke's second condition.

Let us consider one way in which I might, if called upon, justify my assertion that my use of a token of "table" means *table* rather than *tabair*. First, I can, in principle, provide conclusive reasons to think that "table" means *table* on the basis of the proto-theory's methodology. Such reasons will take the form of facts indicating that "table" means (C) in English (rather than (C')) together with simplicity considerations to rule out what is not required to account for the facts. To discover the appropriate facts, we look at the sense of English expressions in which "table" appears. For example, the compositional meaning of "gaming table", "dining table", "operating table", "drafting table", "drawing table", etc. in each case involves the sense of the modifier's specifying the activities for which the surface serves as the locus. Again, "good table" means table whose surface serves well as a locus for the activities appropriate to tables. Or "Nothing designed to serve as a seat and serving solely and exclusively as a seat is a table" is analytic. If "table" had the meaning (C'), then a chair that served solely and exclusively as a seat and was located at the base of the Eiffel Tower would be something to which "table" properly applies, and hence, *per impossible*, it would be a table.

Even without this direct evidence against (C'), we could argue against it indirectly on the grounds that the information it contains over and above that in (C) unnecessarily complicates the definition of "table", since that information is not required to account for any sense property or relation of expressions in which "table" occurs.

Second, I can complete the justification of my assertion that my use of the token of "table" means (C) rather than (C′) by faithfully reporting my communicative intention to apply the token literally and by providing perceptual and other evidence for the truth of my belief that the object to which I applied the token of "table" is in the extension of (C). These justifications seem to do the trick. They contain directions for application which ground my use in an appropriate mixed semantic/psychological fact. Furthermore, my grounds are anything but arbitrary. If I were to give such a justification in an ordinary case of the use of "table", amplifying on each point as required, it would surely be odd for someone to reply, in the face of everything I have said, that my assertion that I mean *table* is arbitrary.

We may now review Kripke's discussion of the paradox to see whether there is anything in it to suggest that the explanation just given is insufficient to satisfy his skeptic—a modest skeptic who does not ask that we plug every logical gap, but asks us only for a specific reason to show why our claim to mean *table* and not *tabair* isn't arbitrary. Kripke writes: "Can I answer the sceptic who supposes that by 'table' in the past I meant *tabair* . . . ? Did I think explicitly of the Eiffel Tower when I first 'grasped the concept of' a table, gave myself directions for what is meant by 'table'? And even if I did think of the Tower, cannot any directions I gave myself mentioning it be reinterpreted compatibly with the sceptic's hypotheses?" (WRPL, p. 49) No doubt we do not think of the Eiffel Tower in first grasping the sense of "table."[5] Nor do we think of it in forming a communicative intention to use the word literally. We grasp the sense of "table", (C), which makes no reference to the Eiffel Tower, the Empire State Building, the Taj Mahal, or any other such things, and on that basis we form and execute the communicative intention to use a token of the word "table" literally, with the sense (C) and with a referent belonging to the type-extension of (C). Since the relation between the sense (C) and its type-extension is an objective relation between an abstract concept and a collection that contains tables but not the Eiffel Tower, it is not necessary for us to think of the Eiffel Tower in forming or executing our communicative intention. No exclusionary thoughts are required to exclude the Eiffel Tower. It is automatically excluded by being outside the type-extension of "table".

Kripke's skeptic's charge here would seem to be that choosing the hypothesis that by "table" we meant *table* is arbitrary because anything we might cite in support of the choice can be reinterpreted as support for the skeptic's hypothesis that by "table" we mean *tabair*. Two things need to be said before I consider this charge. First, as indicated, I will treat it as independent of Quine's argument for indeterminacy. Second, I will treat Kripke's skeptic's charge as independent of Wittgenstein's objections to psychological versions of semantic essentialism. As I made clear in the last chapter, I have no quarrel with Wittgenstein's objections insofar as they are taken to show no more than that the mental provides no linguistic norm with which to determine correct application.

Even the currently most sophisticated conceptions of the mental fare no better than the unsophisticated conception that Wittgenstein's interlocutor tries to defend. Consider a conception like Chomsky's. Chomsky's explanation of language use is entirely in terms of causal consequences of states of a speaker's mind/brain. Now, it doesn't matter that the states can be unconscious, biologically based, or intricately structured in accord with the latest formal theories in linguistics or cognitive science. An explanation of language use in terms of such states is no different from an explanation in terms of the simply structured images that come before our conscious mind with respect to what Wittgenstein had in mind when he referred to "operating a calculus according to definite rules" (PI: 81).

Chomsky has recently discussed Kripke's treatment of Wittgenstein's paradox and tried to show that the paradox does not apply to his own form of linguistic psychologism.[6] But Chomsky's discussion does not come to grips with the paradox. Before considering why this is so, we should note that Chomsky makes no serious attempt to see what Wittgenstein himself is driving at. Chomsky takes it as obvious that Kripke's account of Wittgenstein's paradox is correct and, accordingly, takes it that no examination of "the textual question" is necessary. Philosophers like Winch, Goldfarb, and McGinn would, of course, dispute this, but we can let that pass.

Chomsky confuses the question of whether there is a normative semantic fact of the matter with the question of whether we can build "a complete theory, the best we can, of relevant aspects of how [the speaker] is constructed—of the kind of 'machine' he is—if one likes," where "relevant aspects" include only such biological matters as the language organ, the organization of memory, information-processing mechanisms, etc. (ibid., pp. 236–237). But Wittgenstein's question is whether psychological theories can account for the normative fact that determines whether the speaker means one thing rather than another. The question is not whether there is a causal mechanism inside the speaker's head responsible for speech and whether science can theorize about it. Wittgenstein is certainly not challenging that.

Chomsky writes that the mechanism incorporates a "particular program" which is "part of a more general account of the properties of the mind/brain" and that that account "defines 'malfunction'" (ibid., p. 238). But this does not explain how the challenge to provide an appropriate normative criterion for use has been met. Moreover, proper functioning according to the bioprogram can be improper functioning in accord with rules of the language. This is because the bioprogram's statements about the grammar of the language can be false of the language, as we indicated briefly in chapter 2 in connection with the notion of error (and will develop more fully in chapter 7).[7] Instead of coming to grips with the normative point that Wittgenstein is raising, Chomsky merely repeats the tired truism that the approach he is advocating "leads to confirmable theories."[8] Everything Chomsky says here about "confirmable theories", etc. could just as well be said in connection with astronomy or mechanics where there is nothing normative involved.

There are only two ways of construing the charge of Kripke's skeptic as a challenge to our approach as sketched above. Either the charge is seen as directed against the hypothesis that the word-type "table" means *table* in English, or it is seen as directed against the hypothesis that the sense one grasps in forming the communicative intention to use a token of the type "table" literally is the sense *table*, that is, (C). In the case of the first way of taking the charge, the skeptic is challenging the claim that the semantic evidence adequately supports my hypothesis about the meaning of "table".

The challenge cannot be taken as a challenge similar to standard challenges within linguistics to come up with evidence that selectively supports one hypothesis over another. Given the proto-theory and the kind of broader grammatical theory of which it is to be a part, this challenge poses only practical problems of gathering appropriate evidence. Such problems are the sort that the working linguist encounters every day. We have, moreover, spelled out the nature of the relevant evidence. The proto-theory's general account of semantic evidence tells us that evidence for the hypothesis that "table" means *table* in English takes the form of expressions and sentences containing the word "table" whose sense properties and relations are best accounted for on this hypothesis.

Perhaps I have already given enough examples of such evidence, but the point is important, so it is better to sin in the direction of overdoing it. One example is the intuition of the synonymy of "table" and (C), and, hence, the nonsynonymy of "table" and (C'). A related example is the redundancy of the expression "a table that is a piece of furniture" and the nonredundancy of "a table that is not found at the base of the Eiffel Tower or a chair found there". Another piece of evidence is that Kripke's neologism "tabair" is not synonymous with "table". If this isn't clear intuitively—from the fact that there would not be alternative hypotheses if these words were synonymous—note that "Some tables are tables" is analytic, whereas "Some tables are chairs" is not. Further, note that the sentence "A table is either not found at the base of the Eiffel Tower or found there" is not analytic. (The sentence is, of course, a logical truth insofar as its predicate is universally applicable, but this is not at issue.) Still further, note that "There is a chair at the base of the Eiffel Tower" certainly does not analytically entail "There is a table".[9]

Thus, the challenge must be taken as questioning whether such evidence can, in principle, suffice to rule out every alternative hypothesis about the meaning of "table." Philosophers wise in the ways of skeptics might suppose that even a wide range of semantic evidence might not suffice, because the skeptic could still argue that knowing that an expression type E has a sense with the semantic properties and relations $P_1, \ldots, P_n$ does not determine the hypothesis that E has the particular sense S that it has in the language. If we can permute the associations of colors with color words while preserving positional relations in the color solid, why can't we permute senses with expressions while preserving semantic properties and relations?[10] Couldn't there be a function which associates a different sense S^* having $P_1, \ldots, P_n$ with E and which systematically maps expressions onto senses while preserving semantic properties and relations, so that the hypothesis that E has the sense S is not evidentially distinguishable from the hypothesis that E has S^*?

The cases are different for two reasons, both having to do with the difference between the grammatical structure of a natural language and the geometrical structure of the color solid. First, the assumption that there are just finitely many expressions and sentences whose semantic properties and relations can be looked at in evaluating the hypothesis that E has the sense S is mistaken. Because of the recursive potential of syntax, every expression is a constituent of infinitely many more complex expressions and sentences, and, because of compositionality, there are specific relations between the semantic properties and relations of the expression and the semantic properties and relations of the larger syntactic constructions it enters into. Given that we can always look at further evidence, it is not at all clear that the hypothesis that E has the sense S is evidentially indistinguishable from the hypothesis that E has S^*.

Second, there are also other kinds of relevant grammatical relations. These are relations that hold of sentence-sense pairs on the basis of conditions on the sentence and the sense jointly. One trivial example will explain what is involved. Consider the relation R which holds of an expression E and sense S—think of E = "table" and S = (C)—just in case E rhymes with "Mabel" and S forms an analytic proposition with the application of the predicate 'artifact'. It is clear that such relations can be made as complex and as discriminating of grammatical structure as one likes. For example, one might form the relation R' by throwing in the further conditions that E alliterate with "tabloid" and have just two syllables and that 'S' be a subordinate of 'furniture'. Indeed, the full resources of grammatical representation can be brought to bear in forming such relations. Since the full resources of the grammar are involved, hypotheses that cannot, in principle, be evidentially distinguished with relations in this class must be regarded as equivalent linguistic hypotheses, differing only in the economy with which they express the association between the expression and its sense.

Let us now turn to the second way of taking Kripke's skeptic's charge. Here we are no longer talking about the language; we are talking about its use on a particular occasion. The issue now is, How can I legitimately assert that the sense I grasped in forming the communicative intention to use a token of the type "table" literally is the sense *table*? Kripke writes:

> . . . ultimately the skeptical problem cannot be evaded, and it arises precisely in the question how the existence in my mind of any mental entity or idea can *constitute* 'grasping' any particular sense rather than another. The idea in my mind is a finite object: can it not be interpreted as determining a quus function, rather than a plus function? Of course there may be another idea in my mind, which is supposed to constitute its act of *assigning* a particular interpretation to the first idea; but then the problem obviously arises again at this new level. (A rule for interpreting a rule again.) And so on. For Wittgenstein, Platonism is largely an unhelpful evasion of the problem of how our finite minds can give rules that are supposed to apply to an infinity of cases. Platonic objects may be self-interpreting, or rather, they may need no interpretation; but ultimately there must be some mental entity involved that raises the sceptical problem. (WRPL, p. 54)

Mathematical realists, or 'Platonists', have emphasized the nonmental nature of mathematical entities. The addition function is not in any particular mind, nor is it the common property of all minds. It has an independent, 'objective', existence. There is then no problem—as far as the present considerations go—as to how the addition function (taken, say, as a set of triples) contains within it all its instances, such as the triple (68, 57, 125). This simply is in the nature of the mathematical object in question, and it may be an infinite object. (WRPL, pp. 53–54)

For Kripke's Wittgenstein, Platonism is an "unhelpful evasion" because a mental idea is a finite object and, hence, can only constitute the grasping of a finite part of an infinite object. Since there will always be quus-type functions that share the finite part with the plus function, what I grasp underdetermines the choice of the plus function. No matter how I expand my ideas, they will always underdetermine a particular infinite mathematical object from among all those which have the grasped part in common.

Kripke is surely right that grasp of a finite sequence of triples such as (68, 57, 125), (2, 2, 4), . . . , (n, m, r) does not give us a nonarbitary way of determining a projection to the infinite sequence of triples that is the addition function: any such grasp is as much a grasp of the infinite sequence of triples that is the quus function as it is a grasp of the infinite sequence of triples that is the plus function. However, this concession isn't enough for the conclusion that Platonism is an "unhelpful evasion," that no idea in my mind "can *constitute* 'grasping' any particular *sense* rather than another" (italics mine). The further premise that is required is that the *sense* of "plus" is the infinite sequence of triples in question. This premise is false. The infinite sequence of triples (68, 57, 125), (2, 2, 4), . . . is not the sense of "plus", but rather its reference. Kripke's skeptic, on the present interpretation, is guilty of an old-fashioned sense/reference confusion! Hence, the argument in the above quotation does not show that the skeptical problem is inevitable for the Platonist.

Kripke's argument does, of course, show something. What it shows is that Platonism without intensionalism is untenable. Perhaps Kripke had something like Quine's extensionalist Platonism in mind when he was formulating the argument. Quine countenances abstract objects in mathematics because they are indispensable, but does not countenance them in semantics because, as he sees it, senses play no role in linguistics.[11] On such a Platonism, there are objective mathematical entities and subjective representations of their finite parts, but there are no objective semantic entities and, hence, no subjective graspings of them. The situation is, therefore, parallel to the one in which Wittgenstein originally raised the question of projection, viz., the one in section 139 where he shows that the interlocutor's subjective picture of a cube does determine a unique assignment of tokens of "cube" to physical objects. In the situation to which

Kripke here adapts Wittgenstein's paradox, a domain of infinite objective mathematical objects corresponds to a domain of indefinitely many objective physical cubes, triangular prisms, etc. In both situations, the magnitude of the range of the extensional objects far outstrips our mental grasp. No wonder, then, that Kripke's adaptation of the paradox goes through so smoothly against the extensionalist Platonist.

But everything changes when his skeptic faces the intensionalist Platonist. As was shown in chapter 3, Wittgenstein's projection argument does not work against intensionalist Platonism. Thus, given the parallel, we can expect that the projection argument of Kripke's skeptic will not work against this position either. This is the case. Intensionalist Platonism introduces a new element. In addition to *infinite extensions* like (58, 67, 125), (2, 2, 4), . . . and *open extensions* like the tables, there are also their *finite intensions*, i.e., senses such as the concept of m plus n (i.e., the notion of taking the nth successor of m) and the concept (C). On this intensionalist position, there are inner graspings of senses over and above inner graspings of proper parts of extensions. Platonists are thus no longer in the situation of having to relate a finite mental entity to an infinite objective entity. They have only to relate a finite mental entity (an idea constituting the grasp of a sense) to a *finite* objective entity (the sense itself). The feature of projection, which causes the underdetermination, is absent.

Moreover, the proto-theory provides intensionalist Platonists with grounds for saying that senses are finite entities. According to the theory's decompositional account of the meaning of syntactic simples, the abstract objects that are the senses of words like "table" and "plus" are composed of a finite number of component senses combined in finite superordination or antonymy structures. According to the theory's compositional account of the meaning of syntactic complexes, the abstract objects that are the senses of sentences are formed by a finite number of combinations of finitely many senses.

Therefore, the intensionalist Platonist provides the following account of our grasp of sense in forming communicative intentions. As speakers of English, we have an idea of the sense of words like "table" and "plus" on the basis of which we grasp the objective senses themselves. The projection problem of Kripke's skeptic does not arise here. Thus, we form communicative intentions to use the word "table" or "plus" with respect to the sense *table* or *plus* rather than the sense *tabair* or *quus*. With such intentions, we can use tokens of "table" or "the addition of 68 and 57" literally, that is, with the sense *table* or *the addition of 68 and 57*. (We could, of course, use tokens of them with respect to the senses *tabair* and *quus* if we chose to speak nonliterally.)

Furthermore, our Platonism can not only legitimately assert that the senses I grasp in forming intentions to use "table" and "plus" literally are their senses in the language; it can also legitimately assert, assuming the truth of the relevant beliefs, that the referents I target in forming the intention to use "table" and "plus" literally are their referents in the language, that is, their type-referents. On the "top-down" approach of chapter 2, the sense of an expression determines its type-reference with respect to a domain. Senses objectively determine their type-referents, e.g., tables or infinite sequences of triples of numbers, simply by being true of them. I cannot grasp the type-reference of "table" (when I refer universally) or grasp the type-reference of "plus", but I can target the former collection of objects or the latter infinite object as the type-referents of the senses in question.

The problem of arbitrariness raised by Kripke's skeptic disappears. It arose because, on the Platonist position, the projections we make seem to be indistinguishable from deviant projections. The skeptic accuses us of not being able to justify saying that our finite ideas determine one rather than another infinite object. But, as we have seen, if Platonism is understood to be intensionalist Platonism, we no longer face projections from finite to infinite; accordingly, the need to make arbitrary choices in order to exclude deviant projections disappears.[12] Therefore, only a Platonism like Quine's may be criticized as "an unhelpful evasion."

In closing the last chapter, I put the crux of my solution to Wittgenstein's riddle about following a rule in terms of a variant of the answer that Stephen Albert elicits from the narrator in Borges's "The Garden of Forking Paths": the missing word in Wittgenstein's riddle is "meaning". The same answer expresses the crux of my solution to Kripke's riddle. But, whereas in the former case it was necessary to emphasize the Platonist aspect of intensionalism, in the present case it is necessary to emphasize the intensionalist aspect of Platonism.

5

Quine's Arguments against
Intensionalist Semantics

The present chapter redeems the promissory notes concerning Quine's arguments, issued at a number of points in the previous chapters. It was necessary to postpone the examination of Quine's criticism of the intensionalist underpinnings of non-naturalistic philosophy because Quine's criticism is independent of and quite different from Wittgenstein's. Quine's indeterminacy thesis appears to be similar to Wittgenstein's thesis that semantic essentialism provides no notion of what it is to accord or conflict with a rule, but the similarity does not go very deep.

On the face of it, there is an obvious similarity between Wittgenstein's thesis that the semantic essentialist's explanations allow every application of a word to be in accord with the rule and Quine's thesis that "rival systems of analytical hypotheses can fit the totality of speech behavior to perfection, and can fit the totality of dispositions to speech behavior as well, and still specify mutually incompatible translations of countless sentences insusceptible of independent controls."[1] This similarity has, of course, not gone unnoticed. Quine himself says: "Perhaps the doctrine of indeterminacy of translation will have little air of paradox for readers familiar with Wittgenstein's latter-day remarks on meaning." (W&0, p. 77, note 2) Kripke, as already remarked, makes the comparison, even though he indicates certain reservations about the extent of the likeness, noting that Quine's behaviorism and his conception of how words are learned represent differences with Wittgenstein.[2] Nonetheless, as Kripke himself suggests, Quine's behaviorism may be dispensable in the argument for indeterminacy, and, as seems plain enough, Quine's Skinnerian views about language learning play no role in the argument for indeterminacy. Skinner enters afterwards, as it were, to pick up the pieces.

In fact, the similarity is more a matter of conclusion than of reasoning. Quine's argument for indeterminacy and Wittgenstein's paradox about following rules reach essentially the same conclusion about the prospects for an intensionalist theory of meaning, namely, that the meanings that have to exist for such a theory to be true do not exist; there are no facts about a domain of objective meanings that can validate one set of theoretical claims over another. But the steps by which Quine and Wittgenstein reach this conclusion differ, and these differences reflect fundamental differences between their two brands of naturalism.

Wittgenstein is unique in taking an uncompromisingly deflationary view of all traditional philosophical positions; Quine remains within the Western philosophical tradition, occupying a position which can be thought of as methodologically close to Russell and metaphysically close to J. S. Mill. Quine lacks Wittgenstein's critical emphasis, Wittgenstein's ascientific approach to language and therapeutic approach to philosophy, and Wittgenstein's view of the central role of ordinary use and his hostility to subliming the language. For Quine, the problem with traditional philosophy is not that it is nonsense, but that it is nonscientific. The solution is to turn as much traditional philosophy as possible into natural science and to show that the rest makes no scientific sense.

Thus, contrary to Wittgenstein, Quine argues that intensional concepts are illegitimate because they have no place in a theory of natural science. Quine's naturalistic challenge to the proto-theory is, in a sense, a more direct threat than Wittgenstein's to the basic step of theory construction in chapter 2; for it calls into question the scientific credentials of the semantic concepts on which the proto-theory is based. Accordingly, we cannot rely on our arguments concerning Wittgenstein's paradox to block Quine's fundamentally different line of attack on intensionalist semantics, and, therefore, we have to consider it on its own.

Word and Object, together with the earlier writings in *From a Logical Point of View,* set out Quine's reasons for thinking that one cannot make objective sense of the traditional intensionalist's notions of sense, synonymy, and analyticity.[3] These works have been a watershed for twentieth-century Anglo-American philosophy, radically changing how philosophers think about language, logic, and nearly every other area of investigation. Quine's skepticism, especially as expressed in his indeterminacy thesis, was instrumental in nearly eliminating intensional approaches to language from the contemporary American philosophical scene and in resurrecting philosophical naturalism.

Frege, virtually single-handed, had stemmed the tide of nineteenth-century naturalism in the philosophy of language, logic, and mathematics.[4] Carnap incorporated many of Frege's ideas into Logical

Empiricism, giving that philosophy, on his influential formulation, a significantly non-naturalist cast. Frege's sharp analytic/synthetic distinction, as explicated in Carnap's formal semantics, gave abstract objects and necessary truths sanctuary on the analytic side of the distinction. The distinction stood as the principal barrier to a return of an uncompromising naturalism in the spirit of J. S. Mill, which is why Quine, whose sympathies clearly lie with empiricism, attacks an empiricist doctrine in "Two Dogmas of Empiricism."[5] The arguments in that paper and his deployment of the indeterminacy thesis against the possibility of identity conditions for senses were widely seen as bringing this barrier crashing down, and thereby as opening the way for a neo-Millian naturalism of the sort sketched in "Carnap and Logical Truth."[6] Hence, when the linguistic turn shifted the emphasis in philosophy to language, much subsequent philosophy came to be done within a naturalistic framework which might be described as Humean epistemology minus the category of relations of ideas. Matters of fact are all that matter.

In this chapter, I examine Quine's argument for indeterminacy from a new angle and find that it does not work. If I am right, there is a straightforward sense in which the indeterminacy thesis is refuted. Skepticism about translation, like skepticism about other things of which common sense assures us, incurs a burden of proof in challenging the common-sense view. If the skeptic provides reasons of sufficient strength to discharge the onus of proof, we are presented with an advance in knowledge whose surprising character marks it as a discovery of the most profound sort. Thus, we attach the importance we do to Quine's argument in large part because it threatens to upset our common-sense view that there is always a right and a wrong translation even when the options differ in the way that "rabbit", "rabbit stage", and "undetached rabbit part" do. But, if the skeptic's reasons lack the strength to discharge the onus of proof and can establish only the logical possibility that common sense is wrong, we are presented with nothing more than an "absolute skepticism" which, since it applies to all forms of knowledge, proves too much.[7] In this instance, the skeptic's claim is refuted; for, unchallenged in any specific way, common sense reasserts itself.[8]

Quine wants to show that the notion of translation as expressing the same language-neutral meanings in different languages involves a mistake akin to believing in the gods of Homer. To show this, he sets out to show that the intensionalist tradition from Kant to Carnap, which presupposes that objective sense can be made of such meanings, is, at bottom, no better than mythology. Quine goes right to the heart of the matter: the relation of translation. Translation is critical because it is the only relation that provides interlinguistic identity conditions discriminating enough to individuate intensionalism's maximally fine-grained propositions. It is the ability to individuate such propositions that enables intensionalists to claim that theirs is the only position that does full justice to our ordinary, pretheoretical intuitions about linguistic structure. For example, only conditions for propositional identity based on synonymy account for our ordinary intuition that a sentence like "The sentence '2 is less than 3' means that 2 is less than 3" has a different truth value from a sentence like "The sentence 'The even prime is less than 3' means that 2 is less than 3". Hence, without the relations of synonymy and translation, the intensionalist can claim no advantage in the study of language to offset the introduction of the new intensional entities. Furthermore, without those relations, Frege's argument, in "On Sense and Reference," that such maximally fine-grained propositions are necessary for a complete formulation of the principles of logic, does not get off the ground. Thus, if Quine can establish that no objective sense can be made of equivalence of meaning for sentences of natural languages, he will have discredited intensionalism by showing that it has no more to it than Homeric creation myths.[9]

Some philosophers think there is a quick refutation of Quine. They claim that talk about meaning no more requires a statement of identity conditions to legitimize it than talk about such things as nations or works of art requires statements of identity conditions to legitimize it. But neither Frege nor other intensionalists who hope to vindicate intensionalism as the best scientific account of the semantics of natural language can afford so cavalier an attitude. In particular, my line of argument in this book, which develops semantics within linguistics, cannot tolerate intensional entities without identity. Accordingly, I will accept the need for identity conditions on exactly Quine's terms. If he can show that translation is indeterminate, I will straight off concede that he has shown that sense makes no sense.

The character of Quine's argument for indeterminacy is indicated in such passages as:

> . . . if the posit of propositions is to be taken seriously, eternal sentences of other languages must be supposed to mean propositions too; and each of these must be identical with or distinct from each proposition meant by an eternal sentence of our own. . . . Surely it is philosophically unsatisfactory for such questions of identity to arise as recognized questions, however academic, without there being in principle some suggestion of

how to construe them in terms of domestic and foreign dispositions to verbal behavior. (W&O, p. 205)

The aim of Quine's argument is thus to establish that, in principle,
there is no way to construe questions about identity of intensional
objects in terms of objective facts about verbal behavior. The reason
is that translation is indeterminate in the sense that

> manuals for translating one language into another can be set up
> in divergent ways, all compatible with the totality of speech dis-
> positions, yet incompatible with one another. In countless places
> they will diverge in giving, as their respective translations of a
> sentence of one language, sentences of the other language which
> stand to each other in no plausible sort of equivalence however
> loose. (W&O, p. 27)

I shall make no objection to the issue's being put in terms of speech
dispositions. It seems to me much the same here whether we talk of
expressions or of a speaker's speech dispositions—in particular, dispositions to verbally characterize sentences—or of a speaker's overtly
expressed intuitive judgments about sentences. Hence, if there is no
way to construe questions of identity of sense in terms of speech dispositions, I am prepared to count intensional objects on a par with
Homeric gods.

I shall also make no objection to Quine's statement that "the behaviorist approach is mandatory."[10] Quine writes:

> In psychology one may or may not be a behaviorist, but in lin-
> guistics one has no choice. Each of us learns his language by
> observing other people's verbal behavior and having his own fal-
> tering verbal behavior observed and reinforced or corrected by
> others. . . . There is nothing in linguistic meaning, then, beyond
> what is to be gleaned from overt behavior in overt circumstances.
> (ibid., p. 5)

The behaviorism he has in mind here is not the fierce reductive doctrine of days gone by, but merely a way of putting the study of language on a par with other sciences by requiring the linguist's
theoretical constructions to be justified on the basis of objective evidence. Quine's behaviorism takes linguists out of the armchair and
puts them into the field. Since it merely faces them with the task of
arriving at a theory of language on the basis of the overt behavior of
its speakers in overt circumstances, Quine's behaviorism is a behaviorism we can live with.[11] Thus, instead of challenging Quine's behaviorism, I shall challenge his claim about what can be gleaned from

such behavior in such circumstances, and attempt to show that there is intensional grain to be gathered.

Quine's conclusion that the totality of linguistic evidence cannot eliminate incompatible translation manuals is developed in the situation he calls "radical translation." He illustrates this situation with a jungle story about a field linguist trying to choose among putative translations for the expression "gavagai" in an alien language. Quine argues that the informant's dispositions to verbal response in such a translation situation are "incapable of deciding among 'rabbit', 'rabbit stage', and various other terms as translations of 'gavagai'" (W&O, pp. 71–72). Although nothing near a proof, the argument exhibits an unbreakable symmetry among the evidential considerations that can be adduced to justify the various translations. Whatever we can say on behalf of one translation, we can also say on behalf of the others. The reason is that the ostensive acts of the field linguist and the informant cannot refer to a rabbit without referring to a rabbit stage or an undetached rabbit part, nor any of these without the others, and radical translation contains nothing in the way of evidential controls on hypotheses which might enable the linguist to choose among extensionally equivalent translation options. Thus, Quine's argument leaves the intensionalist with no grounds on which to resist indeterminacy in radical translation.

Quine clearly has such considerations in mind when he claims that reflection on "the nature of possible data and method" in the Quinean radical-translation situation suffices to make us "appreciate the indeterminacy" (W&O, p. 72). He is undoubtedly right in this claim. But what he is undoubtedly right about is much less than is necessary for the philosophical conclusion he wishes to draw. The problem, in a nutshell, is that, although there is no doubt about the rightness of Quine's claim when his argument is made in connection with *Quinean* radical translation, the relation of such radical translation to *actual* radical translation is not clear enough for us to be sure that the claim automatically carries over to the case of actual translation. And, of course, Quine's conclusion must apply to actual translation if indeterminacy is to matter philosophically.

Let us flesh out the nature of the doubts we might have about the step in Quine's argument from his own radical-translation situation to a conclusion about actual translation situations. Quinean radical translation, it might be argued, is Quine's creation. Apart from reflecting the extreme case of actual translation, it has been so constructed that nothing beyond extensional considerations provides evidence for translations. Thus, it is guaranteed that any evidential support for one among a set of referentially indiscernible hypotheses, such as "rabbit", "rabbit stage", and "undetached rabbit part", can be matched with equal evidential support for each of the others. But couldn't Quine's creation fail to mirror relevant evidential features of actual translation situations? Isn't it possible that those situations involve intensional evidence? We have, as yet, no good grounds for rejecting the intensionalist's claim that, in actual translation situations, linguists use evidence relevant to sense differences among the competing hypotheses in order to discriminate among them. If linguists in actual translation situations have such "independent controls," there is no evidential symmetry in those situations, and, hence, no indeterminacy.

My point so far is only that Quine has to say something to make us "appreciate the indeterminacy" for actual translation. He needs to clarify the relation between radical translation, as he defines it, and actual translation, as it exists or could exist in the practice of real linguists. Quine seems to address this need. He presents his own radical-translation situation as the limiting case of actual translation situations, i.e., as the case where historical differences between the languages and cultural differences between its speakers are maximal. Quinean radical translation is presented as the most philosophically perspicuous case of actual translation in virtue of being the case where the issue about meaning is least likely to be confused by historical and cultural similarities.

But the issue is not so easily settled. We have been given likenesses between Quinean radical translation and one class of actual translation situations, but have not as yet been given a reason for identifying them.[12] The acceptability of an identification depends on whether actual translation is *in all relevant respects* like Quinean radical translation. Now, one relevant respect is surely whether or not, in actual translation, the matching of expressions as synonymous also takes place in the absence of "independent controls." For it is the absence of such controls in radical translation which is responsible for evidential symmetry and, hence, for indeterminacy. Therefore, we are owed a reason for believing that such controls are absent in actual translation.

Quine has what he thinks is a reason. The existence of such controls depends on the existence of intensional objects in the way that the existence of independent controls in physics depends on the existence of physical objects. But, as Quine sees it, to suppose that "translational synonymy at its worst is no worse off than physics" is to "misjudge the parallel" (W&O, p. 75). There is a fundamental difference between intensional semantics and genuine sciences like physics: in physics, "the parameters of truth stay conveniently fixed most of the time"; not so with "the analytic hypotheses that constitute the parameter of translation" (W&O, p. 76). Quine explains:

> Something of the true situation verges on visibility when the sentences concerned are extremely theoretical. Thus who would undertake to translate 'Neutrinos lack mass' into the jungle language? If anyone does, we may expect him to coin words or distort the usage of old ones. We may expect him to plead in extenuation that the natives lack the requisite concepts; also that they know too little physics. And he is right, except for the hint of there being some free-floating, linguistically neutral meaning which we capture in 'Neutrinos lack mass', and the native cannot. (W&O, p. 76)

There is no domain of linguistically neutral meanings corresponding to the domain of physical objects, and, consequently, no facts against which to judge the truth of analytical hypotheses which assert that a sentence in the target language expresses the same linguistically neutral meaning as one in the home language. Thus, if there are no meanings, it makes no sense to talk of a scientific choice between competing analytical hypotheses.

As Quine sees it, the correct comparison with physics is this. Theories in physics are underdetermined by the available observational evidence and also by the total possible evidence, but not subject to indeterminacy.[13] Underdetermination is only a matter of "empirical slack" which can be taken up methodologically: genuinely divergent physical theories that survive confrontation with the total evidence can be adjudicated on the basis of methodological canons like simplicity, depth of explanation, etc. The differences between such theories are substantive because there is a physical fact they are about. Intensional semantics, in contrast, suffers from a far worse condition than underdetermination. It suffers from indeterminacy, whose etiology is the lack of a fact of the matter for theories to be right or wrong about.[14] Therefore, whereas the condition of physics can be treated methodologically, the illness of intensional semantics is terminal.

But this reason for thinking that independent controls do not exist in translation is no better than the reason Quine has for thinking there are no linguistically neutral meanings. Obviously, if there are no such meanings, there is no evidence about meaning to use in deciding between rival analytical hypotheses. Hence, it is not enough for Quine just to say that "the discontinuity of radical translation tries our meanings: really sets them over against their verbal embodiments, or, more typically, finds nothing there" (W&O, p. 76). He has to provide a reason for thinking that there is nothing there. Nothing is established by a mere claim.

Moreover, if Quine is employing "the discontinuity of radical translation" to argue for there being no fact of the matter in actual translation, then, once the question is put as we have put it, i.e., in terms of how the step from Quinean radical translation to actual translation is justified, this employment seems to beg the question. At this point, all that Quine can legitimately say is that there is no fact of the matter about meaning in the radical-translation situation that he invented. He is not entitled to say that there are no linguistically neutral meanings in actual translation. Recall that our earlier doubts about the identification of his radical translation with the extreme of actual translation arose because Quine had not shown that the cases do not relevantly differ with respect to the existence of "independent controls." The existence of independent controls, as we have seen, is not unrelated to the existence of meanings.

Furthermore, even if Quine had secured the identification of his radical translation with the limit case of actual translation, he still would not have a basis for claiming that there are no linguistically neutral meanings in actual translation. For, in fact, he never ruled out the existence of meanings in his own radical translation! True enough, there is no evidential basis for choosing between rival analytical hypotheses in Quinean radical translation, but this establishes no more than the unknowability of meanings. Meanings, like Kant's noumena, could exist even if they are unknowable. No mere epistemological considerations such as those we find in Quine's discussion of radical translation entail a negative ontological conclusion such as that which he draws about linguistically neutral meanings. That conclusion introduces an ontological skepticism over and above his already asserted epistemological skepticism. Thus, rather than motivating the claim that actual translation is indeterminate, the ontological skepticism only increases the burden of proof.

Hence, we have a new question: What is Quine's argument for claiming that there are no linguistically neutral meanings?[15] I think, without doubt, that he has one. It is a mistake for Chomsky to represent Quine as simply stipulating that linguistics can have no general theories.[16] It is true that Quine does not at this point explicitly present an argument, or even cite one, but surely a philosopher as acute as Quine sees that an argument is needed to back up his claim that there are no linguistically neutral meanings. He must know that, without one, indeterminacy of translation is unsupported, and intensional semantics can be accused of nothing more serious than underdetermination. In this case, the omnipresence of divergent translations is of no philosophical interest, indicating nothing more exciting than gaps in our knowledge of semantic fact or insufficient application of scientific methodology.

It would also be a mistake to suppose that Quine is simply invoking his behaviorism to back up his claim that there are no semantic facts. As we have seen, that doctrine would not be equal to the task; it is not the militant doctrine that brands as scientific heresy everything that cannot be strictly defined in terms of stimulus and response. Furthermore, Quine couldn't be deriving the claim from an old-fashioned verificationism. If he has verificationist scruples, they have to be rather mild ones in order to allow him to countenance the highly theoretical entities of science, such as the ten-dimensional wonders of contemporary physics and the objects of set theory. Finally, the claim could not be a consequence of physicalism, either. Physicalism allows meanings so long as they are reducible to brain states. Quine's criticism of intensionalists is not that they have been lax in showing that meanings are reducible to physical states or that there are insurmountable problems facing those who attempt to show that meanings are so reducible, but that intensionalists are deluded in thinking there are any such things to be reduced in the first place. Quine's criticism is not that we haven't been given a physicalistic reduction of Homeric gods, but that there are no Homeric gods.[17]

We get a clue to what Quine's argument really is by noting that he makes his claim that there are no linguistically neutral meanings with the full confidence of someone introducing a lemma already proved and widely known. I submit that this is precisely it: Quine thinks he has already given a conclusive argument against such meanings, particularly in his famous paper "Two Dogmas of Empiricism." Indeed, the argument there is directly to the point. That argument aims to show that we can make no objective sense of synonymy. If the argument were conclusive, no respectable theory would quantify over meanings, and considerations of parsimony would oblige us to deny that there are any.

That it is correct to interpret Quine's argument for indeterminacy to have this reference back to his earlier work is shown not only by the tone and logic of his reasoning in *Word and Object*, but also by explicit statements at various places about his overall anti-intensionalist strategy. In the early paper "The Problem of Meaning in Linguistics," Quine makes it clear that, even then, he took his criticism of the analytic/synthetic distinction to show that there is no fact of the matter in connection with meaning.[18] Referring to a restatement of his arguments against synonymy from "Two Dogmas of Empiricism,"

Quine says that construction of a lexicon for translating a language from a radically different culture is not a well-defined task because such a construction suffers from a "paucity of explicit controls."[19] Quine completes the thought:

> The finished lexicon is a case, evidently, of *ex pede Herculem*. But there is a difference. In projecting Hercules from the foot we risk error, but we may derive comfort from the fact that there is something to be wrong about. In the case of a lexicon, pending some definition of synonymy, we have no statement of the problem; we have nothing for the lexicographer to be right or wrong about. (ibid., p. 63)

So, if a definition of synonymy is ruled out by "Two Dogmas of Empiricism," then there is nothing for the lexicographer to be right or wrong about, i.e., no meanings.

In the very recent paper "Indeterminacy of Translation Again," Quine provides further evidence for taking "Two Dogmas of Empiricism" to provide the argument for his claim in *Word and Object* that there are no meanings:

> Considerations of the sort we have been surveying are all that the radical translator has to go on. This is not because the meanings of sentences are elusive or inscrutable; it is because there is nothing to them, beyond what these fumbling procedures can come up with. Nor is there hope even of codifying these procedures and then *defining* what counts as translation by citing the procedures; for the procedures involve weighing incommensurable values. How much grotesqueness may we allow to the native's beliefs, for instance, in order to avoid how much grotesqueness in his grammar or semantics?[20]

The point here is that no comparison between hypotheses about beliefs and hypotheses about meaning is possible because such a comparison assumes an analytic/synthetic distinction. If there were such a distinction, the linguist could, in principle, decide whether a piece of information belongs to the theory of the informant's language or to the theory of his or her extralinguistic beliefs. Without an analytic/synthetic distinction, such decisions involve "weighing incommensurable values."

Given that "Two Dogmas of Empiricism" is intended to supply the argument to show there are no meanings which does not appear in *Word and Object*, Quine's overall argument for indeterminacy of translation can be reconstructed as follows. Given that "Two Dogmas of Empiricism" removes the possibility of a linguistically universal synonymy relation,[21] there can be no identity conditions for intensional objects, and, as a consequence, we must abandon the idea of linguistically neutral meanings serving as the common content of a sentence and its translation. Thus, there is no parallel between semantics as conceived in traditional intensionalism and *bona fide* sciences like physics. In physics, there are objects of study, and so physics suffers only from underdetermination. In semantics, there are no objects of study, and hence, there can be no evidence to provide controls on analytical hypotheses and make objective sense of talk about rational choice among theories of meaning. Thus, there is nothing to distinguish actual translation from Quinean radical translation, and Quine can identify the latter with the limit case of the former. The symmetry argument, developed in connection with Quinean radical translation, now holds for actual translation, and it follows that, in actual translation, divergent systems of analytical hypotheses fit the totality of speech dispositions to perfection. Quine can then say, justifiably, that the limits of possible data for radical translation make the indeterminacy of (actual) translation certain.[22]

　　Having located the "missing" argument, I now want to show that it doesn't work, and as a consequence, that the argument for indeterminacy doesn't work either. The argument in "Two Dogmas of Empiricism" takes the form of a proof by cases. It begins with an enumeration of the areas where it would be reasonable to look for an explanatory paradigm to use in trying to make objective sense of the concepts in the theory of meaning. The areas are definition generally, logical theory, and linguistics. Quine asks whether the methods for explaining concepts in any of these areas can explain synonymy and analyticity. He examines the areas in turn. He argues that the available paradigms in the case of definition either assume prior synonymy relations or else have nothing to do with meaning.[23] In the case of logical theory, he argues that Carnapian meaning postulates and semantical rules shed no light whatever on the nature of synonymy and analyticity (pp. 22–27). In the case of linguistics, he argues that the methods for defining concepts are demonstrably unable to provide noncircular definitions of these concepts (pp. 27–32). Since these cases exhaust the areas where we might expect to find an explanatory paradigm appropriate to logico-linguistic concepts like analyticity and synonymy, Quine concludes that there are no methods for clarifying synonymy and analyticity.

　　Quine's argument in the case of definition is absolutely compelling. So is his argument in the case of logic. But the final argument needed to complete the proof by cases, the argument concerning linguistics, is anything but compelling. Once its structure is revealed, it will be clear that the argument does nothing to establish that attempts to explain analyticity and synonymy in linguistics must fail. I shall discuss this argument in some detail both because of its importance to the issues in this book and because the argument concerns linguistic matters with which many philosophers are unfamiliar. I believe that unfamiliarity with those linguistic matters is responsible for the fact that Quine's argument has gained widespread acceptance in philosophy.

Quine's argument for the case of linguistics begins by identifying *substitution criteria* as the proper linguistic method for defining concepts like analyticity and synonymy. He explains as follows:

> So-called substitution criteria, or conditions of interchangeability, have in one form or another played central roles in modern grammar. For the synonymy problem of semantics such an approach seems more obvious still. However, the notion of the interchangeability of two linguistic forms makes sense only in so far as answers are provided to these two questions: (a) In just what sorts of contextual positions, if not in all, are the two forms to be interchangeable? (b) The forms are to be interchangeable *salvo quo?* Supplanting one form by another in any context changes something, namely, form at least; and (b) asks what feature the interchange is to leave invariant. Alternative answers to (a) and (b) give alternative notions of interchangeability, some suited to defining grammatical correspondences and others, conceivably, to defining synonymy. (*From a Logical Point of View*, p. 56)

It is important to recognize that the substitution criteria Quine borrows from "modern grammar" are not to be confused with the customary substitution operations in logic and mathematics. To be sure, like those operations, substitution criteria specify a concept on the basis of a feature that remains invariant when and only when the elements that replace each other in the chosen context belong to the extension of the concept. But, in the case of the substitution criteria from "modern grammar," there is the special requirement that a description of the context and of the invariance not contain concepts belonging to the family of the concept to be defined. Thus, definitions taking the form of substitution criteria may fail either because the chosen feature does not correlate with all and only expressions in the extension of the concept or because the special requirement is not met, i.e., the feature or the substitution context is statable only using the concept to be defined or a concept in its family.

Given that substitution criteria are the proper method for defining linguistic concepts, Quine has an easy time demonstrating that the concepts of analyticity and synonymy cannot be defined in linguistics. Suppose we wish to define synonymy. The context must be either intensional or extensional. If we choose an intensional context, say "Necessarily, ———", we can use truth as the feature that is to remain invariant in substitutions, but then we violate the noncircularity requirement at the outset because the context has to be characterized using synonymy or other concepts from the theory of meaning.[24] If we choose an extensional context, we get the definition off the ground, but then we can no longer choose truth as the feature that is to remain invariant. For, in extensional contexts, truth does not discriminate synonymous expressions from coextensive but nonsynonymous expressions. We thus have to choose something stronger, like necessary truth or analyticity. But this violates the noncircularity requirement, too, because such notions are defined in terms of synonymy.

This, then, is the argument on which the indeterminacy thesis in *Word and Object* depends. The trouble with the argument is its assumption that substitution criteria are the proper way to clarify concepts in linguistics. This assumption is easily knocked down. There is nothing in favor of the assumption, and strong *a priori* and historical reasons against it.

Quine does not justify his assumption that substitution criteria are the proper way to clarify concepts in linguistics. He merely notes that such criteria have "in one form or another played central roles in modern grammar." This, however, is only to say that substitution criteria occupied a central place in linguistics during the Bloomfieldian period (roughly from the 1930s through the 1950s). Quine offers nothing beyond the place of such criteria in Bloomfieldian linguistics to show that they constitute an indispensable methodology in the science of language and hence a valid approach to defining synonymy. But the fact that one school of thought in the history of a science practiced a certain methodology means very little, given how frequently schools of thought come and go and old paradigms are replaced with new ones. In fact, even as Quine wrote, the positivist foundations of Bloomfieldian linguistics were being eroded by what we now see was a successful critique of logical positivism in the philosophy of science.[25]

An *a priori* reason for thinking that substitution criteria are neither the only nor the preferred form of definition in linguistics is that physics, mathematics, and logic provide examples of another form of definition which can be adapted for concepts in linguistics. This is the familiar approach of defining a concept on the basis of an axiomatic or recursive specification of the relations between it and other concepts in its family, e.g., the Dedekind-Peano axiomatization of arithmetic concepts, or the axiomatization of the truth-functional connectives in a standard sentential calculus. The difference between such *theoretical definitions,* as I shall call them, and substitution criteria is that theoretical definition does not prevent us from using concepts belonging to the same family as the concept to be defined. Effective theoretical definitions explain a concept relative to the other concepts by representing the structure of the primitives in the entire family of concepts. The degree of relatedness exhibited among the concepts in the family is thus a measure not of circularity but of the systematizing power of the explanation.

This difference emerges sharply when we try to impose substitution-criteria definitions on concepts in subjects like logic and mathematics. Suppose, imitating Quine's demand that semantic concepts be defined by substitution criteria, someone were to demand that truth-functional connectives and numbers be so defined. If this demand were legitimate, we would have an argument directly parallel to Quine's, showing that sentential logic and arithmetic make no objective sense. For, as with synonymy, there is no noncircular property that is invariant on all and only substitutions of logically equivalent propositions, on the one hand, and substitutions of numerically identical quantities, on the other. Now, such a conclusion is clearly a *reductio* of the idea that legitimacy of logic and mathematics depends on their identity relations being definable by means of substitution criteria. Thus, intensionalists can say that Quine's argument is similarly a *reductio* of the idea that the legitimacy of the theory of meaning depends on its identity relation being definable by means of such criteria. The circularity that Quine exhibited in attempts to define synonymy and analyticity on the basis of substitution criteria can thus be seen as a product of imposing an inappropriate definitional paradigm on the theory of meaning.

These *a priori* considerations show that there is an alternative definitional paradigm possible for linguistics which lacks just the feature that rules out the definition of synonymy by substitution criteria. It does not matter, given the logic of my argument, whether or not such an alternative ever actually finds its way into linguistics. It could be introduced at any time as another, and preferable, way of defining the family of sense concepts. Nothing could prevent it. Quine's scruples about "misjudging the parallel" could not, since these scruples can have force, as we have seen, only *after* we are given a persuasive argument against linguistically neutral meanings. Only then is there a relevant distinction between intensional semantics and genuine science. At this stage, however, Quine has yet to put together such an argument.

Furthermore, it would do no good to appeal to the arguments Quine used to show that Carnapian meaning postulates and semantical rules fail to explain analyticity and synonymy.[26] Systems of meaning postulates and semantical rules are one way of constructing a theoretical definition for semantic notions, but not the only way. The fact that one way of applying a new explanatory paradigm fails does not show that other ways of applying it will fail as well. Moreover, Carnapian systems have an idiosyncratic feature which makes them subject to Quine's criticism that they are unilluminating about analyticity and synonymy. Such systems mimic the construction of theoretical definitions for logical notions, thereby adopting the Fregean assimilation of analyticity and synonymy to logical truth and logical equivalence. Hence, Carnapian meaning postulates do not describe the structure of senses, but, like the logical postulates on which they are modeled, they just constrain the extensional interpretations of a language. Ironically, so-called meaning postulates are not about meaning, and this is precisely why, as Quine pointed out, they do not explain what analyticity is.[27]

There is also a historical reason for thinking that substitution criteria do not deserve the position that Quine accords them. Quine supposed that the methodology of Bloomfieldian linguistics was an indispensable aspect of the science of language and, hence, something he could rely on in philosophy. This supposition was soon overthrown. In the early 1960s, the field of linguistics underwent what has come to be called the Chomskyan revolution. One of the principal changes the revolution brought about was a paradigm shift from substitution-criteria definition in taxonomic grammars to theoretical definition in generative grammars.[28] Chomsky explicitly modeled his conception of a generative grammar on formal systems in logic. The theorems, instead of being a class of logical truths, are well-formed sentences of a language. An optimal generative grammar for a language L generates all and only the well-formed sentences of L. It is thus a recursive definition of the notion 'sentence of L'. The derivations of a sentence provide a description of its grammatical structure.

Chomsky carried the analogy with logic further. He modeled his conception of general linguistics (i.e., the study of linguistic universals) on metalogic. The definitions of language-neutral concepts were to be given in terms of theoretical definitions stated in the metatheory for generative grammars (i.e., linguistic theory, in Chomsky's terminology). For example, Chomsky defined a syntactically well-formed sentence of a language as a sentence whose syntactic representation can be generated in an optimal grammar of the language, and the concept of two constituents being of the same syntactic type as identity of their syntactic representations in an optimal grammar.[29]

In the context of the present discussion, it is hard to exaggerate the importance of the shift to the new paradigm of generative grammar. The new paradigm, together with the theoretical definitions worked out for concepts in phonology and syntax, provided a model for theoretical definitions in semantics (just as substitution criteria in phonology and syntax had provided for Quine a model for operational definitions in semantics). Of special significance in this connection is the fact that the metatheory for generative grammars opens up the possibility of giving language-independent definitions of language-neutral concepts. This enables us to avoid language-specific definitions such as meaning postulates and thus, as will be explained below, to escape Quine's criticism of such definitions. Theoretical definitions in the metatheory for generative grammars provide a way of defining concepts in the theory of meaning for variable 'S' and 'L' because, in defining a concept at the level of linguistic theory, such definitions specify the concept in terms of features of optimal generative grammars for natural languages generally.

Research in semantics within the generative framework during the 1960s and early 1970s exploited the Chomskyan paradigm of theoretical definition.[30] The aim of this research was to define concepts such as meaningfulness, ambiguity, synonymy, antonymy, analyticity, and other sense properties and relations. Constructing theoretical definitions of these concepts involves two steps. First, it is necessary to develop a conception of the formal representation of sense structure. Such representations would be parallel to the formal representation of constituent structure provided in syntactic markers, but, instead of describing the way sentences are built up from constituents like nouns, verbs, prepositions, etc. as syntactic markers do, semantic representations have to describe the way senses of sentences are built up from the senses of their syntactic constituents (as described in chapter 2). Second, it is necessary, once some progress is made on the first step, to look for formal features of semantic representations which, from sentence to sentence and language to language, correlate with particular semantic concepts.

This research developed decompositional semantic representation, i.e., the semantic representation of the proto-theory in chapter 2, where symbols in formal representations stand for component senses and their relations to one another at every grammatical level, including especially the level of syntactic simples.[31] With the development of such semantic representations, theoretical definitions of semantic concepts like analyticity could be formulated. Such representation was necessary to explicate Kant's narrow concept of analyticity, that is, his concept of judgments that add "nothing through the predicate to the concept of the subject, but merely break . . . it up into those constituent concepts that have all along been thought in it."[32] This is because only decompositional semantic representations mark the presence of the sense of a syntactically simple predicate in the sense of a syntactically simple subject, e.g., in a sentence like "Bachelors are single". Relative to an assignment of such representations to sentences, we can define an analytic sense as a sense whose semantic representation describes it as having the form of a fully saturated n-place predicate where one of the terms contains the full predicate together with each of the other terms.[33] Similarly, we can define meaningfulness and synonymy: semantic well-formedness can be defined in terms of the generability of at least one semantic representation for an expression, semantic identity in terms of sameness of semantic representation for two expressions.

The first thing to note about such a definition of analyticity is that it makes no reference to thought processes and, accordingly, avoids Frege's criticism of Kant's definition of analyticity for psychologism. A second thing to note is that the definition is more general than Kant's, which is restricted to subject-predicate sentences. Our definition covers non-subject-predicate sentences like "Smith marries those he weds" and "Jones buys books from those who sell her books". This broader scope avoids Frege's criticism that Kant's definition applies only to subject-predicate sentences. Finally, note that the definition avoids *both* of Quine's criticisms of Carnap's explication of analyticity. As already indicated, the definition, being in the metatheory of generative grammars, meets Quine's demand that analyticity be defined for variable 'S' and 'L'.[34] It also meets Quine's demand that a definition tell us what property is attributed to a sentence when it is marked 'analytic'. The definition says that the property of being analytic is that of having a redundant predication—the referential upshot of which is that the truth conditions of the sentence (on its analytic sense) are automatically satisfied once its terms take on reference.

Of course, decompositional semantics is in its infancy. We are very far from a full theory of decompositional semantics for natural language. But the incompleteness of the present version of the theory is not something that Quine can use to block the criticism I am making of the argument in "Two Dogmas of Empiricism." In particular, it is not open to him to argue that acceptance of the criticism must be withheld until the theory of decompositional semantics is developed far enough to see clearly whether it works. Since Quine's argument claims to rule out the possibility of making sense of intensional concepts within the science of linguistics, showing that his argument overlooks a possibility for making sense of these concepts in this science *is* showing that the argument fails.

We can now trace the consequences of Quine's failure to support his claim that there are no linguistically neutral meanings. The immediate consequence is that we are free to presume the existence of meanings in the same spirit with which scientists beginning the study of any new field are free to presume there are facts and laws to be discovered. Without a reason to think that the theory of meaning suffers from anything worse than underdetermination, we may pursue the parallel with well-developed sciences. We may take the view that such a course of action is itself the best way to determine whether there are meanings. As with other sciences, trying to construct a theory will, in the long run, show whether the initial optimistic presumption was correct.

As a consequence of our thus being able to pursue the parallel, Quine's argument for the indeterminacy of actual translation breaks down. Recall that this argument depends critically on whether actual translation, like Quinean radical translation, lacks "independent controls." As Quine claims: "When we reflect on the limits of possible data for radical translation, the indeterminacy is not to be doubted."[35] We conceded that the constraints on the choice of analytical hypotheses in Quinean radical translation are too weak to make translation determinate, but we questioned whether actual translation is enough like Quinean radical translation for us to rule out the possibility of stronger constraints in actual translation. Pressing this question, we found nothing to stop us from making the working assumption that there are linguistically neutral meanings. But, on the assumption of a fact of the matter with respect to which analytical hypotheses can be judged, we can say what constraints exist in actual translation over and above those in radical translation and how those constraints can make translation determinate.

The constraints on choices of analytical hypotheses in translation will be the customary blend of data and methodological considerations (i.e., the data must be explained as economically as possible, with as much scope and depth as possible, etc.). The data come from overtly expressed judgments of speakers reflecting their knowledge of the language. In radical translation, the data are restricted to judgments about the reference of expressions. But, on our working assumption, the data in actual translation include judgments about the senses of expressions, too. The linguist can ask whether an expression has a sense (i.e., whether it is meaningful or not), whether an expression has more than one sense (i.e., whether it is ambiguous), whether the sense of one expression is the same as that of another (i.e., whether they are synonymous), whether the sense of one expression is the opposite of the sense of another (i.e., whether they are antonyms), whether the sense of a sentence involves redundant predication (i.e., whether it is analytic), and so on. The possibility of putting such questions to informants automatically provides the possibility of evidential controls like those in other sciences. The informant's answers provide data about sense structure, and the choice of a hypothesis is made on the basis of how well it accounts for the data.[36]

To give some concrete examples of semantic evidence, I will tell a jungle story of my own. Imagine an actual translation situation in which the linguist and informant come from disparate cultures and in which the home and target languages have disparate histories. The linguist is faced with the choice of translating "gavagai" as "rabbit", as "rabbit stage", or as "undetached rabbit part". In my story, but not in Quine's, the linguist simply queries the informant about the senses of expressions. (We shall consider below the question of how they communicate.) The linguist can ask whether "gavagai" is synonymous with one of these English words. The informant may judge it to be synonymous with one of them, judge it not to be synonymous with any, or provide no useful judgment. In the first two cases, the linguist has acquired some data. In the third, the direct approach didn't work. But here, as elsewhere in science, there is a wide range of less direct approaches. For example, the linguist may ask whether "gavagai" bears the same relation to a native expression that "finger" bears to "hand" or "handle" bears to "knife". Or the linguist could ask whether "gavagai" is closer in sense to "infancy" and "adolescence" than it is to "infant" and "adolescent". Or the linguist could ask whether the expression obtained when "gavagai" is modified by the native word meaning "undetached" is redundant like "unmarried bachelor". Or whether the expression obtained when "gavagai" is modified by the native word meaning "detached" is contradictory like "married bachelor". There are indefinitely many further questions to ask and, of course, indefinitely many further informants to ask them of. So why should a body of data obtained in this way, in principle, not settle any question of translation as satisfactorily as a comparable body of data in other sciences would settle comparable theoretical questions?

Two Quinean thoughts arise here. First, there is the problem of how linguists come by the hypotheses which they are supposed to verify by asking such questions about the foreign language. Second, there is the problem of how linguists and informants are able to communicate.

It is hard to see why the first is much of a problem. The hypotheses can be based on guesses based on nothing, hunches educated by experience, prejudices stemming from a cherished theory, or what have you. This is surely how it is in other sciences. Yet Quine views presumptions about the semantics of an alien language deriving from the semantics of one's own language as begging the question.[37] He is surely right in the case of Quinean radical translation. If a linguist in such a situation takes "gavagai" to be an object term, like the English "rabbit", then, in the absence of "independent controls," there is no way to know whether or not the linguist has merely read the grammatical categories of his or her own language into the alien language. But, for the case of actual translation, where, as we have shown, there can be such controls, presumptions about the semantics of the alien language, even those reflecting linguistic chauvinism, beg no question. Evidential controls enable linguists to revise mistaken presumptions and validate correct ones. Falsifications of the category structure of an alien language, accordingly, are on a par with the animistic or anthropomorphic theories of nature in early science. Presumptions on the part of the linguist may retard (or, for that matter, advance) the progress of translation, but, as long as evidence can be brought to bear on such presumptions, they have no philosophical significance.

Although communication between linguist and informant may at first seem a more serious problem, it, too, has a straightforward solution. Quine always represents translation as a situation in which the linguist confronts the informant across an impassable language barrier. Indeed, Quine's assumption that neither knows the other's language has made readers wonder how the informant can even know what the linguist's interests are and how the linguist can know what behavior of the informant to count an assent and dissent. It is Quine's assumption of monolingualism—rather than his behaviorism or anything else—that is the truly unrealistic element in his thinking about translation. Actual translation can no more proceed without a bilingual than grammar construction can proceed without a native speaker.

There is, then, a sense in which the whole question of bilingualism is beside the point. Quine accepts the fact that indeterminacy arises equally well within a single language, between idiolects of different speakers, and, further, that it arises even within a single idiolect, between different temporal stages. Here there is no question of bilinguals, unless, of course, bilingualism is understood as fluency in two idiolects or two idiolect stages. Is Quine to be construed as claiming that English-speaking linguists and their English-speaking informants do not share a language in which they can communicate?

I am, of course, not saying that bilinguals must exist, but only that their existence is an empirical condition for translation. The existence of bilinguals is comparable to the existence of conditions that enable us to conduct the experiments necessary to decide among rival physical theories. Moreover, like such conditions, the absence of bilinguals in the case of some alien language can be overcome by, as it were, creating them in the laboratory. We know a sure method for creating the necessary bilinguals on demand. The method takes rather a long time, and its implementation involves various practical, social, and moral problems, but it works, as those who have acquired bilingual fluency growing up in a bilingual home can attest.

To be sure, Quine thinks that introducing bilinguals begs the question. The feeling that a question is begged is strongest with respect to the possibility of full fluency in both languages, including, as it would, fluency in the meta-linguistic vocabulary of the language, e.g., the expressions for relations like 'translates' or 'is synonymous with'. The idea of an informant or linguist who speaks the whole of the other's language like a native seems to go too far. But why? We are not supposing the actual existence of such bilinguals, but only the possibility of their existence. Accepting the possibility of fluent informants does not settle the question of the existence of meanings, any more than accepting the possibility of reliable meters in a physics experiment settles the question it is set up to decide.

Admittedly, entertaining the prospect of bilingualism is, in itself, entertaining the prospect of translation, since knowledge of translation is what makes a bilingual bilingual. But if there is no harm in entertaining the prospect of translation, there is none in entertaining the prospect of bilingualism.

So no question is begged. But, further, no risk is run. Although bilinguals, like field linguists with presumptions, can cause falsifications in translation, such falsifications, like false grammatical categories read into a target language, can be corrected. As long as we have evidential controls, the difficulties posed by deficient or devious informants are, in principle, no different from those posed by faulty meters in physics experiments.

Let us sum up. Quinean radical translation is indeterminate because it is restricted to using referential features of words. But there is nothing to show that actual radical translation is similarly restricted. With the use of evidence about the senses of words in constructing theories about actual radical translation, the evidential symmetry in Quinean radical translation does not arise in actual radical translation. Intensionalist semanticists may cherish the same hopes for success as other scientists. They are not even required to establish that facts about meaningfulness, ambiguity, synonymy, antonymy, redundancy, etc. are, in principle, sufficient to enable linguists to make a unique selection among a number of translation schemes. Either all but one of the translation schemes can be eliminated, given total evidence and methodological considerations, or else, since synonymy is the identity relation for meanings, the uneliminated schemes count equivalently as ways of expressing the truth about the semantic relation between the languages.

If my criticism of Quine is correct, he has no argument for a skepticism specifically concerning semantics, that is, a skepticism that does not apply equally to all the sciences. This, of course, is not to say that no form of skepticism about determinate translation remains. There is no metaphysical insurance policy against nature's being counterinductive or against linguistic investigation's being counterproductive: linguists can make systematically misleading projections, and informants can produce systematically misleading evidence. But such possibilities lead to nothing more than an absolute skepticism which, because it would obliterate knowledge in all fields, can be discounted. Thus, once Quine's semantics-relative skepticism goes, nothing prevents the common-sense view of translation from reasserting itself.

Life without meaning is not so trouble-free a paradise as it is sometimes made out to be. Quineans have always had trouble explaining in what respect allegedly competing analytical hypotheses compete. It is easy, from a common-sense standpoint, to appreciate the respect in which "rabbit", "rabbit stage", and "undetached rabbit part" represent rival translations, but what, from the standpoint of indeterminacy, is supposed to be the semantic difference? Quine's indeterminacy thesis is predicated on the existence of a conceptual distinction of some sort among such translations; yet the nature of the choice within a Quinean radical-translation situation seems to preclude the possibility of any difference upon which the distinction might rest.

From the perspective of this chapter, the problem is an illusion created by superimposing Quinean radical translation onto actual translation. The conceptual distinctions, on which the framing of rival hypotheses in a case of radical translation depends, derive from the intuitively recognized differences in meaning between "rabbit", "rabbit stage", and "undetached rabbit part". The sense of a distinction without a difference comes from the fact that these differences cannot exist in Quinean radical translation, so they recede into the background when such translation is identified with the extreme case of actual translation. Yet the intuitive recognition of these differences stays with us and reemerges in connection with the indeterminacy thesis to give content to talk of "divergent" or "incompatible" translations (W&O, p. 27). As a consequence, we get the curious duck/ rabbit shift. The illusion disappears if we do not identify Quinean radical translation with a case of actual translation.

Another problem which makes life without meaning less than idyllic is that translational indeterminacy is a slippery slope. Quine's argument from the absence of "independent controls" in the case of translation between languages, if sound, would also show that translation between dialects of a language must be indeterminate. Further, the same argument would show that translations between idiolects of a dialect must be indeterminate. Nor does the slide stop here. We also have to accept indeterminacy in the case of stages of the same idiolect. Hence, in accepting the initial indeterminacy argument, we are buying a linguistic solipsism of the moment: one's own words of other moments stand to one's words of the present in exactly the relation that "gavagai" is supposed to stand to "rabbit", "rabbit stage", and "undetached rabbit part". Quine himself might be willing to live with indeterminacy so close to home, but few others are happy with the prospect.[38] The solution is simply not to take the fatal first step onto the slope, the step of conceding indeterminacy in translation between languages. The present chapter explains why there is no need to take it.[39]

Quine, even more than Wittgenstein, is widely regarded as having terminated the intensionalist program. Those of us who still keep the intensionalist faith are frequently made to feel only slightly less benighted than a philosopher who might still be pursuing Hilbert's program. But, if my criticism of Quine is correct, the indeterminacy thesis does not put an end to intensionalism. Quine cannot be included among those who, like Gödel, did terminate an entire philosophical program. Rather, Quine belongs among the philosophical skeptics who, like Hume, forced subsequent philosophizing to become far clearer about fundamental concepts. Just as Hume did not eliminate the concept of causality, so Quine does not eliminate the concept of meaning.

Appendix: Quine's Replies

Quine has replied to some of these criticisms.[40] The first point he makes is this: "Given analyticity, we can get sameness of meaning within the language but still not between languages. . . . two sentences are equivalent in meaning if the biconditional between them is analytic, but we cannot make a biconditional between sentences of two languages." (p. 198) Let me start with a small matter. Equivalence in meaning, that is, synonymy, is not a matter of the analyticity of the biconditional. Presumably the biconditional between "John is a bachelor" and "John is an unmarried bachelor" is analytic, but these sentences are not synonymous, since only the latter sentence is redundant. Two sentences cannot have the *same* sense if one has a sense property that the other lacks. Synonymy gives the analyticity of the biconditional, but the analyticity of the biconditional does not give synonymy.

A larger matter is that there is no problem about forming sentences that refer to sentences of two languages and saying that they are synonymous. The obvious way to do so is to quote them, as in "The English sentence 'What is his aunt's name?' is synonymous with the French sentence 'Comment s'appelle sa tante?'". Or we might employ the phonetic and syntactic vocabulary of linguistic theory to construct designations of sentences from different natural languages. Clearly, the referential mechanisms that make it possible to do comparative phonology and syntax also make it possible to frame semantic statements about sentences in different natural languages.

Quine next complains that I referred to his argument in "Two Dogmas of Empiricism" as having the form of a proof by cases. He insists that his argument is "not a proof at all" (p. 198). I did not suggest that his argument was intended to be a proof, but said only that it had a form like a proof by cases. My point was that Quine assumed that a certain set of cases is the only area where one might expect to find methods for making objective sense of concepts in the theory of meaning. In any case, Quine's complaint is irrelevant since I did not dispute this assumption, but took on his argument in the most important of the areas he considers.

I think Quine does his own argument an injustice when he writes that the cases were "a few avenues of definition that I or others might have felt were hopeful." In fact, his cases: definition, logic, and linguistics, seem, for all intents and purposes, to be exhaustive, for they are the only areas where one might turn for a way to clarify logico-linguistic concepts. Moreover, the force of his argument depends on the cases being exhaustive. Had there been some other area of science known to deal with the clarification of logico-linguistic concepts, then his argument, having ignored that area, could not have enjoyed the success it did.

Quine repeats his claim from "Two Dogmas of Empiricism" that the explorations of these "avenues of definition" to find a way to clarify meaning "ended in dead ends" (p. 198). This fails to meet my point that his examination of the case of linguistics explored only the dead-end path of operationalist definition, never setting foot on the path of theoretical definition. Quine, quite surprisingly, goes on to endorse a liberal requirement for defining terms, amounting to acceptance of any definitions that "help in systematizing and simplifying a theory" and enable the term to "play a useful role in a theory that meets the test of prediction" (p. 198). This endorsement gives away the store! For it contradicts the claim that the explorations of "avenues of definition" to clarify meaning are all "dead ends," as well as the strong, principled anti-intensionalism he has stood for for decades. Recall that it was just the grudging operationalist requirement that a term had to be defined on the basis of a substitution procedure— which allows no use of other terms in its family—that made it possible for Quine to argue that attempts to clarify analyticity and synonymy in linguistics are doomed to vicious circularity. Without that requirement, there is no argument that linguistics offers no prospect of clarifying analyticity and synonymy, and without that argument, no indeterminacy.

In the paper to which he is replying, I argued that the conception of linguistic definition in "Two Dogmas of Empiricism" is unreasonably strong and should be replaced with something similar to the conception Quine now seems to endorse, and also that such replacement leaves a hole in Quine's argument.[41] Now Quine says he is willing to make the replacement, but he fails to address either the criticism that the replacement leaves a hole in his argument or the criticism that, as a consequence of the hole, his argument for indeterminacy does not go through.

Quine says that his doubts come in connection with whether concepts such as analyticity and synonymy can play a useful role in theory (presumably, linguistic theory) (p. 198). But these doubts are now baseless. There are indefinitely many facts about natural languages which semantic theories in linguistics will need those concepts to explain, e.g., the analyticity of "Squares are rectangles" or the synonymy of "sister" and "female sibling". In the context of "Two Dogmas of Empiricism," Quine's doubts had a basis insofar as he had a reason for thinking that such explanations employed bogus concepts. Now, however, the reason is gone, a casualty of the replacement of the substitution-procedures requirement by a standard which countenances everything that has been done in contemporary linguistics under the name of intensional semantics.

Since, therefore, he cannot fill the gap in his argument for the indeterminacy of translation, Quine is in no position to reassert the old indeterminacy thesis that "right translations can sharply diverge" (p. 198). Quine thinks that he can still assert indeterminacy because he mistakenly thinks that my criticism gets his argument backwards. He says:

> The thesis does not depend on reference to physical objects: 'gavagai' is not characteristic. Nor does it depend on a dogma of there being no such things as intensions. It is the other way around: doubts about intensions come from reflecting on radical translation. They are doubts about how empirical criteria could in general determine what intension is determined by a sentence. (pp. 198–199)

I never supposed that there was an issue about whether the "gavagai" case is characteristic. I was quite clear that "doubts about intensions" are supposed to result from reflection on radical translation and, in particular, on the question of criteria for determining the senses of sentences. This is why the question of "independent controls" was central in my argument. I made it quite clear that I was prepared to grant Quine's conclusions about translation and about semantics if he showed that there are no such criteria, but I argued that he showed no such thing. Quine's reflections on actual translation in the radical case *assume* there are no language-neutral meanings. Of course, without such meanings there are no intensional criteria to provide the necessary "independent controls." But what sanctions this assumption? In *Word and Object*, it comes out of the blue, unless one supposes that it comes from his earlier work, in particular, "Two Dogmas of Empiricism." I put forth evidence for supposing this. Of course, there is room for disagreement here, but nowhere in Quine's corpus is the assumption explicitly established. Quine shows no sign of coming to grips with the fact that his reflections on radical translation involve this indispensable but unsubstantiated assumption.

Alleged doubts concerning how evidence can be brought to bear on questions about "what intension is determined by a sentence" fall into three categories: (i) doubts that arise within the Quinean radical-translation situation where evidence about sense properties and relations is excluded by fiat, (ii) doubts arising from the fact that the use of such evidence seems to presuppose that there are intensions, or language-neutral meanings, and (iii) doubts about the status of concepts like analyticity and synonymy. Quine's objective doubts in all three categories have been put to rest. In the case of (i), it was shown that there is no reason to think that Quinean radical translation coincides with any case of actual translation. This is the question of independent controls. In the case of (ii), it was shown that the supposition that there are intensions or language-neutral meanings is legitimate because it is only provisional and falsifiable. Investigation based on the supposition is the means by which we can find out, *via* the success or failure of theory construction, whether the provisionally supposed objects exist. In the case of (iii), it was shown that Quine provides no basis for doubting the potential scientific status of concepts like analyticity and synonymy. Without such a basis, we have a criterion for determining whether a particular intension is determined by a given sentence based on evidence from informant judgments about the meaningfulness, ambiguity, synonymy, antonymy, analyticity, and other sense properties and relations of the sentence. Given such evidence, it is no trick to specify the criterion for saying that a sentence has a particular intension: the sentence has the intension just in case the best hypothesis to account for the totality of such evidence says so.

Anyone can have personal doubts about the prospects of an infant subject, but, considering the philosophical weight that Quine puts on his skepticism about intensional semantics, his doubts, to be effective, have to be more than personal misgivings. They have to be substantive grounds for dismissing any serious possibility of a theory of meaning which might vindicate Frege's introduction of sense over and above reference. Quine's personal doubts cannot do this.

6
The Domino Theory

1

The standard picture of American philosophy over the last three decades portrays intensionalism as beset by a host of independent arguments which converge to refute it many times over. There is so much overkill on this picture that philosophers who notice that one or another of these anti-intensionalist arguments is not all it is cracked up to be nonetheless have felt that criticizing it would be little more than an academic exercise. But the picture is based on the false assumption that the anti-intensionalist arguments are independent of one another. In fact, there is a tight dependency structure to these anti-intensionalist arguments. One of them, namely, Quine's argument that no objective sense can be made of theories of meaning, supports all the others.[1] Donald Davidson explicitly acknowledges this dependency in his own case: the dedication to Quine in *Inquiries into Truth and Interpretation* reads "without whom not." If the scope of this dedication were sufficiently broadened, it could serve as an epigraph for the present chapter.

The thesis of the chapter is that, because of the dependence of the anti-intensionalist arguments on Quine's argument and since, as we have seen, Quine's argument falls, they all fall, too. The chapter argues for a "domino theory" of extensionalist argumentation during the last three decades: the anti-intensionalist arguments have the structure of dominos so arranged that toppling the first topples them all. This theory, together with the argument in the previous chapter, presents a picture of the logic of the extensionalism/intensionalism controversy very different from the standard picture. Besides showing that the first domino, Quine's argument that no objective sense can be made of theories of meaning, can be knocked down, the previous chapter took the first step toward confirming the domino theory by showing also that the second domino, Quine's argument for indeterminacy, depends on this argument, and therefore, goes down with it. The present chapter will show that the other principal anti-intensionalist arguments—Davidson's argument for abandoning the intensionalist paradigm of analysis, the argument for a purely extensional possible-worlds semantics, Putnam's arguments against traditional intensionalist semantics, and Burge's arguments against semantic individualism—are likewise propped up by Quine's argument and, hence, also go down with it.

2

Davidson's argument for replacing the intensionalist paradigm of analysis, '*s* means *p*', with the extensionalist paradigm (T)

(T) "*s*" is T if and only if *p*

is the linchpin of his entire philosophical program. The argument is as follows:

> Anxiety that we are enmeshed in the intensional springs from using the words 'means that' as filling between description of sentence and sentence, but it may be that the success of our venture depends not on the filling but on what it fills. The theory will have done its work if it provides, for every sentence *s* in the language under study, a matching sentence (to replace '*p*') that, in some way yet to be made clear, 'gives the meaning' of *s*. One obvious candidate for matching sentence is just *s* itself, if the object language is contained in the metalanguage; otherwise a translation of *s* in the metalanguage. As a final bold step, let us try treating the position occupied by '*p*' extensionally: to implement this, sweep away the obscure 'means that', provide the sentence that replaces '*p*' with a proper sentential connective, and supply the description that replaces '*s*' with its own predicate. The plausible result is [(T)].[2]

There are three aspects of this argument to consider. First, there is what Davidson had in mind when he referred to "anxiety that we are enmeshed in the intensional." It is obvious that what he has in mind is largely, if not solely, Quine's arguments. The anxiety to which he refers is that which those arguments are expected to create in anyone contemplating the use of concepts from the theory of meaning, particularly the concept of synonymy, on which the intensionalist paradigm rests. That this is so is confirmed by things Davidson says in other contexts. Examining relations like 'means that' which are reported through indirect discourse, he says: ". . . indeterminacy shows . . . that if there is one way of getting it right there are other ways that differ substantially in that non-synonymous sentences are used after 'said that'. And this is enough to justify our feeling that there is something bogus about the sharpness that questions of meaning must in principle have if meanings are entities."[3]

If Quine's arguments are all that Davidson has in mind, then we could conclude at this point that there is no cause for anxiety about the intensional and, hence, no reason to replace the intensionalist paradigm with convention (T). But before we draw this conclusion we must be sure that Quine's arguments are the only thing Davidson has in mind. There is one thing in "Truth and Meaning" which *prima facie* suggests that there might be something else. Davidson remarks that "wrestling with the logic of the apparently non-extensional 'means that' we will encounter problems as hard as, or perhaps identical with, the problems our theory is out to solve" (ibid., p. 455). And in this connection he mentions the problem of substitution into opaque contexts. The difficulty, as he puts it, is "the standard problem, which is that we cannot account for even as much as the truth conditions of [belief sentences] on the basis of what we know of the meanings of the words in them" (ibid., pp. 453–454).

The question is whether Davidson's reason for thinking that we cannot account for the truth conditions of sentences involving "believe" and other verbs that create opaque contexts falls back on Quinean arguments, specifically in order to deny Fregeans the move of using synonymy as a condition for substitution. It is clear that Davidson is at least not directly appealing to Quine, since "the standard problem" is obviously the problem that Benson Mates raises in his paper "Synonymity."[4] Thus, Davidson's reasons for replacing the intensionalist paradigm of analysis with convention (T) reduce to his reason for claiming that this problem is unsolvable and thus that the replacement enables us to avoid an unsolvable problem. But what, according to Davidson, is supposed to make it unsolvable? In particular, why is Frege's move, as seen by Frege himself or as developed by later Fregean intensionalists, not a solution?

It might seem peculiar that Davidson does not consider the principal intensionalist solutions to the problem. To be sure, he considers Carnap's operationalist explication of belief in terms of affirmative response, and he nicely puts his finger on Carnap's confusion.[5] But criticism of Carnap's explication is really beside the point. What Davidson needs is rather a criticism of the classical Frege-Church solution, which is independent of Carnap's explication. On their solution, inferences like that from "Everyone believes that bachelors are bachelors" to "Everyone believes that bachelors are unmarried men" are valid because those who profess to believe "Bachelors are bachelors" but not "Bachelors are unmarried men" *ipso facto* show themselves to suffer from a linguistic confusion or deficiency which disqualifies them as a counterexample to the inference.[6] It is a supposition underlying the substitution of "unmarried men" for "bachelors" that the expressions are synonymous in English. If this supposition were not accepted for the sake of argument, Frege and Church would not make the substitution and, hence, would not be committed to claiming that the inference is valid. In that case, there would be nothing against which to raise counterexamples.

This solution seems compelling because of the parallel with logic. A judgment of a speaker stemming from defective linguistic knowledge can no more be taken as evidence for invalidity than a judgment of a reasoner stemming from defective logical knowledge can be taken as evidence for invalidity. Genuine evidence about whether an inference goes through, whether a linguistic or a logical inference, cannot be based on incompetence. It might thus seem peculiar for Davidson not to consider the Frege-Church solution. But, of course, Davidson has not simply overlooked or ignored their solution. He has a specific reason for thinking there is no parallel with logic. As emerges clearly elsewhere in his writings, he thinks that, since the parallel and the solution itself both depend on the notions of synonymy and analyticity and since Quine has got rid of those notions, there is no solution to consider. In "On Saying That," Davidson explains that "the lesson" of indeterminacy, which he gives us in the preceding quote, was implicit in Mates's problem. Davidson writes:

> Mates claimed that the sentence "Nobody doubts that whoever believes that the seventh consulate of Marius lasted less than a fortnight believes that the seventh consulate of Marius lasted less than a fortnight" is true and yet might well become false if the last word were replaced by the (supposed synonymous) words "period of fourteen days", and that this could happen no matter what standards of synonymy we adopt short of the question-begging "substitutable everywhere *salva veritate*". Church and Sellars responded by saying the difficulty could be resolved by firmly distinguishing between substitutions based on the speaker's use of language and substitutions coloured by the use attributed to others. But this is a solution only if we think there is some way of telling, in what another says, what is owed to the meanings he gives his words and what to his beliefs about the world. According to Quine, this is a distinction that cannot be drawn.[7]

Since Davidson's reason for thinking that the Frege-Church solution to Mates's problem is not a real solution depends upon Quine's having eliminated the analytic/synthetic distinction, his reason for thinking that there is a cause for anxiety about being enmeshed in the intensional comes down just to Quine's arguments. Therefore, having shown that Quine did not eliminate this distinction, we have shown that the first aspect of Davidson's argument for replacing the intensionalist paradigm with convention (T) is inadequate.

The second aspect of Davidson's argument is his claim that a semantic theory for a natural language will have "done its work" if it just provides the appropriate instances of (T). In making this claim, Davidson is open to the charge of arguing from his own theory, since it is on Davidson's theory of the semantics of natural language in contrast to the intensionalist theories against which he is arguing that there is no work to be done by pairing sentences with meanings in the traditional sense. Frege, for example, thought that there is intensional work to be done, one task being to characterize synonymous expressions in the case of substitution into opaque contexts and another being to distinguish analytic identity sentences from synthetic identity sentences. If Frege is right, a semantic theory that does no more than provide appropriate instances of (T) will not have done all the work.

But Davidson offers no argument to show that there are no such intensional tasks and that the work of a semantic theory can be restricted to providing instances of convention (T). Hence, we again have to interpret him as falling back on Quine. That is, we have to interpret him as supposing that there is no work of accounting for synonymy, analyticity, etc. because Quine has shown those concepts to be bogus. But then the discussion of Quine in the previous chapter removes the second aspect of Davidson's argument for replacing the intensional paradigm of analysis with (T).

The third aspect of Davidson's argument is the assumption of his move of "sweep[ing] away the obscure 'means that'" that the relation 'means that' is, in fact, obscure in some damaging sense. But since Davidson himself offers no reason for assuming this, it seems that the justification, again, must come from Quine's argument that no objective sense can be made of the notion of meaning. Without that argument, there is no reason to think that, even if there is obscurity about the notion of meaning, it is anything more serious than the sort of obscurity that attaches to any complicated concept before it receives careful study. If this is the only sense in which meaning can be charged with obscurity, instead of motivating the replacement of the relation 'means that', such obscurity only motivates a careful study of the relation. Hence, the third and final of reason given for going along with Davidson's proposal to replace the intensionalist program with his extensionalist program disappears.[8]

At this point, we can conclude that there is no reason to go along with Davidson's proposal. But we are in a position to draw an even stronger conclusion. On the basis of what has been said thus far, it also follows that there are positive reasons not to go along with the proposal. For there are certain well-known counterintuitive consequences of adopting convention (T) as our paradigm for the semantic analysis of natural language. In discussing the following three sentences:

(1) Snow is white.
(2) "Snow is white" is T iff snow is white.
(3) "Snow is white" is T iff grass is green.

Davidson himself noted the counterintuitiveness of treating (3) as an account of the meaning of (1) on a par with (2).[9] Other such consequences are that English contains only two meanings, since the truth conditions for every true sentence of English can be given on the basis of any true sentence, and the truth conditions for every false sentence can be given on the basis of any false sentence.

Whether the stronger and more damaging conclusions can be drawn depends on whether Davidson's attempts to mitigate such counterintuitive consequences succeed. Davidson tries to mitigate them by arguing that

> the grotesqueness of [(3)] is in itself nothing against a theory of which it is a consequence, providing the theory gives the correct result for every sentence . . . if [(3)] followed from a characterization of the predicate 'is true' that led to the invariable pairing of truths with truths and falsehoods with falsehoods—then there would not, I think, be anything essential to the idea of meaning that remained to be captured. (ibid., p.457)

Now Davidson would be right to claim that there is nothing remaining to be captured if he had Quine's arguments to rely on, since, if they went through, they would show that there is no fine-grained idea of meaning to offend against in putting (3) on a par with (2) as an account of the meaning of (1). But once Quine's arguments are taken away, Davidson's saying that the grotesqueness is nothing against the theory is simply arguing from his own position. On his position, which says that what is essential for a semantic theory is to pair true sentences with true sentences and false ones with false ones, nothing essential remains to be captured once a theory does this. Defending semantic analyses that capture only co-extension by arguing that nothing essential remains to be captured begs the question of whether semantic analyses need to capture co-intension. Such "grotesque" consequences of the extensionalist paradigm constitute evidence that the paradigm is deficient in being unable to discriminate more finely among putative semantic analyses. Without Quine's arguments, the grotesqueness of such consequences counts against a policy of putting a theory of the truth predicate in place of a traditional theory of meaning.

Recently, Davidson has argued that such criticism fails to note "the essential proviso" in "Truth and Meaning" which requires that theories of the truth predicate give correct results for every sentence.[10] Davidson thinks that sentences like (3) can be ruled out on the requirement of a "reasonably simple theory that also [gives] the right truth conditions for 'That is snow' and 'This is white'" (ibid., p. 26, note 10). Davidson's point seems to be that we will need to employ a nongrotesque instance of (T) for the interpretation of such sentences, and, consequently, the shift to grotesque instances of (T) in the case of sentences where we have the option will produce a more complex overall theory. I am dubious about this for three reasons. First, it seems reasonable to count a theory that replaces "p" with the same single true sentence in all invariably true sentences as simpler or, by a trade-off of complexities, no more complex than one that replaces "p" with a different true sentence in each case. Second, the grotesque pairing of such an identity sentence having an indexical subject with any other sentence having a coextensive predicate nominal—e.g., the pairing of "That's a creature with a heart" with "That's a creature with a kidney"—does not violate Davidson's requirement. Third, even if Davidson could avoid grotesque consequences such as (3)'s being counted on a par with (2), still there will be indefinitely many equivalent counterexamples that cannot be got rid of in this way. Two strains that are resistant to "the essential proviso" are the following. One is the logical and mathematical parallels of (3), such as the example we get by replacing "Snow is white" by "2 is less than 3" and "Grass is green" by "The even prime is less than 3" in the sentences (1)–(3),[11] or, again, replacing "Snow is white" by "There is no largest integer" and "Grass is green" by "There is no even prime greater than 2". The other resistant strain is found among the sentences Quine used to illustrate indeterminacy. Replace "Snow is white" by "Lo, a rabbit" and replace "Grass is green" by "Lo, a rabbit stage" or "Lo, an undetached rabbit part".

Davidson has also introduced a new requirement on instances of (T) which is designed to eliminate grotesque consequences like (3), namely, that instances of (T) "support appropriate counterfactuals."[12] But this is a feeble requirement which, even if it eliminates counterexamples like (3), does little more. Taking the schema for counterfactuals to have the form "If '*s*' were true, then it would be the case that *p*", let us grant that counterexamples like (3) can be eliminated because counterfactuals like "If 'Snow is white' were true, grass would be green" are not appropriate. The idea is, presumably, that lifting the components of the counterfactual from instances of (T) ought not give rise to fàlse counterfactuals. There is no point in raising a question here, since it is child's play to construct equally grotesque consequences that satisfy the requirement. For example, the instance of (T) " 'Snow is white' is true if and only if natural selection produces white polar animals" gives us the appropriate counterfactual "If 'Snow is white' were true, then natural selection would produce white polar animals". Or we can construct counterexamples simply by choosing nonsynonymous expressions that are logically or mathematically equivalent, e.g., "If '2 is a factor of *n*,' were true, then it would be the case that the even prime is a factor of *n*".

We have now seen how the fall of the first domino, Quine's arguments in "Two Dogmas of Empiricism," brings about the fall of the second two: Quine's argument for indeterminacy and Davidson's argument for abandoning the traditional intensionalist paradigm. Let us now turn to the third domino.

3

There have been two species of possible-worlds semantics. Their difference is obscured by the fact that both characterize the notion of meaning and proposition in terms of extensions in possible worlds and both employ the term "intension". But their accounts of possibility differ in that only one of them uses the traditional notion of meaning. The other species employs the term "intension" in an untraditional sense to mean a function from expressions and sentences onto extensions in possible worlds. In the case of this species of possible-worlds semantics, the notion of possibility is under no intensional constraints in the traditional sense of the term "intensional". Accordingly, the two species of possible-worlds semantics have very different notions of meaning and proposition.

Carnap's semantics is the best-known example of the species of possible-worlds semantics whose notion of possibility rests on the traditional theory of meaning. Carnap's semantics derives from Frege's. Carnap streamlined Frege's account of analyticity by eliminating the reference to definitions in favor of logical laws, viz., meaning postulates, which express the extensional force of definitions. This streamlining resulted in a maximal expansion of the logical vocabulary. Not only modals but all other predicates standardly considered extralogical, for example, "is a bachelor" and "is married", are now logical vocabulary.[13] Meaning postulates for such logical vocabulary partially define the notion of a possible world by constraining the model-theoretic interpretation of atomic sentences. So, for example, there is no possible world in which something is a bachelor and married. As Quine was quick to observe, this makes Carnap's possible-worlds semantics a form of traditional intensionalism, and, hence, it faces the same objections as other forms.[14]

In contrast, the account of possibility, meaning, and propositions in extensionalist possible-worlds semantics is based on a distinction between logical and extralogical vocabulary. It puts the notion of possibility under no constraint stemming from the meanings of predicates like "is a bachelor" and "is married". This version of possible-worlds semantics is tailored to conform as much as possible to Quine's scruples about meaning, but Quine's influence is not absolute here as it is in Davidson's case. Extensionalist possible-worlds semanticists give modal concepts a central role in their analyses of the logial form of sentences in natural language, ignoring Quine's objections to modal concepts, because they see the recent advances in modal logic as vindication of such concepts. They think that, by allowing modals into the logical vocabulary, but otherwise treating the semantics of natural language in conformity to Quine's scruples about meaning, they can have the best of both worlds: they escape Quine's criticisms of Carnap, and they establish a more powerful semantics than Davidson's. David Lewis's semantics is an example of this species of possible-worlds semantics.[15]

Quine's arguments provide extensionalist possible-worlds semanticists with the rationale they require for their claim that there is no more fine-grained notion of meaning or proposition than the notion whose identity conditions are expressed in terms of extensions in their possible worlds. Extensionalist possible-worlds semanticists have at times used other arguments for denying the existence of the finer-grained notion of proposition that we get when synonymy is used as the identity condition for meanings. These non-Quinean arguments are based on a caricature of formal representation in a decompositional theory of sense.

The best known of such arguments is David Lewis's objection to a decompositional theory of sense on the grounds that its formal representations are no more illuminating than a translation of one uninterpreted system of formal symbols into another (ibid., pp. 169–170). Lewis claims that hypothesizing decompositional formal representations of sentences reveals nothing about their meaning because it is like translating the sentences into another language, such as Latin. Other philosophers have followed Lewis in making this objection. John Searle writes:

> Suppose we decide to interpret readings as piles of stones. Then for a three-way ambiguous sentence the theory will give us three piles of stones, for a nonsense sentence, no piles of stones, for an analytic sentence the arrangement of stones in the predicate pile will be duplicated in the subject pile, and so on. There is nothing in the formal properties of the semantic component to prevent us from interpreting it in this way. But clearly this will not do because now instead of explaining the relationships between sound and meaning the theory has produced an unexplained relationship between sounds and stones.[16]

A sure sign that these arguments are bogus is that, if they were good, we could use variants of them to do away with all formal theories. If we are allowed to ignore the descriptive character of formal representations, we could also "establish" that logical and mathematical representations are unrevealing about logical and mathematical structure. Following Searle, we could interpret logical and arithmetic formalism as piles and configurations of stones, and conclude from the exercise that formal logic and arithmetic explain nothing.

Clearly, such an argument proves too much. There are two obvious errors in Searle's claim that "the theory has produced an unexplained relationship between sounds and stones." First, a decompositional representation *per se* does not explain the relation between sound and meaning. That is something which is done in the grammar's correlation between representations of senses and representations of sentences. Decompositional representations describe the structure of senses and would do so even in abstraction from their relations to sentences. Second, Searle's claim overlooks the intended interpretation of the formalism. Using a formalism of stones would surely be a clumsy and exhausting business, but, as long as we transfer the interpretive conventions that are employed for the more manageable orthographic formalism, the new stones formalism, too, could, in principle, describe the structure of senses. It is these conventions which turn configurations of formal objects of any sort into a formal description. Ignore them, as Searle does, and formal description seems a mere pile of stones, but recognize them and Searle's criticism is revealed as an attack on a straw man.

Lewis equally ignores the aim of formal representation in a theory of sense. The aim, explicitly stated in the presentation of the theory he is criticizing, is to *describe* the decompositional and compositional structure of sentence meaning. Attention to this aim would prevent him from confusing the relation of description between formal representations of sense and English sentences with the relation of translation. Translation is just a matter of pairing a sentence from one language with a sentence from another language that says the same thing, whereas decompositional and compositional representation is a matter of describing the components of senses, the ways they combine to form complex senses, and the ways that senses, simple and complex, determine ambiguity, synonymy, redundancy, and other sense properties and relations. Translators use their intuitive grasp of the senses of sentences in the two languages to pair sentences that are the same in meaning, but semanticists describe the structure of such shared meanings and the mechanism of their assignment in the languages.

Lewis may have been misled by thinking of semantics exclusively in terms of truth and reference.[17] If he thought that the only semantic structure to be described is extensional structure, he might naturally think that formal representations of intensional structure ignore semantic structure entirely and, hence, are no better than translations into Latin. If this is what is behind his criticism, we are owed an objection to a theory of senses as something over and above reference. As it is, we can only speculate that perhaps Lewis might here be relying on Quine's claim to have shown that nothing can be made of the notion of sense. But, by stating no objections and claiming that representations of the senses of English sentences are no better than Latin translations, he forces us to conclude that he is either relying on Quine, too, or simply ignoring the explicitly presented descriptive aim of the sense theory he is criticizing.

In sum, Lewis and Searle both miss the philosophical woods for the formal trees. They fail to appreciate that the formalism of semantic markers is not an end in itself but is only a means to the end of showing that certain new linguistic and philosophical ideas about the deep structure of language can be coherently and interestingly developed. In the present instance, the means was an adaptation of the marker formalism from syntax, and the end was to show that decompositional semantics provides general statements of compositionality and definitions of sense properties and relations.

Unfortunately, Lewis's and Searle's mistake has been picked up by others. Gareth Evans and John McDowell say that Lewis's "points against 'translational semantics' . . . bear spelling out again."[18] They then proceed to do this.[19] First, in repeating the translational-semantics point, they compare decompositional semantics with Davidson's semantics as an alternative form of so-called "translational" semantics. This compounds the error, since, as we have just seen, it is just senses—the objects whose structure a decompositional theory set out to describe—that Davidson eliminates when he rejects the traditional intensionalist paradigm of analysis in favor of the extensionalist paradigm (T).

Second, Evans and McDowell confuse the question of the aims of a decompositional semantics even further by equating those aims with the prescriptive aims of a Fregean Begriffsschrift theory. They say that the theory's "language" must be "a logically perfect language" if it is to enable the theory to achieve its goals of accounting for meaningfulness, ambiguity, and meaninglessness.[20] Since the semantic theory in question was developed within the strongly antiprescriptivist, pro-descriptivist framework of generative grammar, I am at a loss to explain how Evans and McDowell could go this far wrong. Perhaps this is another example of the difficulty that philosophers have in thinking about intensionalist theory in other than Fregean terms.

Third, Evans and McDowell find the descriptive aim of decompositional semantics—"conceptual breakdown," as they put it—to be objectionable (ibid., p. ix). They have three objections. There is Quine's attack on the analytic/synthetic distinction, which they consider of minor importance. This, in any case, has been dealt with here in chapter 5. Next they say that "conceptual breakdown, if pursued seriously, would be without evident limit."[21] This objection, too, they regard as of minor importance. Even so, they rate it too high. In fact, analysis in sense semantics, as anywhere else, has a clear and well-defined limit, namely, the point at which all the relevant properties and relations of all the objects in the domain have been accounted for on the basis of representations of their structure which cannot be further simplified. When it stops itching, stop scratching.

The objection to which they attribute most importance is this. Engaging in decompositional semantic analysis "conceals from [us] our utter incapacity to do what we ought to be doing," which is "stating something such that, if someone knew it, he would be able to speak and understand the language" (ibid., p. ix). This, as far as I can see, is simply a reiteration of Dummett's claim that we criticized in chapter 2, section 16. As Evans and McDowell offer no independent argument for the claim, it would appear that they rely on Dummett for the argument. But, as we saw, this is a mistake.

Everyone agrees that investigating speech production and understanding speech performance are important. But why ought that be a reason for thinking that everyone ought to be working on the theory of performance? The theory of performance is important for understanding how people make inferences, but no one would regard that as a reason for logicians to pack up and go home. Evans and Mc-Dowell neglect to say what is wrong with the more modest task of trying to construct a theory of the grammatical structure of the language. The task is surely hard enough, as anyone who has worked in generative grammar will readily attest. The only explanation I can think of of why Evans and McDowell might suppose that everyone ought to be studying performance is that they assume that the proper approach to language must be "bottom-up." About this assumption, enough has been said already.[22]

If extensionalist possible-world semantics depends on Quine's arguments, what happens to it as a result of the failure of those arguments? Essentially the same thing that happens to Davidson's semantics. This should not be surprising, since the only advantage over Davidson gained from introducing modal concepts is that extensionalist possible-worlds semanticists can distinguish the different contingent truths and different contingent falsehoods. But, since their possible worlds are extensionally defined, we find essentially the same grotesque consequences as in Davidson's semantics in connection with necessary truths and necessary falsehoods. For example, extensionalist possible-worlds semantics entails that (4) and (5):

(4) 1 is a smaller number than 2.
(5) 1 is a smaller number than the even prime.

are the same in meaning. This is surely as counterintuitive as any grotesqueness of Davidson's semantics. No one would paraphrase or translate (4) and (5) in the same way. No one would take them to contribute the same semantic content to sentences in which they occur as constituents. *Inter alia*, the logical equivalence of (4) and (5) is not sufficient for the logical equivalence of (6) and (7):

(6) Small children know that 1 is a smaller number than 2.
(7) Small children know that 1 is a smaller number than the even prime.

Furthermore, on extensionalist possible-worlds semantics, each necessary truth asserts the same thing as its conjunction with all its logical consequences, and each necessary falsehood asserts everything. Finally, all necessary truths have the same meaning, and all necessary falsehoods have the same meaning. In consequence, there are only two meanings for the English sentences that express logical and mathematical statements.[23]

Without being able to appeal to Quine's criticisms to show that their notion of meaning and proposition is as fine-grained a notion as there can be, extensionalist possible-worlds semanticists have no way to meet the objection, raised by such grotesque consequences, that their notion of meaning and proposition is too coarse-grained. The justification that extensionalist possible-worlds semanticists have given to meet this objection is that there is no finer-grained notion of meaning and proposition, and, hence, asking for a finer-grained notion is not facing up to semantic reality. This "facts of life" rationale collapses once a finer-grained notion becomes a possibility and austerity measures are no longer needed in order to make the best of things. Thus, without Quine's criticisms of meaning to defuse such objections, extensionalist possible-worlds semantics goes the way of Davidsonian semantics.

4

Prima facie, Hilary Putnam's arguments against intensionalism seem to depend on nothing more than a simple exercise of the imagination and, hence, to be independent of Quine's arguments against meaning. In this section, I will show that Putnam's arguments depend on Quine's arguments. They also depend on the conflation of intensionalist semantics with Fregean semantics which was discussed in chapter 2, but this conflation also depends on Quine's arguments, since, if those were good arguments, there would be no alternative to Fregean intensionalism.

Putnam's arguments have a common form. From "It Ain't Necessarily So" to "The Meaning of 'Meaning'," he employs a variety of imaginary situations to try to show that sentences do not have the sense structure that intensionalists suppose them to have. Putnam's idea is that simple thought-experiments about what is possible will show that these sentences can express nothing stronger than contingent connection.[24] Like Quine, Putnam takes analyticity and synonymy to be the basic concepts of the theory of meaning, and, accordingly, he directs his arguments (in the early papers) against analyticity and (in the later papers) against synonymy.[25]

Let us take as our case (8), Putnam's original example of an allegedly analytic sentence:

(8) Cats are feline animals.

Putnam seems to have chosen this example because he saw no reason why Donnellan should have exempted such a case from his criticism of the claim that sentences like "Whales are mammals" are analytic, particularly since both sentences are about natural kinds.[26] Such examples have been the focus of discussion in the subsequent controversy about analyticity, often being treated as paradigm cases. This is unfortunate, since it neglects cases central to the issue between C. I. Lewis and Donnellan, e.g., cases like "Blue is a color" and "Squares are rectangles", which are the toughest for anti-intensionalists to handle. Nevertheless, for the sake of argument, I will assume that intensionalists are restricted to cases like (8). I will also assume that intensionalists are committed to claiming that (8) is analytic, that is, given what we said about analyticity in the last chapter, that the sense of the subject of (8) contains the sense of its predicate.

Putnam's argument against analyticity begins by observing that it is perfectly imaginable that the things referred to in prior uses of "cat" are not feline animals, in virtue of being Martian robots. This observation is quite correct—just as is Putnam's later observation that it is perfectly imaginable that the naturally odorless, colorless, and tasteless liquid that descends from Twin Earth sky as rain and fills Twin Earth oceans and lakes is not something referred to in uses of our word "water", in virtue of its not being H_2O. These observations, I want to stress, are not challenged here. Rather, criticism is directed at the argument that Putnam bases on them.

Putnam tries to argue from the thought-experiment about cats that (8) is not analytic. His idea is that, if (8) were analytic, there could be no case in which (8) is false, but, since the situation in which cats turn out to be Martian robots is imaginable, (8) is possibly false, and hence, not analytic. But does the thought-experiment produce a case in which (8) is false? To answer this question, we have to be clear about what precisely it is that the experiment shows. Putnam's own discussion is open to two quite different accounts of what it shows. On one, it shows something tantamount to (9):

(9) It is possible that the referents of "cat" in all the assertions people have made with it are not animals.

On the other account, the experiment shows straight off that it is possible that cats are not animals.[27]

The former account produces an argument with considerable force. The force of the argument comes from the fact that everyone, even intensionalists, must grant the possibility that the things people have been referring to in the use of "cat" are not animals. If, therefore, (9) can be shown to be incompatible with the analyticity of (8), Putnam has a knock-down argument against analyticity.

On the latter account, in contrast, the thought-experiment directly exhibits things that are cats but not animals. But this account is clearly contentious, as can be seen from the fact that it invites the response "Yeah, and next we'll be hearing about round squares". The problem with the account is that, in trying to get an immediate refutation of analyticity, it contentiously assumes that the thought-experiment by itself establishes the possibility of a robot cat. If the thought-experiment could do that, then some thought-experiment could establish the possibility of a round square (e.g., the Martians can deform the pattern of light rays coming to our eyes from squares). The problem is that the account does not offer a reason to think that we are imagining anything more than a situation establishing (9). What shows that we are actually imagining a case in which *cats* are robots? Or, if we are asked to imagine *that*, that we are imagining anything coherent?

Consider a parallel case. Let us imagine an ancestor of Putnam's in the Salem of 1692 criticizing an intensionalist's claim that (10) is analytic:

(10) Witches possess magical power.

Ebenezer Putnam proposes a thought-experiment in which all the alleged magical powers of the suspected witches have a natural explanation. Surely, it will not do for Ebenezer Putnam simply to assert that the imagined case is a case of something that is both a witch and a woman with no magical powers. The claim begs the question of whether such a case is possible. Ebenezer's intensionalist opponent has the easy and plausible reply that the concocted situation is merely a situation in which there are no witches. Correspondingly, Hilary Putnam's claim that his case is a case of something that is both a cat and a robot is subject to the easy and plausible parallel reply that the concocted situation is merely a situation in which there are no cats.

This point can be reinforced as follows. If "cat" and "feline animal" are synonymous, then, necessarily, (8) is analytic if and only if (11):

(11) Feline animals are feline animals.

is analytic. Now (11) is a straightforward logical truth; so we are not inclined to say that anything is a counterexample to it. It is impossible for something to be both a feline animal and not a feline animal. But what goes for (11) goes for the synonymous (8), and, hence, Putnam's thought-experiment cannot be taken to exhibit a case of something that is both a cat and a nonanimal.

Accordingly, if we wish to construe Putnam's argument as starting where it is on firm ground, we have to adopt the account on which the thought-experiment establishes the undeniable (9). Now the question is whether (9) is, in fact, incompatible with the claim that (8) is analytic. What reason does Putnam have for thinking so? He thinks that intensionalists who accept the analyticity of (8) are committed to denying (9) because of their position that sense determines reference. This commits them to claiming that the analyticity of (8) entails (12):

(12) It is not possible that the referents in all statements people have made with "cat" are nonanimal.

Putnam argues that, since (9) is true, (12) is false, and, therefore, the claim that (8) is analytic is false.

This argument goes through without a hitch if, as Putnam thinks, intensionalists are committed to the position that sense determines reference. It is certainly true that Frege, the father of modern intensionalism, took this position. Frege defined the sense of an expression as the mode of determining its referent; accordingly, the sense of an expression, on his definition, contains the information necessary to fix its reference in statements.[28] But Frege's position is not essential to intensionalism. In chapter 2 and elsewhere I have explained that intensionalists need not go along with Frege on the relation between sense and reference because they need not accept the Fregean definition of sense in terms of reference.[29]

It is curious that Frege's approach to defining sense is like Quine's substitution-criteria approach to defining sameness of sense. Frege's approach, like Quine's, seeks to define a concept in the family of sense concepts in terms of concepts *outside* that family, and, in both cases, the external concepts are from the theory of reference. Thinking that Fregean semantics is the only form of intensionalist semantics rests on the same mistake as thinking that the method of substitution criteria, which, as Quine shows, does not work in the case of synonymy, is the only method of clarifying concepts in linguistics.

Moreover, the alternative to Fregean intensionalism results from the same approach that foils Quine's argument against synonymy, namely, the approach of theoretical definition, on which sense is defined in terms of its relations to other concepts in the theory of meaning, without dependence upon reference or other concepts outside the family of sense concepts. In particular, sense is to be understood as the locus of grammatical properties and relations like synonymy and analyticity, in analogy to the way that syntax is to be understood as the locus of grammatical properties and relations like 'same part of speech' and well-formedness. On this alternative, which is the proto-theory of chapter 2, an understanding of sense comes not from the relation of language to the world, but from relations internal to the grammatical system of the language.[30] The relation of sense to reference is left as a further question to be taken up once significant progress has been made in systematizing sense structure. The proto-

theory's definition of sense is, I believe, a more consistent development of Frege's original distinction between sense and reference than
his own definition.[31]

If the possibility of such a theoretical definition did not exist, intensionalists would be Fregeans by default. In that case, Putnam would
be right in thinking that intensionalists were committed to the position that sense determines reference, and his argument against intensionalism would go through. Thus, Putnam's argument requires a
further premise to the effect that no such theoretical definition of
sense is available to intensionalists. But such a theoretical definition
is surely available if it is legitimate to use concepts like analyticity and
synonymy in the definition of sense. Hence, Putnam needs an argument that such concepts are illegitimate, and what else could this
argument be but Quine's? Therefore, Putnam's argument from the
thought-experiment concerning Martian robots to the conclusion that
(8) is not analytic is either elusive or depends on Quine's arguments.

Let us review the logic of the situation from the perspective of intensionalism without Fregean semantics. Recall that, on our theoretical definition, a sentence is analytic just in case the sense of its
subject, direct object, or any constituent that functions as a term contains the sense of its full predicate together with the senses of the
other constituents functioning as terms.[32] On the basis of such a theoretical definition, the claim that (8) is analytic is only a claim about
the sense structure of (8). There is no claim about the referential structure of (8). To be sure, when we come to relate sense to reference, we
will want to correlate the sense property of analyticity with the referential property that literal uses of analytic sentences that make statements make necessarily true statements. But, when we make such a
correlation, we will be connecting a feature of the grammatical structure of a sentence in a language (a feature of a type) with a feature of
its utterances in a context (a feature of tokens). Thus, the claim that
(8) is analytic, in and of itself, implies nothing about whether some
utterance of "cat" (some token), or even every one, refers to feline
animals or to Martian robots.

Since the claim that (8) is analytic is only a claim about the structure
of the sense of the English word "cat", intensionalists are then free
to take the "top-down" approach to the reference of its utterances,
namely, the view that the utterances take on reference as a function
not only of their sense but also of the conditions of utterance. As a
consequence, intensionalists can avail themselves of Donnellan's insight into reference under a false description: they can say that, in
cases like Putnam's, tokens of "cat" have taken on reference to robots

under the false (semantic) description 'feline animal'.[33] This is a natural account of these cases because, until the news breaks, the utterance conditions involve the belief of speakers that what appears to be a cat is a cat. Thus, the tokens of "cat" have been referring to robots under the false description "cat" because speakers have been living in a collective fool's paradise concerning their true nature. The tokens of "cat" in these cases have literal sense, to be sure, but they have nonliteral reference (see chapter 3, section 3).

Therefore, Putnam cannot take it for granted that the intensionalist claim that (8) is analytic involves acceptance of (12). Putnam's thought-experiment, which establishes the truth of (9), provides no basis for inferring that (8) is not analytic. Putnam has a powerful argument against Fregean intensionalism, but, without Quine's arguments against sense properties and relations, he has no argument against intensionalism *per se*.

"The Meaning of 'Meaning'" is essentially a replay of this drama. This time the argument is recast as an argument against synonymy. The aim, as Putnam explicitly says, is still to refute the traditional intensionalist view of meaning.[34] Here Putnam makes it quite clear that the argument depends on Frege's conception of the relation between sense and reference. He says that the traditional concept of meaning has come to rest on two assumptions:

(I) that knowing the meaning of a term is just a matter of being in a certain psychological state
(II) that the meaning of a term (in the sense of "intension") determines its extension (in the sense that sameness of intension entails sameness of extension).[35]

Given that the traditional concept of meaning rests on both these assumptions, Putnam claims to be able to show that "these two assumptions are not jointly satisfied by *any* notion, let alone any notion of meaning" and, hence, that "The traditional concept of meaning is a concept which rests on a false theory" (ibid., p. 136).

The argument that is to show this again begins with an imaginary situation. This time the science fiction situation is about Twin Earth: "Twin Earth is very much like Earth. . . . In fact, apart from differences we shall specify . . . the reader may suppose that Twin Earth is *exactly* like Earth. He may even suppose that he has a *doppelgänger*—an identical copy—on Twin Earth." (ibid., p. 139) Putnam gives the argument against synonymy in three forms. In the first, there is no H_2O on Twin Earth, and in its place is stuff chemically different from H_2O, namely, XYZ, which is indistinguishable from Earth water under normal conditions. Since my doppelgänger has the same psychological states that I do, but the extension of my English word "water" is H_2O while the extension of his Twin Earth English word "water" is XYZ, (I) and (II) cannot both be true. In the second form of the argument, my words "aluminum" and "molybdenum" refer, respectively, to aluminum and molybdenum, but my doppelgänger's language switches the terms extensionally, so that his "aluminum" refers to molybdenum and his "molybdenum" refers to aluminum (ibid., pp. 142–144). Again, there is sameness of psychological state and difference of extension, and, hence, (I) and (II) cannot both be true. In the third form, the words "elm" and "beech" take the place of the chemical terms, with the slight twist that Putnam puts the reasoning in terms of the fact that his own concepts of elm and beech are the same, but the extensions of "elm" and "beech" in his idiolect differ in the way they do for other speakers of the language (ibid., pp. 134–139). Again, same psychological states and different extensions, and hence, same conclusion.

I concede that this argument, in each form, shows that (I) and (II) are not jointly satisfiable. I concede also that it shows that any theory resting on them is a false theory and, hence, that Frege's theory is a false theory. In making these concessions, I accept (I) as an informal statement of the conditions for knowledge of the meaning of a term, taking the psychological state in question to be one in which the agent grasps the meaning of a term and takes the meaning grasped to be a sense (see also ibid., pp. 134–139). Putnam's argument works because (II), Frege's principle connecting sense and reference, connects them so strongly that possibilities concerning the empirical world can be used to refute Fregean intensionalism.

But Putnam claims more for his argument than just to have refuted one explication of the traditional concept of meaning. He claims to have refuted the traditional concept of meaning itself, to have shown that it "rests on a false theory." This claim is mistaken for reasons that must now be obvious. Since the traditional concept itself does not rest on Frege's principle (II), it has not been shown to rest on a false theory. The fact that (I) and (II) cannot both be true is irrelevant to the explication of the traditional concept within the proto-theory, since it is based on a non-Fregean intensionalism where the joint unsatisfiability is entirely a matter of the truth of (I) and the falsehood of (II).

But we cannot leave the matter here. Recently, Putnam has considered a version of the criticism that his argument doesn't work if intensionalists can drop the claim that sense determines reference.[36] Putnam replies:

. . . if we go the way I went in "The Meaning of 'Meaning'," and take the extension of a term as one of the components of its 'meaning vector', then we have a clear reason for saying that 'grug' has a different meaning in North Ruritanian and in South Ruritanian. Since the word 'grug' clearly has a different reference in the two dialects of Ruritanian, it also has a different meaning. Once we decide to put the reference (or rather difference in reference) aside, and to ask whether 'grug' has the same 'content' in the minds of Oscar and Elmer, we have embarked upon an impossible task. Far from making it easier for ourselves to decide whether the representations are synonymous, we have made it impossible. . . . 'Factoring out' differences in extension will only make a principled decision on when there has been a change in meaning totally impossible.[37]

In this passage, Putnam says three times that the task of determining sameness of content or sense without recourse to reference is impossible. But our non-Fregean definition of sense easily determines the general notion of sameness of sense without invoking reference: two expressions are synonymous just in case any sense property or relation of one is a sense property or relation of the other. The task of determining sameness and difference of sense in particular cases is, then, a matter of inference to the best explanation of the sense properties and relations of the expressions in those cases. The best explanation can be understood to be that explanation which accounts most simply for the available evidence concerning the sense properties and relations in question. For example, it would be evidence for the synonymy of "chair" and "piece of furniture with a back and a seat, serving as a place to sit for one" that "chair which is a piece of furniture serving as a place to sit for one" is redundant, that "chair" and "stool" are antonymous, that "chair" and "bench" are antonymous, that "chair" and "bed" are antonymous, etc. Since we actually have a determination of sameness of sense without invoking reference, it is not impossible to have such a determination.

Why, then, is Putnam so sure that synonymy cannot be determined without recourse to reference? He says nothing about what his reasons might be, but a plausible explanation of his certainty suggests itself when we note that the definition of synonymy, like the definition of sense itself, makes essential use of sense properties and relations, which it is reasonable to think Putnam believes Quine to have completely discredited. I submit that Putnam, who has always been sympathetic to Quine, thinks that, for Quinean reasons, we cannot appeal to such properties and relations. Besides being plausible, this explanation is charitable, since, without it, Putnam would simply be ignoring a proposal for defining sense and sameness of sense which has been in the literature for some time.

But if the explanation is correct, the fall of the first and second dominos undercuts Putnam's reply to the intensionalist who has abandoned the Fregean position. In the absence of that reply, Putnam has no grounds whatever for claiming that the concept of meaning, as explicated within our non-Fregean intensionalism, rests on a false theory.

5

A number of arguments have appeared extending Putnam's line of thinking in "The Meaning of 'Meaning'." The most influential of these are Tyler Burge's arguments against semantic individualism, i.e., the view that the semantics of a natural language is fixed without dependence on social relations within the linguistic community and of other environmental factors.[38] These arguments conflict with our intensionalism, which holds that meaning in natural language is autonomous with respect to such factors and that a speaker's knowledge of the meaning of an expression requires no more than being in the psychological state of grasping its sense. In this section, I want to show that these arguments fail because they depend on Putnam's Twin Earth arguments which depend in turn on Quine's arguments.

In "Other Bodies" Burge imagines a Twin Earth scenario where the focus is not on meanings *per se* but on "belief contents," i.e., the conceptual or semantic aspects of what is believed, or more generally, the proposition associated with the clause functioning as the complement of a verb expressing a propositional attitude.[39] Burge's form of argument can be sketched as follows. Compare my belief contents involving the notion of water with those of my doppelgänger on Twin Earth where there is no H_2O but only XYZ—where there is no water but only twater, to use Burge's convenient way of putting it. Even though there is no difference between my doppelgänger and me with respect to what is in our heads (including non-intensional phenomenal experiences, dispositions to respond, etc.), none of the belief contents containing the notion of water which can be ascribed to me can be ascribed as well to my doppelgänger. For example, my doppelgänger will not have my belief that the drinks have been watered, but will have, rather, the belief that the drinks have been twatered. Since such differences in content can only be a function of the difference in our environments, Burge concludes that semantic individualism is false.

Burge takes Putnam's reasoning in an interesting direction:

When Adam says or consciously thinks the words, 'There is some water within twenty miles, I hope', Adam$_{te}$ says or consciously thinks the same word forms. But there are differences. As Putnam in effect points out, Adam's occurrences of 'water' apply to water and mean *water*, whereas Adam$_{te}$'s apply to twater and mean *twater*. And, as Putnam does not note, the differences affect *oblique* occurrences in 'that'-clauses that provide the contents of their mental states and events. Adam hopes that there is some water (oblique occurrence) within twenty miles. Adam$_{te}$ hopes that there is some twater within twenty miles. That is, even as we suppose that 'water' and 'twater' are not logically exchangeable with co-extensive expressions *salva veritate*, we have a difference between their thoughts (thought contents).[40]

Thus, from the premise that Adam's word "water" means *water* and Adam$_{te}$'s word "water" means *twater,* Burge draws the conclusion that the propositions that express the contents of their hopes are different.

Burge's argument depends on assumption (II) just as much as Putnam's original Twin Earth argument does. Without (II), there is no way to go from the supposition that Adam's utterances of "water" refer to water and Adam$_{te}$'s utterances of "water" refer to twater to the conclusion that "water" means *water* and "twater" means *twater.* Only if Burge takes (II) as a premise can he infer a difference in meanings or belief contents from a difference in the referents of "water" and "twater".

Without (II) it is possible for "water" and "twater" to apply to the very different substances they apply to on Earth and Twin Earth and, nonetheless, be synonymous. "Water" and "twater" could be exact translations because, for example, both have the sense (13):

(13) naturally odorless, colorless, and tasteless liquid that descends from the sky as rain

Thus, "water" and "twater" pick out H_2O on Earth where there is only H_2O, they pick out XYZ on Twin Earth where there is only XYZ, and they pick out both wherever there is both H_2O and XYZ. In each of these cases, the substances are picked out because they are naturally odorless, colorless, and tasteless liquids that descend from the sky as rain. On the assumption that "water" and "twater" are synonymous, Putnam and Burge's hypothetical situations correspond to certain real situations. For example, "anesthetic", which means 'something which causes temporary loss of sensation in a part of the body', picks out chemically different substances such as ether, chloroform, novocaine, etc. because each of those substances has the defining property.

But, clearly, the use of premise (II) in Burge's inference is open to the same challenge as its use in Putnam's inference: not all semantic individualists go along with Frege's acceptance of (II). Rugged individualists have given up Fregean semantics and reject (II). Without Quine's arguments to provide security for this premise, there is nothing to sustain it, and, without the premise, there is no reason to think that the meanings of "water" and "twater" are different or that the belief contents for Adam and Adam$_{te}$ are different. Thus, Burge's criticism of semantic individualism fails along with Putnam's criticism on which it is modeled.

Putnam and Burge have claimed intuitive support for their arguments. These claims are mistaken because my criticism is independent of what set of linguistic intuitions about the imaginary situations in question is accepted. Premise (II) cannot be supported by linguistic intuition, and without that premise linguistic intuition is powerless to support their arguments.

Thus, we may concede that intuition supports Putnam's claim that earthling space explorers reporting back will say that Twin Earth has no water, instead of saying that its water has the chemical structure XYZ.[41] Non-Fregean intensionalists can accept this claim and nonetheless argue that such intuitive evidence about our use of "water" can easily be interpreted as conforming to their position. In the first place, note that intensionalism *per se* says nothing concerning what particular words mean in the language. It is not concerned with descriptive lexicography. Rather, it is a theory of language and a metatheory for grammars. It concerns linguistic universals, the form of the semantic component in grammars, and the question of how semantic evidence is brought to bear in choosing among semantic hypotheses. (For instance, if speakers were to judge that the expression "chemical anesthetic" is redundant, that would be evidence for a definition that excludes hypnosis. Alternatively, if clear literal uses of "anesthetic" apply to hypnosis, that would be evidence for a definition that does not.) Now, assuming that the space explorer's report involves a literal use of "water", i.e., that it is not saying something to the effect of "What they *call* water is not H$_2$O" or "What *passes for* water up here is XYZ", the report is evidence for the lexical hypothesis that the English word "water" means 'substance with the composition H$_2$O'. This is not implausible, since the facts about the chemical nature of water have become so widely known that a meaning change could

well have taken place, so that "water" no longer means (13) or only
(13). Perhaps there has been an addition to the dictionary, so that
"water" now has two senses, a technical, scientific sense referring to
its molecular structure and an ordinary sense like that spelled out in
(13). The usage of the space explorer is explained as stemming from
the fact that, in technical contexts such as space exploration, there is
a natural preference for a technical sense.[42]

So much for Putnam's appeal to intuition. Let us turn to Burge's.
He writes:

> We now consider whether the same natural kind terms should
> occur obliquely in attributions of propositional attitudes to Adam
> and Adam$_{te}$. Let us assume, what seems obvious, that Adam has
> propositional attitudes correctly attributed in English with his
> own (English) natural kind terms in oblique position. He hopes
> that there is some water within twenty miles; he believes that
> sailboat masts are often made of aluminium, that elms are deci-
> duous trees distinct from beeches, that shrimp are smaller than
> mackerel. Does Adam$_{te}$ have these same attitudes, or at least at-
> titudes with these same contents? As the case has been de-
> scribed, I think it intuitively obvious that he does not.[43]

Burge's phrase "as the case has been described" can cover two quite
different things, but in neither does intuition show what Burge supposes. On the one hand, the case has been described as one in which
Adam$_{te}$'s word "water" means something different from Adam's
word "water". Under this description, Burge is correct to say that
Adam$_{te}$ does not have the same attitudes with the same contents as
Adam. Here intuition is idle: it serves merely to reiterate what is already in the description. But the description depends on Burge's argument, which, as we have seen, rests on (II).

On the other hand, there are neutral descriptions that do not include a specification of the alleged semantic difference between
"water" and "twater". Under such descriptions, intuition cannot decide whether Adam$_{te}$ has or does not have attitudes with the same
contents. The case is underdetermined and can be construed along
the lines of whatever semantic view one comes to it with. If we come
with the view that "water" means *water* and "twater" means *twater*,
then we will "intuit" that Adam$_{te}$ and Adam have attitudes with different contents; alternatively, if we come with the view that "water"
and "twater" have the same meaning (say, (13))—but refer to different stuff depending on what there is on Earth and what there is on
Twin Earth (as "anesthetic" can refer to different stuff)—then we will
"intuit" that Adam$_{te}$ and Adam have attitudes with the same content.

Therefore, intuition—pure and simple—can be seen to play no role in deciding whether the same or different concepts occur obliquely in attributions of propositional attitudes to the Adams.

However, Burge does not intend his argument to rest on intuition. He says that "two broad types of consideration back the intuition" that different concepts occur obliquely in such attributions. The first consideration is that "it is hard to see how Adam$_{te}$ could have acquired thoughts involving the concept of water without contact with water, or someone having contact with water" (ibid., pp. 109–110). There are two replies to this consideration. First, one can say that Adam$_{te}$ has had contact with water, since he has had contact with a naturally colorless, odorless, and tasteless liquid that descends from the sky as rain. But this reply begs the question, for Burge has not as yet shown that the rugged individualist is wrong to fix such a liquid as the referent of "water" under the definition (13).

Second, even if we allow that Adam$_{te}$ does not have contact with water, the consideration is totally implausible. It is child's play to see how people could acquire concepts of things that neither they nor anyone else have had contact with. Science fiction stories, scientific treatises, fairy tales, tall stories, novels, etc. are full of concepts without contact. Adam$_{te}$ could acquire the concept of water in the way that scientists develop a concept of something whose existence is a matter of sheer speculation. There would be no point in replying that, in order to imagine abstract concepts, scientists start in contact with natural phenomena and build up theories step by step. Although this is true, the natural phenomena with which scientific theories are in contact may be quite different from and very indirectly connected with the theoretical objects of the theories. Hence, there is every reason to think that the natural phenomena with which Adam$_{te}$ can be supposed to have contact, even though quite different from water, are sufficient for him to imagine water.

The second type of consideration that Burge thinks backs the intuition is that, if we say that Adam$_{te}$ had beliefs involving the concept of water, then "a large number of his ordinary beliefs will be false. . . . But there seems no reason to count his beliefs false and Adam's beliefs true (or vice versa)" (ibid., p. 110). Neither of these considerations has force. As long as an intensional notion of a concept has not been ruled out, it is not sufficient for counting a large number of Adam$_{te}$'s beliefs false that they involve the concept of water. Whether they are counted as false depends on exactly what concept of water figures in Adam$_{te}$'s beliefs. If it is (13), then his beliefs—say, those about the stuff boats sail on and mackerel swim in—will be largely true. Of course, if Adam$_{te}$'s concept of water is the concept 'stuff with the composition H_2O', then a large number of his beliefs will be false. However, even in this latter case, there is good reason for counting $Adam_{te}$'s beliefs largely false and Adam's beliefs largely true, namely that what $Adam_{te}$ designates as stuff with the composition H_2O doesn't have this composition, while what Adam designates as stuff with the composition H_2O does have this composition.

What makes it seem to Burge unreasonable to count a large number of $Adam_{te}$'s beliefs false (while counting Adam's corresponding beliefs true) is that $Adam_{te}$ gets along in ordinary circumstances just as well as Adam does. But this symmetry presents no difficulty. The case of $Adam_{te}$ with his many false beliefs about XYZ corresponds to the case of people in Putnam's fiction with their many false beliefs about catlike robots. There seems to be something unreasonable about counting a large number of $Adam_{te}$'s beliefs false only so long as we overlook the fact that false beliefs, if shared, can be just as good as true ones in ordinary circumstances. Even in Putnam's imaginary situation, if we want to rid the house of mice or to eliminate the horrible meowing from the back fence, we can still use "I'll buy a cat" or "Shoot the cat making that horrible noise". Such utterances achieve the necessary reference under the false description 'feline animal'. The utterances suffice for our purposes, since a properly functioning robot gets us the desired absence of mice, and a nonfunctioning robot gets us the desired absence of horrible noise. Correspondingly, if $Adam_{te}$ wants to obtain something to drink or wants to wash up before dinner, he can use "A glass of water, please" or "Where is the water faucet?". This will do the trick because the utterances will achieve reference to XYZ under the false description 'stuff with the composition H_2O'.

Burge has another influential form of argument against semantic individualism, one in which the notion of arthritis takes the place of the notion of water.[44] People have various and sundry "arthritis thoughts," i.e., thoughts in which the notion of arthritis figures as the object of the propositional attitude. Now suppose that, not knowing the lexical fact that "arthritis" is a condition of the joints, a patient thinks that his or her arthritis has spread to the thigh, i.e., that a painful inflammation in his or her thigh is arthritis. The patient's sense of "arthritis" can be compared to the young child's overgeneralized sense of "daddy" exhibited in its application of the word to all men. Burge contrasts this arthritis case with that of a hypothetical community where everybody applies "arthritis" the way the patient does. (Perhaps arthritis has not yet been isolated as a disease of the joints in this community.) Burge wants to say that, whereas the patient has arthritis thoughts (e.g., the patient might believe that he or she has painful arthritis in an ankle), the patient's doppelgänger in the hypothetical community would lack arthritis thoughts. Burge explains:

> We suppose that in the counterfactual case we cannot correctly ascribe any content clause containing an oblique occurrence of the term 'arthritis'. It is hard to see how the patient could have picked up the notion of arthritis. The word 'arthritis' in the counterfactual community does not mean *arthritis*. It does not apply only to inflammations of the joints. We suppose that no other word in the patient's repertoire means *arthritis*. 'Arthritis', in the counterfactual situation, differs both in dictionary definition and in extension from 'arthritis' as we use it. Our ascriptions of content clauses to the patient (and ascriptions within his community) would not constitute attributions of the same contents we actually attribute. For counterpart expressions in the content clauses that are actually and counterfactually ascribable are not even extensionally equivalent. However we describe the patient's attitudes in the counterfactual situation, it will not be with a term or phrase extensionally equivalent with 'arthritis'. So the patient's counterfactual attitude contents differ from his actual ones. (ibid., p. 79)

The moral of the contrast is supposed to be that the semantic differences must be chalked up to differences in the social environments. But why is there supposed to be a contrast in the first place? True enough, "arthritis", as we use it, expresses the concept of a rheumatoid ailment of the joints; but why think that the linguistically deviant patient should be treated any differently from his or her doppelgänger? Why shouldn't we say that this patient also lacks the attitudes, which are attributed to nondeviant speakers of the language, with content clauses containing "arthritis" in oblique occurrences? Burge gives no reason. Moreover, it is very natural to say this because of the analogy between the linguistically deviant patient who doesn't have the sense of "arthritis" and the young child who does not have the sense of "daddy". Generally, we would not say that a young child who calls every man "daddy" has any attitudes whose description requires the concept of being a father and, correspondingly, it seems correct to deny that the patient has any attitudes whose description requires the concept of arthritis. Just as the child has thoughts about men, the patient has thoughts about inflammations.

We might, in some exceptional cases, say that a lexically deficient young child and a lexically deficient patient have attitudes involving the as yet unacquired conceptual restriction. Without having acquired the word "arthritis", the patient might raise the question "Could my condition be a special rheumatoid ailment that just afflicts the joints?". But, in the corresponding case, we can as well say that people in the hypothetical community have such attitudes. It is easy to see how one of them might pick up the notion of arthritis. Consider an example. There are patients who glory in having many illnesses, and in exploiting them to gain attention. They invest much time and energy thinking about disease possibilities and delight in adding new afflictions to their list. Surely, even a moderately imaginative and medically informed patient of this type could hit on the happy thought that, instead of having an old inflammation spreading to a new spot—a piece of news unlikely to attract much attention—he or she has a new disease, a distinct medical condition consisting of inflammation of the joints.[45]

Burge's second point is that the absence of a word for arthritis in the patient's repertoire is grounds for claiming that the notion cannot play a role in his or her thoughts. The argument purports to explain why no one in the counterfactual community, no matter how neurotically motivated, medically informed, or scientifically imaginative, could come up with the arthritis hypothesis. Aside from ruling out "eureka"-type discoveries, the argument faces a number of counterexamples. The notion of a bad-smelling house was part of many people's thoughts well before Madison Avenue coined the term "houseitosis". English speakers have no trouble forming the thought that dying from lack of water would be worse than dying from lack of food despite the fact that English has no word meaning 'death from lack of water' parallel to "starvation". The speaker recognizes that the meanings of "death", "lack", "water", and the causal preposition combine to form the compositional meaning parallel to "starvation". Thus, Burge's argument does not explain why someone couldn't come up with the arthritis hypothesis.

His own explanation is paradoxical and arbitrary. It is paradoxical because it makes it impossible to understand how novel hypotheses could occur. It is arbitrary because it doesn't provide a reason to show why words should be accorded a special status. Why should absence of a word meaning "arthritis" be critical when, thanks to compositionality, phrases or clauses are available to express the same meaning? Since, obviously, there is no rationale for giving this special status to one syntactic category rather than another, it cannot matter how the patient refers to the condition. Having no word meaning *arthritis*, the patient can coin a new term or construct a phrasal or clausal description to express the meaning. There can be no objection to assuming that a description is synonymous with "arthritis", since we have removed the arguments for supposing that one cannot make objective sense of synonymy. It seems quite straightforward, then, for us to describe the patient as informing everyone that he or she suffers from the newly identified disease arthritis. Describing the patient in this way is no different from describing an early author of science fiction as having written about spaceships.

6

In this chapter I have tried to show that the principal anti-intensionalist arguments over the last three decades of American philosophy are not a collection of distinct criticisms, each standing or falling on its own merits, but have a structure in which Quine's argument against the theory of meaning supports all the others. The chapter also extends the anti-Fregean argument in previous chapters and in some recent papers of mine designed to show that the critics of intensionalism wrongly identified the overall intensionalist position with Frege's position and, as a consequence, mistakenly put their faith in the arguments of Quine and others which underestimate the resources of intensionalism.[46]

There is a striking parallel here to Wittgenstein. As was shown in chapters 2 and 3, he, too, wrongly identified the full range of theoretical positions on meaning with a proper subset to them and, as a consequence, mistakenly put his faith in a critique which similarly underestimates the resources of intensionalism. In both cases, a non-Fregean form of intensionalism, developed within the context of contemporary linguistics, emerges unscathed from the full range of anti-intensionalist criticisms.

One can discern something like the operation of a dialectic in the course of the naturalist/non-naturalist debate in this century. The thesis is Frege's non-naturalistic intensionalism. It temporarily blocks the tide of nineteenth-century naturalism, but, because its conception of sense is tied too closely to logic, his intentionalism, as both he and his disciples developed it, is flawed. Problems to which the flaw gives rise are soon recognized by the two great naturalistic philosophers of our century, who exploit them to launch a rebellion against Frege's intensionalism and nonnaturalism. Wittgenstein sees the underlying flaw as *theorizing* about meaning; Quine sees it as theorizing about *meaning*. But both misdiagnose the flaw. Each exploits his own conception of the flaw to formulate an antithesis to the Fregean position. But the flaw is neither theorizing about nor countenancing the notion of meaning. Rather, it is theorizing in the wrong way about the wrong notion of meaning. Thus, in reaction to Wittgenstein's and Quine's criticisms, a new intensionalism emerges which is a synthesis of some features of Frege's intensionalism and some of their criticisms. The new intensionalism posits senses as necessary for the solution of a wide range of problems in the philosophy of language, including the treatment of names, identity, and opacity, but it theorizes scientifically about a notion of sense, taking the notion as purely grammatical and independent of reference. This intensionalism provides a new and, I believe, more secure basis for non-naturalism than Frege's intensionalism. In the next chapter, I will develop foundations for this non-naturalism in terms of a realist conception of linguistics.

7
The Naturalistic Fallacy

1

Because Wittgenstein's critical philosophy and Quine's naturalized epistemology are the two major forms of contemporary naturalism and because Frege was the principal target of both, contemporary naturalism concentrated on arguing against non-naturalist theories of meaning.[1] The linguistic turn in twentieth-century philosophy was, largely, a novel attempt on the part of naturalists to defeat non-naturalist metaphysics with linguistic arguments. Thus, if my responses in the previous chapters to those arguments are adequate, naturalism does not have the substantiation it is widely taken to have, and at this point there is a standoff in the controversy between naturalism and non-naturalism. Even though this is in itself a significant advance for non-naturalism, considering where it was at the outset, nothing in my arguments precludes another, as yet unimagined philosophical turn which succeeds where the linguistic turn failed. Since it is unsatisfactory to leave things in this undecided state, the present chapter tries to supplement those arguments with a further argument showing that philosophical attempts to establish naturalism are fundamentally mistaken.

2

A standard account of naturalism is given in Arthur Danto's essay in the *Encyclopedia of Philosophy*, where naturalism is characterized as

> a species of philosophical monism according to which whatever exists or happens is *natural* in the sense of being susceptible to explanation through methods, which, although paradigmatically exemplified in the natural sciences, are continuous from domain to domain of objects and events. Hence naturalism is polemically defined as repudiating the view that there exists or could exist

any entities or events which lie, in principle, beyond the scope of scientific explanation.[2]

Danto's account characterizes what I shall call "scientific naturalism"; I shall distinguish it from "philosophical naturalism" shortly.

To understand scientific naturalism, some minor shortcomings of Danto's characterization need to be considered. The main one is that, in explaining the term "natural", Danto refers to "natural sciences". This means that his methodological delimitation of the objects and events that the monism allows is specified circularly. This circularity carries over to the "polemic definition" as well, since Danto means to repudiate objects and events beyond the scope of scientific explanation *in the natural sciences*. Clearly, the reference to scientific explanation would not have its intended force if "scientific" were not understood in this restricted sense. Danto subsequently removes the circularity by indicating that natural objects and events are those which "exist within the spatiotemporal and the causal orders." Thus, the objects repudiated are those which are claimed to exist outside the spatiotemporal and causal nexus, that is, those with which we cannot become acquainted through direct causal contact or through causal contact with objects and events in causal relations to them.[3]

This still leaves questions like these: Do pains, afterimages, and thoughts have a spatial locus in a clear enough sense for them to count as natural objects? Can the intended notion of cause be specified without the notion of a natural object? Are we to dismiss claims, like Gödel's, that mathematical intuition acquaints us with the non-natural objects of set theory? Is the universe as a whole—the entire spatio-temporal order—a natural object? But, even though these are serious questions, I will not try to pursue them, since an absolutely complete and flawless definition of naturalism is no more necessary for my purposes than for those of the naturalist.

Danto emphasizes the importance to naturalism of a continuity of methods of explanation. Some naturalists put the point more directly by saying that every object in the world is a natural object. Other naturalists talk about a continuity of knowledge and belief, and still others put the thesis in terms of a continuity of subject matter—every special science is continuous in subject matter with physics, chemistry, and biology, perhaps even saying that all the sciences are about configurations of matter and energy and their transformations. Such claims need not commit the naturalist to one or another of the common unity-of-science doctrines or to one or another form of reductionism. No naturalist qua naturalist has to claim that the natural uniformity extends upward to a unity of the various scientific ways of studying phenomena or to claim that there is a special class of natural objects in terms of which all others have to be understood. The fundamental thesis of scientific naturalism is that there is a continuity of natural objects and events across the entire range of special sciences: the world is a natural world, and there is no place in it for non-natural objects or events. This is Danto's point that naturalism is a monism. This thesis is meant to proscribe at least three classes of things: supernatural beings, Cartesian mental substances, and abstract objects or universals. I shall not be concerned with the attempt to ostracize the supernatural and Cartesian mental substances. I am concerned only with the attempt to deny abstract objects a place in the world.

The designation of naturalism as a monism is obscured by the fact that some of those who take the naturalist position countenance abstract objects and universals, sometimes even making use of them in their philosophy. I do not have in mind those who make use of the terminology without having *bona fide* abstract objects or universals in their ontology. I mean those who are generally considered or consider themselves to be naturalists but who countenance such objects understood in the standard way: as objects that lack spatial relations, cannot come into and go out of existence, cannot cause change, and cannot be caused to change. The problem is exacerbated by the fact that these philosophers are sometimes among the most illustrious naturalists. Aristotle and Quine are examples.[4]

Aristotle, as I understand him, believes that there are universals, only that they are somehow natural; that is, natural objects actually have such geometrical properties as straightness and circularity. Aristotle thinks that we arrive at universals by abstracting away from other aspects of concrete things, such as their material, and considering them just as circles or squares. This is all well and good if we can assume knowledge of circularity or squareness and if certain natural objects are truly circular or square. But both assumptions are dubious. On the one hand, it has never been explained how this abstraction process is supposed to work in bringing us knowledge of universals if the process really involves no appeal to universals. On the other hand, no natural object is perfectly circular or perfectly straight. Every object in nature deviates to some extent from perfect circularity or perfect straightness.

W. V. Quine believes that sets are to be counted among the furniture of the world. The example of such a philosopher, who has served as a model naturalist but countenances abstract objects—which he makes no effort to reduce to something concrete in the causal nexus— seems to raise a question about the characterization of naturalism as a monism. This is only because of our reluctance to accept so stark an inconsistency or so radical a shift in the thought of so prominent a figure in twentieth-century naturalism. But there can no more be a species of naturalism that is consistent with belief in the existence of abstract objects than there can be a species of atheism that is consistent with belief in the existence of God. Naturalists cannot countenance the existence of universals and abstract objects, whose existence is independent of natural objects, without contradicting their monism, which denies that anything exists over and above natural objects.

Philosophers like Aristotle and Quine are not in fact the thoroughgoing naturalists that they first seem to be. This construal preserves the monistic element in the characterization of naturalism and, thereby, keeps naturalism and non-naturalism as opposed positions. There is no alternative. A dualism that puts a premium on doing justice to scientific knowledge, accepting abstract objects in order to do justice to the mathematical sciences, while rejecting Cartesian minds and supernatural spirits in order to do justice to the natural sciences (i.e., to keep their notion of causation coherent), is no naturalism. It is the very non-naturalism that I am arguing for in this book. In accepting abstract objects, such a dualism accepts much of traditional metaphysics and, in particular, its claim to provide knowledge of the most abstract aspects of reality. On this dualism, the principal metaphysical issues between Plato and Aristotle, between nominalists, conceptualists, and realists in Medieval philosophy, between Mill and Frege, between Meinong and Russell, and between Wittgenstein and Wittgenstein are still with us. This dualism is simply another name for non-naturalism.

How is it, then, that naturalists like Aristotle and Quine come to countenance abstract objects? I think the same deep respect for science which leads them to become naturalists in the first place subsequently leads them to admit abstract objects. This respect for science puts these naturalists in the position of having to countenance all the objects that science countenances. A naturalist like Quine who recognizes science as first philosophy has to accept the existence of the objects that science says exist; so he has to admit the abstract objects of set theory into his fundamental ontology. The source of the problem is, I think, a conflict at the very heart of this conception of science as first philosophy. Since this is a conception on which science is the final arbiter on all matters, including philosophical matters, and yet on one matter, namely, the issue of naturalism itself, the decision is made on independent philosophical grounds, the (naturalistic) decision arrived at can subsequently conflict with what science says exists. I shall argue that this conflict reflects a fallacy in this attempt to make the philosophical preference for naturalism square with the First Philosophy picture of science as universal arbiter.

Per se, scientific naturalism is a bare claim about what there is. It allows nonnatural objects as a possibility, but denies that they are an actuality. Scientific naturalism can be distinguished from the doctrine, referred to above as "philosophical naturalism," which seeks to establish philosophically a preference for scientific naturalism. Philosophical naturalism argues on the basis of philosophical considerations, together perhaps with scientific ones, that a complete description of the spatio-temporal-causal realm is a complete description of everything. Philosophical naturalism can be thought of as carrying this naturalistic message to theory construction in the special sciences and in other disciplines concerned with what there is. The issue of philosophical naturalism, especially the philosophical reasons for and against imposing naturalistic constraints on theories of the world, is the issue with which the present chapter is concerned. The issue of scientific naturalism comes within the purview of philosophy only as part of philosophical naturalism.

3

Non-naturalists sometimes claim that the application of philosophical naturalism in certain disciplines involves a fallacy. Frege saw a fallacy of psychologism in attempts to define logical concepts psychologically.[5] G. E. Moore saw a "naturalistic fallacy" in attempts to define moral concepts naturalistically.[6] Both were on what seems to me the right track in suspecting a basic definitional fallacy of some kind, but neither of their criticisms are satisfactory as they stand. Each criticism contains only a piece of the diagnosis, and, even together, they fall short of the whole truth about philosophical naturalism. The pieces need reshaping, integration, and supplementation.

Frege and Moore each focus on one discipline to the exclusion of others where the same issue of naturalism arises, and, as a consequence, their treatments neglect the general features of the problem with philosophical naturalism. Also, their treatments exclude the discipline of linguistics, whose subject, language, soon became the central battleground in the twentieth-century controversy between naturalism and non-naturalism. Frege was even prepared to accept a psychological—or perhaps a sociological—view of natural languages; his conception of imperfections in natural language is, very likely, the source of this view.[7] Such a view seems to have come from his thinking of imperfections of language in terms of biological limitations.

Finally, Frege and Moore make certain errors which limit or blunt their criticism. One such error of Frege's was his simplistic picture of the options open to psychologizers of logic. Frege's narrow focus on a psychologism based on individual subjectivity allows naturalists to exploit the model of idealization in physical science to formulate a psychologism which appears to escape his charge that psychologism sacrifices objectivity and necessity.[8] Below we shall examine Chomsky's and Dummett's attempts to go this route.

Over the years, a number of errors have been found in Moore's argument against naturalistic definitions of moral concepts. At present, the consensus among philosophers is not only that ethical naturalism cannot be refuted with Moore's original argument but that no refutation along the lines of Moore's argument is possible either. I agree with the first of these assessments, but, on a liberal understanding of what counts as "along the same lines," not with the second. I concede that basic problems with Moore's original argument cannot be overcome, but I think they are peculiar to his linguistic way of understanding the naturalistic fallacy and of running the argument. If I am right about this, it ought to be possible to construct a new argument in the spirit of Moore's, but sufficiently different to sidestep its problems.

I will develop a new conception of the naturalistic fallacy and, based upon it, a new argument that philosophical naturalism commits a naturalistic fallacy. I will illustrate this fallacy in the cases of linguistic and logical naturalism. The naturalistic fallacy in the form in which I shall identify it in linguistic and logical naturalism is, in a nutshell, psychologistic definition—but "psychologistic" and "definition" in what, as we shall see, are very different senses from the senses that "definition" and "psychologistic" have in Frege's and Moore's work. Since the fundamental issue of philosophical naturalism transcends the special cases of linguistics and logic, I will try to defuse some of the problems in transferring the argument to other cases, in particular, to ethics, where Moore first argued for a naturalistic fallacy.

4

Moore believed that the attempts of ethical naturalists to define basic ethical concepts like 'right' and 'good' in terms of naturalistic concepts like 'productive of pleasure', 'what is desired on reflection', 'conducive to the greatest overall happiness', and 'what is most highly evolved' would always fail and, moreover, that there is a general way to show this. He wrote:

. . . whoever will attentively consider with himself what is actually before his mind when he asks the question 'Is pleasure (or whatever it may be) after all good?' can satisfy himself that he is not merely wondering whether pleasure is pleasant. And if he will try this experiment with each suggested definition in succession, he may become expert enough to recognize that in every case he has before his mind a unique object.[9]

Given a naturalistic definition identifying an ethical property with a naturalistic one, Moore asks whether something's having the naturalistic property closes the question of whether it has the ethical property. Moore reasons that if the naturalist's definition were correct, the question would be closed. The question, "This thing is P, but is it good?" would be self-answered in the same way as "This thing is P, but is it P?". According to Moore, one can see that naturalistic definitions are incorrect from the fact that such questions are not closed semantically. For instance, the question "This thing is productive of pleasure (what is desired on reflection, etc.), but is it good?" is not self-answered in the manner of a question like "John is a bachelor, but is he an unmarried man?".

Moore's "open-question argument" has come in for much criticism. Some criticisms can be answered.[10] But one that cannot is that Moore's argument misconstrues naturalistic definitions, because, typically, they are not put forth as lexical definitions. Putnam states the criticism as follows:

. . . Moore conflated *properties* and *concepts*. There is a notion of property in which the fact that two *concepts* are different (say 'temperature' and 'mean molecular kinetic energy') does not at all settle the question whether the corresponding *properties* are different. (And discovering how many fundamental physical properties there are is not discovering something about *concepts*, but something about the *world*.) The *concept* 'good' may not be synonymous with any physical concept . . . , but it does not follow that *being good* is not the same as *being P*, for some suitable physicalistic (or, better, *functionalistic*) P. In general, an ostensively learned term or property (e.g., 'has high temperature') is not synonymous with a theoretical definition of that property; it takes empirical and theoretical research, not linguistic analysis, to find out what temperature is (and, some philosopher might suggest, what *goodness* is), not just reflection on meanings.[11]

Moore did construct his argument in terms of linguistic meanings and linguistic analysis. I think this is clear not only from his statement of the argument, but also from his discussion of definition and analysis in his Schilpp volume.[12] Definitions, in Moore's sense, break down the complex meaning of a word into its parts: they can be seen as the ordinary-language equivalent of the proto-theory's decompositional representations of senses.[13] Hence, an adequate definition is analytic and in its interrogative form is a self-answered question.[14] As a consequence, Moore's open-question argument casts ethical naturalists as lexicographers of the moral vocabulary. But this is surely not the position many ethical naturalists take, nor one that any must take. Ethical naturalists can legitimately object that Moore misrepresents their claim. They can protest as follows: "We are not especially concerned with the meaning of moral terms in the language. Rather, our concern is with the extralinguistic reality that such terms denote, that is, with the good and with right action. We put forth theories about the nature of the good and right action. Our concern is ethics, not language."

5

It is clear that the ethical naturalist's claim is not a lexical claim; it is even clearer that logical naturalist's, mathematical naturalist's, and linguistic naturalist's claims are not lexical claims either. Had Moore taken a broader perspective on philosophical naturalism and viewed ethical naturalism as simply one among many species of the genus *naturalism*, he would surely have recognized the ethical naturalist's claim as a claim about moral reality rather than as a claim about language. The first order of business facing us in developing a new form of the naturalistic fallacy is, then, to move the discussion from the investigation of language to the investigation of reality. To do this, I will apply the language/theory distinction which the proto-theory vouchsafes, in order to express the fact that naturalistic definitions, in ethics and elsewhere, are put forth as theoretical conceptions.

This distinction provides us with a basis for saying that the naturalist's definition does not express an analytic identity of properties like "Bachelors are unmarried men" but expresses rather a synthetic identity of properties like "Temperature is mean molecular kinetic energy". To obtain a new conception of the naturalistic fallacy, we need to look further into the difference between analytic and synthetic identity statements. In the case of a true analytic identity statement, the expressions flanking the identity sign are just linguistic labels for one and the same concept (in Putnam's sense), while in the case of a true synthetic identity statement, the expressions label different concepts that pick out the same thing. This difference correlates with

differences in the use of such statements. The serious purpose in using an <u>analytic identity statement</u> is to inform someone about the
<u>meaning of a term</u>; in using a <u>synthetic identity statement</u>, it <u>is to put
forth an account of the nature of the reality to which a term refers</u>. To
mark this difference, I will distinguish between *concepts*, that is, senses of words or expressions in the language (the sense in which
Putnam uses the term), and *conceptions*, that is, accounts of the nature
of something which result from identifying extensions of concepts or
properties (usually within a theory).[15]

This distinction explains why it makes perfectly good sense to
speak of true or false conceptions, but not of true or false concepts,
that is, true or false senses. For example, it makes sense to say that
the conception of water as H_2O is the true conception of water. This
is to say, this conception gets the composition of water right. Similarly, it makes sense to say that the conception of women as too fem-
inine for political leadership is false. This conception says that female
gender and fitness for political office do not coincide empirically, and
it is refuted by examples such as Golda Meir, Indira Gandhi, Margaret
Thatcher, and Benazir Bhutto. In contrast, it does not make sense to
speak of concepts, senses of words and expressions, as true or false—
except when the term "concept" is used to refer to what we are calling
"conceptions", as, for example, in "the Freudian concept of neu-
rosis". It is semantically deviant to say that the sense of the English
word "bachelor" is true, or that some but not all of the senses of the
ambiguous word "bank" are false. The reason for the deviance is that,
since there are no synthetic property identities in senses, <u>the senses</u> of terms
<u>involve no assertion about the nature of anything in reality, and so
there is nothing for the predicates</u> 'true' and 'false' <u>to endorse or re-
pudiate</u>. Since there is nothing in senses to be true or false, there is
nothing to which there can be a counterexample.[16]

If we put conceptions in place of concepts, we can develop a notion
of the naturalistic fallacy that does not involve Moore's misrepresen-
tation of the claims of naturalists as linguistic claims. Since conceptions express synthetic identities, this step removes the naturalistic
fallacy from the area of language, putting it in the area of theory
(broadly construed), where it belongs. In the cases with which we
shall be concerned, conceptions are stated as theoretical definitions,
and, hence, the naturalistic fallacy will concern not statements about
the lexical meanings of words in the language but statements of a
theory which provide that theory with its account of the nature of the
objects in the domain, and which the theory then employs in its explanations of phenomena.

Conceptions may be naturalistic or non-naturalistic. A naturalistic conception postulates only natural objects; a non-naturalistic conception postulates non-natural objects. The physicist's conception of temperature as mean kinetic molecular energy is naturalistic because molecules are spatio-temporal objects which enter into causal interactions. Frege's conception of propositions and Gödel's conception of sets are non-naturalistic because those objects are presented as abstract.

It is still possible to speak of the naturalistic fallacy as a definitional mistake, only we now have to take the definitions to be theoretical definitions rather than lexical definitions. This difference changes the nature of the error. It is no longer, as Moore thought, an attempt to analyze linguistically what is unanalyzably simple. It must now be some error in the attempt to philosophically impose naturalistic conceptions on the theories in a discipline. The crux of our explanation of the new notion of the naturalistic fallacy will be to make clear in what sense the basic notions in certain fields, although theoretically definable, are not naturalistically definable, so that the philosophical naturalist's commitment to so defining them leads to trouble. Since the trouble must have to do with the conditions on the synthetic identity of properties in theories within certain special sciences, the naturalistic fallacy, as I will construe it, is similar to other fallacies in that it arises when conditions on proper reasoning are not met.

What kind of conditions are in question in the case of such synthetic identity of properties? In the case of lexical definition, the conditions are expressed in the sense principles that determine the synonymy of the definiens and the definiendum. In the case of deductive inference, the conditions are expressed in logical principles. In the case of inductive inference, they are expressed in probability principles. Extending this line of thought, we can say that, in the case of theoretical definition, the conditions are expressed in principles for evaluating scientific theories with the theoretical definitions they contain. Thus, the conditions for the theoretical identity of properties in theories are simply the standard methodological canons for determining how well theories account for the phenomena in the domain, e.g., familiar canons like 'save the phenomena', 'do not multiply entities beyond necessity', etc. As Putnam notes, the adequacy of a theoretical definition is judged by its role in research, that is, in terms of the contribution it makes to a theory's ability to explain phenomena.[17]

Thus, methodological canons for evaluating scientific theories take the place of linguistic intuition in Moore's open-question argument. Instead of being exhibited in conflicts between a naturalistically preferred linguistic analysis and linguistic intuition, the naturalistic fallacy will be exhibited in conflicts between the naturalistically preferred theory and the scientifically best theory—when the conflicts stem from the use of naturalistic theoretical definitions. The naturalistic fallacy is, then, the violation of standard methodological principles which is implied by a commitment to naturalistically preferred theories in spite of the sacrifice of methodological canons. There is no general specification of scientific methodology on which philosophers of science agree, but in practice methodological criteria are understood well enough for us to identify the scientifically best theory as long as we stick to clear cases. We may formulate the new notion of the naturalistic fallacy as follows:

> (NF) A naturalistic fallacy is committed when philosophical considerations lead to imposing naturalistic conceptions on theories of a domain with the result that the best theories that contain those conceptions conflict with the best scientific theories of the domain.

6

There are three kinds of theories involved in my argument against philosophical naturalism. First, there are the *philosophical theories;* in the present case, we are concerned with philosophical naturalism. Second, there are the theories that translate the claim of a philosophical theory into constraints on theories in a special science. These are *metatheories.* Third, there are theories in a science on which such constraints are imposed. These are *object-theories.*

Object-theories determine ontological commitments. Quibbles side, we can say with Quine that acceptance of a theory commits us to the existence of the objects it quantifies over. That is: "Our acceptance of an ontology is . . . similar in principle to our acceptance of a scientific theory . . . we adopt, at least insofar as we are reasonable, the simplest conceptual scheme into which the disordered fragments of raw experience can be fitted and arranged."[18] However, the matter is not as straightforward as it may seem at first. What is quantified over in object-theories can depend not only on the phenomena they explain, but also on the nature of the conceptions they use in explanation, and these, in turn, can depend on a philosophical theory which sponsors certain conceptions over others. Ontological questions can be muddied by the role that philosophical theories can play in the choices of scientists with philosophical views about the nature of their subject.

Metatheories link object-theories in a special science with philosophical theories. The intervening metatheory provides a channel through which the success or failure of object-theories can be brought to bear in evaluating a philosophical theory. The metatheory imposes constraints on object-theories which reflect the philosophical theory's conception of the world. Since such constraints steer theory construction toward the philosophical theory's conception of things and away from the conceptions of competing philosophical theories, the success or failure of object-theories conforming to the constraints of a metatheory can be used to judge the adequacy of the philosophical theory whose conception of the world the metatheory expresses.

There are familiar examples of philosophical theories which provide metatheories to constrain theory construction. One is behaviorism with its various metatheories expressing constraints on the definition of mental notions in psychological theories. Another example is empiricism with its metatheories based on notions like verifiability, falsifiability, and operational definition. There are also examples in the formal sciences, such as Hilbert's nominalism with its metatheory restricting mathematical conceptions to those which are about a finite stock of discriminable expressions, and Brouwer's conceptualism with its metatheory restricting logical conceptions to those which can be based on appropriately constructable proofs.[19]

These examples also illustrate the way the success or failure of object-theories can be used to evaluate metatheories and, in turn, to evaluate a philosophical theory. If the constraints of a metatheory prove too strong for the construction of adequate object-theories, the metatheory loses creditability, and, as a consequence, the philosophical theory that sanctions the metatheory loses creditability, too. For instance, when psychological theories constructed in accord with behaviorist metatheory turned out not to handle facts reflecting relations in higher linguistic and cognitive processes, behaviorism lost creditability.[20] To take another example, it is generally felt that the viability of intuitionistic foundations of mathematics depends, in part, on whether its conceptions can account for a sufficiently wide range of entrenched classical mathematics. The view I am taking of philosophical naturalism as giving rise to metatheories for certain of the special sciences, which puts theory construction under the constraint of having to conceive of phenomena in those sciences naturalistically, is based on a familiar practice of evaluating philosophical theories.

One further observation needs to be made. The indirect assessment of a philosophical theory via the implications of the metatheories it sanctions need not wait until the object-theories formulated in accord with those metatheories are actually evaluated in the relevant sciences. Logical Empiricism illustrates this. Its claim that all nonanalytic knowledge comes from experience was translated into a number of different metatheories, presenting somewhat different notions of the relation a theory must bear to observation in order to be significant. Philosophers were able to evaluate such a metatheory by asking how faithful to the scientific facts object-theories would be in various hypothetical situations if those theories conformed to the constraints of the metatheory. Many metatheories expressing Logical Empiricism's claim about knowledge were found to impose intolerable constraints on scientific theory because the best account of the scientific facts would be precluded in a wide range of hypothetical cases.[21]

7

The argument to the effect that philosophical naturalism commits the naturalistic fallacy as defined by (NF) thus exploits a philosophical theory's responsibility for the metatheories it sanctions and a metatheory's responsibility for the object-theories that conform to its constraints. The argument would show that philosophical naturalism gives rise to metatheories whose constraints on object-theories are unreasonable in light of our commitment to the (methodologically) best scientific theories. In one sense, such an argument is straightforward. Because naturalism is a monism, it makes a general claim about the special sciences. Hence, the argument that it commits the naturalistic fallacy need only be made in connection with one special science. If it can be established that there is at least one special science where object-theories conforming to naturalistic metatheories conflict with the best scientific theories, philosophical naturalism is fallacious.

But, in another sense, setting up the argument in a special science is not straightforward. One difficulty is that, for any chosen discipline, there will, in general, be more than one naturalistic metatheory. Although naturalists might have reasons to prefer one metatheory over the others, qua naturalists, they have no more preference for one or another of the possible naturalistic metatheories than you or I have for one or another new dollar bill we might receive at the bank. Moreover, the class of available metatheories seems open-ended. Hence, a conclusive argument for (NF) has to show that, with respect to a given special science, every naturalist metatheory leads to object-theories that conflict with the best scientific theories. Otherwise conflict might be due to some inadequacy in a proper subset of metatheories and, hence, not reflect on philosophical naturalism itself. I will call this "the problem of open-endedness."

This problem, like many others in philosophy which arise from the option of reformulation, cannot be entirely solved; hence, there can be no conclusive argument for (NF). But the problem can be mitigated to the point where a forceful argument can be given against philosophical naturalism. To put this case into perspective, let us consider Logical Empiricism again. Its general claim that all nonanalytic knowledge arises from experience translates into an open set of criteria of significance for concepts in scientific theories, just as philosophical naturalism's claim that knowledge is natural knowledge translates into an open set of different constraints. But, in spite of the fact that only a small number of the possible criteria were actually shown to be wrong, the argument against Logical Empiricism was forceful enough to remove it from the philosophical scene. This example suggests that it is not necessary to deal with every possible naturalist metatheory. So long as we deal with the most plausible metatheories, our argument can still be persuasive in spite of being inconclusive.

The other difficulty is that the special science chosen for the argument has to be characterized in sufficient detail to specify the phenomena that object-theories have to account for and in sufficiently neutral a way to make the comparison of object-theories acceptable. Arguments for or against a philosophical theory in connection with a special science cannot be convincing if there is no general agreement on what phenomena fall within the boundaries of the science. There are two concerns here. One is that the chosen discipline may not be sufficiently developed for it to be clear whether certain critical facts are within its boundaries. The other, which can interact with the first, is that scientists who are developing the discipline may have a philosophical axe to grind and, as a consequence, may draw its boundaries along partisan lines; e.g., they may delimit aspects of its boundaries in a way that excludes phenomena that their object-theories have trouble handling. I will call this difficulty "the problem of delimitation."

Consider an example. In the case of logic, solving the problem of delimitation would require us to say what facts are in the domain of theories of implication. Which operators belong to logic proper? Quine would have us exclude modal operators and, hence, modal logic from "definitive science." Quine is a good example of a scientist with a philosophical axe to grind. He thinks that notions like essence, possibility, and necessity are troublesome both from a technical standpoint (in connection with quantifying in) and from a philosophical standpoint (such notions threaten to commit the logician to obscure entities).

I am not saying that interventions by scientists with a philosophical axe to grind are always illegitimate, but only that they complicate matters. Interventions do not make argument impossible because they too can be evaluated. Interventions are only as legitimate as the reasons put forth on their behalf. An intervention cannot simply stipulate that a fact does or does not belong in the domain without begging the question. Imagine a behaviorist stipulating that the only psychological facts are behavioral facts, or an American structuralist stipulating that the only grammatical facts are physical properties of the speech signal. If interventions are to count in circumscribing the subject matter of a science, they must be supported by arguments with some substance—they cannot be circular arguments that collapse when they are closely examined. In this connection, Quine's attempt to exclude modal facts from logic is instructive. Although his attempt was motivated by an aversion to essences, possibilities, and necessity, it avoided circularity by containing arguments which even his severest critics had to take seriously.

The Quine example is also instructive in showing the kind of considerations that determine the acceptability of an intervention. From the philosophical standpoint, the issue between Quine and his critics was whether his anti-modal arguments were strong enough to overcome the traditional involvement of logic with modality. In general, the criteria for the acceptability of arguments supporting an intervention is whether their reasons for excluding (or including) phenomena are strong enough to overcome the traditional involvement (or lack of involvement) of the discipline with those phenomena. If the involvement is superficial, then even a relatively weak argument can establish a delimitation of the domain excluding the phenomena, but if the involvement is deep, then there may be no argument strong enough to do so.

Such a principle is indispensable for rationally settling issues about interventions and issues about philosophical theories which turn on them. Without it, any philosophical theory can make itself secure against criticism simply by introducing appropriate delimitations of the phenomena, that is, delimitions which ensure that the discipline in question contains no phenomena that undermine the object-theories for which the philosophical theory is responsible. I shall try to show that, given such a principle, the problem of delimitation, like the problem of open-endedness, can be mitigated sufficiently to enable us to construct an argument to show that philosophical naturalism commits (NF).

8

I have postponed explicit discussion of the classical positions of *nominalism, conceptualism,* and *realism* because their relations to naturalism and non-naturalism are best appreciated after the problem of open-endedness has been presented. This is because these ontological positions determine the range of metatheories involved in the problem of open-endedness and because our discussion of the mitigation of this problem best begins with an account of how, in particular, nominalism and conceptualism expand the range of naturalistic metatheories.

Nominalism expresses the naturalistic view that the world contains no abstract objects or universals, in the form of a claim that general terms are mere vocables which come to denote things or classes of things through use. Nominalists share with other naturalists the doctrine that all the objects there are are concrete natural individuals, but the nominalist solves the problem of how generality is achieved in the application of language by making similarity of application a matter of resemblance among the referents of linguistic forms. The classical form of nominalism derives from medieval philosophers like William of Occam and modern philosophers like Hobbes and Berkeley. It differs from the doctrine that Nelson Goodman calls "nominalism", which tolerates anything in the way of individuals, including Platonic forms.[22] Hartry Field is the most vigorous contemporary proponent of nominalism.[23]

Conceptualism differs from nominalism in two ways. First, conceptualists deny that general terms are mere vocables. They claim that the mind frames concepts which are the source of generality in the application of general terms. The mind supplies the general concepts under which things are grouped together into kinds.[24] Second, conceptualists need not be naturalists. Because conceptualism *per se* adopts no specific conception of the mind or of mental concepts, it may take a naturalistic or a non-naturalistic form. A conceptualism that identifies mental objects with Cartesian substances or with souls takes a non-naturalistic or supernaturalistic form, whereas one that identifies mental objects with constructions out of physical matter takes a naturalistic form.

The first of these differences, coupled with naturalistic conceptualism, provides naturalist metatheories different from those in nominalism. Briefly, naturalists can bring their philosophical theory to bear on object-theories by imposing either nominalistic or conceptualistic constraints on them, and this choice between these two types of constraint, together with the choices in each of these types, presents the naturalist with a wide range of metatheories to choose from.

Realism is the position that there are abstract objects. Realism *per se* does not say what kinds of abstract objects there are, only that the world contains them. A realist view of an object-theory says that it is about abstract objects and that its truth consists in the abstract objects' having the properties and relations that the theory ascribes to them. Realism in this sense must be distinguished from two other positions bearing the same name. One is the anti-instrumentalist view of theories in empirical science, which holds that entities such as photons are not convenient fictions but actual objects in the physical universe. This position is clearly irrelevant to our present con- *how so?* cerns. The other is the position Hilary Putnam calls "mathematical realism."[25] On this position, a mathematical theory is true or false in virtue of something external to us, but its assertions are not about the existence of anything (especially, abstract objects). Rather, mathematical statements assert that some things are possible and others impossible. Mathematics is a form of applied modal logic. On Putnam's mathematical realism, mathematical theories are interpreted naturalistically; i.e., their modal statements are about natural objects, though they play no favorites. Since Putnam's mathematical realism is not intended to provide a contrast with naturalism, it, too, is irrelevant here. (It will, however, become relevant in another way, and we will return to it below.)

Just as there are different forms of naturalist metatheories, so there are different non-naturalist metatheories. For obvious reasons, I am taking non-naturalism exclusively in its realist form in this book, but, *and not a supernaturalistic version?* since there can be non-natural objects, such as Cartesian substances or supernatural entities, which are not abstract objects, technically speaking, there can be non-realist forms of non-naturalism. Realist non-naturalism both conflicts with naturalism and is independent of non-naturalist conceptualism and supernaturalism, insofar as it claims that abstract objects can exist without consciousness or mind, whatever its nature, and without supernatural beings. Given the nature of the argument that I am constructing against philosophical naturalism, there is no corresponding problem of open-endedness for non-naturalism. *ie problem of alternative formulations (?)*

9

Before we can mitigate the problems of open-endedness and delimitation, it is necessary to choose some special science(s) with respect *how wd.* to which to construct the argument against philosophical naturalism. *this work* I have choosen linguistics. Because of the close relation of this dis- *for history* cipline to logic and because of the role of logic in Frege's non- *or* naturalism, I will construct the argument with reference to logic as *theology* well.

are there abstract entities to be used/ analyzed by historians, indep. of mind but not supernatural?

The choice of linguistics is apropos for a number of reasons. One is that the central issue in the controversy between nominalism, conceptualism, and realism is a linguistic issue: what is at issue is the semantics of general terms. Thus it is only fitting that the linguistic claims of these doctrines be required to prove themselves in the science whose subject is language. Another reason that the choice of linguistics is apropos is that, as we have seen, Wittgenstein, Quine, and nearly every other major naturalist philosopher in twentieth-century Anglo-American philosophy based a very large part of their case against non-naturalistic metaphysics on language. But linguistics is apropos in still another respect. The two most important formative events in twentieth-century American linguistics were controversies between a nominalist and a conceptualist metatheory for grammars of natural languages. In the first, the Bloomfieldian revolution, a mentalist conception of natural language inspired by Wundtian psychology was replaced with a nominalist conception inspired by the then new Logical Empiricist school.[26] Bloomfield fashioned a nominalistic metatheory which construed the reality of natural languages as acoustic and grammars as catalogues of the distributional regularities in speech. In the second of these revolutions, the Chomskyan revolution, this nominalist conception was replaced with a more sophisticated form of mentalism. Chomsky proposed a conceptualistic metatheory on which the reality of natural languages is a matter of the psychological states of fluent speakers, and grammars are generative theories of such internal states.

These revolutions in linguistics show us something about how a philosophical theory can be translated into different metatheories. In the case of Bloomfield's metatheory, naturalism is translated into the nominalist requirement to interpret grammars as theories of co-occurrence relations among segments of speech in a corpus. In the case of Chomsky's metatheory, naturalism is translated into the conceptualist requirement to interpret grammars as theories about the psychological states that instantiate the linguistic rules children acquire in becoming fluent speakers.[27]

At the early stages of the Chomskyan revolution, it was unclear whether Chomsky's conceptualism was Cartesian or materialist.[28] But he has subsequently made it clear that his position is a materialist conceptualism in which linguistic structure has its reality in human biology, in particular, in a "language organ."[29] Thus, ignoring a possible early Cartesian phase of Chomsky's thinking, we can say that naturalism, of one form or another, has been the orthodox foundational position in American linguistics throughout this century. The choice that linguists faced during this period was between translating this position into a nominalist metatheory on which linguistic structure is a certain type of wave phenomenon or into a conceptualist metatheory on which it is psycho-biological structure.

Conceiving of linguistics as a branch of applied physics or treating it as a branch of psychology/biology are the only choices available within naturalism. They are not, however, the only choices. Logically speaking, there is also the possibility of conceiving of linguistics as a branch of mathematics, realistically conceived. In an earlier work, *Language and Other Abstract Objects*, I developed this possibility.[30] Grammars were interpreted as theories of the structure of sentences taken as abstract objects. On this view, linguistics is neither applied physics nor psychology nor biology. Rather, linguistics is an autonomous discipline which studies sentences in a way analogous to the way that mathematics studies numbers. Beyond elaborating this view, I argued that it offers linguists the advantages of nominalist and conceptualist views without their disadvantages. The rationale for taking the next step from conceptualist linguistics to realist linguistics was analogous to Chomsky's rationale for taking the step from nominalist linguistics to conceptualist linguistics. Chomsky criticized the nominalist's interpretation of grammars for confusing language with concrete phenomena of speech. I criticized the conceptualist interpretation of grammars for confusing language with concrete phenomena in the brains of speakers.[31] Chomsky's point is that Bloomfield confuses the result of exercising linguistic knowledge with the knowledge exercised; mine is that Chomsky confuses knowledge of the language with the language that it is knowledge of. If this distinction is correct, then Chomsky, too, takes grammars to be about something other than and more concrete than what is their proper object of study, i.e., the sentences that comprise the language. This, I want to claim, leads to conflict with the canons of scientific methodology.

The issue I raised in *Language and Other Abstract Objects* echoes the issue between Frege's and Husserl's realist view of logic and the conceptualist view of logic at the time. Chomsky has his logical counterparts in Lipps, Sigwart, B. Erdmann, and Wundt. The linchpin of Chomsky's conceptualism is his claim that grammars are theories of *linguistic competence*, i.e., theories of the ideal speaker-hearer's knowledge of the language. Chomsky writes:

> Linguistic theory is concerned primarily with an ideal speaker-listener, in a completely homogeneous speech community, who knows its language perfectly and is unaffected by such grammatically irrelevant conditions as memory limitations . . . in applying his knowledge of the language in actual performance.[32]

Husserl characterizes the psychologism against which he is arguing as the claim that a logic is a theory of *logical competence,* i.e., the ideal reasoner's knowledge of logical implication. Husserl writes:

> Let us imagine an ideal person, in whom *all* thinking proceeds as logical laws require. Naturally the fact that this occurs must have its explanatory ground in certain psychological laws. . . . I now ask: Would the natural laws and the logical laws in this assumed situation be one and the same?[33]

The resemblance between Chomsky's formulation of conceptualism and Husserl's is striking, but, on reflection, not all that surprising. Conceptualism, of both the linguistic and the logical variety, has naturalism as its philosophical starting point. Both psychological interpretations are motivated by the recognition that nominalist metatheories are too restrictive to provide adequate object-theories— that behavior and its physical effects constitute an insufficient basis for the representation of human cognitive potential. Both model their conception of theory on idealizations in the empirical sciences.

As Chomsky's linguistic conceptualism is akin to the logical conceptualism of Lipps, Sigwart, Erdmann, and Wundt, so my linguistic realism is akin to Frege's logical realism. I take non-naturalism as a philosophical starting point. I think human cognitive potential, regardless of how idealized, is an insufficient basis for the representation of languages and their inherent sentence-forming potential. I reject idealization, with its empirical starting point, as a suitable model for theories, modeling them instead on mathematical theories. Finally, I think that the picture of linguistic knowledge as self-knowledge mistakenly characterizes its object: linguistic knowledge is not about subjective experience or inner states, but rather about objective facts such as that "Have you a book on logic?" is an English sentence whereas "Read you a book on logic?" is not.

cf. Hegel's method of exaltation.

10

Frege characterizes logical knowledge as based on "an activity that does not create what is known but grasps what is already there. . . . it is essential for grasping that something be there which is grasped; the internal changes alone are not the grasping."[34] Like Frege's logical realism, my linguistic realism takes what is grasped to be an objective fact about abstract objects. This characterization has both descriptive and philosophical virtues, as rationalist philosophers have pointed out. On the descriptive side, the characterization seems to present the simple, unvarnished truth about how logicians, mathematicians, and linguists actually discover basic facts. The characterization seems to report their practice veridically. On the philosophical side, insofar as logical, mathematical, and linguistic truths do not depend on basic facts obtained from sense experience, it is possible to account for them as necessary truths.

The explanation of necessary truth in logic and mathematics has traditionally been the skeleton in philosophical naturalism's closet. The attractiveness of Wittgenstein's and Quine's philosophies is, I believe, due in no small measure to the fact that they do not require naturalism's empiricist epistemology to explain necessary truths. Since every philosophical theory has its skeleton, it is a mistake for naturalists to argue, as they frequently do, that the bête noire of realism is that, while it claims that what is known in logic and mathematics is based on grasping abstract objects, it does not explain how natural objects like ourselves can grasp non-natural objects. I have no desire to underplay the seriousness of this problem, but I want to make it clear that naturalists who have tried to use this problem as a knock-down argument against realism are overly optimistic about Wittgenstein's and Quine's claims to have shown that the naturalist's closet is empty. If realism must go because of its unsolved epistemological problem, then naturalism must go because of *its* unsolved epistemological problem.

It will be worthwhile to say a bit more to make clear how intractable the epistemological problem is that naturalism faces. There is no need to add anything to what has already been said about Wittgenstein's or Quine's semantic arguments against necessity. But, since some naturalists have had high hopes for Putnam's so-called mathematical realism in connection with the epistemological problem facing naturalists, let us now consider Putnam's position. If it is to be comprehensible, its assumption that mathematical statements about possibility and impossibility are true or false of natural objects must be coherently put together with its assumption that mathematical truths are necessary. But, as Putnam himself notes, this raises Hume's objection that a conclusion expressing a necessary connection cannot be derived from premises about a finite sample of actual connections.[35] Putnam does not, in fact, address this objection. Instead, he refutes Hume's positive view that necessity is a subjective matter, arguing that modal notions figure in science as objective notions and that their legitimacy cannot be reasonably challenged on the grounds that they are not among the observables.[36] Although this refutation may undercut Hume's subjectivist view of necessity, it does not get around Hume's objection. Nothing Putnam says explains how truths with the superstrength of necessity can be based on nothing more than a finite amount of contingent information about natural objects. Thus, it is just as hard *prima facie* to see how Putnam's naturalistic assumption can fit together with his assumption that mathematical truths are necessary as it is *prima facie* to see how we can grasp facts about non-natural objects like numbers.

The problem of how knowledge of necessary truth can be got from observation of the natural world is not unique to Putnam's view of mathematics. It exists for any naturalism that concedes the existence of *bona fide* necessary truth. For such a naturalism has to explain how we can get truth with the superstrength of necessity on the basis of sensory acquaintance with natural objects and inductive projection. Since naturalists have got no further with this problem than realists have with the problem of how we grasp truths about abstract objects, the proper assessment is simply that epistemology in general has not solved the philosophical problem occasioned by the fact that the natural world presents us only with contingency, while our best example of knowledge is knowledge of necessary truth in logic and mathematics.

11

We are now in a position to explain how the problems of open-endedness and delimitation can be mitigated. In the present section I will consider the problem of open-endedness. This problem presents itself in two specific forms. First, philosophical naturalism translates into nominalist as well as conceptualist metatheories for logic and linguistics. To mitigate here, we will rely on Chomsky's criticisms of linguistic nominalism to provide grounds for asserting the inadequacy of nominalist metatheories for linguistics.[37] Philosophers with the aim of showing that all the sciences can be nominalistically formulated would be well advised to acquaint themselves with the Bloomfield tradition in American linguistics and Chomsky's criticisms of it. It is hard to see how a program for formulating linguistics nominalistically could be essentially different from the program of the more sophisticated Bloomfieldians.

It is worth pointing out that Chomsky's criticisms of linguistic nominalism, if sound, undercut logical nominalism as well. This is a consequence of the need of naturalists and non-naturalists alike to provide an ontology for logic which is the same as the ontology provided for linguistics, since the objects of which logical laws hold are linguistic objects. To deny this overlap is to deny logic relevance to the inferences we make in natural languages, that is, the inferences we make in doing mathematics, logic, and everything else.

I will assume that, since we may rely on Chomsky's criticisms of nominalist metatheories in linguistics, we can confine the argument for (NF) to conceptualist metatheories.

The second form of the problem of open-endedness arises from the fact that conceptualism itself makes more than one metatheory available. To mitigate, I will introduce an umbrella doctrine covering a wide variety of psychological constraints on object-theories in linguistics and logic and expressing the basic conceptualist commitment to identifying linguistic and logical structure with psychological structure. In formulating such a doctrine, we take our cue from Chomsky's conceptualist metatheory, on which object-theories are theories of linguistic competence, but leave out the controversial features of his special notion of competence. In this way, we arrive at the following:

> Object-theories in linguistics and logic are empirical theories of the psychological or biological states that instantiate the linguistic and logical information speakers use, in the one case to speak and understand language, and in the other, to produce and comprehend deductive reasoning.

We will assume that the competence of speakers and reasoners takes the form of an idealization. In the case of linguistics, the ideal speaker knows what is necessary for linguistic communication, whatever that is, and, in the case of logic, the ideal reasoner knows what is necessary for deductive reasoning, whatever that is.[38] Thus, although a competence/performance distinction is assumed, it can be far more inclusive than Chomsky's.

Some competence/performance distinction is necessary in order to prevent every causal influence on speech and inference from becoming part of the subject matter of grammar and logic. A notion of competence distills the proper psychological states from the motley of factors encountered in empirical data, thereby preventing the study of linguistics and logic from turning out to concern such things as the belch or hiccup mechanism, brain tumors, high levels of controlled substances in the blood, etc. In serving to exclude grammatically or logically irrelevant factors, as in physics and other sciences, idealization functions to simplify the statement of laws.

12

The problem of delimitation is less difficult in the case of logic than in the case of linguistics. The parts of the boundary of logic that are disputed—for example, in connection with Quine's dissatisfactions about modality—are small, and so the delimitation of logic is sufficiently agreed on for our purposes. Thus, I will discuss only the case of linguistics.

The difficulties about delimitation in that case arise from the fact that linguistics has only recently emerged as a formal science. As a consequence, formalization and systematization have not progressed far enough to stabilize the boundaries of linguistics, in contrast with logic. Accordingly, there is comparatively wide scope for conflicting proposals about how to fix the boundaries of linguistics, even proposals that entertain removal of what have been traditional features of the discipline. Still, as we pointed out above, there is a principle that governs such interventions: delimitations that exclude central features of the discipline as traditionally understood are acceptable only if supported by arguments of sufficient strength to offset the centrality of the features.[39]

This said, it should be observed that, in fact, there is reasonable agreement on the central kinds of grammatical facts within linguistics. Linguistics has a long tradition going back to ancient Greek and Indian science. There is a substantial body of practice which circumscribes a wide range of phenomena as linguistic, providing a notion of the subject matter of grammar clear enough to specify what kind of phenomena rival object-theories of a natural language must account for. In this practice, grammar is the study of languages and the sentences belonging to them. Its aim is to discover the structure of sentences and the relations among them under which collections of sentences constitute languages.

Thus, linguistic tradition provides a relatively clear-cut picture of the kinds of facts that grammatical theories must account for, namely, facts about the grammatical structure of sentences. One kind of fact concerns the distinction between strings of words that are sentences, i.e., grammatical, and strings that are not, i.e., ill-formed. A fact of this kind is that "Have you a book on philosophy?" is a sentence of English, while "Read you a book on philosophy?" is not. Another kind of fact concerns degree of ambiguity. A fact of this kind is that "Visiting relatives can be annoying" is two ways ambiguous, in contrast to "Visiting relatives is annoying". Still other kinds of facts concern the syntactic relations within and among types of sentences. In the former case, we have the fact that "John" is the direct object in "John is easy to please" but the subject in "John is eager to please". In the latter case, we have such facts as the active and passive relation, the declarative, imperative, and interrogatory relations, etc. Examples of this kind are the relation between an active sentence like "John loves Mary" and a passive sentence like "Mary is loved by John", and the relation between "You will go", "Go!", and "Will you go?". Agreement is another kind of syntactic fact. An example is "John overlooked himself", in contrast with "John overlooked themselves". Synonymy and antonymy are two other kinds; for example, "sister" is synonymous with "female sibling", and "sighted" is antonymous with "blind". Finally, analyticity and analytic entailment are still another kind; for example, "John killed Bill" analytically entails "Bill is dead".[40]

These examples illustrate both the kinds of grammatical facts that have played a central role in the investigation of sentence structure and particular facts belonging to each kind. As with other sciences, linguistics must account for both the different kinds of facts and particular facts of each kind. The account of a kind of grammatical fact is a definition of a grammatical property or relation in terms of the structure in expressions and sentences which is necessary and sufficient if they are to have the grammatical property or relation in question. The account of a particular grammatical fact is an explanation of why some expression(s) or sentence(s) have a grammatical property or relation, in terms of an account of its (their) structure and a definition of the grammatical property or relation in question. Thus, the particular fact that "flammable" and "inflammable" are synonyms, rather than antonyms, might be explained by an account on which the former derives from the noun "flame" whereas the latter derives from the verb "inflame".

The account of particular grammatical facts corresponds to the account of particular logical facts in logical calculi; the account of kinds of grammatical facts corresponds to the account of logical concepts, e.g., consistency, in metalogic.

Accordingly, we may say that linguistics and logic seek to answer questions of the form (Q1) and (Q2):

(Q1) What are the extensions of the properties and relations P_1, . . . , P_n for English, French, Chinese, Russian, Japanese, and other natural languages?

(Q2) What are the definitions of P_1, . . . , P_n?

where in the case of linguistics P_1, . . . , P_n are properties and relations like grammaticality and synonymy, and in the case of logic P_1, . . . , P_n are properties and relations like consistency and implication.

Grammars address themselves to parts of the question (Q1), and a theory of language, or a linguistic theory (as it is also called), addresses itself to the question (Q2). Logical calculi address themselves to parts of the question (Q1), and a meta-logical theory addresses itself to (Q2). For example, a generative grammar of a language L

(which generates a set of sentences) is, *inter alia*, an answer to the question 'What is the extension of the property of grammaticality in *L*?'. Corresponding examples in logic are familiar.

13

On the basis of this sketch of what sort of facts grammars and logical calculi explain and what sort linguistic theories and metalogics explain, we can specify the notion 'the best scientific theory' as used in our formulation of (NF) as follows:

> The best scientific theory is the theory that accounts for the widest range of facts in the domain in the most methodologically satisfactory manner (i.e., with the least apparatus, etc.).[41]

Given this specification, it might seem as if we could show that conceptualism in linguistics and logic commits the naturalistic fallacy by showing that the best psychological theories of these domains diverge from the optimal scientific theory.[42] The best theory of the English speaker's psychogrammar will say that some complex property *G* expresses the empirical truth about linguistic competence in English, and, correspondingly, the best psychological theory of human reasoners will say that some complex property *L* expresses the empirical truth about human logical competence. Conceptualism claims that the empirically true theory of competence in English, *T(G)*, is the best conception of English and that the empirically true theory of competence in logic, *T(L)*, is the best conception of implication. At this point, we can ask, echoing Moore, whether *T(G)* and *T(L)* are the best scientific theories for linguistics and logic. In the present context, this amounts to asking whether *T(G)* is the proper basis for answering the grammatical questions in (Q1) and (Q2) and whether *T(L)* is the proper basis for answering the logical questions in (Q1) and (Q2). Is well-formedness in the sense of *T(G)* a satisfactory conception of grammaticality in English? Is inference in the sense of *T(L)* a satisfactory conception of implication? If we can find reason to answer such a question in the negative, we have reason to think that the theories having the most going for them as psychology diverge from the theories having the most going for them as linguistics and logic.

Let us consider an argument of this form. Recently, Chomsky has acknowledged that the phenomenon of analytic entailment falls within the scope of grammar. He writes: ". . . I agree with Katz that certain analytic connections exist among linguistic expressions, certain truths hold solely by virtue of linguistic facts; for instance, the relation between 'I persuade him to leave' and 'He intends to leave'."

Chomsky also writes: "The statement that to persuade John to do something is to cause him to intend to do that thing is necessarily true. It is true by virtue of the meaning of its terms, independently of any facts; it is an 'analytic truth' in technical jargon."[43] But since a theory of the speaker's linguistic competence is an empirical theory of the mind/brain and since the mind/brain is a contingent object, the mental/neural relations that have to be meant by "analytic connections" in the case at hand are contingent and could be otherwise. But, if so, a conceptualist will have to say that it is not necessary that the sentence "He intends to leave" be true whenever the sentence "I persuade him to leave" is true, and that the sentence "To persuade John to do something is to cause him to intend to do that thing" is not necessarily true. Therefore, the conceptualist construal of theories of human linguistic competence as theories of the language contradicts Chomsky's recent acknowledgments about analytic sentences and analytic entailments. Since these acknowledgments are, in effect, the concession that the best scientific theory of English says that such analytic statements are necessary and analytic entailments are valid, the construal can be taken to conflict with the best scientific theory of English.[44]

Although this argument is a problem for Chomsky, other conceptualists might evade it by embracing a position like his earlier one on which alleged analytic connections are part of general knowledge outside of sentence grammar. Conceptualists might be willing to go along with Quine in denying that there are necessary truths. Faced with such a move on the part of conceptualists, the natural response would be to try to restate the argument in terms of some other grammatical property or relation. But once we move to some other grammatical property or relation, there is a problem. The beauty of analyticity and analytic entailment is that an argument using them requires only the triviality that facts about the psychology of human beings are contingent facts in order to exhibit a contradiction. Once we move to other grammatical properties and relations, we require significant knowledge about human psychology which puts us in the position of having to rely on the best available theory of the ideal speaker's knowledge of English. The problem is not that there is no satisfactory psychological theory available at present or foreseeable in the future, though that is certainly true. It is that such a theory would do us no good even if it were available. Even if there were a theory in psychology as irresistible as the best in physics, we still couldn't use it in our argument because the argument would then falsify the linguistic naturalist's position as effectively as Moore's open-question argument falsifies the ethical naturalist's. Linguistic naturalists, qua naturalists, no more claim that some particular psychological theory is correct than ethical naturalists, qua naturalists, claim that some particular definition of a moral concept is correct. Qua naturalists, they commit themselves to the claim that grammars are theories of psychological states, but not to anything about the details of such empirical states. The point might be put by saying that if God were to tell us only that true object-theories in linguistics are theories of psychological states, naturalists could immediately claim victory—they would not have to wait around to hear more.

Since the same considerations apply in the case of logical naturalism as well, we cannot employ an argument that ties the fate of linguistic and logical naturalism to the empirical fate of particular psychological theories, no matter how good the theories might look on present evidence. But this generality of linguistic and logical naturalism in itself suggests a way of arguing that they commit the naturalistic fallacy (NF). Recall that these positions are philosophical theories concerning the nature of linguistics and logic. They specify classes of metatheories which, in turn, impose particular constraints of one psychological sort or another on object-theories in these special sciences. Thus, linguistic and logical naturalism are, as it were, two levels up from the empirical psychological theories themselves. As a consequence, both those philosophical theories and their metatheories are chosen behind a "veil of ignorance" about the empirical truth.[45] Once the philosophical theories have specified metatheories that allow only object-theories about psychological phenomena, they have had their say. The question of choosing an optimal metatheory, e.g., a nominalist one or a conceptualist one, is a further question; they say nothing for or against any particular metatheories, much less any particular object-theories that fall under the constraints of those metatheories. Hence, by their nature, linguistic and logical naturalism *can play no favorites* with respect to empirical theories of the psychology of speakers and reasoners.

Although linguistic and logical naturalists do not claim that grammatical structure and logical structure are this or that kind of facet of human psychology, they do claim that they are a facet of human psychology *whatever human psychology might turn out empirically to be*. Since they are betting that the best empirical theories of linguistic and logical competence are the best grammars of natural languages and the best theory of implication, no matter what the empirical facts might turn out to be, we can call their bet on the basis of possibilities concerning what human linguistic and logical competence might be. We can argue that linguistic and logical conceptualists lose their bet that the best empirical theories of the psycho-grammar or psycho-logic inside people's heads are the best grammar of a language and the best logic.

We will argue this by running our own "open-question argument." First, we fix the optimal psychological theories $T(G)$ and $T(L)$ on the basis of an assumption about the psycho-grammar and psycho-logic inside people's heads. We can then pose the questions 'Is English grammar G?' and 'Is logic L?' If we like, we can make these questions more specific by asking about a consequence of $T(G)$ or $T(L)$ for some particular property like grammaticality or logical truth. Such questions ask whether the set of optimal theories of the language contains $T(G)$ and the set of optimal theories of logic contains $T(L)$. Finally, to answer these questions, we determine the optimal scientific theories with respect to the linguistic and logical facts and scientific methodology. There is a naturalistic fallacy if $T(G)$ or $T(L)$ is not among the scientifically optimal theories, that is, if $T(G)$ is incompatible with the optimal theories of English with respect to its consequences for some grammatical properties or relations in $P_1, \ldots, P_n$ or if $T(L)$ is incompatible with the optimal theories of logical implication with respect to its consequences for some logical properties and relations $P_1, \ldots, P_n$.

I will present two cases of such incompatibility. The first is one in which the conflict between conceptualist theories and best scientific theories arises with respect to simplicity. It is possible that human linguistic and logical competence represents some information redundantly. (Redundancy might well be functional, achieving heuristic advantages over corresponding more concise systems.) For example, there might be more formal operations than required for formulating certain syntactic rules. Rules that move symbols around can be formulated with the two operations of copying a symbol in a new position and deleting it from the old position, but also with a single operation of permutation. Since any rule that can be formulated with permutation can be formulated as well with copying and deletion, a psycho-grammar using all three operations will involve redundancy.

However, from the perspective of the study of human linguistic competence and language processing, the existence of a psycho-grammar containing cases of all three operations of symbol movement is simply an empirical fact. A theory of the psycho-grammar which does not represent all three would be like a model of human physiology that does not represent both kidneys. But a grammar of English that employs all three operations is uneconomical, since any of the grammatical properties and relations $P_1, \ldots, P_n$ of English sentences which are accounted for with all three operations can be more simply accounted for with only copying and deletion operations. Since the accounts are otherwise identical, the simpler account is preferable, by Occam's razor, and hence, is the best scientific theory of English. Thus, put forth as a theory of English, the best theory of the psycho-grammar of English speakers conflicts with the best scientific theory of the language.

Similar examples are available in the case of logic. It is possible that human logical competence in propositional inference involves distinct psycho-operators not only for negation, disjunction, conjunction, material implication, and material equivalence, but for all other sentential operators as well. Such a psycho-logic might well offer heuristic advantages over one having only Sheffer's stroke, but it offers no logical advantages over it. Again, a logical competence with superfluity of inference rules might offer heuristic advantages over one equivalent in logical power, but it would offer no logical advantages over the more parsimonious system. Thus, put forth as a theory of propositional logic, the best empirical theory of the psycho-logic in our heads conflicts with the best scientific theory of propositional logic.

The second case I want to consider is one in which the conflict between the best theory of competence and the best scientific theory arises with respect to truth, so that the former makes false predictions about English or about implication. Now it might seem on the face of it that such a case is impossible. How could the ideal speaker of English be wrong about the grammatical structure of English, or the ideal reasoner wrong about implication? It might seem as if, *by definition*, they could not be. But a closer look at the nature of idealization shows that it is perfectly coherent to have a notion of an ideal speaker who is wrong about aspects of the language and a notion of an ideal reasoner who is wrong about certain implications.

The notions of an ideal speaker and reasoner are idealizations from actual speakers and reasoners in the same way that the notion of an ideal gas is an idealization from actual gases. An idealization in science eliminates aspects of a phenomenon which would complicate the statement of laws and theories, but does not change the nature of the phenomenon. Just as an idealization of mechanical phenomena removes friction or smoothes out unevenness in a surface, so the competence idealization filters out performance factors, thereby adjusting for idiolectical differences among speakers, discounting memory limitations, etc. But idealization cannot change the system inside the speaker's head from a system of the sort it is to a system of another kind. If it changed the basic nature of actual phenomena, it wouldn't be an idealization *of* the phenomena.

Thus, to say that a representation is an idealization of a phenomenon is to say no more nor less than that it is a representation of the phenomenon in which it is made to assume an ideal form. Idealization of the mechanical yields an ideal mechanical; idealization of the mental yields an ideal mental. The ideal speaker and the ideal reasoner are, therefore, ideal only in the sense of having a perfect form of a particular kind of actual human competence, that is, a form free of the adulterations that obscure its character, e.g., in the way that memory limitations obscure the recursive character of syntactic rules. The notion of an ideal speaker is a perfection of the kind 'actual human speaker,' and the notion of an ideal reasoner is a perfection of the kind 'actual reasoner'.

Now to see how the ideal speaker and the ideal reasoner could have false beliefs, consider the analogous case of human geometrical knowledge. It is plausible that the geometrical competence on which our sensory and motor skills depend is Euclidean. But, being perfect knowledge of Euclidean space, the psycho-geometry inside human heads does not capture the structure of actual space—though it approximates closely enough to that structure to guide behavior within the range of everyday experience. Thus, put forth as a theory of actual space, an optimal theory of our geometrical competence makes predictions inconsistent with those of the best scientific theory of actual space. That is, in virtue of being a true theory of our psycho-geometry, it makes false statements about physical space outside the range of everyday experience.

In the same way, the ideal speaker's competence can be wrong about the language, and the ideal logician's competence could be wrong about implication. Consider a linguistic case parallel to this geometrical case. It is possible that the human mind is innately programmed to organize linguistic experience in the form of a huge finite list of sentential paradigms, one for each of the English sentences $S_1, \ldots, S_n$. The speaker's psycho-grammar is such a finite list of paradigms, where each paradigm contains a specification of the phonological, syntactic, and semantic structure of the sentence to which it corresponds. Let n be so large that there is a paradigm on the list for every sentence that could actually occur in speech or writing. Thus, the psycho-grammar will enable speakers to produce and understand novel sentences, i.e., sentences they haven't as yet encountered, since any encountered sentence will be short enough to fall within the range of linguistic experience.

Since the facts on which a science bases its choice of a best theory must derive from observations of sentences that are short enough to be encountered in experience, the conditions for choosing a best theory in this possible case are the same as the conditions in actual cases. Since the supposition that speakers of English have such a list-psycho-grammar changes nothing about the conditions under which a best scientific theory of English is chosen, the same theory would be chosen as the best scientific theory of English in the hypothetical case as is chosen in actual cases. That is to say, linguists will make the same straightforward inductive projection to an infinity of English sentences from a sample of English sentences which exhibit recursive sentence construction. For example, observing the regularity that, for any well-formed sentence S_i, we get another well-formed sentence S_j when S_i is prefixed by "I know that" or the regularity that, for any well-formed sentence S_i of the appropriate type, we get another well-formed sentence S_j when S_i is conjoined with "Snow is white", the linguist generalizes the recursive process and projects an infinite class of well-formed English sentences. Hence, in the possible case, too, the linguist projects an infinite class of well-formed English sentences.

Thus, the best scientific theory of English in our hypothetical case predicts that there is no longest English sentence. But since the true theory of the English speaker's psycho-grammar predicts that there is a longest English sentence, the theory conceptualists put forth as the best theory of English, in virtue of reflecting the psychological truth about the competence of English speakers, is inconsistent with the best scientific theory of English.

This case automatically carries over to logic by putting propositions in place of sentences.

Consider another kind of example. It is possible that the human mind is innately programmed to extrapolate from experience on the basis of a system of grue-like predicates.[46] The speaker's knowledge of English or of implication would then consist of rules that assign grammatical or logical descriptions reflecting observed regularities to sentences of length n or less, but descriptions reflecting grue-like departures for sentences longer than n. Again, n may be taken to be so large that nothing in linguistic experience suggests that our innate learning mechanism is making grue-like projections. Thus, given the present state of psychology/neuroscience, we have no inkling that, in the case of sentences longer than n, the rules of the psycho-grammar and the psycho-logic assign sentences to semantic and logical categories in essentially arbitrary ways; e.g., sentences that are ambiguous would be represented as unambiguous, sentences that are synonymous would be represented as nonsynonymous, sentences that express logical truths would not be represented as such, sentences would be assigned to the wrong consequence sets, etc.

Again, the conditions under which scientists choose a best theory in the hypothetical case are the same as those in actual cases, and, hence, they will extrapolate semantic or logical theories in the standard inductive way: rules for the assignment of expressions and sentences to semantic and logical categories will be straightforward generalizations from regularities in sentences encountered in experience. Thus, the best scientific theories make predictions about semantic and logical properties and relations of sentences longer than *n* which are incompatible with the predictions of the theories that the conceptualist puts forth as the best theories of properties and relations in these sentences. Hence, here too there is conflict between the best scientific theory and the best conceptualist theory.

I don't follow this argument that support this in philos.

G. E. Moore asks whether what is before our mind when we question a naturalistic definition of "good" or "right" is an open or a closed (self-answered) question. We asked whether the theoretical definitions of linguistic and logical properties and relations which naturalistic metatheories allow are the best scientific conceptions of them. As a consequence, our naturalistic fallacy is a matter of the inconsistency of the best naturalistic conceptions of the phenomena in certain disciplines with the best scientific conceptions of those phenomena. Instead of appealing to linguistic intuition to show that the philosophical naturalist is trying to define indefinably simple notions, our argument appeals to scientific methodology to show that philosophical naturalists lose their presumptive bet on the naturalistic definability of linguistic and logical properties and relations because their definitions cannot be naturalistically constrained in the general case without being scientifically deficient in particular cases. To put the point another way, philosophical naturalism commits a fallacy because, in imposing metatheories requiring that the best empirical theories of competence be *ipso facto* taken as the best scientific theories, it closes options for theory construction which scientific methodology obliges us to leave open.

14

In this section, I consider a number of responses that might be made to the argument that philosophical naturalism commits the naturalistic fallacy.

Call Foul
This move claims that my argument employs a question-begging distinction between 'linguistic' and 'psychological' facts in determining the best theory of English because it restricts attention to grammatical

facts about well-formedness, ambiguity, grammatical relations, etc. This is not the case. Certainly I think of such facts as linguistic, but linguistic naturalists, for their part, think of them as linguistic too, though, of course, they also think of them as psychological, which I do not.

This point can perhaps be made clearer by distinguishing *linguistics proper* from the *foundations of linguistics*.[47] The former is principally concerned with formally systematizing the facts about the structure of sentences in individual natural languages and natural language in general, whereas the latter is concerned with philosophically explaining the nature of such facts. The distinction is analogous to the distinction between mathematics proper and the foundations of mathematics. The systematization can go on without knowledge of or agreement on what kinds of things these facts are facts about. The sorts of facts I used in section 12 to determine the best theory of English are central to traditional linguistics and widely accepted in contemporary linguistics. The determination itself, although part of an argument within the foundations of linguistics, assumed nothing outside of linguistics proper.

Now the complaint that my argument begs the question is also based on the claim that I don't consider psycho-linguistic facts to be on a par with the facts I consider linguistic, that I have ignored facts about the relevant states of a speaker's mind/brain. This is not so. In the cases considered, it was shown that the best account of those facts presents a picture of English sentence structure incompatible with the picture of it that we get from the facts about the grammar of English sentences. If we imagine ourselves taking both sets of facts under consideration together, the result would be the same, since this incompatibility would then appear as an obstacle to obtaining a coherent theory of the combined set of facts. When we try to include both in a common theory of English, we would find the systematization of one set irreconcilable with that of the other.

It Can't Happen Here

This move denies that the best theory of the psycho-grammar or the psycho-logic could take an uneconomical form, or the form of a list, or contain rules employing grue-like predicates, or have any form that conflicts with the best scientific theory. But what force is there to this denial? The reason for the claim cannot be that the cases used in the argument are impossible, for even the cases of a world in which there exists no English psycho-grammar and no psycho-logic are possible. Nothing weaker would support an attempt to block the argument for the naturalistic fallacy. Moreover, the claim cannot be inferred from the philosophical naturalist's *a priori* identification of the theory of a natural language with a theory of the competence of its speakers, since that identification is precisely what has been challenged. Nor can it be inferred from an empirical identification, since the necessary information for such an identification is not available behind the veil of ignorance.

Bite the Bullet
This move claims that the object-theories conforming to conceptualist metatheory are acceptable in spite of what appears to be stubble untrimmed by Occam's razor, or a conflict with the inductive projection that, for every sentence, there is a longer one, or arbitrary assignments of English expressions to grammatical categories for indefinitely many sentences. In connection with the case where the psycho-grammar is found to be a finite list of sentential paradigms, one linguistic conceptualist suggested to me that the proper response for linguistic conceptualists is to say that this proves that there is a longest English sentence and then to claim credit for a great scientific discovery.[48]

Presumably, this means that conceptualists also wish to take credit in the grue-predicates case for discovering that structure dependence breaks down in the megasentences of English. Here, however, it seems clear that the bullet is just too hard to bite, since it means accepting crazy categorizations for English megasentences. Typical of such categorizations would be assignments like "ruthlessly" to the category preposition, "cabbage" and "dust" to the extension of the synonymy relation, and "bear" and "silver" to the extension of the rhyme relation. Also grammars would mark constituents inconsistently, e.g., "cabbage" and "dust" as nonsynonymous and synonymous, and "bear" and "silver" as nonrhyming and rhyming. Since crazy categorizations like these would clearly finish any grammar of English containing them in the case of sentences of standard lengths, how can they be tolerated in the case of sentences that are simply longer? How can a difference in the length of the sentence matter? It can't. Marking ungrammaticality grammatical or grammaticality ungrammatical is no more acceptable when it occurs in connection with sentences of one length than when it occurs in connection with sentences of another length. The length of a sentence cannot in and of itself be an excuse for false or inconsistent predictions.

Given that all sentences are on a par with respect to their potential to serve as confirming or disconfirming evidence, the predictions of the theory of the psycho-grammar in the case of megasentences must count against it in both of the other cases as well—no matter how good a face the linguistic naturalist tries to put on it. But if excessive apparatus and conflict with inductive projection count against it as a theory of English, the only recourse for the conceptualist that scientific methodology offers is to plead in extenuation that there is no better theory of English available. This plea cannot be made in the present circumstances, since there is a theory of English which is more economical and which, if anything, handles the observed facts better.

Join the Intuitionists

Another possible move in the finite-list-grammar case is for the conceptualist-linguist to adopt a position analogous to the position of the intuitionist in mathematics and logic. Chomsky himself has drawn the analogy between the intuitionist views of Brouwer, Heyting, and Dummett and his own views about grammar.[49] Presumably, Chomsky is suggesting that, just as intuitionists think there is a number n just in case it has been constructed, so he thinks there is a sentence S_n just in case it has been constructed, and, consequently, there is no actual infinity of numbers or sentences, merely a potential infinity. Let us look at such a position.

There are two intuitionist positions in mathematics and logic, and linguistic conceptualists who go this route must choose one as their model. One is the position of A. S. Yessenin-Volpin, as commonly understood, on which there are only finitely many objects in the domain of arithmetic. Yessenin-Volpin denies that arithmetic is about the numbers, claiming instead that it is about what he calls "the series F of *feasible* numbers, i.e., of those numbers up to which it is possible to count."[50] He thus denies that there is a number series containing 10^{12}. Linguists who choose this model have to say that English grammar is about what, in analogy, we might call "the series F' of *feasible* sentences, i.e., those which can actually be produced in speech" (or perhaps those for which there is a paradigm in the list-psycho-grammar). Thus, correspondingly, they deny that there are sentences of English of the length 10^{12}.

I think one would be hard pressed to find a more counterintuitive position. Our notion of a well-formed sentence is one on which well-formedness is a purely structural notion, having to do with syntactic relations among sentential constituents. Ill-formedness arises when such relations are not what they are grammatically required to be. Thus, as long as such relations remain undisturbed, we can always increase the length of a sentence by adding a modifier or conjoining the sentence with another: length increases cannot *per se* disturb the relations on which well-formedness depends. Furthermore, a linguistic position based on the Yessenin-Volpin model would have essentially the same difficulty that has led to the widespread rejection of ultra-intuitionism in the foundations of mathematics. The difficulty is that abandonment of mathematical induction would leave mathematics without a well-defined concept of number. Moreover, arithmetic, then being about a subseries of the numbers, seems hardly to be mathematics in the true sense. Correspondingly, the linguistic counterpart of Yessenin-Volpin's position, abandoning induction too, would leave linguistics without a well-defined concept of sentence, and such a linguistics would hardly be linguistics in the true sense.

Linguistic conceptualists who choose to model their position on the more conventional form of intuitionism can say that there is a potential infinity of sentences. But this position incurs another set of problems, namely, those concerning the intuitionist's conception of logical and mathematical truth. For the notion of potentiality has to be cashed in terms of what it is possible for us to prove. Of course, the intuitionist need not hold that logical and mathematical truth is relativized to actual achievements or to the capacities of particular mathematicians. As Dummett points out, the relativization can be to what the human mathematical community can, in principle, prove.[51] But this does not help. Since we are mortal as a collectivity, too, it merely substitutes collective human contingency for individual human contingency.

The problem is that, since, even on Dummett's improvement, intuitionism sacrifices the idea that logical and mathematical truth are independent of us, the position relativizes logical and mathematical truth in a way that forfeits objectivity and necessity. How can logical and mathematical truth be relative to human proof capacities without the existence and nature of logical and mathematical objects and facts being dependent on the existence and nature of the creatures with those capacities? How can logical and mathematical truth be necessary if logic and mathematics thus share in our contingency? Of course, this will not seem much of a sacrifice to philosophers who have Wittgensteinian or Quinean reasons for thinking there is no absolute (e.g., community-independent) objectivity and necessity. But, presumably, except for such reasons, those philosophers, like the rest of us, think that doing justice to mathematics and logic requires us to recognize the objectivity and necessity of their truths. Thus, if this book shows that the reasons that Wittgenstein and Quine have given are inadequate, the sacrifice is too great.

Moreover, Dummett's improvement in the relativization does not get around the other facets of the subjectivity problem. For example, corresponding to how relativization to individual mathematicians makes proof variable with respect to differences among individuals, relativization to the human community would make proof variable with respect to differences among (human and other) communities. Imagine a community of Martian mathematicians. The Martians, whose proof capacities are greater than ours, can, in principle, prove things that human mathematicians cannot. But, now, consider a mathematical proposition that they can prove, but we cannot, i.e., a proposition that is within their proof capacities but beyond ours. Is the proposition true for them but untrue for us? What about propositions that we can prove and they can refute? For Dummett's intuitionist, there is no higher law than the combined resources of a community, and, hence, nothing precludes the situation where p is a theorem (provable in community A) and not-p is a theorem (provable in community B). Suppose that (owing to space travel) the communities merge; which is the truth in the new melting-pot community? If the community with its internal logical inconsistency is irrational overall, nothing has really been accomplished by trading in individualistic relativism for community relativism.

It might be tempting to say that p rather than not-p is the truth for the melting-pot community because p was proved by the smarter members of the community. But we cannot say that those who write out derivations of p are the smarter ones without begging the question. Notions like proof and smartness presuppose logic as a criterion. Which logic serves as the criterion here? If there is no higher logical law and the two logics are inconsistent, it is circular to assume those using p-logic are writing out genuine proofs and are actually the smartest.

Quibble
Another move runs as follows: Your argument does not address the position it should address because the notion of competence that it uses to formulate Chomsky's metatheory is weaker than Chomsky's own notion. His notion is that of the ideal speaker's *perfect* knowledge of the language.[52] You have left out the all-important qualification 'perfect'. On a properly formulated version of the conceptualist metatheory for linguistics, no system can be perfect if it fails to account for more than a proper subset of the infinitely many sentences of the language, nor can any system constitute knowledge if it falsely predicts semantic or logical properties.

The crux of this move is to replace the notion of an idealization of actual competences with that of a representation of the language as the thing to which the qualification 'perfect' applies. Thus, applying the qualification no longer gives us the notion 'perfect form of human psycho-grammar' (i.e., the notion of the perfection of a kind), but yields instead the notion 'perfection qua knowledge of the language' (i.e., the truth, the whole truth, and nothing but the truth about it). Putting aside the question of whether this move distorts Chomsky's own position, it is clear that the move is self-defeating because the replacement concedes the existence of an external, psycho-grammar-independent language whose faithful representation is what perfect knowledge consists in. If there were no language beyond a psycho-grammar inside our heads, it would make no sense to speak of faithful representation.

Furthermore, the move doesn't help. The revision of the notion of competence simply makes it a necessary condition on competence that the speaker's information be perfectly true (with respect to the language). Instead of improving the situation for the linguistic conceptualist, the introduction of this necessary condition leads to an equally strong objection in the cases considered, since the psycho-grammar and the psycho-logic in those cases turn out to be false (with respect to the language). The objection is now that speakers have no competence. Object-theories in linguistics and logic which are framed in terms of this replacement are about nothing. But, since optimal theories of English are about English sentences and optimal theories of implication are about implication relations, we can still draw the conclusion that no theories that conform to the conceptualist's meta-theory are among the best scientific theories.

Try Levels

It might be claimed that generalization can do what idealization cannot. The conceptualist might argue that there are various levels of generality at which theories of a phenomenon may be developed. Those called "psycho-linguistic" and "psycho-logical" are close to the empirical phenomena, while those we call "linguistic" and "logical" are at a higher level of generality. As we ascend, features of the phenomena that are significant at lower levels drop out. Thus, at the level of competence, performance factors drop out, and, at the level of grammar or logic, features reflecting the peculiar characteristics of human psychology drop out. But theories at higher levels are about the same empirical phenomena as theories at the lowest.

But why suppose that theories at higher levels are about the empirical phenomena at the lowest level? If empirical constraints applying to theories at the lower, psychological level are removed at the highest level, there is no longer any reason for taking the theories at the highest level to be about something empirical. What content can there be in the claim that the grammars and logical calculi at the highest level are empirical, psychological theories when those theories are under no empirical or psychological constraints?[53] Rather than supporting conceptualism, this move saws off the limb on which it sits.

The argument was clearly too good to be true. If such a conception of levels worked in the present case, naturalistic philosophers of mathematics could show that talk about sets is nothing but talk about physical things, simply by stipulating a hierarchy with physics at the bottom and set theory at the top.

The Argument from Miracles

A conceptualist might argue as follows: Why worry about what goes wrong in possible cases? It's the actual case that counts, and nothing has been established about psycho-grammars and psycho-logics in it. We conceptualists are betting that psycho-grammars and psycho-logics in the actual world coincide with the best scientific theories in linguistics and logic. That is our faith. Yours is that they do not. This is the real issue, and *a priori* arguments won't settle it.

Given the pressures on the human psycho-grammars and psycho-logics to take a form suitable to their role in speech production and comprehension, it would be a miracle if the true theories of these psychological objects were to coincide with theories of sentence structure and implication shaped by none of those pressures.[54] Still, such a miracle might happen. Insofar as the cases on which my argument turns are mere possibilities, nothing derived from them bears on what is actually true of English speakers or of reasoners. Hence, nothing in my argument implies that there couldn't be such a coincidence. But the conceptualist is mistaken in thinking that the issue is whether speakers and reasoners actually have inside their heads something which coincides with grammars and logics. As far as the issue with which we are concerned here goes, non-naturalists could take the same side as conceptualists in the bet about coincidence.

The argument from miracles confuses the issue of philosophical naturalism, with which we are concerned here, with the issue of scientific naturalism, with which we are not. The former concerns whether there can be a philosophical, hence, *a priori*, argument that the conception of theories proper for linguistics and logic represents them as theories of psychological states. In contrast, the latter concerns whether the objects in the world are all natural objects. The former primarily involves philosophical theories and their meta-theories, and depends on philosophical argument; the latter is primarily about object-theories, and depends on scientific investigation. Particular instances of the issue of scientific naturalism can be put as questions of theoretical identity within one or another special science.

Thus, it might be asked within linguistics, or logic, whether the objects in the domain of linguistics, or logic, can, given what is known about them in these disciplines, be identified with certain objects in the domain of psychology. My argument for a naturalistic fallacy does not address this question at all.

Since the issue concerning scientific naturalism is a question of theoretical identity, the argument from miracles is immediately forfeit. According to the argument's version of the conceptualist's bet, the bet makes sense only if we do not take the question of philosophical naturalism to be already settled in favor of conceptualism. For, if theories 𝓁 in linguistics and logic have been philosophically shown to be psychological theories, there is only one kind of object-theory, not the two kinds which are required to raise the question of identification. What question of identity is there for Chomsky, who starts out with a philosophical position that defines a grammar as a psychological theory? Since those who use the argument from miracles take there to be a genuine question of theoretical identity for the science in question, they must agree with me that there is no prior demonstration that linguistic and logical theories are psychological theories. Thus, the argument from miracles, instead of replying to my criticism of philosophical naturalism, actually seems to concede its conclusion that psychological theories and theories in linguistics and logic are not philosophically identifiable.

15

I have tried to establish that philosophical naturalism is fallacious because its metatheories preclude the best scientific theories. This means that the claim of scientific naturalism cannot be supported philosophically and, consequently, cannot be used in philosophical arguments in the ways that some philosophers have tried to use it. It does not, of course, mean that scientific naturalism's claim that there is nothing in the world but natural objects is false, but shows only that naturalism is in a sense no longer a philosophical issue. The issue becomes an issue in the special sciences, where there is a choice between object-theories free of ontological commitment to the existence of abstract objects and object-theories with such commitments. In this section, I would like to consider a reason for thinking that linguistics is committed to abstract objects and a recent attempt to show that there is no such commitment.

If the history of the Chomskyan revolution has shown one thing, it is that it is hopeless for linguistics to take the sentences of natural language to be concrete acoustic events produced in speech.

Chomsky and the other critics of American structuralism established beyond doubt that the theoretical goals of linguistics cannot be achieved if sentences are construed as utterances. This is not to say that sentence tokens play no role in linguistic investigation, but to say rather that they are not the objects that grammars are theories of.

Even without these criticisms, it is easy to see that tokens are not the objects grammars are theories of. Recall from chapter 2 C. S. Peirce's distinction between linguistic types and tokens. It is "the" in the type sense, that is, the unique "the", which is the object of study in grammatical investigations of the role of the definite article in sentence structure. The focus on linguistic types is what provides linguistics with a common, enduring subject matter from one linguist to another and from one blackboard cleaning to the next. Moreover, the attempt to obtain such a subject matter by identifying sentences with sets of linguistic tokens is known to fail, first, because the use of sets is self-defeating unless we have some way of understanding set theory without commitment to abstract entities, and, second, because only a comparatively few sentences are fated to have tokens, so that the basic laws about the structure of sentences break down.[55]

Given that linguists study sentences in the type sense, the objects of their study, as Peirce observes, cannot "lie visibly on a page or be heard in any voice." Just as sentences can have no spatial location, they can have no temporal location, either. It is just as impossible for the English sentence "Flying planes can be dangerous" to have a location in time (e.g., to occur sometime during the first day of the year 2000 A.D.) as it is for that sentence to be located in space (e.g., at Times Square in New York City). Furthermore, sentences cannot have causal properties. Unlike their tokens, they can neither break fragile crystal nor be produced by the movements of the vocal apparatus. But if sentences in the type sense are outside time and space and are causally inert, they are *by definition* abstract objects.[56] Hence, once we recognize that the objects of study in linguistics are types, it follows immediately that linguistics is about abstract objects, that is, that all grammars in linguistics quantify over abstract objects. Since we may assume that some of those theories are true, there are abstract objects, and, therefore, scientific naturalism is false.

In a recent article Sylvain Bromberger has argued that it is still possible to claim that the study of linguistics is about human psychology, even conceding that linguistics in the sense of the synchronic study of sentence structure is about abstract objects.[57] He tries to show that this concession is compatible, on the one hand, with the view that information about sentence types is obtained from information about sentence tokens and, on the other, with the view that the linguist's knowledge of the properties of sentence types is obtained from facts about "people's mental makeup." Let us consider these attempts in turn.

Bromberger says initially that information about types comes from "attending to one's senses" (ibid., p. 58). This seems to be a lapse. One might, in principle, obtain all the information necessary for constructing a grammar of one's language with eyes closed and ears plugged up, simply by attending to one's own linguistic intuitions. Bromberger presumably disagrees with Platonists who think that intuition presents us with types themselves; he presumably thinks that the sentences presented to us in linguistic intuition are tokens within the mind and that intuition is merely another sense. Let us accept this for the sake of argument, noting, however, that Platonists will think that Bromberger begs the question at the very outset.

Bromberger's idea is that, for the cases where types have tokens, the information that a type T has property P must be obtained from observing that tokens of T have P. (Information about the properties of types that do not have tokens can be inferred from the structure of the concept space to which those types belong on the basis of hypotheses obtained from observing tokens of other types in the space and of reasoning about mental things; ibid., p. 85). This route to knowledge of the properties of types, as Bromberger sees it, is secured, in part, by requiring that tokens of a type share a fixed set of properties which are also the properties of the type (ibid., pp. 62–73). Properties of types are thus properties of their tokens promoted from exemplifier to exemplified.

There are two problems with this idea. One is that it seems to assume a "bottom-up" conception of grammatical properties. From a "top-down" approach like that in chapter 2, it can be objected that the grammatical properties that empiricists (see chapter 8) take to be observed in tokens (to be inherent in them) are really properties of the types that have been associated with those acoustic events in the process of categorizing them as tokens of types. The "top-down" approach denies that sound waves and piles of chalk, ink, etc. have any grammatical properties in and of themselves. This denial is supported by the fact that utterances (and inscriptions) in themselves can be physically indistinguishable from acoustic events (and physical objects) occurring in nature; e.g., Polly might discover that what she took to be a flattering remark about her looks was actually just the sounds "polly", "is", and "pretty" spoken by a parrot. If the reference to types in the communicative intentions underlying the production and the recognition of utterances (and inscriptions) is what infuses them with the grammatical properties of types, then obtaining information about the language by observing that tokens of its sentences have one or another grammatical property shows nothing. It may be true that properties of tokens are the basis on which we come to know properties of types, but the tokens are the basis only because they, as it were, are the mirrors in which we see the reflection of our own antecedent knowledge of the properties of types. In this case, properties of tokens do not have the epistemic priority that is assumed in Bromberger's conception of our route to knowledge of properties of linguistic types.

a priori

Besides failing to consider this objection, Bromberger says nothing about the fact that grammatical properties, like other properties, are acknowledged to be universals. Perhaps he has in mind something like Aristotle's position on universals, but in that case there is the objection in section 2 of this chapter, which needs to be answered.

The other problem with Bromberger's idea is that the structure of tokens is not a sufficient ground for grammatical properties. The token of the English imperative "Run home!" which you have just read is constituted of deposits of ink. What sense can it make to say that *it* on its own has a second-person-pronoun subject when it doesn't even contain a subconfiguration of ink deposits that can be identified as a second-person pronoun? It seems quite impossible for *tokens* simpliciter to have grammatical properties that depend on constituents and relations with no surface realization.

Bromberger's reply to the objection that tokens in and of themselves have none of the underlying grammatical properties and relations that his account of the token/type relation requires is that utterances and inscriptions "are produced by agents with phonological, syntactic, semantic, and pragmatic intentions. They embody and manifest such intentions. And they have attributes that encode such intentions." (ibid., p. 73) No doubt, tokens are indeed produced by agents with all the appropriate intentions and may be seen as "embodying" or "manifesting" the speaker's intentions, but how is this supposed to show that the tokens themselves have attributes like having a grammatical subject? The mystery is not solved by Bromberger's claim that they do have them unless the intentions of the agents refer to unreduced types.

Although it is true that we impute attributes like 'having an understood second-person subject' to tokens of imperatives, the attribution must be understood as something like 'is a token of a type which has a second-person subject in its underlying structure', since it makes no sense to say that a token of a sentence has an attribute like having a second-person subject unless some part of the token can be the object of the attribution. But the token in question has no such part.

Its parts are configurations of ink deposits, and although it contains ink deposits that might be said to manifest verbhood or direct-objecthood, none can be said to manifest subjecthood. In this case, it seems better to understand such attributions as I have indicated than to say that tokens can have attributes in the sense required by Bromberger's reply.

It does not help for Bromberger to tell us that scientists attribute temperature and acceleration "with the help of theories" (ibid., p. 74). The cases are entirely different. The sample of mercury with the temperature of 356.6° Celsius *has* molecules in its constitution, only they are too tiny to be seen with the naked eye, whereas the token of "Run home!" has no (tiny) configuration of ink particles of the required sort in its constitution. Whereas, in the case of the mercury, there is something for us to make a theoretical inference about, in the case of the token of "Run home!" there is not.

Bromberger offers one other argument for his claim that "linguistics must concern itself with psychology" (ibid., p. 58). He claims that the study of "people's mental makeup" is "the only plausible interpretation of soundness and completeness for theories" in linguistics, that is, the only way for linguists to determine the significant grammatical properties and relations for a language (ibid., p. 84). To support this claim, Bromberger first states that the study of psychology is at least a way of doing this, and he then considers a possible objection to the effect that the psychological way has to assume that there are "minds, brains, organisms, wetware." But since the linguistic realist certainly does not deny this assumption or the fruitfulness of scientifically studying minds, brains, organisms, and wetware and since it is hard to imagine who would deny any of this, one wonders why Bromberger bothers to raise the objection.

The real objection for Bromberger to answer is why the realist's rival interpretation of the soundness and completeness of theories in linguistics is not plausible. On this interpretation, the linguist evaluates theories about significant grammatical properties and relations on the basis of standard methodological criteria, i.e., coverage of the facts, simplicity, and other criteria that are in general use in science. Bromberger anticipates an objection based on such a non-psychological approach, but, surprisingly, his answer is to challenge the idea that theories in linguistics can be certified by the rules of induction and simplicity. His response is: "Why maximum simplicity and certification by the rules of induction? Why not maximum complexity and certification by some rules of counter-induction?" (ibid., pp. 83–84) Of course, the linguistic realist can no more produce a justification of induction than anyone else. But why should Bromberger think heavy-duty philosophical skepticism is at all relevant? Why should only realists have to solve the deep philosophical problems that Hume and Goodman have raised before their conception of theory evaluation in linguistics can be considered plausible? Those philosophical problems do not have to be solved for the sake of linguists, who, like scientists in other fields, get along fine with an implicit grasp of induction, Occam's razor, etc. Since there is no reason to think that linguists cannot determine the significant grammatical properties and relations of the language on the basis of methodological know-how, why should the realist interpretation have to include philosophical knowledge that no one has?

Moreover, it is a good thing for Bromberger's own approach that there is no general requirement on interpretations to solve such problems. If the requirement for the plausibility of an approach *were* its ability to solve them, Bromberger's own psychological approach would be as implausible as the linguistic realist's. Obviously, "maximum complexity" and "counterinduction" will play hell with the study of minds, brains, organisms, and wetware. It may be that Bromberger has the answer to Hume and Goodman up his sleeve, but, even so, it does him no good in connection with the present issue. The answer will only explain why scientists are philosophically justified in trusting simplicity rather than complexity and induction rather than counterinduction, and such an explanation gives as much or as little aid and comfort to linguistic realism as it does to linguistic conceptualism.

16

In this concluding section, I would like to say something about the source of naturalism's troubles in connection with sciences like linguistics and logic. In a nutshell, it is that these sciences trade in the abstract while naturalism insists that everything be concrete. Naturalism pushes commitment to the concrete to the point where theoretical definition in the special sciences must be definition in terms of conceptions of the concrete. One can see this reflected directly in definitions of grammars and linguistic theory such as Chomsky's and also indirectly in Quine's assumption that concepts in the theory of meaning must be defined by substitution procedures which extensionally correlate such concepts with the behavior of speakers and other aspects of the natural environment.

In this connection, it is interesting to recall Chomsky's own criticism of linguistic nominalism for constraining grammars to be theories of an acoustic reality and, as a consequence, preventing

vs psychological reality?

grammars from being optimal theories of the language.[58] His criticism was that adequacy of grammatical description requires more abstraction than nominalistic metatheories allow. But, although Chomsky's conceptualist replacement for nominalistic metatheory is a considerable liberalization, perhaps as much as a naturalistic framework will permit, it is by no means a complete liberalization. In fact, it replaces constraints based on one concrete reality with constraints based on another. Hence, there is still a ceiling on the level of abstraction in theories of natural languages, and this raises the prospect that the ceiling may still be too low if such theories are to adequately describe the structure of natural languages.

What makes this prospect a reality is that sciences like linguistics and logic are about structures which are maximally abstract, and so any ceiling on the level of abstractness for theoretical definitions will distort grammatical and logical structures. Thus, it is easy to see generally why the best scientific theories in these disciplines cannot be brought under constraints interpreting them as theories of concrete objects like mind/brains. In requiring that a theory of English or a theory of implication be a theory of a concrete psychological reality, conceptualism presents us with theories that do not describe the structure of English sentences or implication relations themselves, but describe, as it were, the shadows they cast on the walls of our mental/neural cave.

Appendix: On Ethics

In this appendix, I want to explain why the reformulation of the naturalistic fallacy in connection with linguistic and logical naturalism need not preclude (NF) from applying to ethical naturalism. This explanation should not be taken as a direct argument for ethical non-naturalism. That is well beyond the scope of the book.

Ethical naturalism and ethical non-naturalism are the two principal forms of cognitivism. Cognitivism says that ethical terms express properties and relations and that ethical sentences are true or false in the standard correspondence sense. For example, cognitivists hold that the sentence "One ought to keep a promise" is true in virtue of the fact that one ought to keep a promise. Cognitivism holds it to be a fact, other things being equal, that promise keeping is obligatory. The controversy between the two forms of cognitivism is over the nature of ethical facts. Ethical naturalism takes them to be facts about the natural world, e.g., facts about what is productive of pleasure. An ethical non-naturalism in line with the linguistic and logical non-naturalism of this chapter takes them to be facts about values, e.g., the value of treating people as far as possible as _ends_, conceived of as abstract objects. Like other abstract objects, they express an aspect of the significance of things in the natural realm. The value of an act is a measure of its moral worth, just as the number of a collection is a measure of its plurality. But, like other abstract objects, values belong to a part of reality independent of the natural realm.

Thus, beyond simply endorsing the autonomy of ethics, ethical non-naturalism, in our sense, provides an explanation of autonomy in terms of its conception of ethics as being about abstract values belonging to a non-natural realm. The autonomy of ethics has always been an attractive thesis, as is clear from the fact that many philosophers of different persuasions defend it, but it is unsatisfying without an explanation of why ethics should be autonomous. Ethical non-naturalism provides a reason. Of course, ethical naturalism provides a reason why it should not be autonomous, but, insofar as ethical non-naturalism provides the only explanation for the autonomy of ethics, to the extent that autonomy is an attractive thesis on its own, ethical non-naturalism gains in attractiveness.

The autonomy of ethics is customarily expressed in terms of the slogan that _ought_-statements cannot be derived from _is_-statements. However, this slogan is well known to lead to a number of undesirable consequences. Since naturalists exploit them to undermine the autonomy claim, I want to pause briefly to show that these consequences arise only from the customary formulation of the claim.

Typical of such consequences are examples of derivations of _ought_-statements from _is_-statements like "Socrates is a philosopher; therefore, Socrates is a philosopher or one ought to keep a promise" and "Socrates is a philosopher; therefore, if philosophers ought to keep promises, then Socrates ought to keep promises". Such consequences arise, as I see it, entirely because the notion of derivation in the formulation of the autonomy of ethics is understood as logical derivation. Logical derivation has various means at its disposal for producing valid arguments whose conclusions contain novel extralogical predicates of _any_ sort whatever. Thus, for example, the same features of the logical operators which give rise to "counterexamples" to the autonomy of ethics can just as well give rise to "counterexamples" to the autonomy of logic, mathematics, or any other subject. Although it is possible, as the naturalist urges, that no subject is autonomous, this way of establishing it seems a bit too easy.

Philosophers have, of course, recognized that such "counterexamples" are too gimmicky to refute a philosophically interesting claim, but, because the philosophical theory that all valid consequences rest on logical relations has been so widely accepted, they have been unaware of any alternative to understanding the notion of derivation in terms of logical derivation. However, from discussion in chapters 2 and 5, we can see that an alternative is provided by the proto-theory's analytic entailment, which involves the "beams in the house" relation of containment instead of the "plant in the seed" relation involved in logical entailment. Construing the notion of derivation in the slogan as analytic entailment blocks just the feature responsible for the "counterexamples" because it permits only conclusions whose predicates are literally contained in the sense of the premise. Thus, all the "counterexamples" to the autonomy of ethics are removed at one stroke.[59]

analytic entailment v/. logical entailment.

On our non-naturalism, the underivability of an ethical *ought* from an *is* is of a piece with the underivability of a logical, linguistic, and mathematical *ought* from an *is*.[60] The irreducibility of value to fact is an irreducibility of value to *natural* fact. The explanation for the irreducibility is thus the same for all cases, namely that the *ought*-statements in these disciplines express claims about the intrinsic properties and relations of abstract objects, whereas the *is*-statements express claims about natural objects and events.

value vs = natural fact

It is a corollary of this explanation that the basic principles of ethics, logic, linguistics, and mathematics are necessary truths. Just as it is true in every possible world that 2 plus 2 is 4, so it is true in every possible world that intentionally causing pain to the innocent and unwilling simply for one's own sadistic amusement is morally wrong. One significant feature of this corollary is that it offers us a way to handle philosophically proposed or anthropologically discovered cases which are alleged to be moral behavior in their own context in spite of conflicting with our deepest convictions about what is morally wrong. We can handle them in the same way we handled the cases in the *Remarks on the Foundations of Mathematics* with which Wittgenstein tries to show how instances of inference, counting, and calculation can conflict with our deepest convictions about logical and mathematical truth. That is, we can deny that such philosophically concocted or anthropologically discovered cases are even possible cases of moral behavior, since they conflict with necessary truths. This line of argument in ethics is promising because, if notions like fascism and slavery can be properly formulated, we can hope to provide a reason for thinking that they are wrong absolutely, no matter when, where, or under what circumstances they occur.

i.e. relativism

but these seem to be natural phenomena, not abstract entities.

It follows from the necessary truth of the basic principles of those disciplines that knowledge of these principles is something that we could not have if all knowledge came from the study of contingent relations in the natural world. I shall discuss this consequence at

OR REVELATION IN
THEOLOGY ?

rational
intuition
cf.
Spinoza ?

some length in the next chapter; here I want to indicate the three sorts of consideration that lead the non-naturalist to accept intuition as an indispensable source of our knowledge of basic facts in ethics, logic, linguistics, and mathematics. One consideration is simply the fact that these disciplines are unlike the common natural sciences in that intuitive judgment plays a validating role in them. Another consideration, stressed by Kant, is that knowledge concerning contingent relations in the natural world by itself cannot deliver knowledge of necessary connection.

The third is that, if there is an argument that the best account of a subject is one on which it is about abstract objects—for example, the standard argument from the plentitude of sets—then, since basic facts about such objects are beyond the range of perception, this argument is at the same time an argument for intuition as the means for obtaining knowledge of such facts. This is because perception is an information channel that works through causal contact with concrete natural objects; hence, we cannot acquire information about abstract objects like values, sentences, propositions, or sets through perception, since we cannot make causal contact with them.[61] Since we have knowledge of basic ethical, linguistic, logical, and mathematical facts, there must be a faculty that provides such knowledge without causal contact. The faculty must provide *a priori* knowledge, as does the faculty of reasoning, but, since the knowledge in questions is *ex hypothesi* basic, the faculty in question cannot be the faculty of reasoning. Introspection, too, is ruled out, since it reports only on our subjective states, while the faculty in question provides information about objective fact. Since we know of no other alternative, we arrive, by a process of elimination, at the traditional rationalist's faculty of intuition.

This is just a sketch of converging lines of argument which, as I see it, form the case for taking intuition to be a necessary factor in explaining the source of our knowledge of basic facts in ethics, linguistics, logic, and mathematics. I have introduced these considerations to supplement remarks elsewhere in the book which serve as a corrective to misrepresentations of the case for a faculty of intuition of the traditional rationalist sort.[62]

These features of ethical non-naturalism suggest one feature which is critical for extending the argument in this chapter to ethics. This further feature is that knowledge in ethics can be presented as a theory which is like theories in logic, linguistics, and mathematics in being based on inferences designed to explain facts supplied by intuition and evaluated by the familiar methodological standards. This is, of course, a controversial suggestion, but, if it can be sustained against the best available objections, the argument in this chapter stands a good chance of being made applicable to ethics.

There is, of course, no prospect of defending this conception of ethical non-naturalism against all the objections that might be raised even after taking account of the objections that are directly answered on the basis of what this book has already argued and will argue in the next chapter. However, there is one set of objections that must be answered because of their wide acceptance in meta-ethics. These are the objections stemming from the view that appeals to intuition and theory in ethics have been completely discredited. This view commonly occasions impatient dismissals of meta-ethical talk about intuition, but I think it can be shown that the view rests on little more than a picture of the world in which there is no place for a rationalist faculty of intuition, and that this picture is based on no more than Wittgenstein's late philosophy or Quine's naturalized epistemology. Examining this view will, I think, show that this book's arguments against Wittgenstein and Quine have implications which indirectly answer the major objections used to discredit earlier forms of ethical non-naturalism. Moore, Ross, and Prichard have, in a sense, been the victims of developments in Anglo-American meta-ethics entrained by the events in the philosophy of language and logic with which we have been concerned in the previous chapters.

A convenient synopsis of the arguments against ethical intuition is found in Bernard William's book *Ethics and the Limits of Philosophy* which purports to show that "the model of intuition in ethics has been demolished."[63] Williams claims first that the model "failed to explain how an eternal truth can provide a practical consideration" (ibid., p. 94). But I find it unclear why the model should be required to provide such a consideration, since intuition is properly invoked only to explain knowledge of *theoretical* fact. Pure theory in mathematics and logic does not require a practical payoff. Why should it require one in ethics? Furthermore, even assuming such a requirement, it is not clear why there is supposed to be a problem about how eternal truths inform us on practical matters. This seems straightforward in many cases. The ethical truth expressing the obligation to help others when they are in serious need and when we can do so with no trouble to ourselves informs us that we ought to drop the life preserver to the drowning child.

Moreover, Williams does not make it clear whether he thinks that the model of intuition in logic and mathematics also fails to explain how their eternal truths provide "a practical consideration" and, if so, whether mathematical and logical intuition are to be condemned along with ethical intuition. Logical and mathematical truths provide practical considerations to indicate what one ought to do in inference and calculation, and ethical truths provide practical considerations to indicate what one ought to do in moral decision. What is the relevant difference? No doubt, our knowledge of ethical truths is far less substantial than our knowledge of logical and mathematical truths, but this difference can amount to no more than a matter of degree. As far as I can see, every kind of defect found in our knowledge of ethics is also found in our knowledge of logic and mathematics.

This can perhaps be better appreciated by making the same claim in connection with linguistics, since it is an interesting intermediary case where the extent of such defects is greater than in logic and mathematics but less than in ethics. Williams himself addresses the case of linguistics, and so we shall return to it below.

Second, Williams claims that "it is wrong to assimilate ethical truths to necessities" (ibid., p. 94). He thinks that this claim is established by "cultural disagreement." Williams says that if members of another culture disagree with us about a mathematical truth, we think first of running to the linguist, but, if they disagree with us about an ethical truth, our first thought would not be that we need a better translation. This, of course, is right, but not for any reason that matters to the issue of the necessity of ethical truths. As Williams surely recognizes, it is quite possible that the linguist will be of no help even in the cases of mathematics and logic because the native might actually believe a logical or mathematical falsehood. (Frege once did.) Alternatively, a linguist, or perhaps an anthropological linguist, might be of help in showing that a disagreement about what ought to be done is really at bottom not an ethical disagreement, but only seems so owing to differences in language, belief, or custom. (Whether an act is patricide or honoring one's father can depend on the community's religious beliefs.)

This is not to deny Williams's point that there is a difference in our initial diagnosis of the disagreements. But the difference is easily explained in terms of the fact that people's logical and mathematical knowledge, in our culture as well as in others, is generally less degraded and less confused with extraneous matters. On this explanation, the existence of such a difference provides no support for Williams's claim that ethical disagreement is different in kind from logical or mathematical disagreement.

Williams claims that "it is wrong to assimilate ethical truths to necessities," but it seems no less dubious that there is a possible world in which it is moral for Nazi guards to amuse themselves making innocent and unwilling concentration camp inmates suffer than it is that there is a possible world in which seven marbles plus five marbles is seventeen marbles. It is not easy to see how a philosopher might impose a relevant theoretical distinction between these cases. The standard Wittgensteinian view that the certainty we have that such a possible world does not exist is just a matter of our inability to conceive of it from within our particular form of life does not make the needed distinction, because Wittgenstein's view, as he himself makes amply clear, applies to both kinds of case. Finally, there is enough in this book to show that general naturalistic grounds do not suffice to establish such criticisms of necessity.

Third, Williams claims that "above all, the appeal to intuition as a faculty explained nothing" (ibid., p. 94). Given the three sorts of consideration which underlie the non-naturalist's acceptance of a faculty of intuition, this claim requires that it be already shown that ethical truths are not necessary truths. For, if this is not already shown, non-naturalists can argue that appeals to ethical intuition have an explanatory role like that of appeals to perception. Non-naturalists can argue that, just as without perception we have no source for our basic knowledge of contingent truth, so without intuition we have no source for our basic knowledge of necessary truth. So, since Williams has not shown that ethical truth is not necessary truth, there is, putatively at least, something for the faculty of intuition to explain.

Williams seems to rest his claim about the unexplanatoriness of intuition on cultural disagreement. But, as we have seen already, such disagreement can be explained by differences in belief and other nonmoral factors underlying the apparent conflicts between judgments about the rightness or wrongness of behavior. No case has been presented where we must explain such disagreement in terms of different ultimate moral values.

Williams presents an argument which is intended to block a revival of the notion of an ethical intuition and which is based on the current widespread use of the notion of a linguistic intuition (ibid., p. 97). This argument thus bears directly on my claims about the relations between intuitive judgment in ethics and linguistics. His claim is that putative intuitions about the right thing to do in a moral situation are not analogous to intuitions about the right thing to say in a language (ibid., p. 97). But the only support Williams gives for this claim is the Wittgensteinian view that linguistic judgments depend on nothing more than the ability to recognize similarities, which he says "must be right" (ibid., p. 97). But if the discussion in chapters 2 and 3 is correct, Williams's confidence in this nominalistic view is misplaced.

Williams also claims a disanalogy between conflicts of intuition in linguistics and conflicts of intuition in ethics, because, according to him, in the former we say there are two different dialects whereas in the latter we seek to show that one intuition is more reasonable (ibid., p. 98). This claim seems to me to be wrong about conflicts of intuition in both cases. There is something corresponding to dialect in ethics, namely, manners. Manners seem to me to blend ethics with convention in a way similar to the way that a dialect blends fixed language pattern with regional convention. But this is, admittedly, speculative. The clear defect in Williams's claim is that it rests on too simple a picture of linguistics. Often linguists seek reasons to show that one of the conflicting intuitions is better. The linguist knows that dialect difference is only one possible hypothesis about the source of a conflict. Alternatively, one of the conflicting intuitions might be explained away as arising from an idiosyncratic linguistic mistake on the part of the informant. Or the conflict might stem from the unconscious influence of the informant's pet linguistic views. It might also reflect a competence/performance confusion. In these cases, linguists will offer reasons to show that one of two intuitions is better, e.g., that that intuition makes more sense because it fits into the overall theory of the language better than the other intuition.[64] Finally, it is worth noting that there are numerous conflicts in linguistics which no one is willing to see resolved on a live-and-let-live basis. These are conflicts on which a significant theoretical issue depends, e.g., the scope of transformational rules in syntactic description or whether sentences such as "Bachelors are unmarried" are analytic.[65]

Thomas Nagel, though sympathetic to "the example of mathematics" in constructing "a realism about the existence of reasons or values which we can discover by certain processes of thought," comes to reject the example because he thinks that ethics and mathematics differ insofar as "parts of [mathematics] govern the physical world."[66] Nagel's point, as I understand it, is that mathematical truths restrict the way the world can be, so that, for example, it cannot be a world where seven things plus five things are seventeen things, but ethical truths do not, since the world is a place where Nazis do sadistically torture innocent people. If Nagel is right that ethical truths do not restrict the world in the way that logical and mathematical truths do, considerable doubt is cast on the transferability of the naturalistic-fallacy argument to ethics.

I think Nagel's rejection of a mathematical model is based on a mistake about what kind of restriction moral truths impose on the world. Moral truths do not preclude acts of sadistic torture or wanton promise breaking; they preclude *moral* acts of sadistic torture or wanton promise breaking. The difference between the mathematical truth that 7 plus 5 is 12 and the ethical truth that sadistic torture is morally wrong concerns only the kind of property whose exemplification is precluded.

It might help to contrast the way mathematical law restricts the world with the way that natural law does. Natural law restricts by narrowing down the logical possibilities in specifying the actual, whereas mathematical law does not choose among possibilities, but restricts the world at a prior point, by ruling out some things as possibilities. Mathematical law carves the impossible away from the meaningfully expressible, e.g., Frege's least convergent series. But, given that ethical law is necessary, it restricts the world in the same sense as mathematical law. It carves the ethically impossible away from the meaningfully expressible, e.g., excluding morally acceptable acts of torturing the innocent and unwilling for sadistic amusement. Mathematical and ethical law restrict possible worlds in the same way, i.e., by precluding things which are incompatible with them.

[handwritten margin note: yes but, people don't seem to accept the authority of ethics as they do what . . .]

There is a further question of whether it makes sense to talk about truths or laws "restricting" or "governing" the world even in the case of mathematics. It seems to me that this might be a misleading metaphor and that it might be better to say that such truths or laws describe a universal feature of possible worlds. In this case, the objection to "the example of mathematics" disappears entirely.

Another difference between ethics and subjects like logic, linguistics, and mathematics is that the latter are sciences but ethics is not. Isn't the term "moral science" an anachronism—no more the name of a real science than "political science"? Ethics is certainly no science today, and I have no idea whether it will ever achieve that status. But the transferability of the naturalistic-fallacy argument to ethical naturalism does not depend on ethics' meriting the honorific "science". The only question that matters for transferability is whether theory in ethics is enough like theory in science. For example: Is there a similar enough notion of theoretical definition in both? Do methodological considerations, e.g., coverage of the facts, simplicity, etc., apply in a way similar enough to the way they apply in such subjects?

Whether one thinks that ethics is sufficiently like science depends on one's conception of ethics. Obviously, ethics on Williams's conception bears little resemblance to a science, since he is skeptical even about the notion of theory in ethics.[67] On the other hand, it is clear that the term "theory" is widely used in ethics to refer to systems of principles—utilitarianism, contractarianism, Kantian theory, ideal-observer theory, etc.—designed to explain facts about goods, rights, and obligations. On the traditional cognitivist conception of ethics, which many naturalists and non-naturalists share, there is a notion of theory which bears enough of a likeness to the notion of theory in certain sciences. On this conception, in trying to find the conditions for moral obligation, ethical inquiry is trying to discover facts about the world. Non-naturalists can plausibly construe attempts in ethics to discover such conditions as similar to attempts in mathematics to discover the conditions for being a set. Furthermore, when we look at such attempts to settle controversies about whether utilitarianism, contractarianism, Kantian theory, or some other system of principles best accounts for facts about goods, rights, and obligations, it is clear that considerations of coverage of cases, simplicity, depth of explanation, etc.—which are typically used in humanistic studies generally—are accepted standards of evaluation.

The transferability of the naturalistic-fallacy argument to ethical naturalism need not even depend on showing that ethics is enough like science. As long as notions of theory and methodology are involved in ethics, we can treat the reference to scientific theory and scientific methodology in (NF) simply as a convenience in running the argument in connection with logic and linguistics. (NF) could be reformulated to make no reference to scientific theory or scientific methodology. Less conveniently, I could have used the more general notions of theory and methodology already in use in the humanities, namely, the notion of theory understood as a systematically developed conception of the nature of the entities in a domain, and the notion of methodology understood as a set of criteria for evaluating theories in terms of their coverage of the facts, simplicity, depth of explanation, etc. Given such general notions, we can define the notion of the best theory for the facts about goods, rights, and obligations. Thus, although we can concede real differences between ethics and the sciences, the concession neither, in principle, prevents the naturalistic-fallacy argument from being applicable to ethics, nor, in practice, prevents us from having a promising way of applying it.[68]

8

Conclusion: The Problems of Philosophy

1

Kant's formulation of the task of metaphysics as explaining the possibility of synthetic *a priori* knowledge, together with the failure of his own explanation, set philosophy on a course which led in the twentieth century to the linguistic criticism of metaphysics. This formulation was proposed in order to rescue metaphysics from Hume's charge that it falls between the two stools of *a priori* conceptual analysis and *a posteriori* experimental reasoning. Kant believed that Hume failed to recognize the synthetic nature of mathematics and, therefore, failed to see that metaphysics could not be abandoned without sacrificing mathematics.

Kant expresses the general form of the problem by cross-classifying propositions on the basis of two distinctions: the analytic vs. the synthetic and the *a priori* vs. the *a posteriori*. The former is a semantic distinction, contrasting propositions whose predication is explicative with propositions whose predication is ampliative. The latter is an epistemological distinction, contrasting propositions that can be known independently of all experience with propositions that can be known only through experience. The result is the familiar four-celled matrix in which the synthetic *a priori* cell contains mathematical and metaphysical propositions.

Kant's aim in this cross-classification was to show that Hume's empiricism cannot account for all of our knowledge. It may account for the content of the analytic *a priori* and the synthetic *a posteriori* cells, but not for the content of the synthetic *a priori* cell. Knowledge of propositions in the analytic *a priori* cell is unproblematic. Because they have explicative predicates, *a priori* knowledge of their semantic structure suffices to show that the condition under which we pick out the things the propositions are about guarantees that those things have the properties predicated of them. Knowledge of propositions in the synthetic *a posteriori* cell is also unproblematic. Because the propositions are *a posteriori*, empirical knowledge of the way the world is suffices to show that the things the propositions are about have the properties predicated of them. However, the propositions in the synthetic *a priori* cell pose a problem for Humean empiricism. Since the propositions in this cell have ampliative predicates, their truth value cannot be learned from examining their semantic structure. But, since these propositions are also *a priori*, their truth value cannot be learned from observing the way the world is, either. Since Humean empiricism countenances only relations of ideas and matters of fact, an account of our knowledge of mathematical and other propositions in the third cell is beyond Humean empiricism.

Kant thinks that, once we distinguish synthetic propositions like those of mathematics which apply to objects that never appear in experience from synthetic propositions like those of empirical science which apply to objects in experience, it is clear that something more than Humean empiricism is required to account for our knowledge. Kant's alternative to the empiricist's claim that experience is the source of our synthetic knowledge was that the mind itself is "the author of the experience in which its objects are found." Kant explains our synthetic *a priori* knowledge in terms of the conformity of objects to our sensibility and understanding rather than in terms of their conformity to external objects presented to us through the senses. Kant believed that his Copernican Revolution uncovered the source of our synthetic *a priori* knowledge because it explains how synthetic propositions can apply to objects that never appear in experience.

Although Kant's transcendental idealism was remarkably successful in satisfying many philosophers for a substantial period of time, eventually deep troubles began to emerge. First, despite Kant's protests, transcendental idealism does not seem enough of an improvement on ordinary idealism to solve the basic metaphysical problems about knowledge. Transcendental idealism seems, in the final analysis, as much a surrender to the Cartesian skeptic as empirical idealism. Second, Einstein's relativistic physics refuted Kant's claim that Euclidean geometry expresses synthetic *a priori* knowledge of space, thereby not only depriving Kant of an account of geometrical knowledge, but also, and more importantly, putting his entire account of synthetic *a priori* knowledge under a cloud of suspicion. Third, persistent difficulties with the distinctions, apparatus, and argumentation in the *Critique* eroded confidence in Kant's reformist cure. The accumulation of such difficulties over the years has left little confidence in its early promise to, once and for all, put metaphysics on a sure course where, leaving behind the interminable squabbles of earlier times, it can make progress comparable to that in the sciences.

These troubles disillusioned many philosophers with Kant's explanation of the possibility of synthetic *a priori* knowledge, which, in turn, created skepticism about Kant's explanation of the task of metaphysics. Because of this skepticism and because of the unflattering pace of progress in metaphysics in comparison to the pace of progress in science, many philosophers eventually soured on Kant's reformist cure for metaphysics, with the result that a radical cure in the Humean spirit came to seem attractive once again. The flourishing of deflationary naturalistic and positivistic philosophies in the nineteenth century was one consequence. Very early in the twentieth century, the work of Frege, Moore, and others for a time checked the influence of these philosophies, but, by the middle of the century, resistance to them had all but disappeared, and Logical Positivism's neo-Humeanism, Wittgenstein's radical critical philosophy, and Quinean naturalism came to dominate the scene.

Ironically, it was Frege, who was sympathetic to Kant and in part concerned with improving Kantian philosophy, who provided the impetus and the tools for undermining Kant's reformist cure. The strength of Kant's position derived from the fact that his sense-containment conception of analyticity links the fate of metaphysics with that of mathematics by characterizing both as synthetic. Frege revealed various shortcomings in Kant's notion of analyticity and in the theory of meaning on which it rests. He hoped, of course, to remove these shortcomings, and, in this spirit, he defined analytic propositions as consequences of logical laws plus definitions. But the Fregean conception of analyticity together with Frege's logicism created the possibility of cutting the link that Kant had forged between the fate of metaphysics and that of mathematics. This conception of analyticity expands sense containment from "beams in the house" containment to "plant in the seeds" containment, thereby allowing the predicate of a logical proposition—and, with logicism, of a mathematical proposition—to be "contained" in its subject. The Logical Positivists were quick to try to cut the link between metaphysics and mathematics by using Frege's semantics in an effort to show that mathematical and logical truth is nothing more than analytic truth in something like Frege's broad sense.

Contrary to the general opinion, the disastrous feature for non-naturalism in Frege's work is not the absence of an epistemology suitable for his realist ontology, but rather the presence of a semantics that reconstructs analyticity in a way which, unlike the traditional theory of meaning, provides no basis for the Kantian formulation of the task of metaphysics. At the time, the traditional theory of meaning was nowhere near sufficiently developed to take on Frege's semantics or to bear the weight that the Kantian account of metaphysics puts on it. Once Frege's work focused the issue of the existence of synthetic *a priori* knowledge on questions of language and meaning, making the philosophy of language the central area in philosophy and meaning the central topic in the philosophy of language, positivists and naturalists were able to exploit both the underdevelopment of the traditional theory of meaning and Frege's contributions to philosophy, logic, and mathematics in order to undercut the Kantian account of metaphysics. The underdeveloped state of the traditional theory was the Achilles' heel of Kant's reformist cure for metaphysics, and Frege's semantics was Paris's arrow.

Indeed, the main course of Anglo-American philosophy in this century can be charted in terms of the three distinct ways in which the underdeveloped state of this theory or Frege's work, and particularly, his semantics, was exploited to mount linguistic attacks on metaphysics. One was the way in which the Logical Empiricists exploited both. Schlick writes:

> The meaning of a word is solely determined by the rules which hold for its use. Whatever follows from these rules, follows from the mere meaning of the word, and is therefore purely analytic, tautological, formal. The error committed by the proponents of the factual *a priori* can be understood as arising from the fact that it was not clearly realized that such concepts as those of the colors have a formal structure just as do numbers or spatial concepts, and that this structure determines their meaning without remainder. . . . Thus, [sentences which are the showpieces of the phenomenological philosophy] say nothing about existence, or about the nature of anything, but rather only exhibit the content of our concepts, that is, the mode and manner in which we employ the words of our language. . . . they bring no knowledge, and cannot serve as the foundations of a special science. Such a science as the phenomenologists have promised us just does not exist.[1]

As Schlick indicates in this quotation, he believed that a logical semantics, presumably based on Frege's work (as developed by Russell and Wittgenstein), could account for allegedly factual *a priori* truths as "purely analytic," thereby making otiose a special science of intuition such as Husserl and the phenomenologists were advocating.

This program seemed promising because, with the underdeveloped state of the traditional theory of meaning, nothing appeared to stand in the way of using Frege's broad notion of analyticity to refurbish Hume's category of relations of ideas and thereby deny the synthetic nature of logic and mathematics. Logical Empiricists could thereby revitalize British Empiricism.

The two other ways in which naturalists exploited the underdevelopment of the traditional theory of meaning to undermine the Kantian formulation of the task of metaphysics have been extensively discussed in previous chapters. Wittgenstein's critique of theories of meaning in the Frege-Russell tradition paved the way for the new version of his radical critical philosophy in the *Philosophical Investigations*. My argument in chapter 2 to the effect that the proto-theory escapes Wittgenstein's critique can in part be read as an account of why the underdeveloped state of the traditional theory of meaning—particularly, in encouraging philosophers to see Frege's semantics as simply an explication of the traditional theory—made the theory seem vulnerable to his critique.

The third way in which philosophers exploited the underdevelopment of the traditional theory was, of course, Quine's attack on the analytic/synthetic distinction, which paved the way for his attempt to naturalize epistemology. The argument in chapter 5 to the effect that Quine's criticisms of intensionalist semantics overlook the most natural form for an intensionalist theory to take within the framework of linguistics can in part be read as an account of why the underdeveloped state of the theory of meaning made intensional theory seem vulnerable to Quine's criticisms—particularly, in encouraging philosophers to see Quine's picture of the Bloomfieldian grammatical paradigm as the only one for theories in linguistics.

In all three of these ways, the aim was to undercut the Kantian formulation of the task of metaphysics by emptying the synthetic *a priori* cell of the Kantian matrix. The Logical Positivists like Schlick sought to empty it by moving all the propositions that Kant had put there over into the analytic *a priori* cell. Wittgenstein sought to empty it by getting rid of metaphysical propositions as pieces of nonsense and moving the remaining mathematical and logical propositions down into the synthetic *a posteriori* cell. According to Wittgenstein, what we should say about a logical or mathematical proof is "this is simply what we *do*. This is use and custom among us, a fact of our natural history" (RFM: 61). Quine sought to demote all *a priori* propositions, analytic and synthetic alike, down to the synthetic *a posteriori* cell. "Epistemology," Quine writes, "is best looked upon . . . as an enterprise within natural science," and in natural science there are "only Hume's regularities, culminating here and there in what passes for an explanatory trait or the promise of one."[2]

It is now generally recognized that the Logical Empiricist attack on metaphysics failed both because its various verificationist doctrines could not be made to work and because, as Quine acutely saw, Carnap's attempt to provide a suitable explication of the notion of synonymy in Frege's definition of analyticity on the basis of "meaning postulates" fails.[3] As we can see from the previous chapters, this attempt to assimilate semantics to logic, rather than reconstructing traditional semantic theory, deforms that theory in a way which sacrifices the very features that explain what analyticity is for natural languages generally. In particular, casting the theory of meaning in the form of postulates modeled on logical postulates sacrifices the decompositional sense structure which underlies the "beams in the house" notion of containment and, with it, the narrow analytic/synthetic distinction.

Given the arguments in the previous chapters, the other two ways of trying to undercut the Kantian conception of metaphysics can also be seen to have failed. Given the arguments in chapters 2, 3, and 4, Wittgenstein's attempt to get rid of metaphysical sentences and to show that logical and mathematical facts are nothing more than facts of "our natural history" fails because his critique of theories of meaning does not eliminate them all and so does not leave the field clear for his new conception of meaning. Furthermore, given the arguments in chapters 5 and 6, Quine's attempt and that of his followers to show that all propositions are *a posteriori* also fail, and, as we shall see, their case for a naturalized epistemology, as a consequence, collapses. Therefore, my arguments in the course of this book are arguments to show that none of these attempts succeeds in emptying the synthetic *a priori* cell.

Just as the arguments in those chapters show that what allowed these attempts to get as far as they did was the underdeveloped state of the traditional theory of meaning, so they also show that what blocks these attempts from succeeding is the development of the proto-theory. Many of the critical features of that theory—for example, decompositional structure—were latent in the traditional theory of meaning, for example, in Locke's and Kant's notion of concept inclusion. The development of a theory that explicitly contains these and other features which distinguish it from the Fregean theories that Wittgenstein, Quine, Putnam, etc. were criticizing is already enough to remove the vulnerable point in Kant's formulation of the task of metaphysics. It is clear, from what has been said in this book and in the works about the proto-theory to which I have referred, that none of those criticisms shows that the theory cannot bear the philosophical weight of Kant's cross-classification of propositions into analytic vs. synthetic and *a priori* vs. *a posteriori*. Moreover, on the proto-theory, the content of the cells comes out quite close to what it is on Kant's original description of the cross-classification. The propositions of mathematics and metaphysics which Kant put in the synthetic *a priori* cell can remain, and, given the narrow notion of analyticity in place of Frege's broad notion, we can even augment Kant's examples of synthetic *a priori* truths with truths of logic.

An interesting conclusion emerges: the arguments in this book take twentieth-century philosophy full circle round, back to the point prior to the Logical Positivist, Wittgensteinian, and Quinean attacks on metaphysics. The three attacks that challenged the Kantian foundations for metaphysics by trying to transfer the contents of the synthetic *a priori* cell over to the analytic *a priori* cell, erasing them or demoting them to the synthetic *a posteriori* cell, were unsuccessful. But their supposition that the traditional theory of meaning is the soft underbelly of the Kantian move to provide new foundations for metaphysics misjudged the condition of that theory. Its vulnerability reflected not inherent, fatal defects in the theory, but only the neglect the theory had experienced over the centuries. Thus, proper attention to the theory brings us back to facing the problems of metaphysics as Kant formulated them.

Of course, this is not to say that we are led back to Kantian theory. My arguments endorse only Kant's question of how knowledge of synthetic *a priori* truths is possible. They do not endorse Kant's answer that the objects of knowledge have to conform to our sensibility and understanding. Nothing I have said saves that answer from the difficulties it has been found to have over the years. Thus, we are once again faced with metaphysical problems, but without Kant's transcendental idealism as a way of solving them, without the linguistic turn as a way of dissolving them, and without naturalized epistemology as a way of recasting them. In this chapter I want to explore some aspects of this situation. Among the questions that naturally arise at this point are: How worthwhile are the accounts of knowledge as *a posteriori* knowledge of natural objects in this situation? How should we conceive of explanations of how synthetic *a priori* knowledge is possible? What attitude should we take toward the legendary obstinacy of metaphysical problems?

2

The argument in the last chapter used examples of the divergence of naturalistic theories from optimal scientific theories, on standard dimensions of theoretical evaluation like coverage of the evidence, inductive projection, and simplicity. It was possible to use standard principles of scientific methodology because the argument assumed no more than their acceptance as criteria for evaluating theories in the special sciences—on which there is sufficient general agreement. But once we go beyond such uses and try to say something about the philosophical justification of such principles, that is, about the foundations of the special sciences, agreement ends. The question of the status of such epistemologically central principles is at the very heart of the issue between naturalism and non-naturalism.

Although both positions regard philosophical reflection on scientific methodology as epistemology of a standard sort, naturalists and non-naturalists tell quite different stories about its nature and ground. The Quinean wing of contemporary naturalism, in advocating naturalized epistemology, claims that knowledge of scientific methodology is *a posteriori* knowledge. Its principles inform us of that part of nature which guides the investigation of nature. They are the products of natural science practiced on instances of its own practice. The principles are more general than the empirical results of ordinary investigations in natural science, but no different from them in epistemological status.

Non-naturalists refuse to swallow the idea that our basis for accepting the criteria we use to judge the acceptability of scientific claims generally is the product of particular empirical investigations. What standards of acceptability were used in those empirical investigations to show that the criteria are acceptable for judging scientific claims? The criteria themselves cannot have been so used because, aside from the blatant circularity, what would be the point of trying to show them acceptable if they already counted as acceptable enough for this purpose? Other criteria merely introduce a regress, since they need to be shown acceptable. Thus, the implausibility of the naturalist's story has led the non-naturalist to see the principles of scientific investigation as synthetic *a priori* conditions for the acceptability of knowledge claims.

For non-naturalists, epistemology is an *a priori* study of those conditions. In this sense, non-naturalism takes a foundationalist approach to knowledge. Foundationalism has come in for hard times in recent years, but the criticisms do not stand up without the support of naturalist metaphysics. Either they assume the arguments of anti-foundationalists like Wittgenstein and Quine, or, when they do not, they work only against a straw man which connects foundationalism in the narrow sense I have specified with some dubious view like the view that claims about the foundations of knowledge are infallible. Often we hear the criticism that the search for foundational explanations is misguided because, as naturalists are fond of reminding us, "Explanations come to an end somewhere" (PI: 1). Non-naturalists can agree that philosophical explanation stops at some point, and yet deny both that it never starts and that philosophical understanding comes from any source other than a terminated foundational explanation. Moreover, non-naturalists are right to emphasize that, in interesting cases, it is usually not clear just where the stopping point is. As often happens in the sciences, what looks like an ultimate principle may turn out not to be. And, even if something is taken as ultimate, there is a sense in which it can still be justified; e.g., Church's thesis may turn out to be ultimate, yet various considerations justify it.

Since the *a priori* conditions for scientific theory are not a matter of analytic property identity, they do not simply reflect the semantic categories of the language, and accordingly, violations of such conditions, as in the case of theories that arbitrarily sacrifice phenomena or make counterinductive projections, cannot be explained as category mistakes. That is, they are not deviations from the necessary sense structure of the language. Hence, non-naturalism claims that such conditions take the form of *a priori* constraints on synthetic property identity. Non-naturalism claims that we can know *a priori* synthetic conditions on scientific theories, because we can know conditions involving necessary synthetic property identities, i.e., conditions reflecting more than the contingent relations that can be learned from *a posteriori* investigation. This claim is one of the principal things at issue between naturalism and non-naturalism, as I will explain when we consider the relation between empiricism and naturalism.

Naturalists claim that we can know of no conditions on scientific theories save what *a posteriori* investigation can discover via observation of nature. Non-naturalists challenge this claim because they think that the principles for demonstrative and nondemonstrative inference cannot be got from information about natural objects, since even the concept of such an object presupposes those principles. Canny naturalists like Quine recognize that "physical objects are conceptually imported into the situation . . . as irreducible posits comparable, epistemologically, to the gods of Homer," and, accordingly, recognize the necessity of adopting nativism in some form.[4] Thus, they assume, as a basis for our predicting future experience from past experience, some biologically imposed structure which disposes us to posit objects with enduring properties. But even a nativist assumption is not enough to meet the non-naturalist's challenge. As the naturalistic-fallacy argument shows, the naturalist must do more than simply assume that the principles with which we happen to be natively endowed lead us eventually to posit the *right* objects. The considerations in sections 14 and 15 of the last chapter show that, even throwing in evolution, being the innate concept of an object for the human species is no guarantee of being the correct concept of an object. Genetic might does not make epistemological right.

Therefore, beyond the scientific question of what concept of an object is innate, there is the further philosophical question of what grounds there are for thinking that that innate concept corresponds to objects as they are in the world. The great promise of naturalized epistemology was that it held out the hope of identifying the former question, which concerns scientific theories of human native endowment, with the latter question, which concerns epistemological theories of justification. But, to justify identifying the two, naturalism had to remove the traditional philosophical understanding of the latter question as a question about what we ought to accept as knowledge over and above what we do accept. To remove it, naturalists tried either to show that the only substantive form of the question is a question in natural science or to show that the only sensible form of the question is an ordinary, unphilosophical one. If the arguments in this book are right, the question has not been removed.

Since it exists, it has to be answered. But naturalism is impotent to answer the traditional philosophical question of justification. Naturalism was, in fact, compelled to try to invalidate the distinction between knowledge of the principles we do use and knowledge of the principles we ought to use, because it has no resources with which to explain the distinction—no resources to explain, for example, why we are justified in positing emeralds and roses rather than, say, emeroses and rosealds. Naturalism has only explications of past practices available to it in positing emeralds and roses. No wonder then that naturalists like Quine and Goodman are so fond of conservatism, and that the specter of circularity always arises when naturalists try to address traditional questions in epistemology.

Quine, the leading naturalist of our day, tried to escape the criticism that naturalized epistemology is circular by arguing as follows:

. . . surrender of the epistemological burden to psychology is a move that was disallowed in earlier times as circular reasoning. If the epistemologist's goal is validation of the grounds of empirical science, he defeats his purpose by using psychology or other empirical sciences as the validation. However, such scruples against circularity have little point once we have stopped dreaming of deducing science from observations. If we are out simply to understand the link between observation and science, we are well advised to use any available information, including that provided by the very science whose link with observation we are seeking to understand.[5]

But the circularity criticism does not depend on a dream of deducing science from observation. Non-naturalists can agree with Quine that to ask for more than an understanding of the actual link between observation and science is unreasonable. As we have seen, "scruples against circularity" do not arise in connection with describing the link found in the natural history of science, but do arise in connection with validation, which is a matter not of deducing science from observations, but of justifying the principles used in establishing the link. Validation is part of the understanding of that link. It is the part that explains why it is *those* principles and *that* link, and not, as the skeptic would have it, other principles and another link. Quine does not reject this question of validation, since, as we shall see below, he admits the legitimacy of the skeptic's doubts about our principles.

Quine seems to think that the new descriptive psychology, which naturalists put in place of the old normative epistemology, not only can exhibit the epistemological principles underlying scientific theory but can also validate them. But since naturalized epistemology can exploit only the naturalistic content of theories like those in empirical psychology, how can the naturalist hope to answer the skeptic's challenge to our principles and to the theories that those principles link to observation? What is required to answer the skeptic is some way of justifying the principles that we have used to specify the link between theory and observation as those which we *ought* to use to specify the link. But it is just this normative element that is lost when the "epistemological burden" is surrendered to empirical psychology.

Some naturalists conceive of language, deduction, induction, or ethics in a way that makes it seem as if there is nothing normative to account for. Kripke has called this conception "*inversion* of the conditional":

Many philosophers can be summed up crudely (no doubt, not really accurately) by slogans in similar form: "We do not condemn certain acts because they are immoral; they are immoral because we condemn them." "We do not accept the law of contradiction because it is a necessary truth; it is a necessary truth because we accept it (by convention)." "Fire and heat are not constantly conjoined because fire causes heat; fire causes heat because they are constantly conjoined" (Hume). "We do not all say 12 + 7 = 19 and the like because we all grasp the concept of addition; we say we all grasp the concept of addition because we all say 12 + 7 = 19 and the like."[6]

The strategy of inverting the conditional is clearly designed to absolve naturalism of the responsibility for giving an account of immorality, necessary truth, etc., which, as we have seen, it is unable to do. Hence, instead of being required to account for the *ought* of ethics, logic, etc. without going beyond the bounds of empirical psychology, naturalists are required only to give an account of such natural phenomena as conventional agreement, condemning behavior, acceptance, etc. The "inversion of the conditional" thus makes it seem as if naturalism has nothing especially difficult to account for.

Kripke is right to reject this inversion.[7] Two considerations show this. One emerges when we note that condemnation of an immoral act is not in and of itself sufficient. Condemnation can be morally inappropriate; e.g., when people condemn a thing because everyone is condemning it or because they have been raised to condemn it. Thus, an immoral act must be condemned *for the right reason*. Since the right reason for condemning it is that it is immoral, it must be condemned because it is immoral. But, if so, appropriate condemnation contains the normative element seemingly lost in the inversion. Hence, the fact that naturalistic accounts of condemning behavior (acceptance, constant conjunction, agreement) can capture purely descriptive notions means nothing, since those accounts fail to capture the conditions under which such responses (or events) occur for the right reason. These considerations suggest that the inversion strategy, as practiced, begs the question, since an account of condemning behavior (etc.) has to capture such conditions if it is to provide the right reasons.

But even in cases of appropriate condemnation, inversion makes the mistake of putting the determiner in the place of the determined and the determined in the place of the determiner. That this is so is perhaps clearest in the cases of logic and mathematics, where the inversion sacrifices the necessity of logical and mathematical principles, as should be clear from the discussions in the previous chapters. If the discussion of ethics in the appendix of the previous chapter is on the right track, the inversion also sacrifices the necessity of moral principles and, as a consequence, assimilates morality to something like manners. Licking one's plate is ill mannered because society condemns it, and, on the inversion, sending the innocent to the gas chamber is immoral also because society condemns it. Of course, the naturalist can say there is a difference in strength of condemnation. But such differences are no more than differences in how we feel, which, with changes in our attitudes toward the acts, can disappear. I think that only on the basis of a link between necessity and the *ought* of morality, such as was discussed in the last chapter, can we do justice to the distinction between morality and manners. For, on this basis, even if every society turns Nazi, such murders, praised though they would be, would still be immoral.

The point is, in fact, a general one: only on the basis of a link between necessity and the *ought* of logic can we do justice to the distinction between acceptance of a convention and logical truth. For a convention, by its nature, can be changed, leaving us a different convention, but a logical necessity, by its nature, cannot be changed, leaving us a different logical truth. Quine's treatment of logical laws illustrates the problem naturalists face in attempting to naturalize logic in the face of this distinction. Quine vacillates between two positions. One is the position he takes in "Two Dogmas of Empiricism": that logical laws are at bottom empirical principles in natural science. They are central beliefs in our overall system, but they, too, can be revised for implying something false about observation. The other is the position he takes in *Word and Object* and reaffirms in his reply to Stroud: logical laws are conventions of intelligible expression.[8] The latter position takes the denial of a logical law (e.g., excluded middle) to be unintelligible gibberish, whereas the former takes it to be possibly true.

Neither position is satisfactory. Both fail to explain the force of a standard logical principle like noncontradiction. The latter fails to explain the intelligibility of alternative logics; the former has to fall back on the necessary truth about noncontradiction that it was introduced to replace.[9] If Quine does not make use of the principle of noncontradiction in formulating the notion of revisability, what are the conditions under which noncontradiction has to be revised? On the one hand, there must be such conditions, since Quine claims that all principles of logic are revisable in principle, but, on the other, there cannot be, since, under those conditions, there is no obligation to reject the principle as false because it *conflicts* with true observation statements.

Let us put aside Quine's attempts to naturalize deductive logic for a moment and look at Nelson Goodman's attempt to naturalize inductive logic. Goodman tells us that the old riddle, the task of explaining why we ought to make inductive projections, has been laid to rest, and urges us to occupy ourselves instead with his new riddle, the task of explicating the projections we do make.[10] But Goodman's dismissal of the old riddle is too quick. No one not already convinced that such metaphysical problems are, to use Goodman's own word, spurious can be convinced by his rehearsal of the familiar Humean moves. (Deductive justifications don't work because inductive conclusions do not follow from statements about past experience, and inductive justifications don't work because they beg the question.) The implication is, presumably, that inductive projection is beyond justification, but this conclusion doesn't follow unless it is further supposed that deductive and inductive justification exhaust the modes of justification. To see that there is a fallacy here, note that Goodman fails to consider a number of approaches to solving the old riddle against which he should have had an argument. Such approaches start with the opposite assumption: that standard deductive and inductive justifications do not exhaust the options.[11] For example, Goodman never mentions approaches like those of Peirce and Reichenbach and those of Salmon and Strawson.[12] My point is not that any of those approaches are actually successful. Rather, it is that the approaches are serious attempts to explore the possibilities of justification beyond the standard deductive and inductive options, and that Goodman's failure to consider them shows that his dismissal of the old riddle is too hasty.

Of course, on a view like Hume's, where knowledge divides exhaustively into relations of ideas and matters of fact—that is, into the categories of analytic *a priori* and synthetic *a posteriori* knowledge—the supposition that deductive and inductive justification exhaust the modes of justification can seem appealing. For those who hold such a view, Goodman has needed no argument to support his dismissal of the old problem, since they already think that something which is neither about relations of ideas nor about matters of empirical fact is spurious metaphysics. For anyone else, however, an argument is required to establish that the category of synthetic *a priori* knowledge does not provide a further mode of justification.

If the old riddle of induction had been eliminated, Goodman's approach to the new riddle would make sense. According to Goodman, we should approach the justification of inductive inferences on analogy with the justification of deductive inferences, where deductive inferences are justified by conformity to deductive rules, which, in turn, are justified by conformity to "accepted deductive practice."[13] Goodman's view is that, if such mutual adjustment of deductive rules and practices, which, he supposes, involves no traditional metaphysical issues, is good enough for deduction, it ought to be good enough for induction as well.

But Goodman is wrong to suppose that reaching reflective equilibrium in the justification of deductive rules is free of metaphysical issues. We find such issues, for example, in the disputes between supporters of standard logic and supporters of alternative logics. We cannot hope to settle these issues on the basis of a sanitized process of mutual adjustment between practice and theory. The divisions between standard logic and the alternatives are too deep-going, and the contending theories can too easily claim an acceptable equilibrium between theory and practice. Ordinary practice cannot easily be enlisted on one side of the issue or the other, while specialized practice and theory divide into a collection of robust, incompatible reflective equilibria. Metaphysical argument about the nature of meaning and truth is required to choose between them.

Without the assumption that the old riddle has been eliminated, Goodman's new riddle becomes a version of the old riddle of justifying standard inductive practice as against counterinductive alternatives. Since the equilibrium we reach is no better than the principles employed to reach it, Goodman's picture of mutual adjustment now seems question-begging in the way that is familiar at this point. The supposition that justification consists in having a place within the final reflective equilibrium seems to contain the same philosophical problems we saw in Quine's discussion of deduction. What principles are supposed to guide the process of adjustment? Standard inductive rules would produce circularity. The appeal to conservatism is of no help, either. We may have got off on the wrong foot and now simply be entrenching and, perhaps, amplifying past errors. We thus have the parallel problem in non-demonstrative inference of how we know that an "accurate codification of accepted inductive practices" is not leading us down a garden path, into an orthodoxy of accepted inductive mistakes. A version of this problem can be posed by asking how we know that, by taking the council of conservatism, we are not heading for inductive disaster in the future because, in fact, we live in a grue-type world? Here we can clearly see that we have the old riddle of how to justify inductive rules dressed up in the new clothes of predicates.

The above criticisms of Quine and Goodman are criticisms of their naturalism rather than of the conception of reflective equilibrium. The criticisms are intended to apply not to the idea that justifying a principle can be a matter of showing that reflection reaches a stable equilibrium with that principle rather than its rivals, but only to naturalistic versions of that idea on which the process of reaching reflective equilibrium excludes metaphysical reflection. I am sympathetic to such a conception of justification so long as it is allowed that metaphysical problems can stand in the way of equilibrium and that progress toward equilibrium can be made by metaphysical speculation.[14] Once we allow metaphysical speculation into the reflective process, the claim that reflective equilibrium is a justificational process is no longer contentious, but reflective equilibrium itself is no longer the naturalist's exclusive possession.

When Quine's and Goodman's attempts to naturalize epistemology are set side by side, we gain a revealing perspective on the shortcomings of the enterprise. On the one hand, for all his emphasis on naturalizing epistemology, Quine seems more cognizant than Goodman of the fact that the old philosophical puzzles arise within naturalized epistemology, that is, within science. Referring to the Cartesian skeptic, Quine writes: "I am not accusing the skeptic of begging the question; he is quite within his rights in assuming science in order to refute science; this, if carried out, would be a straightforward argument by *reductio ad absurdum*. I am only making the point that skeptical doubts are scientific doubts."[15] Quine also remarks that "the Humean predicament is the human predicament."[16] Since this is to say that the old riddle of induction is still with us, Quine clearly thinks that, whatever the advantages of treating epistemology as an "enterprise within science," escaping the old riddles is not one of them. On the other hand, Goodman seems more cognizant than Quine of the fact that naturalized epistemology lacks the resources to solve traditional philosophical problems. Goodman's attempt to dismiss "the Humean predicament" seems motivated by a recognition of the limits of naturalized epistemology which make deflationary treatments of traditional philosophical problems necessary.

As I see it, Quine and Goodman each have a piece of the truth. Quine is right that traditional philosophical problems arise within a naturalized epistemology, and Goodman is right that its resources do not suffice to solve them. As Quine recognizes, nothing stops the Cartesian skeptic from donning the white laboratory jacket of the scientist and asking whether external reality is really the way we take it to be on the basis of how it impinges on our sensory surfaces. But, as Goodman seems to see more clearly—e.g., in connection with affirming Hume's skepticism concerning inductive justification—natural science cannot justify its own methodological principles because the results that might be used for that purpose would themselves have been obtained with those principles. Taking Quine's and Goodman's points together, the conclusion is that, if naturalized epistemology were all we had by which to distinguish the link between scientific phenomena and scientific theory that we ought to accept from links that we have accepted, are disposed to accept, or are urged by the skeptic to accept, then we could not stop the skeptic from "assuming science to refute science."

3

Given this conclusion, the naturalistic account of knowledge that philosophers would be giving up in returning to traditional metaphysics, being no better than metaphysics at its worst, is hardly worth holding on to. This makes very clear the wisdom of Wittgenstein's conception of naturalism with its emphasis on showing that philosophical problems are nonsense. Although there is no need to consider Wittgenstein's radical critical philosophy any further, we do need to consider another variety of deflationism which has not yet been considered.[17] This is the framework-relativity which is most often thought of in connection with Carnap's view that we cannot know foundational principles because, since these are external to the maximal frameworks within science, there is nothing on the basis of which they can be known.[18]

Let us begin with Carnap. According to him, traditional philosophers argue interminably about justification because such questions are "framed in the wrong way."[19] The grounds that Carnap offers for supposing that questions of justification are improperly framed are that such questions cannot be answered empirically.[20] To be properly framed, the propositions in question would have to satisfy the verifiability criterion—but the never-ending philosophical arguments about them should make it amply clear that no sense experience is relevant to their truth or falsehood. Carnap holds that the notion that there is something to explain rests on a confusion between the genuine practical question of whether to employ a linguistic framework and the bogus theoretical question of whether the world of things depicted in the framework is real.[21]

Again we encounter the two alternatives of Humean empiricism, and again we reply that no argument has been presented which shows that the synthetic questions that cannot be answered empirically are improperly framed. From today's perspective, Carnap's support for his claims is paltry to say the least. The only ground for them is Vienna-style verificationism. But if there is one doctrine about the meaningful which has been given its chance and found wanting, verificationism is it.[22] Had something like Schlick's line been able to handle synthetic *a priori* truths, Carnap would not be open to this reply. But the line that such truths are "purely analytic, tautological, formal" came to grief, and, as we have seen, the logical principles on which it was based themselves turn out to be further synthetic *a priori* truths. Moreover, as some philosophers pointed out early on, Carnap's doctrine is self-refuting: since the doctrine is about linguistic frameworks as wholes, it cannot itself be confirmed or disconfirmed by any possible sense experience, and, hence, it condemns itself as meaningless.[23]

Verificationism is not the only doctrine that can be used to establish a framework-relativity like Carnap's. Any doctrine that accords sense only to internal propositions because they are internal, withholding it from external propositions because they are external, will establish one, too. The essential point is that these doctrines preclude any basis for assigning meaning which is framework-neutral. Wittgenstein's and Quine's criticisms of traditional intensionalism try to preclude the possibility of a universal semantics of natural languages that would serve as a basis on which external propositions can receive a sense apart from particular linguistic frameworks. Frege's language-independent senses are clearly one of Wittgenstein's prime targets, and Quine makes it quite explicit that he wishes to preclude "language-neutral meanings." In Wittgenstein's case, the relativity is to a language embedded in a form of life, and, in Quine's, to a language conceived of as a seamless web of beliefs.

Wittgenstein and Quine provided the prototype and also arguments for more recent conceptions of framework-relativity. The most influential framework-relativity to be built on this prototype is Kuhn and Feyerabend's conception of theory change in science. Feyerabend puts the semantic core of the conception as follows: "the meaning of every term we use depends upon the theoretical context in which it occurs. Words do not 'mean' something in isolation; they obtain their meaning by being part of a theoretical system."[24] Kuhn and Feyerabend draw the conclusion that there can be no propositions external to the particular theories involved in a scientific revolution which express the conflict between the theories in neutral terms. This conclusion challenges the standard view of scientific progress, on which successful theories refute unsuccessful ones. On their view, successful theories merely replace unsuccessful theories.

Elsewhere, I have argued that the significant alternative to the Kuhn-Feyerabend view that words obtain their meaning within a theoretical system is not that words mean something in isolation, but that their meaning derives from the semantics of natural language in general which is common to rival theoretical systems.[25] I argued further that the only thing standing in the way of such an alternative was the mistaken idea that Quine's criticisms of the analytic/synthetic distinction and of language-neutral meanings is successful. The present book completes my argument by completing its arguments against Quine and by adding arguments against Wittgenstein, whose work equally supports the Kuhn-Feyerabend view.

Recently, Putnam has proposed a framework-relativity which he calls "internal realism."[26] He imagines two frameworks for determining the number of objects there are, a Carnapian framework which counts objects in the ordinary way and a Polish framework which mereologically counts the sum of any two objects as a third object. Putnam claims that there is no "neutral description" of "a world with three objects" over and above these partisan counts, because there are only the logical primitives of the ordinary framework and the logical primitives of the Polish one (ibid., pp. 18–19). He claims that the primitives of these systems "have a multitude of different uses rather than one absolute 'meaning'" (ibid., p. 17). Spelling this claim out, he says that questions like 'Does the Carnapian or the Polish framework give the correct count?' do not make sense. "[T]here is a limit to how far questions make sense" imposed by the fact that object terms are meaningless if not relativized to a framework (ibid., pp. 19–20).

It is hard to see this as anything more than Wittgenstein on family resemblance, or, more likely, Quine on indeterminacy. Corresponding to Quine's radical-translation situation with rabbits scurrying by the feet of linguist and native informant is the world of three objects. Corresponding to the translations "rabbit" and "undetached rabbit parts" are the Carnapian and Polish counts. Corresponding to my distinction between Quine's radical translation and actual radical translation is the distinction between Putnam's situation in which there are only the Carnapian and Polish systems with their own special formation rules and actual situations where such logistic systems are framed within natural languages. Corresponding to the absence of independent semantic controls in Quine's radical translation is the absence of a linguistic means of arriving at a "neutral description" in Putnam's situation of the Carnapian and Polish theorists. Corresponding to my challenge to show that Quinean radical translation does not ignore a significant feature of actual translation by ignoring the independent controls found in actual translation is a challenge to Putnam to show that his situation does not ignore a significant feature of the actual situation in science by ignoring the linguistic means for arriving at "neutral descriptions."

Quine's response was that independent controls assume "linguistically neutral meanings," and there are none. Putnam's response to the corresponding challenge must be the same: a "neutral description" assumes "absolute meaning[s]," and there are none. Thus, the critical question for Putnam, as it is for Quine, is: What argument is there to show that there are no absolute (language-neutral) meanings? In the work under consideration Putnam fails to give an argument for the claim that there are no "absolute meaning[s]." His remark that the notions of 'object' and 'existence' are "logical primitives" with "a multitude of different uses" is, of course, uncontentious if it is simply asserted as truth about these notions within the Carnapian and Polish systems, but the remark begs the question if asserted as a truth about the senses of the English words "object" and "existence" (ibid., p. 19). On a theory of meaning like that developed in chapter 2, "logical primitives" in artificial languages or theoretical systems can have decompositional meaning in a natural language. Furthermore, on the "top-down" approach to pragmatics, the decompositional meaning of an expression type can participate in "a multitude of different uses" without the existence of those uses being any evidence against the expression type's having that one meaning.

Therefore, Putnam's denial that there are "absolute meaning[s]" requires an argument against the analytic/synthetic distinction, a decompositional theory of meaning, and such a conception of pragmatics. Of course, Putnam has been making such an argument for almost his entire philosophical career, and, accordingly, he has to be understood as basing his claim that there are no framework-transcendent meanings on that earlier argument. But, as section 4 of chapter 6 has shown, the argument in question, although adequate for dismissing Fregean "absolute meaning[s]," is not adequate against the non-Fregean "absolute meaning[s]" of the proto-theory. Quine's argument against meaning and synonymy, as section 4 also showed, is needed to block the formulation of such a non-Fregean alternative. As we saw in chapter 5, however, Quine's argument does not hold up because it underestimates the potential for theories of meaning within linguistics; in particular, the argument overlooks exactly the proto-theory. So, with the fall of these dominos, Putnam has no reason for rejecting (non-Fregean) "absolute meaning[s]."

To see the role of the analytic/synthetic distinction in saving us from framework-relativity, we need only look for a moment at how its absence gets us into it. Wittgenstein's metaphor of language as an ancient city with ever more modern suburbs expresses the same rejection of the traditional language/theory distinction as Quine's holistic picture of our system of belief. With the rejection of this distinction, languages are taken to contain information of all kinds, including information belonging to the theories in the special sciences. In this way, languages are divided along the lines that divide such theories and are, accordingly, limited by the conceptual resources of particular theories. The result is incommensurability and indeterminacy. Thus, the language/theory distinction is essential to any notion of a language with conceptual resources that are expressively rich enough to avoid incommensurability and indeterminacy.

The language/theory distinction is, in effect, the analytic/synthetic distinction. This is because the language/theory distinction is drawn in terms of a notion of language on which the semantics of languages is principally determined by a set of analytic propositions and in terms of a notion of theory on which its truths about the domain are principally determined by an axiomatic system of synthetic propositions. Given the analytic/synthetic distinction, we have the language/theory distinction. Given that we have the language/theory distinction, we can say, within the semantics of natural languages, that conflicting theoretical claims, whether scientific or philosophical, reflect incompatibilities between fundamental synthetic propositions of theories.

In Putnam's example, the Carnapian theorist has a theory about the world on which there are fewer objects than there are on the Polish theorist's. But, once we move from Putnam's encapsulated situation (which parallels Quine's artificial radical-translation situation) to the actual situation in which theories are framed within natural languages, the appearance of framework-relativity disappears. Each theory would be translatable into the natural language in which the other theory can also be expressed. The languages are *ex hypothesi* English (or German) and Polish, and, therefore, in Putnam's example, the Carnapian theorist's statement that there are three objects can be translated into Polish, and the Polish theorist's statement that there are seven can be translated into English (or German)—Putnam does so. And both statements are true, since the mereological statement is true just in case there are three objects. This account assumes, of course, that English, German, Polish, and other natural languages are intertranslatable or expressively complete in the sense of section 8 of chapter 2. But, given the arguments of that chapter, the only non-Quinean reasons that proponents of framework-relativity have given against intertranslatability or expressive completeness are inadequate. Since there are no Quinean reasons, there are no grounds for framework-relativism.

4

Naturalists are fond of saying that the metaphysical attitude prevents us from dealing with philosophical problems. But, if the arguments in this chapter concerning naturalized epistemology are correct, it is clearer that the naturalistic attitude prevents us from dealing with them than that the metaphysical attitude does. Methodological principles or philosophical propositions such as that there is an external world are *a priori*, and, hence, they are beyond the range of the *a posteriori* discoveries of natural science.[27]

Ironically, then, it is non-naturalism, which recognizes the *a priori* character of philosophical propositions, that opens up the possibility of explaining our knowledge of philosophical propositions by treating their explanation as itself a matter of *a priori* philosophical theory. Non-naturalism holds out the prospect of obtaining appropriate grounds for such propositions because it permits synthetic *a priori* philosophical grounds for methodological principles and other synthetic *a priori* propositions. Thus, when the promise of naturalized epistemology and the hopes for deflating metaphysics fade, what recourse is left but to adopt an approach that offers the possibility of dealing with the problems? If the naturalistic alternatives have been ruled out and if we are not prepared to accept skepticism, then it seems there is no choice but to pursue a non-naturalist approach to the justification of foundational principles.[28]

These reflections suggest not only that the problem of explaining our knowledge of synthetic *a priori* truth should be restored to its former central place in philosophy, but also that the problem will not take the form it took in the Kantian framework. I have already indicated why I think that its solution does not lie in Kant's transcendental idealism. But there are also more specific features of the problem that are got wrong in the Kantian framework. One, which I will not rehearse here, is the account of analyticity itself.[29] Another is a mistake in Kant's formulation of the problem of how synthetic *a priori* knowledge is possible, namely, his idea that necessity is the hallmark of the synthetic *a priori*.[30] To say that a proposition is necessary is to say that it is true in every possible world, but philosophical skepticism presents us with examples of possible worlds in which synthetic *a priori* propositions are false. Since there is nothing incoherent in supposing the falsehood of the inductive principle or the proposition that the external world is the way we perceive it, the synthetic *a priori* propositions in question are not necessary truths.

Since some synthetic *a priori* propositions are contingent, the explanation of how knowledge of synthetic *a priori* truth is possible must make a place for the contingent synthetic *a priori*. This point is buttressed by the fact that, since we are allowing the meaningfulness of external questions, there is a perfectly meaningful notion of objective reality, that is, of what things are like apart from us and how we may think about them. If so, we have to count it as possible that objective reality is different from what we think it is, even when we have done everything we can to think in the best scientific way. It follows that it is possible that skepticism may prevent us from knowing reality with complete and absolute certainty even with respect to its most abstract aspects.[31] But this hardly implies that we do not know it. *intermed. position betw. Maim. + Spinoza ?*

Let us recapitulate. The problems of philosophy involve explaining how contingent synthetic *a priori* knowledge is possible. The *a priori* element means that these problems are not solvable on the basis of empirical investigation and, hence, are beyond the scope of natural science. The synthetic element means that they are not solvable on the basis of semantic investigation and, hence, are also beyond the scope of linguistics and linguistic philosophy. The contingent element means that they are not solvable on the basis of logical investigation. The proper conclusion is, I think, that their solution depends on philosophical investigation.

I have no account of philosophical investigation to offer. As a non-naturalist, I think that, since our knowledge of foundational principles cannot be explained on the basis of *a posteriori* reasoning from observations of natural objects, it must be understood on the basis of *a priori* reasoning from intuitions about the structure of non-natural, abstract objects. I cannot at present be more specific than I have been about such reasoning, intuition, or abstract objects. But within the scope of this study the absence of such an account is not a problem. The study is concerned with criticizing naturalistic conceptions of philosophical investigation, such as that it is empirical investigation of a special sort or that it is Wittgensteinian linguistic investigation. The study aims to show that these are misconceptions arising in an attempt to reduce philosophy to something else; they constitute reductionism applied to philosophy itself.

This attempt is motivated by a mistaken diagnosis of why philosophical progress moves at so relatively slow a pace. But what of the conditions that make reductionists and critical philosophers impatient with the pace of philosophical progress? Even those who are not reductionists or critical philosophers at times feel such impatience: metaphysicians seem to be endlessly wrangling among themselves, while scientists make steady progress. I will consider this natural feeling of impatience below. But before I do I want to examine the assumptions of critical philosophers and reductionists which take them beyond such general concern, leading the former to insist that something is wrong with the way metaphysical problems are conceived and the latter to insist that something less like traditional philosophy and more like science is necessary to set things right.

There are two assumptions: one is that there is some substantive notion of how fast philosophy ought to be progressing, and the other is that philosophy and science can be measured with the same scale, so that philosophical progress can be compared with scientific progress and the rate of the one used as a measure of the performance of the other. These assumptions are rarely, if ever, singled out and critically examined, but, once they are, it is rather easy to show they are mistaken.

The rate at which a discipline progresses is the rate at which it closes the gap between some initial stage of investigation when certain problems are unsolved and some later stage when definite results or solutions for them have been obtained. To judge the rate of progress in a discipline, then, we would have to know something about how hard the problems are, since, without that, the absence of results might show nothing. The problems might be so hard that, with many times the number of investigators, many thousands of years might be a drop in the bucket. Now, although it is safe to say that the problems of philosophy are very hard, we have no idea of what their order of difficulty is. We have no notion of the kind and degree of complexity we are facing in such problems, nor, for that matter, do we have much idea of the power of human intelligence in such circumstances. Hence, we have no notion of how fast philosophy should be progressing, and, consequently, it makes no more sense to claim that philosophical progress from the time of Socrates to the present has been exceedingly slow than it does to claim that it is par for the course or even that it is exceedingly fast. Therefore, the diagnoses of critical philosophers and reductionists that there is something wrong cannot be based on a rational assessment to the effect that there has been appropriate effort which has failed to achieve results in appropriate time.

Furthermore, dissatisfaction with philosophical progress assumes that philosophical investigation is sufficiently like scientific investigation for comparison, but the difference in the rate at which results are achieved in the two investigations is as much an argument against a relevant similarity as it is an argument for the view that metaphysics is a basically unsound enterprise. Given all the historical evidence, one can conclude that science and philosophy are very different, which *prima facie* is a plausible enough thing to say, and has been said by a large number of philosophers, including Wittgenstein.

Moreover, critical philosophers like Kant could not reasonably hold that science and philosophy are similar because they concede that philosophical propositions are *a priori*, whereas the propositions of natural science are *a posteriori* and those of mathematical science are about far simpler matters than philosophy. Philosophers like Quine are in a better position to make the assumption of similarity. Quine's view is that philosophy is self-reflective natural science, so bad philosophy like Frege's is bad natural science and good philosophy like Mill's and Hume's is good natural science. But, even though Quineans have no trouble making the assumption, they have had no success in defending it.

On the basis of the above reflections, the critical philosopher's and the reductionist's dissatisfaction with traditional philosophy and their insistence that it is time for a change appear in a quite different light. They now seem to stem either from a deeply confused notion that the problems of philosophy are easy enough for us to have gotten significant results by this time or from an unjustified identification of philosophy with some form of natural science. There is, then, no rationale for taking traditional philosophy to task because its problems remain unsolved while scientific problems get solved at a great rate.

The aspects of the history of philosophy which the critical philosopher and the reductionist interpret as signs of deep trouble can be interpreted instead as supporting our view of philosophical propositions as special. These propositions are different from the propositions of the natural sciences in virtue of comprising their metaphysical foundations and being synthetic *a priori*, and different from the propositions in the mathematical sciences in virtue of comprising their metaphysical foundations and being contingent. Some indication of this special character of philosophical propositions can even be gleaned from features of the various views that have been criticized. Quine's conception of philosophical propositions as close to scientific propositions, but constituting a more abstract epistemological structure of natural science, expresses something of their role as the metaphysical foundations of science—except for their not being *a posteriori*. Carnap's conception of philosophical questions as external questions expresses the absolute character of philosophical propositions—except for their not being meaningless because unverifiable. Wittgenstein's conception of philosophy as somehow prior to and independent of empirical science expresses their autonomy—except for their not thereby transcending the limits of language. Kant's conception of problems of philosophy as problems about how it is possible to know synthetic *a priori* truth expresses the proper semantic and epistemological status of philosophical propositions—except for his idealistic view of them and his linking of the *a priori* with the necessary.

The attempt on the part of the early Wittgenstein, Schlick, Carnap, and their followers to show that metaphysical questions are meaningless can be seen as a mistaken response to a genuine feature of such questions. The explanation of their alleged meaninglessness was that philosophical propositions are not about anything and, hence, cannot be true or false. (This, in effect, is also the line Quine takes about the propositions of the theory of meaning in claiming that there is no fact of the matter in translation.) Mistakenly treating philosophical propositions as about something when they are about nothing, so the deflationary explanation runs, is responsible for the sad state of metaphysics. But the mistake is to think of philosophical propositions as having to be about something in the natural realm, like truths of natural science. Unless it is assumed along with the naturalist position that everything there is is part of the natural realm, there is no basis for claiming that philosophical propositions are about nothing.

According to the non-naturalist position, instead of saying that philosophical questions cannot be answered because they relate to nothing in the world, we can say that they are immensely difficult to answer because they relate to everything. Such generality is suggested by the skeptic's ability to call all our beliefs about the world into question by challenging a single philosophical proposition. Accordingly, I submit that philosophical questions still remain unanswered, despite all of Western philosophy, because of their universal scope. The speculation that philosophical propositions comprise the metaphysical foundations of the sciences offers an explanation of why the scope of philosophical questions should make it so hard to answer them. Given the foundational role of philosophical propositions in scientific investigations, the answer to a philosophical question will, at some level, be part of the scientific answers forthcoming from such investigations, and further, the scientific answers will, at an initial stage at least, be relevant to the answer to the philosophical question.

This intimate involvement can be seen in the way in which philosophical propositions about causality enter into contemporary debates about the interpretation of quantum-mechanical phenomena, the way in which philosophical propositions about truth and necessity enter into debates between classical and constructivist mathematicians, the way in which philosophical propositions about the nature of mind enter into debates about the computer model in the emerging cognitive sciences, and the way in which philosophical propositions about abstract objects enter into debates about the character of linguistics. But beyond this dependence of scientific propositions on philosophical propositions, there is the further dependence of philosophical propositions upon one another. Given these wheels within wheels, no special hypothesis like the critical philospher's or the reductionist's is needed to explain why philosophical problems require a radically different time scale from the problems of science and, accordingly, far more patience than would be appropriate in the sciences. Perhaps full solutions to the problems of philosophy can no more be expected even in the long run than can a full scientific theory of everything. Perhaps, like the latter, a comprehensive metaphysical theory that does justice to the unity of philosophy is an ideal of reason which we can approximate but not attain.

5

At the very beginning of this book I quoted a passage in which Kripke describes himself as vascillating between a Chomskyan and a Wittgensteinian approach to natural language. I suggested that Kripke had put his finger on a dilemma for a large segment of contemporary philosophy. The choice between those approaches forces us to go either against our best scientific impulses or against our best philosophical impulses and, consequently, either to sacrifice the benefits of a scientific understanding of language or to embrace a conceptual scheme which, philosophically, seems like *Luftgebäude*. I conjectured that we can go between the horns of the dilemma by denying its assumption that the only approaches to natural language open to us are one or another form of naturalism. In the course of the book, I have tried to show that the arguments that appear to restrict us to naturalist approaches turn out, on close examination, to be inadequate.

If I am right that there is a viable non-naturalist approach to language and meaning, the dilemma itself becomes an argument against naturalism, because it unnecessarily sacrifices either the advantages of the Chomskyan approach or the advantages of the Wittgensteinian approach. Non-naturalism offers philosophers the benefits of a scientific approach to language of the sort we find in contemporary formal linguistics without requiring them to pay the intolerable price, as far as their own subject is concerned, of reneging on their commitment to its problems. On Chomsky's approach to linguistics, concepts like 'deep structure' amount to little more than *Luftgebäude* in application to philosophical problems because they are part of the machinery set in motion by speakers who "operate a calculus according to definite rules." Such internal models, as we have seen, can no more determine the correct use of language than external models.

Another way to appreciate the philosophical uselessness of linguistic concepts when they are understood psychologically in accord with Chomsky's linguistic conceptualism is to note that linguistic conceptualism is a special case of Quine's naturalized epistemology. As with Quine, philosophical questions for Chomsky, like the question that divides rationalists and empiricists, arise and are allegedly solved in the exclusively empirical context of *a posteriori* investigations. But if, as I have argued, philosophical questions are *a priori* questions, then, as we have seen in the earlier discussion of Quine and Goodman, a Chomskyan approach is not only incorrect about their origin but ineffective for their solution.

Chomsky frequently calls himself a rationalist, but, in fact, his approach is as empiricist as Quine's. To see this, we have to see why Quine is an empiricist despite the notion of an innate quality space presented in *Word and Object*.[32] This notion commits Quine to a very strong assumption about innate structure, it is true, but to draw the moral from this commitment that Quine is as much of a rationalist as Chomsky would be wrong. The right moral is that Chomsky is as much of an empiricist as Quine. To appreciate this, we just have to remind ourselves of what an empiricist is, viz., someone who thinks that all our knowledge comes through our sensory channels and is about the natural objects which are the source of the information that passes through those channels. Chomsky certainly thinks this, since he thinks that our linguistic knowledge comes from the information we get, internally, from our innate linguistic structures and, externally, from the speech to which we are exposed as language learners; he thinks that linguistics is about our biological capacity for language, our language faculty in the form of a neural organ, and physical instances of speech which are the data for acquiring such a faculty.[33]

What has led to the wrong moral is the idea that nativism and empiricism are opposites. Nativism, in some form, is always part of empiricism, and indeed must be, since, without some innate structure, no stimulus would be re-identifiable and no empirical generalizations could be made. Furthermore, one cannot get beyond empiricism to rationalism by strengthening one's nativism. In order to cross over to rationalism, one must instead change one's view about knowledge, to allow that some knowledge does not come through any sense channel, even an internal one, and is not about natural objects, even neural ones.

Moreover, there is a good reason why naturalists are empiricists and vice versa: naturalism and empiricism depend upon each other. Empiricism serves naturalism by providing an epistemology that restricts what we can know to what naturalism says there is to be known, and naturalism serves empiricism by guaranteeing that empiricism covers all the kinds of knowledge there can be.

The non-naturalist approach frees linguistic concepts like 'deep structure' from the stigma of *Luftgebäude* by construing linguistics as an *a priori* discipline. Accordingly, it construes the philosophical problems concerning linguistics as arising about *a priori* principles which belong to the foundations of the discipline. Thus, non-naturalism provides a clear conception of how philosophical problems about the foundations of the science of language can be related to but different from scientific problems about the structure of natural languages in linguistics proper.[34] As a consequence, linguistics and its concepts can be of a piece with the *a priori* problems of philosophy. Accordingly, it is possible, as we have seen in chapter 2, for linguistic concepts like 'deep structure' to contribute to philosophical investigation. This being so, such linguistic concepts cannot be philosophically stigmatized as *Luftgebäude*. Thus, we secure the advantages of scientific linguistics without reneging on the philosopher's commitment to the problems of philosophy.

We have also avoided the disadvantages of Wittgenstein's approach. Since he wants to argue that philosophical problems can be dissolved by showing that the sentences expressing them have no meaning, it is necessary for him to fashion a notion of meaning so inclusive that it can deal with all the matters with which philosophical problems are concerned. Only if everything on which the critical uses of language depend is packed into meaning will meaning be broad enough to support Wittgenstein's argument that all metaphysical sentences go beyond the limits of language. But, when the notion of meaning is made broad enough to serve this purpose, it becomes bloated with all manner of extralinguistic fact, and, as a consequence, it goes far beyond the notion of meaning in natural language (for reasons of the sort mentioned in chapter 2, section 7). Such broadening of the notion of meaning takes it beyond the limits of the linguistic.

If I am right that the limits of the linguistic coincide with the boundary between language and theory, then, on the proto-theory's narrow notion of meaning as well as on Wittgenstein's broad notion, philosophical questions lie beyond the limits of language. But this no longer means that philosophical questions are nonsense. It only means that they are extralinguistic questions, concerning the metaphysical foundations of the sciences and other disciplines. This, in turn, means that the philosopher's task is roughly the task that Kant, the great reformist critical philosopher, formulated in order to show what questions were ignored in Hume's empiricist and naturalist philosophy, namely, the task of explaining the possibility of synthetic *a priori* knowledge.

On the basis of this conception of the nature of the commitment to the problems of philosophy, I claimed that we can preserve what is best in both the Chomskyan and the Wittgensteinian approaches and avoid what is worst. But, left at that, this claim is bound to be haunted by Wittgenstein's ghost. His enterprise of showing that philosophical problems cannot be meaningfully posed was a novel and heroic attempt to "[give] philosophy peace". Once we give up on Wittgenstein's radical critical philosophy, we are again face to face with these most obstinate of all intellectual problems. The task of solving them is bound to seem daunting, and we are bound to think often of the solace Wittgenstein offered.

Thus, in order to exorcise Wittgenstein's ghost, it may seem necessary to provide some assurance of philosophical success. No one can give such assurance. There is no way to obtain assurance short of continuing in the direction which is still left open to us of seeking metaphysical understanding. So I do not think that it counts against the non-naturalist approach that philosophizing based upon it will continue, for the foreseeable future, to be "tormented by questions which bring *itself* in question" (PI: 133).

The situation, as I see it, is this. The linguistic turn explored a promising alternative to the metaphysical paths in the great maze that is philosophy. That alternative path seemed, at the time, to lead the way out. But, in fact, the path led us back into the depths of the labyrinth, landing us at nearly the point where the turn was first taken. In spite of the fact that now we have to return to the exploration of metaphysical paths, the philosophers who took the linguistic turn contributed something of genuine value to philosophy in discovering a new path. No matter that the path turned out to be a dead end; in marking it as such, we fill in one more detail of the map that we, together with philosophers of the past and future, are making of the maze.

Notes

Preface

1. Saul Kripke, "Substitutional Quantification," in *Truth and Meaning*, J. McDowell and G. Matthews, eds., Oxford University Press, 1976, p. 412. "Luftgebäude" is, literally translated, "buildings of air."
2. For present purposes, I am lumping various approaches together with the Chomskyan and (late) Wittgensteinian (e.g., Quine's with Chomsky's and Ryle's with Wittgenstein's). In the course of the book it will be clear why, in spite of certain differences, this grouping is reasonable.
3. F. P. Ramsey, *The Foundations of Mathematics and Other Logical Essays*, Kegan Paul, London, 1931, pp. 115–116.
4. Noam Chomsky, "Some Conceptual Shifts in the Study of Language," in *How Many Questions? Essays in Honor of Sidney Morgenbesser*, L. Cauman et al., eds., Hackett Publishing Co., Indianapolis, 1983, pp. 156–157.
5. Ludwig Wittgenstein, *Remarks on the Foundations of Mathematics*, Basil Blackwell, Oxford, 1956, section 61. I will have more to say about Wittgenstein's naturalism in the next chapter.
6. Hao Wang, *Reflections on Gödel*, MIT Press, Cambridge, Mass., 1987, pp. 212–218.
7. J. J. Katz, *Language and Other Abstract objects*, Rowman & Littlefield, Totowa, N.J. 1981; D. T. Langendoen and P. Postal, *The Vastness of Natural Languages*, Basil Blackwell, Oxford, 1984; *The Philosophy of Linguistics*, J. J. Katz, ed., Oxford University Press, 1985; J. J. Katz and P. Postal, "Realism vs. Conceptualism in Linguistics," to appear.

Chapter 1

1. Whether, and if so to what extent, Wittgenstein's critical philosophy reflects the thinking of earlier German naturalistic philosophers are questions that go beyond the scope of the present study. See Hans Sluga, *Gottlob Frege*, Routledge & Kegan Paul, London, 1980, pp. 19–26.
2. Ludwig Wittgenstein, *Tractatus Logico-Philosophicus*, Routledge & Kegan Paul, London, C. K. Ogden, trans., with F. P. Ramsey, 1922; D. F. Pears and B. F. McGuiness, trans., 1961; section 6.53. Citations hereafter will be by section number, and quotations will be from the Pears and McGuiness more recent translation.
3. Gottlob Frege, *Conceptual Notation and Related Articles*, T. Bynum, ed. & trans., Oxford University Press, 1972. Alfred North Whitehead and Bertrand Russell, *Principia Mathematica*, Cambridge University Press, 1910; 2d ed., 1925.

4. Wittgenstein, *Philosophical Investigations*, Basil Blackwell, Oxford, 1953, section 133. Henceforth references to this book appear in the text, in the form of parentheses enclosing its initials and the number of the section in question. References to other works of Wittgenstein's are given in the same way wherever possible. In the case of a book like Wittgenstein, *Culture and Value*, G. H. Von Wright, ed. and P. Winch, trans., University of Chicago Press, 1984, where Wittgenstein's remarks are not organized into numbered sections, I will use the initials of the title and page numbers.

5. René Descartes, *Meditations on First Philosophy*, L. J. Lafleur, trans., Bobbs-Merrill, Indianapolis, 1951, p. 23.

6. For some time, philosophers have been developing a serious appreciation of the significance of Wittgenstein's thought on meaning and language. See, for example, Michael Dummett, "Wittgenstein's Philosophy of Mathematics," *Philosophical Review*, Vol. LXVIII, 1953, pp. 324–348, and, more recently, Crispin Wright, *Wittgenstein on the Foundations of Mathematics*, Harvard University Press, Cambridge, Mass., 1980, Saul Kripke, *Wittgenstein on Rules and Private Language*, Harvard University Press, Cambridge, Mass., 1982, and Colin McGinn, *Wittgenstein on Meaning*, Basil Blackwell, Oxford, 1984. Given that it is now clear what is at stake in the philosophy of mind, the philosophy of logic and mathematics, the philosophy of language, and metaphilosophy if Wittgenstein's arguments against theories of meaning do hold up, it is, I believe, a measure of the pervasiveness of naturalism that no full-scale effort has been made, particularly on the part of philosophers who oppose his late philosophy, to put those arguments to the kind of test that could determine whether they really do hold up.

7. Frege, *Conceptual Notation and Related Articles*.

8. See Peter Winch, "Facts and Super-facts," *Philosophical Quarterly*, Vol. 33, No. 133, 1983, pp. 393–404; Paul Horwich, "Saul Kripke on Rules and Private Languages," *Philosophy of Science*, Vol. 51, No. 1, 1984, pp. 163–171; McGinn, *Wittgenstein on Meaning*; and Warren Goldfarb, "Kripke on Wittgenstein on Rules," *Journal of Philosophy*, Vol. LXXXII, No. 9, 1985, pp. 471–488.

9. Moritz Schlick, "Is There a Factual *A Priori*?", in *Readings in Philosophical Analysis*, H. Feigl and W. Sellars, eds., Appleton-Century-Crofts, New York, 1949, pp. 277–285.

10. Kripke's *Wittgenstein on Rules and Private Language* has played an important role in bringing the relation between Wittgenstein and Hume to the attention of philosophers. McGinn's *Wittgenstein on Meaning* clarifies this relation (see pp. 39–42 and 136–138).

11. Wittgenstein supposed that the grounds for our fundamental beliefs are provided by the habits formed by the operation of experience on human nature (PI: 25, 415). Wittgenstein's account of following a rule is based on the idea that the use and understanding of language rests on "unreflective habit" in very much Hume's sense of that term.

12. Quine, "Semantics and Abstract Objects," in *Proceedings of the American Academy of Arts and Sciences*, July 1951, pp. 95–96.

13. Quine, "Two Dogmas of Empiricism," in *From a Logical Point of View*, Harvard University Press, Cambridge, Mass., 1953, p. 45.

14. Quine, "Necessary Truth," in *The Ways of Paradox and Other Essays*, Random House, New York, 1966, p. 56.

15. Quine, "Two Dogmas of Empiricism," pp. 42–46.

16. Bertrand Russell, "The Philosophy of Logical Atomism," in *Logic and Knowledge*, R. C. Marsh, ed., Macmillan, New York, 1956, pp. 175–281.

17. Quine, *Word and Object*, MIT Press, Cambridge, Mass., 1960, p. 275.

18. The philosopher's proper concern with language is to make conceptual improvements in the psychologist's theory of linguistic behavior. Quine thinks that language is best understood within a reinforcement theory of the kind developed by Skinnerian psychology, and he sees his own work on stimulus meaning as a contribution to the theory and methodology of such a behavioristic psychology (ibid., chapter III).

19. Chomsky's naturalism is a special case of Quine's naturalized epistemology. His disagreements with Quine over grammatical questions such as analyticity are merely family squabbles within naturalism, mostly having to do with the issue of how much innate structure has to be postulated as the biological basis for language acquisition. I will say more on this point in chapter 8. I will discuss Quine's naturalism in connection with his countenancing of abstract objects in mathematics in chapter 7.

20. Quine, "Epistemology Naturalized," in *Ontological Relativity and Other Essays*, Columbia University Press, New York, 1969, p. 82.

21. Frege's explication of analytic statements as statements derivable from logical truths plus definitions (with no assumptions from a special science) removed the outstanding flaws in Kant's formulation, and Carnap's explication of Fregean analytic statements as statements derivable from logical postulates and meaning postulates removed the heterogeneous element in Frege's explication (i.e., the reference to definitions). See Frege, *Foundations of Arithmetic*, J. L. Austin, trans., Basil Blackwell, Oxford, 1950, p. 3^e-4^e; Rudolf Carnap, "Meaning Postulates" in *Meaning and Necessity*, University of Chicago Press, 1947 (enlarged ed., 1956), pp. 222–229. Actually, Carnap's explication contributed to the disrepute of Kantian metaphysics by putting analyticity in a form that was easy prey for Quine. See J. J. Katz, "The New Intensionalism," to appear.

22. Carnap, "Intellectual Autobiography," in *The Philosophy of Rudolf Carnap*, Library of Living Philosophers, P. A. Schilpp, ed., Open Court, La Salle, Ill.,1963, pp. 3–67.

23. Quine, *From a Logical Point of View*, pp. 20–46.

24. Donald Davidson, "Truth and Meaning," *Synthese*, Vol. XVII, 1967, pp. 304–323.

25. Quine's arguments shield those theories from criticisms such as, for example, that their notion of proposition is counterintuitive because it entails that "The number 2 is greater than the number 2" and "The even prime is greater than the number 2" express the same proposition. Quine's argument that one cannot make objective sense of the concept of synonymy, in precluding the use of this maximally fine-grained notion as the condition for propositional identity, assures us that such counterintuitive consequences are to be accepted as a fact of life. Without Quine, it is doubtful that many philosophers would be willing to tolerate theories with such consequences.

26. Quine, *From a Logical Point of View*, pp. 20–46, and Quine, "Carnap and Logical Truth," in *The Philosophy of Rudolf Carnap*, pp. 385–406.

27. Chomsky, *Aspects of the Theory of Syntax*, MIT Press, Cambridge, Mass., 1966, pp. 1–9.

28. J. J. Katz and J. A. Fodor, "The Structure of a Semantic Theory," *Language*, Vol. 39, 1963, pp. 170–210, and Katz, *Semantic Theory*, Harper & Row, New York, 1972.

29. See the works cited in the previous footnote, plus J. J. Katz and P. Postal, *An Integrated Theory of Linguistic Descriptions*, MIT Press, Cambridge, Mass., 1964.

30. Katz, *The Philosophy of Language*, Harper & Row, New York, 1966.

31. Katz, "Some Remarks on Quine on Analyticity," *Journal of Philosophy*, Vol. LXIV, No. 2, 1967, pp. 36–52.
32. Katz, "Mentalism in Linguistics," *Language*, Vol. 40, 1964, pp. 124–137.
33. I no longer think this option is completely tenable. See Katz, *Language and Other Abstract Objects*, and also Katz and Postal, "Realism vs. Conceptualism in Linguistics," to appear.
34. G. E. Moore, *Principia Ethica*, Cambridge University Press, 1903, p. 16.

Chapter 2

1. In this connection it is interesting to note Chomsky's conception of the child as a "little linguist." Chomsky says that "the child who learns a language has in some sense constructed the grammar for himself on the basis of his observations of sentences and non-sentences" and that "this grammar is of an extremely complex and abstract character [so that] the young child has succeeded in carrying out what from the formal point of view, at least, seems to be a remarkable type of theory construction." This conception also underlies Chomsky's inferential model of speech comprehension and his anti-structuralist view of the linguist as theoretical scientist rather than taxonomist. See, for example, Chomsky, *Aspects of the Theory of Syntax*, pp. 18–62, and *Language and Mind*, enlarged ed., Harcourt, Brace, Jovanovich, New York, 1972, pp. 25–64 and 115–120.
2. This point is very nicely made in Goldfarb, "I Want You to Bring Me a Slab: Remarks on the Opening Sections of the *Philosophical Investigations*," *Synthese*, Vol. 56, 1983, pp. 268–269.
3. I have stressed appearance, to make it clear that I am not assuming a compositional conception of the sense of syntactically complex constituents, i.e., the view that the senses of the individual words in idiomatic sentences like "Cat got your tongue?" are literally components of the sense of the sentence. This is a position for which I will argue below. But here I would beg the question flagrantly if I were to assume a conception that is so controversial in the context of Wittgenstein's critique of theories of meaning and, in particular, of Frege's theory, which is the starting point for modern thinking about compositionality. See Frege, "Compound Thoughts," *Mind*, Vol. LXXII, 1963, pp. 1–17; reprinted in *Essays on Frege*, E. D. Klemke, ed., University of Illinois Press, Urbana, 1968, pp. 537–558; citations are to the Klemke version.
4. J. V. Canfield, *Wittgenstein: Language and World*, University of Massachusetts Press, Amherst, 1981, pp. 70–72.
5. Ibid., p. 71.
6. The fact that theories in linguistics will nowadays use technical apparatus in order to express such conditions ought not, in and of itself, be taken to prove that such theories cannot deal with the same things that ordinary semantic disputes are about. If the use of technical apparatus invariably had the consequence of leading away from ordinary phenomena, we would have to say that the phenomena of temperature which thermodynamics addresses are not the ordinary phenomena of temperature. If technical apparatus in linguistics alone is supposed to have this consequence, we have to be given a relevant difference, and one, moreover, that explains why, when linguists are doing phonology rather than semantics, technical linguistic apparatus doesn't lead them away from ordinary phenomena (of sameness and difference in pronunciation).

7. Carnap, *The Logical Syntax of Language*, Routledge & Kegan Paul, London, 1937, pp. 51–52, and also p. 321.

8. Russell, *Introduction to Mathematical Philosophy*, George Allen & Unwin, London, 1919, pp. 167–180; also "On Denoting," in Russell, *Logic and Knowledge*, R. C. Marsh, ed., Macmillan, New York, 1956, pp. 39–56.

9. Frege was the first philosopher to see that theories of meaning must accept the consequences of their account of meaning for the explication of synonymy and meaningfulness and to argue on the basis that extensionalist theories of meaning provide the wrong account. His famous criticism of extensionalism for being unable to explain why truths of the form $a = a$ and $a = b$ differ in cognitive value is a special case of the criticism that extensionalism is unable to distinguish between synonymy and nonsynonymy. See his "On Sense and Reference," in *Translations from the Philosophical Writings of Gottlob Frege*, P. Geach and M. Black, eds., Basil Blackwell, Oxford, 1952, pp. 42–78.

10. It might be worthwhile to say a bit more about the strategy of leaving the nature of this relation entirely open for the time being. First, a general observation. It is possible that the linguistic pegs on which to hang referential structure do not emerge until after sufficient progress has been made in systematizing sense structure. In this case, premature attempts to specify the referential structure of language would run into unnecessary trouble. Second, an anticipation. Frege's influence is immense. So much so that most philosophers automatically equate intensionalist semantics with Fregean semantics. Since I am going to reject Frege's semantics and his conception of the relation between sense and reference, I should here and now make this clear. I will argue below that Frege's intensionalism is the source of much of the intensionalist's troubles and should be resisted. Frege took the position he did because he defined sense as mode of referential presentation. I shall argue that a proper development of our commonsense notion of sense—namely, as that which is the same in synonymous expressions, opposed in antonymous expressions, duplicated in redundant expressions, etc.—does not lead to the notion of mode of presentation of the referent.

11. C. S. Peirce, *Collected Papers of Charles Sanders Peirce*, Volume IV, C. Hartshorne and P. Weiss, eds., Harvard University Press, Cambridge, Mass., 1958, p. 423.

12. J. L. Austin, *How to Do Things with Words*, Harvard University Press, Cambridge, Mass., 1962.

13. J. R. Searle, *Speech Acts*, Cambridge University Press, Cambridge, 1969, and H. P. Grice, "Meaning," *Philosophical Review*, Vol. 66, 1957, pp. 377–388.

14. I owe this courtroom example to George Bealer (in conversation).

15. The linguistic literature is now quite large, but see Katz, *The Philosophy of Language*, pp. 121–122; Chomsky, *Aspects of the Theory of Syntax*, pp. 10–15, and Langendoen and Postal, *The Vastness of Natural Languages*.

16. This argument that there are meaningful megasentences and, hence, sentences that can have no use, is based on an intuition like that on which the claim that there is no largest number is grounded. Each new step presents exactly the same situation as every preceding step, thus requiring exactly the same conclusion. The reason each new step presents the same situation in the case of conjoining sentences is that well-formedness is a structural property. The structure that makes the conjoined sentence well formed is independent of the size of the conjuncts conjoined to produce it.

17. Chomsky, *Aspects of the Theory of Syntax*, pp. 11–14.

18. These examples of the divergence between meaning and use are parallel to Frege's examples of the divergence between meaning and reference. For example, just as Frege's example of "the least convergent series" argues that meaningfulness does not coincide with having a referent, so the examples of megasentences and multiply center-embedded sentences argue that meaningfulness does not coincide with having a use.

19. This discussion is incomplete insofar as more has to be said about how syntactic aspects of grammatical structure which enter into the correlation between sentences and their senses can be distinguished from semantic aspects of grammatical structure. If, as seems to be the case, information about grammatical relations like 'subject of' and 'direct object' plays a role in the compositional meaning of a sentence and if the compositional process is the process that effects the correlation between sentences and their senses, then how is such information distinguished from sense information *per se*? In a nutshell, the answer is that such information is not required in the definitions of semantic properties and relations. But this is a complex matter which goes beyond the scope of the present discussion. See Katz, *Semantic Theory*, Harper & Row, New York, 1972.

20. Grice, "Logic and Conversation," in *Syntax and Semantics, Vol. III*, P. Cole & J. L. Morgan, eds., Academic Press, New York, 1975, pp. 41–58.

21. Someone, failing to understand the words of our esteemed president, might ask us to repeat them. But requests to repeat what someone has said can only be requests for us to produce another token of the same sentence type(s) as the original, since the words that weren't understood were tokens and, hence, one-time affairs.

22. It must have this reference, since, as Peirce points out, "it is impossible that [a sentence type] should lie visibly on a page or be heard in any voice."

23. Frege, "Compound Thoughts," p. 537.

24. Alfred Tarski, "The Concept of Truth in Formalized Languages," in *Logic, Semantics, and Metamathematics*, Oxford University Press, 1936, p. 164.

25. Katz, *Semantic Theory*, pp. 109–116.

26. Katz, *Language and Other Abstract Objects*.

27. See, for example, Chomsky, *The Logical Structure of Linguistic Theory*, Plenum Press, New York, 1975, pp. 30–32. This source provides the best description by Chomsky himself of the steps leading up to his development of generative grammar.

28. Chomsky, *Aspects of the Theory of Syntax*, pp. 3–15.

29. Chomsky, *Cartesian Linguistics*, Harper & Row, New York, 1966, pp. 31–51.

30. Frege, *Conceptual Notation and Related Articles*, pp. 112–113.

31. Russell, *Introduction to Mathematical Philosophy*, George Allen & Unwin, London, 1919, pp. 167–180.

32. An exception is the pragmatic investigations of H. P. Grice, whose ideas go a long way toward resolving many of the questions about the relation of logical operators to their natural-language counterparts which were raised in P. F. Strawson, *Introduction to Logical Theory*, Methuen, London, 1952, pp. 78–92.

33. Carnap, *Meaning and Necessity*, p. 8.

34. Quine, *Word and Object*, MIT Press, Cambridge, Mass., 1960, p. 159.

35. Discussion of this issue has been inconclusive. See, for instance, the essays in Part III of *The Linguistic Turn*, R. Rorty, ed., University of Chicago Press, 1967, pp. 173–268.

36. See Chomsky, "Current Issues in Linguistic Theory," Mouton, The Hague, 1964. The treatment in this work is, of course, quite different from the current treatment, but this does not matter for our purposes.

37. Chomsky, *Aspects of the Theory of Syntax*, pp. 63–74.

38. It is sometimes suggested that we can represent an *n*-ways-ambiguous expression by relating it to *n* expressions, each of which marks a distinct term of the ambiguity. But, since to do this we must know that no expression is meaningless and that none are synonymous with any of the others, such a representation of ambiguity can hardly be taken as a syntactic reduction of ambiguity.

39. There is a certain justice in associating the view with Frege, though, of course, nothing hangs on the association. Frege did not carry the analysis of sense beyond the boundaries of syntactic structure. See Geach and Black, *Translations from the Philosophical Writings of Gottlob Frege*, pp. 51–52.

40. It should be noted that the presentation of my view of semantics in this chapter is necessarily abbreviated and that it is far more fully presented in publications like *Semantic Theory, Propositional Structure and Illocutionary Force*, and other works of mine referred to here.

41. For discussion, see Katz, *Semantic Theory*, pp. 157–171, and Smith and Katz, *Supposable Worlds*, chapters II and IV, to appear, Harvard University Press.

42. Frege, "On Sense and Reference."

43. Wittgenstein, *Tractatus Logico-Philosophicus*, section 4.002; the passage quoted is from the 1961 translation.

44. The falsehood of a proposition *P*, according to Wittgenstein's picture theory of meaning in the *Tractatus*, consists in the fact that the picture that *P* conveys depicts nothing in the world. *Tractatus*: 2.06, 4.064, 4.0641.

45. Wittgenstein, *Tractatus*: 4.0641.

46. Wittgenstein, *Tractatus*: 6.375 (first paragraph) and 6.3751 (last three paragraphs).

47. Wittgenstein, "Some Remarks on Logical Form," *Aristotelian Society*, Supplementary volume IX, 1929, p. 168.

48. Wittgenstein, *Philosophical Remarks*, R. Rhees, ed., R. Hargreaves and R. White, trans., Basil Blackwell, Oxford, 1975.

49. Quine, "Two Dogmas of Empiricism," in *From a Logical Point of View*, pp. 20–46; D. Davidson, "Truth and Meaning," *Synthese*, Vol. XVII, No. 3, 1967, pp. 304–323.

50. Immanuel Kant, *Critique of Pure Reason*, N. K. Smith, trans., Humanities Press, New York, 1929, pp. 48–49.

51. Frege, *The Foundations of Arithmetic*, p. 4ᵉ.

52. That there should be some basis is plausible, since the two types of sentence seem different on the face of it. An aspect of this difference is that the simple sentence is about unmarried men while the complex sentence, as logically construed, is about everything.

53. Kant, *Critique of Pure Reason*, p. 49.

54. Wittgenstein, *Tractatus*: 5.557.

55. It is important to note that the third way out does not challenge the fundamental step Frege took in creating predicate logic, that is, the step of using the truth-functional operators from propositional logic to express relations among the propositional components of quantificational formulas. Hence, this direction does not entail a denial of Frege's logical heritage. Rather, it challenges the widespread practice of paraphrasing simple sentences from natural lan-

guage into a canonical logical notation. It also challenges the permissive attitude, expressed by Carnap and Quine, of letting logicians decide questions of
such paraphrase on the basis of what best serves their ends. It is doubtful
whether anyone in fact takes such a *laissez-faire* attitude in practice. Quine himself was unwilling, in the case of analyticity and synonymy, to let Carnap
"judge outright whether his ends are served by the paraphrase."

56. One example of this is the problem that the fallacious inference "Ruth is good
and Ruth is a dancer; hence, Ruth is a good dancer" poses for Davidson's theory of action sentences. See J. J. Katz, C. Leacock, and Y. Ravin, "A Decompositional Theory of Modification," in *Actions and Events*, E. LePore and
B. McLaughlin, eds., Basil Blackwell, Oxford, 1986, pp. 207–234.

57. The principle in taking this step was that phenomena are best accounted for
when their treatment offers the widest coverage of them with the least apparatus. The preference for descriptive accounts over explanatory accounts in
cases where descriptive accounts are possible is based on this principle, since
in those cases the descriptive account achieves the same coverage without the
loss in economy resulting from adding apparatus to represent underlying
structure. In cases where, because of a dearth of structure accessible to description, descriptive accounts cannot achieve full coverage of the phenomena, the
added apparatus does work and, consequently, is not uneconomical. At this
point, the comparison between descriptive and explanatory accounts becomes
strictly a matter of coverage, and, on these grounds, the explanatory account
is preferable.

58. It is plausible to suppose that lurking in the background is Frege's conception
that the source of our ability to understand novel linguistic communication
depends on the possibility of distinguishing "parts in the thought corresponding to the parts in the sentence, so that the structure of the sentence serves as
an image of the structure of the thought" (Frege, "Compound Thoughts," p.
537).

59. Ignoring this distinction allows Wittgenstein to treat the question at the beginning of section 19 of whether "Slab!" in the example of section 2 is a word or
a sentence in the *laissez-faire* way he does. He is wrong to say that one can, in
any strict sense, call that utterance a sentence. The general's utterance "Attack!" is a token of an imperative sentence type, but the builder's utterance
"Slab!" is a token of the noun "slab" with an intonation that is understood in
context to express a desire to have a referent of that noun brought to him.

60. See also Katz, *Language and Other Abstract Objects*.

61. The anti-realist applications of the ideas about meaning presented in the *Philosophical Investigations* are found in Wittgenstein, *Remarks on the Foundations of
Mathematics*, Basil Blackwell, Oxford, 1956, and also in *Wittgenstein's Lectures
on the Foundations of Mathematics*, C. Diamond, ed., Harvester Press, Hassocks,
Sussex, 1976.

62. Dummett, *Frege: Philosophy of Language*, Harper & Row, New York, 1973, p. 92.
This view is widely endorsed. See, for instance, John McDowell, "On the
Sense and Reference of a Proper Name," in *Reference, Truth, and Reality*,
M. Platts, ed., Routledge & Kegan Paul, London, 1980, p. 148.

63. Dummett, "What Is a Theory of Meaning?" in *Mind and Language*, S. Guttenplan, ed., Clarendon Press, Oxford, 1975, pp. 100–101.

64. In fact, such a conception of a theory of understanding, incorporating some
version of an independent theory of grammar, is a common working assumption in the study of sentence processing within psycholinguistics.

65. Frege, "The Thought: A Logical Inquiry," in *Essays on Frege*, Klemke, ed., p. 513.

66. Frege, "On Sense and Reference," pp. 57–60.

67. Frege, "On Sense and Reference," pp. 56–78.

68. In chapter 6 we shall consider objections to Frege's semantics from the reference side and explain how our proto-theory avoids them. But it is worth noting that there are also objections to his semantics from the sense side. One counterexample to Frege's definition of sense is a pair of expressions like "a bachelor" and "an unmarried bachelor" which express the same mode of presentation, yet are not identical in meaning since one is redundant and the other is not. This example is not troublesome for the proto-theory's definition of sense. On that definition, expressions like "bachelor" and "unmarried bachelor" will be nonsynonymous because the extra meaning of the adjective "unmarried" introduces a duplication into the compositional meaning of the latter expression.

69. This term is taken from Katz, "Has the Description Theory of Names Been Refuted?", in *Meaning and Method*, G. Boolos, ed., Cambridge University Press, 1990, pp. 31–61.

70. Tyler Burge, "Sinning against Frege," *Philosophical Review*, Vol. 88, 1979, p. 400.

71. See Chapter 3 and also Katz, "Has the Description Theory of Names Been Refuted?"

72. See Grice's papers "Meaning" and "Logic and Conversation" for discussion of the principles in question.

73. Our "top-down" approach provides a natural way to make a number of important distinctions concerning properties of utterances. We may distinguish two different ways in which an utterance can be meaningless. One way is for the utterance to be a token of a semantically deviant type, e.g., Chomsky's "Colorless green ideas sleep furiously". The other way is for the utterance to be a token of a meaningful sentence but used in a context where it cannot be correlated with a meaningful sentence type, e.g., an "off the wall" remark, a remark that we can't take literally and can't figure out how else to understand. The former way directly reflects the meaninglessness of a sentence; the latter reflects the absence of the necessary contextual information.

An utterance can be situationally ambiguous in the same two ways. It can be a token of an ambiguous sentence type which occurs in a context where there is no clue to how it should be disambiguated. The cagey speaker who says simply, "I'm going to the bank" by way of concealing his or her future whereabouts is a case in point. Alternatively, the utterance of an unambiguous sentence type can occur in a situation where it can have either a figurative or a literal meaning, without its being clear which of these is intended.

Utterances can also be situationally vague. The classic instance of such vagueness is the statement of the Delphic Oracle to Croesus, "If Croesus went to war with Cyrus, he would destroy a mighty kingdom". Situational vagueness differs from situational ambiguity. In situational vagueness, the utterance is a token of an unambiguous sentence or an ambiguous sentence all but one of whose senses can be contextually eliminated, yet, in spite of there being only one sense to contend with, pragmatic considerations are too weak to determine a unique path to a sentence type from which to obtain a proper sense for the context. We are left with a number of possible correlations to nonsynonymous sentence types which have semantically similar senses.

74. See G. P. Baker and P. M. S. Hacker, *Wittgenstein: Understanding and Meaning*, Vol. 1, University of Chicago Press, 1980, pp. 144–146.

75. Katz, *Propositional Structure and Illocutionary Force*, Harvard University Press, Cambridge, Mass., 1980.

76. There is a pejorative connotation to terms like "superfluous" and "redundant". But this is entirely a matter of pragmatics. Speakers do not need the rewritten form because the unrewritten form is a more concise way to make the same assertion in nearly every circumstance, and they are properly averse to using the rewritten form because utterances with such sense duplication would seem bizarrely pointless in most circumstances (though, of course, not in all, as the use of expressions like "free gift" to attract attention shows).

77. Chomsky, *Aspects of the Theory of Syntax*, pp. 3–9.

78. Chomsky, *Cartesian Linguistics*.

79. Lexical gaps represent no deficiency in the expressive power of the language because they can be compensated for by the compositional principles of the language. It seems plausible to think that, for each such gap, there is a syntactically constructible expression whose sense is the meaning of any word that would fill it. That the sense primitives and their modes of combination fully specify the semantic types of the language is something that must, I think, be part of the foundations of a "top-down" approach. It is one of the things that gives such approaches their rationalistic flavor. Although this will be a controversial conception of the semantic potential of languages, there is no need to defend it further at this point, since it is not challenged by any arguments that Wittgenstein has as yet succeeded in establishing.

80. See Katz, "Has the Description Theory of Names Been Refuted?" for a presentation of an alternative to both the view that the meaning of a name is the object it denotes and the view that the meaning of a name is its use in the language-game. The alternative, like Frege's view, says that the meaning of a name is its sense, but, unlike Frege's view, it gives an account of the sense of a name that is not open to the standard (e.g., Kripkean) objections.

81. Moore discusses his conception of analysis in his replies to his critics in *The Philosophy of G. E. Moore*, P. A. Schilpp, ed., Open Court, La Salle, Ill., 1942, 3rd. Edition 1968, pp. 660–667. He makes it clear that he understands analysis to be a process of paraphrase which exposes the decompositional sense structure of words. Moore's analyses expose the sense components of a word by expressing them each in terms of an explicit constituent of the paraphrase. For further discussion, see Katz, *Cogitations*, Oxford University Press, Oxford, 1986, pp. 145–150.

82. It is not, in fact, impossible to speak of orders themselves having parts. Military orders, for example, have parts. It is likely that, since we do not customarily encounter orders with parts needing to be distinguished, we have come to find it strange to refer to the parts of orders. Be this as it may, whether orders that people give each other do or do not have parts has no direct bearing on the issue about analysis in the present sense. An order to bring a broom, being what is given *in* the use of language, is not an analysandum for such analysis.

83. Prescriptive principles are part of a program to rationally reconstruct natural languages or replace them with an ideal language. Such a program sees natural languages as imperfect because we cannot read the structure of reality off of their grammatical structure. (We cannot, as Frege complained, read off the existence of an object from the grammatical well-formedness of a referring

expression.) In contrast, the proto-theory takes the very strong stand of denying that even the most general structure of reality, that is, its conformity to the condition of logical possibility, can be read off of natural languages. This is the ultimate significance of the analytic/synthetic distinction: a natural language contains no theory because it is a theoretically neutral means of expressing theories. The only things that can be read off of the sense structure of natural languages are sense properties and relations. See Smith and Katz, *Supposable Worlds*.

84. It is possible that there is more than one set of semantic simples, but semantics is no worse off for allowing equivalent sets of simples than are other disciplines where the same possibility exists.

85. It is also why the very first thing Wittgenstein focuses on in the *Philosophical Investigations* is the notion of the essence of language.

86. *Translations from the Philosophical Writings of Gottlob Frege*, Geach and Black, p. 46.

87. *Webster's New International Dictionary of the English Language*, 2nd ed., G. & C. Merriam, Springfield, Mass., 1961, p. 1030. An example of the homonymy of "game" is its sense 'prey of a hunter'. I have even simplified somewhat in the case of sense (A). *Webster's* qualifies the notion of contest as 'mental or physical', and mentions the possible purposes of the participants (for participating) over and above the purpose of the activity (as a contest), but I have eliminated these irrelevancies.

88. There is no point here in presenting a serious argument for the dictionary's claim that (A) and (B) are distinct senses of "game", that is, trying to show that hypothesizing them is necessary to account for sense properties and relations of sentences in which the word occurs. Since my argument here is basically concerned with showing that Wittgenstein's findings do not refute the proto-theory, by showing what happens in the pragmatic projection of semantic structure, I can assume that *Webster's* is correct.

89. It is sometimes said that an explanation of family resemblance based on ambiguity won't work. Some philosophers make this claim because they think that Wittgenstein's arguments prior to section 65 eliminate the only notion of sense appropriate for such an explanation. This would be a good reason for dismissing such an explanation if the prior arguments were successful, but, since they are not, the claim is unfounded. Baker and Hacker say that an ambiguity explanation won't work because Wittgenstein has counterexamples to it that are "obvious in the text" (see Baker and Haker, *Wittgenstein: Understanding and Meaning*, pp. 329–330), but the passages they cite, viz., PI sections 67, 69, and 77, do not even address the question.

90. We can, of course, have a word in English "scair" which means 'chair that comes and goes at seemingly arbitrary times'. This would be a word that differed semantically from "chair" in the way that "board game" or "card game" differs from "game". But, in this case, the question for physics is whether the extension of "scair" is empty or not.

91. "On Sense and Reference," p. 60.

92. We have already mentioned semantic vagueness, a form of pragmatic inexactness in which an utterance is associated with a number of nonsynonymous sentences and hence receives a number of senses, because the context is too weak to provide a unique sentence.

93. For a formal presentation, see Katz et al., "A Decompositional Theory of Modification," pp. 207–234; also Katz, "Common Sense in Semantics," in *New Di-*

rections in Semantics, E. LePore, ed., Academic Press, London, 1987, pp. 157–234.

94. This discussion ignores the compositional combination of subjects, direct objects, etc. with verbs. See Katz, *Semantic Theory* and also the references in note 93 above.

95. Katz, *Semantic Theory*, pp. 450–451.

96. See Katz, "Has the Description Theory of Names Been Refuted?" for an account of names which shows that intensionalism is not so restricted.

97. Chomsky, *Aspects of the Theory of Syntax*, pp. 3–9.

98. Of course, Wittgenstein's own view of mathematics is contrary to this, but it must be kept in mind that his view rests on the supposition that his critique of theories of meaning has successfully replaced theoretical notions of meaning with considerations of the use of words. Hence, it cannot be invoked at this point to argue against entertaining this prospect.

99. Frege, *The Basic Laws of Arithmetic*, pp. 13–14. Not only does Frege offer no good reason for his conceptualist view of language, but it is inconsistent on one reading of him where he is identifying propositions with senses of sentences and, hence, saying that senses are the objects of which the laws of truth hold. What is the ontological status of senses, which, as linguistic, are supposed to be natural objects, and which, as logical, are supposed to be non-natural objects?

100. See Katz, *Language and Other Abstract Objects*.

101. Peter Winch, *The Idea of a Social Science*, Routledge & Kegan Paul, London, 1958; Saul Kripke, *Wittgenstein on Rules and Private Language*, 1982; Barry Stroud, "Wittgenstein and Logical Necessity," *Philosophical Review*, vol. LXXIV, 1965, pp. 504–518; Colin McGinn, *Wittgenstein on Meaning*, 1984, pp. 84–92.

102. *Wittgenstein's Lectures, Cambridge, 1930–32*, D. Lee, ed., Basil Blackwell, Oxford, 1980, p. 59.

103. *Wittgenstein's Lectures, Cambridge, 1932–35*, A. Ambrose, ed., Basil Blackwell, Oxford, 1979, p. 51.

104. Kripke, *Naming and Necessity*, Harvard University Press, Cambridge, Mass., 1980, pp. 60–97.

105. Keith Donnellan, "Criteria and Necessity," *Journal of Philosophy*, Vol. LIX, No. 22, 1962, pp. 647–658; Hilary Putnam, "It Ain't Necessarily So," *Journal of Philosophy*, Vol. LIX, No. 22, 1962, pp. 658–671, and "Is Semantics Possible?", *Metaphilosophy*, Vol. 1, 1971, pp. 187–201.

106. Katz, *Semantic Theory*, pp. 157–197, and Smith and Katz, *Supposable Worlds*.

Chapter 3

1. M. O' C. Drury reports Wittgenstein once having remarked, "It has puzzled me why Socrates is regarded as a great philosopher. Because when Socrates asks for the meaning of a word and people give him examples of how that word is used, he isn't satisfied but wants a unique definition. Now if someone shows me how a word is used and its different meanings, that is just the sort of answer I want." *Recollections of Wittgenstein*, R. Rhees, ed., Oxford University Press, Oxford, 1984, p. 115.

2. Those familiar with Wittgenstein's discussion of mathematics will recognize his use of these ideas in arguing against mathematical Platonism and the conception of absolute necessity. He writes: "So much is clear: when someone

says: 'If you follow the rule, it *must* be like this,' he has not any *clear* concept of what experience would correspond to the opposite. Or again: he has not any clear concept of what it would be like for it to be otherwise. And this is very important." (RFM, III: 29) The *Remarks on the Foundation of Mathematics* is studded with examples of how signs might be used otherwise than the ways in which we use them. These examples, like the one above, are intended to show that there is no absolute necessity even in our most rigorous proofs. We *could* follow inferential practices different from our actual ones; hence, contra Platonism, the rules of the practices we actually do follow are contingent, even though we might have no real choice in the matter. I shall not directly consider these ideas from the *Remarks on the Foundations of Mathematics* in the present context. My strategy is to argue against them indirectly, by criticizing the portions of the *Philosophical Investigations* which provide the semantic underpinnings for the criticisms of necessity in *Remarks on the Foundations of Mathematics*. My argument will be general enough so that its application to Wittgenstein's anti-Platonist criticisms in that book are straightforward. The classical discussions of Wittgenstein on mathematics and necessity are Michael Dummett, "Wittgenstein's Philosophy of Mathematics," *Philosophical Review*, Vol. LXVIII, 1959, pp. 324–348, and Barry Stroud, "Wittgenstein and Logical Necessity," *Philosophical Review*, Vol. LXXIV, 1965, pp. 504–518.

3. The naturalized notion of content is supposed to make meaning more ontologically tractable, but the real effect is rather, as Wittgenstein's paradox shows, to produce something semantically impotent. McGinn points out that Fodor's psychosemantics is open to Wittgenstein's argument because it conceives of understanding as nothing but transduction into a special vocabulary of signs in the language of thought: "Wittgenstein's question about such a system of signs would be how it acquires a meaning, seeing that syntax alone cannot add up to semantics" (*Wittgenstein on Meaning*, p. 118).

4. The logic of my argument does not require that I compare my solution to the paradox with Wittgenstein's; hence, I have not done so. I hope to make this comparison on another occasion, for I think it will show that what Wittgenstein says about following a rule does not actually constitute a solution to the paradox; it will show, in particular, that the events to which we are exposed in the acquisition of language, comprising concrete as well as mental images, cannot restrict us to one family resemblance rather than another.

5. It is mistaken to go on to conclude, as many philosophers have, that, beyond the sort of fact about application that Wittgenstein has in mind, there is no objective fact in virtue of which a speaker means one thing rather than another. One consideration which leads those philosophers to draw this conclusion is the supposition that the line of anti-intensionalist criticism from Wittgenstein through Putnam or the anti-intensionalist criticisms due to Quine refute every form of intensionalism. This is false. Here let me issue a promissory note, to be redeemed in chapters 5 and 6, for a demonstration that the proto-theory is not refuted. Without this supposition, all that can be concluded is that the fact in question is neither a purely grammatical fact nor a purely psychological one.

6. With a definition of the sense relation of analytic entailment, we can replace the containment clause with a clause requiring that there be a sentence type T such that the meaning of T is the meaning of the utterance in question and the meaning of T analytically entails the meaning of the sentence type of which the utterance is a token. An early formulation of the definition of analytic entailment

is found in Katz, *Semantic Theory*, pp. 188–189, and a more recent, fuller formulation is found in Smith and Katz, *Supposable Worlds*.

7. There are, of course, problems about application in connection with sentences,
for example, how RLS applies in the case of the literalness of performative utterance meanings. It seems correct to say that uses of "The door is open" to
state the fact that the door is open are literal, but uses of it to request someone
to close the door are nonliteral. Moreover, it also seems correct to say that the
use of "I request that you close the door" to ask someone to close the door is
literal. Hence, the literalness/nonliteralness distinction relates to performative
character as well as propositional content. Literalness is a matter of sameness
of appropriate components from sense of utterance to sense of sentence, and
nonliteralness can occur because of a difference in either performative character
or propositional content. But what is the appropriate component in the case of
"The door is open"? There seems to be no grammatical element in the sentence
which expresses its character as an assertive proposition, that is, no element
whose relation to an assertion made with it makes that use literal and whose
relation to a request made with it makes that use non-literal. The problem here
is, I believe, only that the element does not appear in the surface structure of
the sentence. A solution to this problem is forthcoming on a deeper analysis of
the grammatical structure of "The door is open," which shows that the sense
of such sentences contains an element that gives them an assertive force. See
Katz, *Propositional Structure and Illocutionary Force*, pp. 37–134.

8. The failure to distinguish literal and nonliteral sense from literal and nonliteral
reference, and then to distinguish between the two ways in which nonliteral
reference can take place, is, I believe, one of the principal factors responsible
for thinking that Putnam's robot-cat case and similar cases are counterexamples
to intensionalism. Without these distinctions, it does not appear possible for the
application of a word to have a literal sense but not a literal reference. So, the
critic of intensionalism, correctly thinking that the word "cat" has been used
with a literal sense, incorrectly concludes that its reference is literal, too, and
hence, given the reference to robots, the critic concludes that the sense of "cat"
cannot be 'feline animal'. This is ironic, since such critics seem to accept Donnellan's account of reference under a false description which involves the same
distinctions (see Keith Donnellan, "Proper Names and Identifying Descriptions," in *Semantics of Natural Language*, pp. 356–379). Clearly, in Donnellan's
examples of a use of "the person drinking champagne" to refer to someone
drinking ginger ale out of a champagne glass, the speaker is using the expression with its literal sense, but it is taken to refer nonliterally to the ginger-ale
drinker. See chapter 7 for an examination of the argument of these critics.

9. H. P. Grice, *Studies in the Way of Words*, Harvard University Press, Cambridge,
Mass., 1989, pp. 1–144. Nothing hangs on this choice. Grice's theory is widely
known and works well for present purposes.

10. The fact that constitutes a speaker's having such an intention is just the speaker's being in some psychological state which *is* the having of this structured
intention. I have no particular axe to grind about the character of such a state,
and hence, for the sake of argument, I am prepared here to accept any account
of psychological states which realizes such an intention. However, in the context of Wittgenstein's problem about following a rule, someone might think that
there is a corresponding problem for such intentional states, whatever their
character, since, if there were none, Wittgenstein's problem would have a trivial
solution: we could solve it simply by talking about what the speaker intends to

mean when he or she applies the word "cube". But this is not the case because the intention must involve a specification of what meaning the token of "cube" is to have on the occasion, and, if the specification is given just in terms of some image, picture, etc. that comes before the speaker's mind, then there is no solution. As we have seen, an intention with such specification can be realized by a method of projection on which the token refers to a triangular prism. What distinguishes the solution I am constructing from such a pseudo-solution is that the specification of what meaning the speaker intends the token of "cube" to have is given in terms of the meaning of the word type "cube" in English, that is, the abstract property of being a regular solid with six equal square sides, with which the word is corrected in the grammar of English.

11. There is a kind of conflict that occurs in certain nonliteral uses, but it is not an opposition of the sort Wittgenstein had in mind. It is rather the vehicle by which a linguistic token is assigned a nonliteral meaning. This is the conflict that, on Grice's pragmatics, occurs when assignment of literal meaning to a token cannot be squared with knowledge that the speaker is conforming to the conversational maxims. For example, such a conflict occurs in Grice's case of the man who refers to a trusted associate who has just stabbed him in the back in a business venture as a "fine friend." Such conflicts are the tip-off that the speaker does not intend the token literally and thereby initiate the listener's reconstruction of the speaker's communicative intention ("Logic and Conversation," p. 51).

12. Furthermore, it is no argument against our position that there can be Donnellan-type cases in which the referent of "cube" is not a cube; e.g., someone may refer to a triangular prism by saying, "That cube is a beautiful red color". The speaker in such cases commits a linguistic error, viz., a violation of RLR. The cases are labeled "reference under a false description" because the referent does not fit the meaning of the referring expression. Thus, the speaker in our example does not refer literally with "cube". He or she is taken to refer to a triangular prism because the audience charitably forgives the error in the interests of saving the speaker's assertion.

13. Stroud, "Wittgenstein and Logical Necessity," pp. 504–518.

14. Frege, *The Basic Laws of Arithmetic*, University of California Press, Berkeley, 1967, p. 14.

15. See Katz, *Language and Other Abstract Objects*.

16. In particular, the thesis of solipsism, which Wittgenstein was so concerned to show could not be expressed in language, falls safely within these limits of language.

17. There are also views of intuition on which we are not required to have the direct acquaintance that the perception analogy implies and, hence, views that avoid the well-known epistemological problem. See Katz, *Language and Other Abstract Objects*, pp. 192–220, for a discussion of the realist conception of linguistic intuition.

18. McGinn, *Wittgenstein on Meaning*, pp. 99–100.

19. There is support for Wittgenstein's and McGinn's reading of Frege in passages where he explains his doctrine of sense with analogies like his telescope case ("On Sense and Reference", p. 60). Such analogies present senses as spatiotemporal particulars and our grasp of them as like the grasp of an image in the mind. But, despite these ways in which Frege plays into the hands of his critics, I think that a better reading of Frege, which brings his realism to the fore, makes the reading of his critics questionable.

20. See Katz, *Language and Other Abstract Objects* for further discussion.

21. McGinn, *Wittgenstein on Meaning*, p. 102, note 16.
22. I want to avoid a confusion that can arise about the argument in this chapter. The development of the proto-theory, which provides the basis for the argument, is carried out within formal linguistics; hence, the fully developed theory will be a formal theory of sense structure. I want to make clear that the fact that the theory is formal does not in itself make the version of semantic essentialism based on the theory vulnerable to Wittgenstein's paradox. Psychologized versions of semantics essentialism are vulnerable because the objects to which they assign the role of essences are concrete formal objects. This is not the case with our version. Although representations of senses in the proto-theory are formal objects, the senses they represent are not. Formal objects like deposits of ink, piles of graphite, excavations in a physical surface, constructions of wire, etc. are concrete objects and, hence, necessarily spread out over regions of space and time (even if only the phenomenological space in which imagery occurs). But senses, as the proto-theory conceives them, are abstract objects and, hence, not formal, concrete objects.
23. J. L. Borges, *Labyrinths*, New Directions, New York, 1964, p. 27.

Chapter 4

1. Kripke, *Wittgenstein on Rules and Private Language*, Harvard University Press, Cambridge, Mass., 1982.
2. Goldfarb, "Kripke on Wittgenstein on Rules," p. 474. In *Wittgenstein on Meaning* (p. 62). McGinn interprets the epistemological challenge as having little significance for Kripke beyond its function of providing a way of introducing the metaphysical challenge. McGinn (pp. 177–179) makes essentially the same point that Goldfarb makes in the quotation in the text.
3. McGinn, *Wittgenstein on Meaning*, pp. 68–71.
4. Ibid., p. 69, note 12.
5. Grasping will involve a speaker's tacit knowledge of the semantic structure of the language. The nature of such knowledge has long been a controversial topic in the foundations of linguistics, but it is not directly relevant here.
6. Chomsky, *Knowledge of Language: Its Nature, Origin, and Use*, Praeger, New York, 1985, pp. 221–243.
7. This point was made as far back as Katz, *Language and Other Abstract Objects*, pp. 87–92.
8. Chomsky, *Knowledge of Language: Its Nature, Origin, and Use*, p. 240.
9. It is perhaps worth stressing that the point of these examples is to *illustrate* the claim that it is a reasonably straightforward matter to produce the evidence necessary to justify our hypothesis against skeptical challenge. The aim behind their presentation is not to give a full-fledged linguistic argument for the hypothesis that "table" means *table* in English. It is unnecessary to give such an argument to show that the skeptic is wrong to claim that choice between our hypothesis and the hypothesis that the English word "table" means *tabair* is arbitrary. To show that the claim is wrong requires no more than examples of the kind of evidence which can discriminate the two hypotheses. It seems clear that, supposing that we can make objective sense of properties and relations like synonymy and analyticity, the examples show this.
10. I am indebted to Mark Johnston for this question.
11. Quine, "On What There Is," in *From a Logical Point of View*, pp. 1–19.

12. The issue here should be kept separate from that of how spatio-temporal creatures such as ourselves can have knowledge of abstract objects. Non-naturalists
cannot assume that knowledge of abstract objects is continuous with knowledge
of empirical objects, deriving from a causal relation between knower and known
as in the case of perception. A sketch of a non-naturalistic view of how we can
know abstract objects is found in Katz, *Language and Other Abstract Objects*. I
return to certain aspects of this issue in the last two chapters, and I hope to
provide a full treatment in a later work.

Chapter 5

This chapter is an expanded version of "The Refutation of Indeterminacy," *The Journal of Philosophy*, Vol. LXXXV, 1988, pp. 227–252. Reprinted with permission of the
editors.

1. Quine, *Word and Object*, p. 72; hereafter, W&O.
2. Kripke, *Wittgenstein on Rules and Private Language*, p. 57.
3. *Word and Object*, p. 205, and *From a Logical Point of View*.
4. Sluga, *Gottlob Frege*, pp. 17–34.
5. Quine, *From a Logical Point of View*, pp. 42–46.
6. Quine, "Carnap and Logical Truth," in *The Philosophy of Rudolf Carnap*, P. A.
   Schilpp, ed., pp. 385–406, and also, of course, at the end of "Two Dogmas of
   Empiricism."
7. This notion is adapted from G. E. Moore, "The Refutation of Idealism," in his
   Philosophical Studies, Routledge & Kegan Paul, London, 1922, p. 30.
8. It is, of course, one thing to have the common-sense view of translation and
   quite another to have the kind of justification for it that would be provided by
   a full-fledged linguistic theory of translation. Although having both is clearly
   more desirable than having only the former, the latter is not necessary to refute
   the skeptic's claim.
9. Quine, *Philosophy of Logic*, Prentice-Hall, Englewood Cliffs, N.J., 1970, p. 3.
10. Quine, "Indeterminacy of Translation Again," *Journal of Philosophy*, Vol.
    LXXXIV, No. 1, 1987, pp. 5–10.
11. Indeed, if it were not, it would be too controversial in the present cognitive
    climate to bear the weight of the indeterminacy argument. But there are ques-
    tions here which ought to be raised. Why doesn't Quine think that behaviorism
    is mandatory for the psychologist as well? Doesn't he think linguistics is a
    branch of psychology? And if so, why is psychology divided in this way?
    Doesn't he suppose that we learn more than just languages by observing others
    and being corrected by them? Is "introspective semantics" (ibid., p. 9) no good,
    but introspective psychology all right?
12. Note, for example, how in "Indeterminacy of Translation Again" Quine slides
    unhesitatingly from speaking of "translation" and "our linguist" (pp. 5–6) to
    speaking of "radical translation" and "our radical translator" (p. 7).
13. W&O, pp. 75–76; updated in "On the Reasons for Indeterminacy of Transla-
    tion," *Journal of Philosophy*, Vol. 67, No. 6, 1970, pp. 178–183.
14. W&O, pp. 76–79, and also earlier in *From a Logical Point of View*, p. 63.
15. We need not interpret Quine as taking the discontinuity of radical translation to
    be a basis for inferring the absence of linguistically neutral meanings. Perhaps
    all he means is that such discontinuity helps us see that there are no meanings.
    But, even on this interpretation, the question of the text stands, since, here too,
    without a justification Quine's case would come down to a bare assertion.

16. Chomsky, "Quine's Empirical Assumptions," in *Words and Objections*, D. Davidson and J. Hintikka, eds., D. Reidel, Dordrecht, 1969, p. 62.

17. Thus, I think McGinn's dismissal of Quine is mistaken about Quine's reasons for thinking there is no fact of the matter about meaning (*Wittgenstein on Meaning*, p. 152). Quine does, of course, represent his attitude as the inverse of Brentano's (W&O, p. 221), but Quine's reason for taking this attitude is not the simplistic one attributed to him. Rather, Quine thinks that the reduction of meanings to aspects of the physical world, say, to neural structures in human brains, makes no sense because there is nothing to be reduced in the first place. He writes, for example: "I want to relate physicalism to my perennial criticisms of mentalistic semantics. Readers have supposed that my complaint is ontological; it is not. If in general I could make satisfactory sense of declaring two expressions to be synonymous, I would be more than pleased to recognize an abstract object as their common meaning. . . . Where the trouble lies, rather, is in the two-place predicate of synonymy itself; it is too desperately wanting in clarity and perspicuity." Quine, "Facts of the Matter" in *Essays on the Philosophy of W. V. Quine*, R. W. Shahan and C. Swoyer, eds., Harvester Press, Hassocks, Sussex, 1979, pp. 166–167. See also "On the Reasons for Indeterminacy of Translation," pp. 180–181.

18. Quine, *From a Logical Point of View*, pp. 47–64.

19. Ibid., p. 63. Note that we even have the same notion of absence of controls which figures so prominently in chapter II of *Word and Object*.

20. Quine, "Indeterminacy of Translation Again," p. 8.

21. Another line of argument is this. Quine's aim is to show, contra Frege, Church, and Carnap, that there are no intensional objects for intensionalists to use in their statement of principles of logic. Because it is into logic that intensionalists propose to introduce senses, the relation of synonymy that provides the identity condition must be specified, as Quine puts it in "Two Dogmas of Empiricism" (pp. 33–34), for variable '*S*' and '*L*'. The reason is that principles of logic express a language-neutral implication relation. That is to say, logic concerns a notion of implication which is specified for variable '*S*' and '*L*', not a notion like implication-in-Italian. Thus, if Quine can show there is no linguistically universal notion of synonymy, there will be no linguistically neutral meanings, and hence, nothing for intensionalists to appeal to extend logic in a naturalistically dubious direction.

22. Quine, "Indeterminacy of Translation Again," p. 9.

23. Quine, *From a Logical Point of View*, pp. 24–27.

24. Quine observes that Carnap's possible-worlds account of necessity uses meaning relations among state descriptions to guarantee logical independence (*From a Logical Point of View*, p. 23).

25. To see how important a role positivism played in shaping Bloomfield's reconstruction of linguistics, see L. Bloomfield, "Language or Ideas?", *Language*, Vol. 12, 1936, pp. 89–95; reprinted in *The Philosophy of Linguistics*, Katz, ed., pp. 19–25.

26. Quine, *From a Logical Point of View*, pp. 32–36.

27. It is important to note that Carnap's work represents a significant break with the Fregean tradition preceding it. Whereas that tradition characterized analyticity in terms of intensional notions (e.g., Frege characterized it in terms of laws of logic plus definitions, i.e., statements of sameness of sense), Carnap abandons the use of intensional notions in his meaning-postulates approach, characterizing analyticity exclusively in terms of extensional notions. This is

why Quine rightly criticizes him for failing to explain what analyticity is. If analyticity can be explained, you have to talk about sense structure to do it. This is also why Quine's criticism doesn't apply to other intensionalist accounts of analyticity. See Katz, *Cogitations*, pp. 41–97.

28. One of the most influential examples of theoretical definition in the early stages of generative syntax was Chomsky's rule for the English auxiliary system. See Chomsky, *Current Issues in Linguistic Theory*, p. 36.

29. See Chomsky, *Syntactic Structures*, Mouton, The Hague, 1957, pp. 49–60, and especially pp. 53–55 for discussion of theoretical definitions.

30. See Katz, *Semantic Theory; Propositional Structure and Illocutionary Force*, Harvard University Press, Cambridge, Mass., 1980; and "Common Sense in Semantics," pp. 157–233.

31. Katz, *Cogitations*, pp. 75–90.

32. Kant, *Critique of Pure Reason*, N. K. Smith, trans., Humanities Press, New York, 1929, p. 49.

33. This is but the sketchiest of presentations, but see Katz, *Cogitations*, cited above. A full presentation is to be found in Smith and Katz, *Supposable Worlds*.

34. Quine has somehow not seen the point that a theoretical definition of analyticity framed in the metatheory of generative grammars does define the notion for variable 'S' and 'L', a point which I first made in "Some Remarks on Quine on Analyticity," *Journal of Philosophy*, Vol. LXIV, 1967, pp. 36–52. See Quine, "On a Suggestion of Katz," same issue, pp. 52–54, and also "Methodological Reflections on Current Linguistic Theory," in *Semantics of Natural Language*, D. Davidson and G. Harman, eds., D. Reidel, Dordrecht, 1972, pp. 449–450. In these papers, Quine confuses a theoretical definition of analyticity with a technique for questioning informants to elicit judgments about analyticity for the sentences of a particular natural language.

35. Quine, "Indeterminacy of Translation Again," p. 9.

36. Note that our approach can adopt a holism which insists that translation schemes can be tested (or even constructed) only as components of a comprehensive grammatical theory of natural languages.

37. In *Word and Object* (p. 72), Quine writes: "To project [analytical hypotheses] beyond the independently translatable sentences at all is in effect to impute our sense of linguistic analogy unverifiably to the native mind."

38. See Quine, "Ontological Relativity," in *Ontological Relativity and Other Essays*, p. 46, where he remarks, "On deeper reflection, radical translation begins at home." The full force of such deeper reflection is brought out by the "theorem" that Putnam proves from the indeterminacy thesis. See Hilary Putnam, *Reason, Truth, and History*, Cambridge University Press, 1981, pp. 22–48. A side benefit of the refutation of indeterminacy in this chapter is that one no longer needs to accept Putnam's "theorem."

39. I have said nothing in the text about what Quine calls "pressing from below." As he puts it: "By pressing from below I mean pressing whatever arguments for indeterminacy of translation can be based on inscrutability of terms. I suppose that Harman's example regarding natural numbers comes under this head, theoretical though it is. It is that the sentence '3 ∈ 5' goes into a true sentence of set theory under von Neumann's way of construing natural numbers, but goes into a false one under Zermelo's way." Quine, "On the Reasons for Indeterminacy of Translation," p. 183.

But Quine is wrong in thinking that the nature of the choice between the two ways of construing natural numbers puts pressure on us to recognize indeterminacy. The consideration he raises is relevant if, and only if, it has already been shown that the analytic/synthetic distinction cannot be drawn. If the distinction can be drawn, pressing from below is ineffective. For it can hardly matter to questions of translation, which are on the analytic side, that a mathematical sentence comes out true within one set of synthetic statements and false within another. On the other hand, if the distinction cannot be drawn, pressing from below is unnecessary. For then, as we have already seen, the gap in Quine's argument in *Word and Object* is filled, and the argument goes through without a hitch. Hence, my criticism of Quine's argument in "Two Dogmas of Empiricism" is a criticism as well of his claim that examples like Harman's are a consideration in favor of indeterminacy.

40. Quine, "Comments on Katz," in *Perspectives on Quine*, R. Barrett and R. Gibson, eds., Basil Blackwell, Oxford, 1990, pp. 198–199.

41. The paper in question is "The Refutation of Indeterminacy," which is reprinted in *Perspectives on Quine* and appeared originally in *Journal of Philosophy*, Vol. LXXXV, No. 5, 1988, pp. 227–252.

Chapter 6

This chapter is a considerably revised and expanded version of "The Domino Theory," *Philosophical Studies*, Vol. 58, 1990, pp. 3–39.

1. Quine, "Two Dogmas of Empiricism," in *From a Logical Point of View*, pp. 20–46.

2. Davidson, "Truth and Meaning", *Synthese*, Vol. XVII, No. 3, 1967, pp. 304–323; reprinted in *Readings in the Philosophy of Language*, J. F. Rosenberg and C. Travis, eds., Prentice-Hall, Englewood Cliffs, N.J., 1971, p. 455 (references to this paper are to this reprint).

3. Davidson, *Inquiries into Truth and Interpretation*, Clarendon Press, Oxford, 1985, p. 101.

4. Benson, Mates, "Synonymity," in *Semantics and the Philosophy of Language*, L. Linsky, ed., University of Illinois Press, Urbana, 1952, pp. 101–136.

5. Davidson, "Truth and Meaning", p. 461.

6. Alonzo Church, "Intensional Isomorphism and Identity of Belief," *Philosophical Studies*, Vol. 5, 1954, pp. 65–73.

7. Davidson, *Inquiries into Truth and Interpretation*, pp. 101–102.

8. Thus, not only is Davidson's constructive program a direct implementation of Quine's recommendation of the Tarskian paradigm at the end of his paper "Notes on the Theory of Reference," in *From a Logical Point of View*, p. 138, but Davidson's rationale is Quine's rationale that the theory of truth is preferable to the theory of meaning on the grounds that truth is free of the ills that allegedly plague meaning.

9. Davidson, "Truth and Meaning," p. 457.

10. In Davidson, *Inquiries into Truth and Interpretation*, p. 26, note 10.

11. Katz, "Logic and Language: An Examination of Recent Criticisms of Intensionalism," in *Language, Mind, and Knowledge, Minnesota Studies in the Philosophy of Science*, Vol. VII, K. Gunderson, ed., University of Minnesota Press, 1975, pp. 63–76.

12. Davidson, *Inquiries into Truth and Interpretation*, p. 26, note 11.

13. Carnap, "Meaning Postulates," in *Meaning and Necessity*, pp. 222–229.

14. Quine points out (*From a Logical Point of View*, p. 23) that Carnap's broader notion of possibility falls within the scope of his criticisms because the specifica-

tion of possible worlds assumes knowledge of the incompatibility of predicates like "bachelor" and "married".

15. D. Lewis, "General Semantics," in *Semantics of Natural Language*, Davidson and Harman, eds., pp. 169–218.

16. Searle, "Chomsky's Revolution in Linguistics," originally in *The New York Review of Books*, 1972; reprinted in *On Noam Chomsky*, G. Harman, ed., Anchor Books, New York, 1974, pp. 2–33; the quote is from p. 27.

17. Lewis, *Convention*, Harvard University Press, Cambridge, Mass., 1969, pp. 170–171.

18. G. Evans and J. McDowell, "Introduction," in *Truth and Meaning: Essays in Semantics*, Clarendon Press, Oxford, 1976, pp. vii–viii.

19. Evans and McDowell consider only very early formulations of the decompositional theory of meaning, ones over ten years old at the time of their writing.

20. Evans and McDowell, "Introduction," *Truth and Meaning*, p. viii.

21. Ibid., p. ix. This strikes me as a variant of the argument in Renford Bambrough, "Universals and Family Resemblances," *Proceedings of the Aristotelian Society*, Vol. LXI, 1960–61, pp. 216. Bambrough first concedes that brothers have in common that they are male siblings and then, perhaps noticing that he is giving away too much, says, "Even a concept which can be explained in terms of necessary and sufficient conditions cannot be *ultimately* explained in such terms. To satisfy the craving for an ultimate explanation of 'brother' in such terms it would be necessary to define 'male' and 'sibling', and the words in which 'male' and 'sibling' were defined, and so on *ad infinitum* and *ad impossible*." The response to this is that asking for "ultimate explanation" *is* crying for the moon, but that all that is required is a revealing analysis of the senses of expressions in terms of what is, in relation to their structure, a small set of semantic simples.

22. Let us take the parallel with logic a step further. In logic, no one would insist that concern with logical structure *per se* "conceals from [us] our utter incapacity to do what we ought to be doing," which is to state something such that, if we knew it, we would be able to produce good arguments ourselves and properly evaluate the arguments of others. Even though we are all well enough acquainted with the gap between theory and practice in logic not to think that logic courses significantly raise the proficiency of students in practical reasoning, we do not, for that reason, think there is no point to teaching logic. The question that Evans and McDowell beg is the question raised by the parallel gap between theory and practice in the case of language. They presuppose that a theory of sense structure that does not pay off directly for the understanding of linguistic practice is illegitimate despite how informative the theory is for its own domain.

23. See F. M. Katz and J. J. Katz, "Is Necessity the Mother of Intension?," *Philosophical Review*, Vol. LXXXVI, 1977, pp. 70–96. The revision of possible-worlds semantics known as "situation semantics" improves matters somewhat, but it doesn't address the basic problem. See Jon Barwise and John Perry, *Situation Semantics*, MIT Press, Cambridge, Mass., 1983. Situation semantics introduces the idea that the interpretation of a sentence is a situation type, a set-theoretic construction out of pieces of actual situations, which may or may not reflect an actual situation. The idea avoids the Fregean move of taking sentences to designate truth values and, as a result, enables those who adopt this position to avoid having to say that there are only two necessary propositions. But this does

not help much with the general problem of having an exclusively extensional characterization of the notion of a proposition. The same situation type of John being a bigamist has to interpret the nonsynonymous sentences "John has two wives" and "The number of John's wives is equal to the even prime." Furthermore, having cut themselves off from anything like the Fregean device of referring to the sense of a sentence in an opaque context, Barwise and Perry have to allow substitutions on the extensional condition of sameness of situation type, leading to familiar counterintuitive results in connection with verbs of propositional attitude. Barwise and Perry bite the bullet, taking the position that there are no semantic reasons for a reluctance to make inferences on the condition of sameness of situation type, but only pragmatic reasons for that reluctance (pp. 199–200). They claim that the semantic notion of a proposition which underlies the appeal of those familiar counterintuitive results is misguided, based on our having lost our blessed state of semantic innocence in which expressions stand directly for objects in the world and sentences for situations. But this claim flies in the face of a wide variety of observations about our ordinary linguistic talk which show it to be shot full of intensionalist idiom. See Scott Soames, "Lost Innocence: Comments on Situations and Attitudes," *Linguistics and Philosophy*, Vol. 8, No. 1, 1985, pp. 59–71. See also my "Why Intensionalists Ought Not Be Fregeans," pp. 90–91, where I discuss the way that Frege's narrowing of the scope of a theory of meaning has encouraged extensionalists to think there are very few pretheoretic semantic phenomena that semantic theories must do justice to. As well, note the semantic facts (i)–(viii) in chapter 2, section 3, pp. 28–29.

24. Putnam, "It Ain't Necessarily So," *Journal of Philosophy*, Vol. LIX, No. 2, 1962, pp. 658–671; "Is Semantics Possible?", *Metaphilosophy*, Vol. I, 1970, pp. 187–201; "The Meaning of 'Meaning'," in *Language, Mind, and Knowledge, Minnesota Studies in the Philosophy of Science*, pp. 131–193.

25. That is to say, analytic in the full-blooded intensionalist sense. Putnam introduces his own notion of analyticity in "The Analytic and the Synthetic" in *Minnesota Studies in the Philosophy of Science*, Vol. III, H. Feigl and G. Maxwell, eds., University of Minnesota Press, Minneapolis, 1962, pp. 269–317, but this is a pale copy, offering no basis for necessary truth. Putnam's claim to be relying to Quine seems to misunderstand the Kantian and Fregean focus of Quine's criticisms. Putnam's notion of analyticity would be quite acceptable to Quine.

26. Keith Donnellan, "Necessity and Criteria," *Journal of Philosophy*, Vol. LIX, No. 22, 1962, pp. 647–658.

27. Putnam, "It Ain't Necessarily So," p. 659.

28. Frege, "On Sense and Reference," pp. 56–78. I use the term "determine" rather than the more usual "present" as closer to Frege's intent. See Sluga, *Gottlob Frege*, pp. 150–153. Note that Frege took it as an imperfection of natural languages that their meaningful expressions often do not determine a referent.

29. See, in particular, Katz, "Why Intensionalists Ought Not Be Fregeans."

30. Frege's definition of sense in terms of the notion of reference, together with the role he accords truth in his overall conception of logic, has encouraged critics of intensionalism to think that any theory of sense is somehow deficient if it doesn't contain an account of truth and reference. For example, David Lewis makes this objection in *Convention*, pp. 170–171.

31. Frege, *Foundations of Arithmetic*, pp. 3–4.

32. This is the conception in Katz, *Semantic Theory*, pp. 171–182, developed further in *Cogitations* and in Smith and Katz, *Supposable Worlds*.

33. Donnellan, "Reference and Definite Descriptions," *Philosophical Review*, Vol. LXXV, 1966, pp. 261–304.

34. Putnam, "The Meaning of 'Meaning'," p. 136.

35. Ibid., pp. 135–136. Thus, if there were any doubts about my analysis of Putnam's conception of the intensionalist position that he sees himself attacking, there cannot be any now.

36. Putnam neglects the earliest and most complete form of the criticism that it is open to intensionalists to drop the principle that sense determines reference (see Katz, "Logic and Language: An Examination of Recent Criticisms of Intensionalism," especially, p. 98). The form of the criticism that he responds to makes it easy to come up with a response, for this form of the criticism is not accompanied with a positive account of how intensionalists can determine relations among senses apart from reference. Without such an account, Putnam can respond, as he does, that, if the principle is dropped, such relations cannot be determined. See the text for a discussion of what happens when there is an account explaining how sense relations can be independently determined.

37. Putnam, "Computational Psychology and Interpretation Theory," in Putnam, *Realism and Reason, Philosophical Papers, Volume 3*, Cambridge University Press, 1983, p. 149.

38. The argument is presented in a number of places, with a number of twists. I shall consider two papers: T. Burge, "Individualism and the Mental," in *Midwest Studies in Philosophy*, Vol. IV, P. A. French, T. E. Uehling, Jr., and H. K. Wettstein, eds., University of Minnesota Press, Minneapolis, 1979, pp. 73–122; and "Other Bodies," in *Thought and Object*, A. Woodfield, ed., Clarendon Press, Oxford, 1982, pp. 97–120.

39. Burge, "Other Bodies," pp. 100–101.

40. Ibid., p. 101. Burge rejects Putnam's claims about the indexicality of common nouns like "water", which I believe he is right in doing. I shall ignore this issue because, as Burge himself says, it "tends to divert attention from major implications of [Putnam's] examples" (p. 107).

41. Putnam, "The Meaning of 'Meaning'," pp. 139–142.

42. This is confirmed by the fact that the intuition changes when we move from the case of "water" to other cases. Take the word "food". It is intuitively clear that earthling space explorers reporting back from Twin Earth will not say that there is no food there because the stuff that people on Twin Earth eat to nourish them is chemically different from our food. When we consider a range of cases like "food" it starts to look very much as if the intuitions are meaning-driven, that is, that what we say about what space explorers will say is largely a function of our grasp of the meaning of the word in question. (I owe this example to George Bealer, in conversation.)

43. Burge, "Other Bodies," p. 109.

44. Burge, "Individualism and the Mental," pp. 77–79.

45. If patients are presumed not to be in the proper position to identify a new disease, we can imagine that, rather than a neurotic patient, our subject is a hero of medical science.

46. Katz, "Why Intensionalists Ought Not Be Fregeans," and "Has the Description Theory of Names Been Refuted?"

Chapter 7

1. P. F. Strawson, in *Skepticism and Naturalism: Some Varieties*, Columbia University Press, New York, 1985, seems to suggest that there is another form of naturalism, one he calls "non-reductive," "catholic," "liberal," and "soft." On his account the Quinean and Wittgensteinian forms of naturalism that I have been discussing are two forms of "reductive," "strict," or "hard" naturalism. I find it puzzling that Strawson considers the "non-reductive" or "soft" naturalist position to be a form of naturalism at all. He says that, according to nonreductive naturalism, "the notion of existence in this region [of reality] is extended to include what we so readily speak of, or appear to speak of, viz., thought-objects, not locatable in nature, though sometimes exemplified there" (p. 94). Strawson makes it quite clear that such objects are full-blooded abstract entities (p. 73). Although it is true that, at one point, he seems to disavow "a special faculty of intuition" (pp. 40–41), at another point he seems to embrace it (p. 88). And, in expressing his sympathy for nonreductive naturalism, Strawson writes that his allegiance "lies with the realists or catholic naturalists rather than the nominalists or strict naturalists" (p. 94). Thus, it seems that the position Strawson calls "non-reductive naturalism" is naturalism only in name and that it is more properly called "non-naturalism." I think that Strawson's interesting line of argument in these Woodbridge Lectures becomes immediately clearer and more cogent as soon as we recognize that the conflict is between naturalism of a Quinean or Wittgensteinian variety and non-naturalism of the tradition that includes Leibniz, Descrates, and Frege.
2. A. Danto, "Naturalism," in the *Encyclopedia of Philosophy*, P. Edwards, ed., MacMillan, New York, 1967, Vol. 5, pp. 448–450.
3. "Naturalism," p. 448.
4. Aristotle, *Metaphysics*, XIII.3, 1078a21-2, 28-9; Quine, *Quiddities*, pp. 25–29.
5. Frege, *The Basic Laws of Arithmetic*, pp. 1–25.
6. Moore, *Principia Ethica*.
7. Frege, *The Basic Laws of Arithmetic*, pp. 12–13; see the discussion in Katz, *Language and Other Abstract Objects*, pp. 161–166.
8. Frege, "The Thought," in *Essays on Frege*, Klemke, ed., pp. 507–535.
9. Moore, *Principia Ethica*, p. 16.
10. One criticism is that word meanings in natural language are too unclear and ambiguous for Moore's test to work. This seems to be simply false on the face of it. There is no unclarity of meaning or ambiguity in the cases Moore considered which prevents us from concluding that the question in them is open. It is evident that the sense of "thing productive of pleasure" contains nothing to rule out the possibility of bad pleasures in the way that the sense of "bachelor" contains something to rule out married bachelors. But if there is doubt in some case whether the question is open, we always have the option of varying the form of the question. A question may be self-answered negatively as well as positively, and in the negative form intuition is often more clear-cut. Thus, it is plain that the question "Is what is productive of pleasure ever bad?" is not self-answered negatively, in contrast to "Are bachelors ever single?"

    This criticism might be a reason for thinking that, even after exploring every option for varying the question, there are some cases where semantic structure might not be transparent enough for Moore's test to apply. But this is only an objection to a claim that the test is directly applicable in every case. No such claim need be made. It is a truism of research in linguistics that direct linguistic intuition can fail when grammatical structure becomes complex and subtle. This is a fact of life in the study of language, and it is taken to show that intuition needs supplementation by less direct methods, i.e., theory construction. At best this criticism shows that Moore's test cannot be applied in the simple way he supposed.

Another criticism is that Moore's open question itself is linguistically deviant. This isn't plausible, since such questions are instances of a common way of questioning the adequacy of a definition, and in the case of some of the naturalistic definitions that Moore criticizes, he seems quite right to claim that his experiment turns out the way he thinks it does.

11. Putnam, *Reason, Truth, and History,* Cambridge University Press, 1981, p. 207. It seems peculiar to find Putnam presupposing the analytic/synthetic distinction in this quotation. Since, as we saw in chapter 6, Putnam accepts Quine's criticisms of the distinction and since much of Putnam's work in the philosophy of language is devoted to inventing arguments of his own against it, he seems to be in no position to distinguish between synthetic and analytic identities—between linguistic analysis, i.e., just reflection on meanings, and empirical/theoretical research. I suppose he would appeal to the "one-criterion concept" notion of analyticity in Putnam, "The Analytic and the Synthetic" in *Minnesota Studies in the Philosophy of Science,* Vol. III, H. Feigl and G. Maxwell, eds., University of Minnesota Press, Minneapolis, 1962, pp. 358–397. But I doubt that this notion, whose extension is at the mercy of empirical/theoretical research, draws the distinction between synthetic and analytic identities which is intended in the quotation.

12. Moore, "A Reply to My Critics," in *The Philosophy of G. E. Moore,* P. A. Schilpp, ed., Vol. I, Open Court, La Salle, Ill., 1942, pp. 660–667.

13. See Katz, *Cogitations,* pp. 144–152, for a discussion of Moore's notion of semantic analysis in relation to decompositional theory.

14. See Katz, *Semantic Theory,* chapter 5, for a discussion of the relation between analytic and contradictory statements, on the one hand, and positively and negatively self-answered questions, on the other.

15. See ibid., pp. 450–452, for another discussion of these notions.

16. Counterexamples to a claim that a sense is the sense of a certain expression in a natural language are not at issue here.

17. Putnam, *Reason, Truth, and History,* p. 207.

18. Quine, "On What There Is," in *From a Logical Point of View,* pp. 16–17. In adopting the substance of Quine's view, certain provisos are necessary. First, I am obviously not also adopting the philosophical views that go along with it in Quine's presentation of the view expressed in the slogan "To be is to be the value of a variable." Rather, I am adopting the general thought that commitment to an ontology for a scientific theory is essentially a matter of a rational choice among theories. Second, I assume that a comparison of rival theories in terms of simplicity can be made only after they are equated with respect to their degree of faithfulness to the facts. If one theory better accounts for the facts, the greater simplicity on the part of the other cannot normally be a basis for preferring it.

19. David Hilbert, "On the Infinite," in *Philosophy of Mathematics,* P. Benacerraf and H. Putnam, eds., Prentice-Hall, Englewood Cliffs, N.J., 1964, pp. 134–151; L. E. J. Brouwer, "Intuitionism and Formalism" in *Philosophy of Mathematics,* pp. 66–77.

20. This was the upshot of the critique in Chomsky, "Review of *Verbal Behavior*," *Language*, Vol. 35, 1959, pp. 26–58.

21. Carl G. Hempel, "Empiricist Criteria of Cognitive Significance: Problems and Changes," in *Aspects of Scientific Explanation*, Free Press, New York, 1965, pp. 101–119; and Hempel, "The Theoretician's Dilemma," in *Minnesota Studies in the Philosophy of Science*, Vol. II, H. Feigl, M. Scriven, and G. Maxwell, eds., University of Minnesota Press, Minneapolis, 1955, pp. 37–98.

22. Goodman, "A World of Individuals," in *Problems and Prospects*, Bobbs-Merrill, Indianapolis, 1972, pp. 155–172.

23. Field, *Science without Numbers*, Princeton University Press, 1980.

24. Although, for this reason, it is sometimes claimed that nominalism is a simpler form of naturalism than conceptualism, it would seem that, since nominalism requires some psychological account of how resemblance is recognized, it may not in fact be simpler. Nominalism would collapse into naturalistic conceptualism if its account of such recognition could not be given without having to locate the source of generality in categories of the mind. But even if it remains a separate doctrine, there is little chance of being able to make any serious simplicity comparison.

25. Putnam, "What Is Mathematical Truth?" in *Philosophical Papers*, Vol. I, Cambridge University Press, 1975, pp. 60–78.

26. Bloomfield, "Language or Ideas?", *Language*, Vol. 12, 1936, pp. 89–95.

27. Chomsky, *Aspects of the Theory of Syntax*.

28. As far as I can see, books like Chomsky's *Cartesian Linguistics* leave the question open.

29. For example, Chomsky, *Rules and Representations*, Columbia University Press, New York, 1980.

30. Katz, *Language and Other Abstract Objects*.

31. Ibid., pp. 76–93.

32. Chomsky, *Aspects of the Theory of Syntax*, p. 3.

33. Edmund Husserl, *Logical Investigations*, Vol. I, J. N. Findlay, trans., Humanities Press, New York, 1970, p. 103.

34. Frege, "The Thought," pp. 507–535.

35. Putnam, "What Is Mathematical Truth?", pp. 70–71.

36. Ibid., pp. 71–76.

37. Chomsky, *The Logical Structure of Linguistic Theory*, pp. 1–59.

38. Given the looseness of the notion of competence as we are using it, every psychologically constrained theory of syntax and a wide variety of views about meaning fall under conceptualist metatheory. The semantic views include views of Sellars, Quine, Chomsky, Searle, Harman, Dennett, Fodor, Block, Loar, Field, Lycan, McGinn, and Schiffer, and other so-called "conceptual-role semanticists." Of course, some of these philosophers present their semantic views not as theories of natural languages, but as views about the content of thoughts or beliefs. But most of them see their views as part of a theory of natural language, and even in the case of those who don't, their views can be, and have been, taken in this way.

Looking at these views as ways in which a conceptualist metatheory might conceive of semantic competence, the common doctrine uniting the different versions of conceptual-role semantics is that the meaning of a sentence is to be understood in terms of its function in cognitive processes like thinking, speaking, understanding, inference, etc., and that the meaning of an expression is its contribution to the roles of the sentences in which it appears. Conceptual-role semantics is a blend of the familiar conception of meaning as use with a functionalist view of mind, of the sort we associate with Turing and Putnam. The conception of meaning as use is basic, but the notion of use is subject to various construals. In any case, use is not put out in the open, as it would be in Wittgensteinian or strictly behaviorist approaches, but is located in the realm of the mental, functionally conceived, and perhaps slated for biological reduction.

39. For example, Chomsky once drew the boundaries of sentence-grammar to exclude the meaning of words and the compositional meaning of sentences from sentence structure; see Chomsky, *Reflections on Language*, Pantheon, New York, 1975, pp. 104–105, and *Rules and Representations*. He did this, it seems, because he had an axe to grind in linguistics. The principal driving force behind Chomsky's theoretical work in linguistics has always been to develop the general theory of language as a theory of language acquisition. The salient feature of language acquisition is the fact that it occurs so extremely rapidly, without requiring very high intelligence, and without a rich input. Thus, Chomsky has sought models which represent acquisition as an automatic process. The difficulty is that the learning of word meanings does not seem to work this way. It is far slower, and more dependent on intelligence and input. Faced with this empirical fact, Chomsky avoids saying that language acquisition is not homogeneous by saying instead that meaning is not part of language.

It should be noted, however, that recently Chomsky has reversed himself on this delimitation, and now seems to fully include meaning in sentence-grammar. See Katz and Postal, "Realism vs. Conceptualism in Linguistics," to appear, sections 6 and 7. This reversal is puzzling because now Chomsky has to say that language acquisition is not homogeneous. He doesn't explain how he can now maintain his long-standing position on the rapid, automatic nature of language acquisition.

40. For a more extensive discussion, see Katz and Postal, "Realism vs. Conceptualism in Linguistics."

41. It should be noted, of course, that, even with full knowledge of the facts, there may be no single best theory. More than one theory may surpass the others but, compared to one another, may be equally faithful to the facts, equally simple, and equally good on the other methodological dimensions. Some of these co-optimal theories will express the same conception of the phenomena in the sense in which an arithmetic in binary notation and one in decimal notation express the same conception of numerical structure or in which equivalent propositional logics express the same conception of implication. But others need not. (That is, there can be some which express different conceptions of phenomena in the sense in which von Neumann's and Zermelo's ways of construing numbers do.) This is no problem. All such theories can be counted as expressing the best conception of the facts, since, for our purposes, we need nothing more than a notion of a set of optimal theories.

42. On the basis of the discussion in the previous note, I shall often make the simplifying assumption that there is only one best theory, but nothing hangs on this. If there is more than one, the argument will show divergence from them all.

43. Chomsky, *Language and Responsibility*, Pantheon Books, New York, 1977, p. 145, and also "Prospects for the Study of Language and Mind," unpublished lecture, Israel.

44. A more complete statement of the argument is found in "Realism vs. Conceptualism in Linguistics." Someone might think that the argument can be got

around by claiming that what is necessary is that if "I persuade him to leave" and "He intends to leave" have the meanings they have in English, then the first entails the second. This is to criticize the argument for failing to distinguish between the (true) claim that the relations between the meanings of the sentences are necessary from the (false) claim that the relations of those meanings to the English sentences is necessary. The relation between the meanings holds necessarily, even though it is a contingent fact that the meanings in question happen to be expressed in one orthographic, phonetic, or neural form rather than another. But my argument makes a stronger claim than it is being given credit for. The argument claims that, since on the conceptualist position relations between meanings, too, must be taken to be contingent neural structures, there cannot be a necessary entailment even between the meanings of the sentences. The point may perhaps be made clearer by observing that conceptualism precludes conceptions of meaning that would represent contingent neural connections as necessary connections. Thus, on allowable conceptions of meaning, e.g., Quine's conception of stimulus meaning, it is not necessary that the meaning 'He intends to leave' be true whenever the meaning 'I persuade him to leave' is true.

45. This notion is adapted from John Rawls, *A Theory of Justice*, Harvard University Press, Cambridge, Mass., 1971, pp. 136–142.

46. Goodman, *Fact, Fiction, and Forecast*, Bobbs-Merrill, Indianapolis, 1955, pp. 59–83.

47. For further discussion of this distinction, see Katz and Postal, "Realism vs. Conceptualism in Linguistics."

48. Norbert Hornstein made this suggestion in his comments on my paper "The Irrelevance of Psychological Representations," at a session of the conference "Representation, Realism, and Research," Columbia University, December 2–4, 1988.

49. N. Chomsky, R. Huybregts, and H. van Riemskijk, *Noam Chomsky on the Generative Enterprise*, Foris, Dordrecht, 1982, part I, chapter 1, pp. 15–16.

50. A. S. Yessenin-Volpin, "The Ultra-intuitionistic Criterion and the Anti-traditional Program for the Foundations of Mathematics," in *Intuitionism and Proof Theory*, North-Holland, Amsterdam, 1970, pp. 3–45.

51. Dummett, *Elements of Intuitionism*, Oxford University Press, 1977.

52. Chomsky, *Aspects of the Theory of Syntax*, p. 3.

53. This move can be seen as in the spirit of Quine's picture of knowledge as a seamless fabric of fundamentally empirical truths. But if our criticism of Quine's attack on the analytic/synthetic distinction is right, then the reason for believing this picture is eliminated and we are left with just the picture. Without Quine's arguments that there is no seam between the analytic and the synthetic, talk about levels is merely a misleading metaphor.

54. Scott Soames, "Linguistics and Psychology," in *The Philosophy of Linguistics*, Katz, ed., pp. 204–226.

55. Quine, *Quiddities*, pp. 216–219.

56. I am speaking of the grammatical core of the field, and do not deny that sociolinguistics, historical linguistics, etc. concern psychological matters.

57. Sylvain Bromberger, "Types and Tokens in Linguistics," in *Reflections on Chomsky*, A. George, ed., Basil Blackwell, 1989, pp. 58–89.

58. Chomsky, *The Logical Structure of Linguistic Theory*, pp. 28–35.

59. A somewhat different account of the proper way to formulate the autonomy of ethics is found in Frank Jackson's excellent paper "Defining the Autonomy of

Ethics," *Philosophical Review,* Volume LXXXIII, 1974, pp. 88–96. My account is simpler in making the one adjustment of taking derivation as analytic entailment. Of course, the greater simplicity is achieved only by using more intensionalist theory, but I use nothing that would not also have to be used for a complete statement of Jackson's definition, that is, a statement that sets out the full theory required to support the intensionalist notions on which the definition rests.

Two more general points need to be made in connection with the use of intensionalist theory in this connection. First, the present instance of philosophical difficulties produced by treating derivability as an exclusively logical relation is not an isolated case. As I have argued elsewhere, the philosophical theory that all valid consequences rest on logical relations is also responsible for confusions about the nature of the *cogito* and about Descartes's understanding of the argument and its place in his philosophy. See *Cogitations.* Therefore, the rationale for the use of intensionalist theory in the present instance goes beyond the case of ethics.

Second, other aspects of intensionalist theory play an important role in providing an understanding of the full range of objections to the autonomy of ethics. One example is that the theory provides the most satisfying way of handling the influential objection to the autonomy of ethics raised in Searle, *Speech Acts,* pp. 175–198. Searle argues that *ought*-statements about obligations can be inferred from *is*-statements about speech acts of promising. Given the intensionalist theory in question, we can reply that this derivability argument is circular because the sense of "promise" decompositionally contains the moral concept of undertaking an obligation. Hence, the sentences in which the verb occurs are not truly *is*-sentences, as is required in a derivation that refutes autonomy. See the decompositional account of the meaning of performative verbs in Katz, *Propositional Structure and Illocutionary Force.*

60. For example, we find a counterpart of the meta-ethical nonobtainability thesis in linguistics. We might express it in the slogan *sense cannot be obtained from sensa.* Ironically, Quine's argument in "Two Dogmas of Empiricism" illustrates this semantic nonobtainability thesis. The substitution procedures that he invokes to show that any attempt to determine the extension of the synonymy relation will be circular are an appropriate definitional apparatus for trying to reduce concepts in the theory of meaning to a set of acknowledged naturalistic concepts, where the property preserved in substitution belongs to this set. Thus, Quine's argument can be recast as an argument that no naturalistic explanation of sense concepts is possible and, hence, a demonstration of the semantic case of the general non-naturalist nonobtainability thesis. In the case of logic, we have the thesis that the *ought* of logical inference cannot be derived from the *is* of natural connection. This could be argued for simply by recasting Quine's argument against the possibility of using substitution procedures to define concepts in the theory of meaning as an argument against the possibility of using them to define the logical operators. In this connection, see Katz, *Cogitations,* pp. 44–51.

61. This is why it is a mistake for a mathematical realist like Gödel to explain our knowledge of mathematical truth as a kind of perception. It is a strange mistake for a rationalist, since it amounts to taking *a priori* knowledge to have an empiricist explanation! So, perhaps Gödel does not mean actual perception.

62. I have made some suggestions about intuition in *Language and Other Abstract Objects,* pp. 192–220. I hope to develop them elsewhere.

63. Bernard Williams, *Ethics and the Limits of Philosophy*, Harvard University Press, Cambridge, Mass., pp. 93–119.

64. Chomsky, *Syntactic Structures*. Chomsky's view is that a generative grammar of *L* is an explication of the notion 'sentence of *L*' and that its construction should proceed on the basis of the clear cases of sentences and nonsentences. The strategy for handling unclear cases that do not become clearer as we learn more is to have the grammatical rules that work for the clear cases decide them when those rules become applicable. Williams spends much time arguing about the difficulty of deciding unclear cases, but, although it is true that such cases can at times be difficult, it is also true that generative linguists have been doing remarkably well with Chomsky's explication strategy over the last three decades. Aside from warmed-over Wittgensteinianism, there is nothing in Williams's discussion arguing against this strategy in linguistics—or, in ethics, for that matter. In this connection, see Thomas Nagel's review of *Ethics and the Limits of Philosophy* in *Journal of Philosophy*, Vol. LXXXIII, No. 6, 1986, pp. 351–360.

65. The case here is slightly more complex, owing to the supposition that there is nothing corresponding to dialect differences in ethics. This supposition might be denied, or, accepting it, we might explain such differences in the linguistic case on the "analytic geometry" conception of languages in my *Language and Other Abstract Objects*.

66. T. Nagel, Review of *Ethics and the Limits of Philosophy*, p. 359.

67. In his review of *Ethics and the Limits of Philosophy*, Nagel argues, I believe correctly, that Williams has too strong a notion of what theories in ethics would have to be.

68. Of course, there will be a far greater number and variety of unclear cases facing theory construction in ethics than in logic, linguistics, and mathematics, because of the far greater complexity of the subject. This makes discovering and formulating the underlying principles in ethics orders of magnitude more difficult than in those subjects, but, as far as I can see, it makes no difference to the issues discussed in the text. I will return to aspects of this matter in the next chapter.

Chapter 8

1. Schlick, "Is There a Factual *A Priori*? in *Readings in Philosophical Analysis*, H. Feigl and W. Sellars, eds., Appleton-Century-Crofts, New York, 1949, p. 285.

2. Quine, "The Nature of Natural Knowledge," in *Mind and Language*, S. Guttenplan, ed., Oxford University Press, 1975, p. 68, and "Necessary Truth," in *The Ways of Paradox*, Random House, New York, 1965, p. 56.

3. Carnap, "Meaning Postulates," in *Meaning and Necessity*, pp. 222–229; and Quine, "Two Dogmas of Empiricism," in *From a Logical Point of View*, pp. 20–46. See Katz, *Cogitations and "The New Intensionalism"*, for further discussion of the criticisms of Carnap's semantics in the text.

4. Quine, "Two Dogmas of Empiricism," p. 44.

5. Quine, "Epistemology Naturalized," in *Ontological Relativity and Other Essays*, pp. 75–76.

6. Kripke, *Wittgenstein on Rules and Private Language*, pp. 93–94, note 76.

7. Ibid., pp. 93–94.

8. I have in mind the notion of convention that Quine introduces in his "Reply to Stroud," in *Words and Objections*, Davidson and Hintikka, eds.

9. See Katz, "Semantics and Conceptual Change," *Philosophical Review*, Vol. 88,

1979, pp. 327–365. See also Strawson, *Skepticism and Naturalism: Some Varieties*, pp. 89–90.

10. Goodman, *Fact, Fiction, and Forecast*, 1965, pp. 62–66.

11. Ibid., p. 62.

12. See Hans Reichenbach, *Experience and Prediction*, University of Chicago Press, 1938, pp. 348–386, *The Theory of Probability*, University of California Press, Berkeley, 1949, pp. 469–484. For a critical analysis, see Katz, *The Problem of Induction and Its Solution*, University of Chicago Press, 1962.

13. Goodman, *Fact, Fiction, and Forecast*, pp. 63–64.

14. I adopted this conception for knowledge of necessary truth in linguistics, logic, and mathematics in *Language and Other Abstract Objects*, pp. 192–220.

15. Quine, "The Nature of Natural Knowledge," p. 68.

16. Quine, "Epistemology Naturalized," p. 72.

17. Thus, I have ignored Wittgenstein, *On Certainty*, Basil Blackwell, Oxford, 1969.

18. Carnap, "Empiricism, Semantics, and Ontology," in *Meaning and Necessity*, pp. 207–213.

19. Ibid., p. 207.

20. Ibid., p. 215. Here Carnap harks back to the views about pseudo-problems that philosophers of the Vienna Circle once held.

21. Ibid., p. 207.

22. Hempel, "Empiricist Criteria of Cognitive Significance: Problems and Changes," in *Aspects of Scientific Explanation*, pp. 101–122.

23. I do not know who first pointed out the self-refuting nature of the verifiability doctrine. Barry Stroud presents an interesting extension of the point in which he considers the consequences for Carnap of taking the doctrine internally; see Stroud, *The Significance of Philosophical Scepticism*, Clarendon Press, Oxford, 1984, pp. 194–196. Stroud notes that it is "no doubt misguided" to understand the doctrine internally, but sees the fact that skepticism is meaningless taken externally as forcing this understanding (p. 193). I differ with Stroud in thinking that Carnap's formulation of the doctrine precludes its being understood internally. I should add that trying to exempt this doctrine from its own domain of application (e.g., as a matter of convention) won't help. This is not to say that the doctrine couldn't be reformulated to say that all external propositions are ill-framed except this proposition itself, but the reformulation robs it of its rationale, since it is then no longer externality that causes such propositions to be ill framed.

24. Paul Feyerabend, "Problems of Empiricism," in *Beyond the Edge of Certainty*, R. Colodny, ed., Prentice-Hall, Englewood Cliffs, N.J., 1965, p. 180.

25. Katz, "Semantics and Conceptual Change," *Philosophical Review*, Vol. 88, 1979, pp. 327–365.

26. Putnam, *The Many Faces of Realism*, Open Court, La Salle, Ill., 1987.

27. I have not bothered to discuss recent criticisms of the notion of *a priori* knowledge, principally, Philip Kitcher, *The Nature of Mathematical Knowledge*, Oxford University Press, 1984, because I have already said enough to indicate why their assumptions should be rejected. In Kitcher's case, there are two principal assumptions. One is a general requirement concerning the causal basis for belief. As Kitcher expresses it, this requirement is open both to a strong construal on which it is a version of the causal theory of knowledge and to a weak construal on which it is not. On the former construal, mathematics and logic would be ruled out, and, on the latter, the requirement is too weak for naturalistic purposes. I have argued this generally in *Language and Other Abstract Objects*, pp.

206–212; also see B. Hale, *Abstract Objects*, Basil Blackwell, Oxford, 1987, pp. 126–148, for an argument replying to Kitcher specifically. Kitcher's other assumption is Quine's argument in "Two Dogmas of Empiricism," etc. We have seen those arguments do not work.

28. The arguments of skeptics do not show that those propositions cannot be known *a priori*. Although Hume's skeptical argument does show that inductive conclusions do not follow deductively from necessary truths, this is hardly the same as showing that they cannot be given any sort of *a priori* justification. Similarly, although Descartes's skeptical argument shows that the existence of the external world is not a deductive consequence of any body of observational evidence, this does not show that its existence cannot be given an *a priori* justification. See Stroud, *The Significance of Philosophical Skepticism*, for a demonstration of how little progress the arguments of Moore, Kant, Malcolm, Carnap, and Quine have made against Descartes's skepticism in the *Meditations*.

29. See the earlier chapters of this book and also Katz, *Cogitations*.

30. Kant, *Critique of Pure Reason*, pp. 50–51.

31. A similar point about skepticism is made in T. Nagel, *The View from Nowhere*, Oxford University Press, 1988, pp. 67–68.

32. Quine, *Word and Object*, pp. 83–84.

33. Chomsky, *Knowledge of Language: Its Nature, Origin, and Use*, pp. 13–50.

34. This conception is modeled on the familiar conception of the relation between philosophical problems about mathematics and mathematical problems themselves. See my introductory essay for the collection *The Philosophy of Linguistics*, pp. 1–16, and Katz and Postal, "Realism vs. Conceptualism in Linguistics."

Index

Alston, W., 40
Ambiguity, situational, 329n 73
Analysis, 101–107
  depth of, 105
Aristotle, 237, 238
Assertion, 94–96
Augustine, 23, 87
Austin, J., 40, 41

Baker and Hacker, 331
Bambrough, R., 341n 21
Barwise, J., 342n 23
Bealer, G., 343n 42
"Begriffsschrift Theories," 8
Berkeley, G., 250
Bloomfield, L., 252, 253
Bloomfieldian linguistics, 188, 190
Bloomfieldian revolution, 252
Bromberger, S., 276, 277, 278, 279, 280
Brouwer, L. E. J., 270
Burge, T., 19, 91, 224, 225, 226, 227,
  228, 229, 230, 231

Canfield, J. V., 31, 32
Carnap, R., 10, 11, 14, 32, 56, 67, 158,
  176, 177, 210, 307, 308, 316
Chomsky, N., vii, ix, x, 16, 17, 18, 50,
  51, 52, 56, 59, 64, 97, 122, 123,
  168, 169, 183, 190, 252, 253, 260,
  261, 270, 275, 276, 318, 347n 39
  conceptualism, 252–254
  necessity argument against, 261
  as rationalist, 318–319
  and "top-down" approach, 50–52
Chomskyan revolution, 190–191, 252
Church, A., 206
Cognitivism, 281–282
Compositionality, 83

Concepts
  "broad," 121
  "narrow," 121
  vs. conceptions, 243–244
Conceptualism, 250–251

Danto, A., 236
Davidson, D., x, 19, 203, 204, 205, 206,
  207, 208, 209
  and Mates's problem, 205–207
Definition
  and essential/inessential properties,
    114–115
  lexical, 244
  substitution criteria, 189
  theoretical, 189–192, 242, 244
Democritean tradition in linguistics and
  logic, 54–56
Descartes, 6
Dewey, J., 10
Donnellan, K., 128, 143, 216, 217
Drury, M. O'C., 333n 1
Dummett, M., 270, 271
  on theories of meaning, 84–86

Ellipsis, 52–66, 79
  directionality, 75–80
  and theoretical inference in
    semantics, 52–66
  and underlying syntactic structure,
    52–66
Empiricism, and rationalism, 319
Epistemology, naturalized, 298–307
Erdmann, B., 253, 254
Ethics, 281–290
  autonomy of, 283, 349n 59
Evans, G., 213, 214, 215
Exactness, 115–121

Family resemblance, 110–113
Feyerabend, P., 308
Field, H., 250
Fit, 152–153
Fodor, J., 17
Folk semantics, 29–30
Framework-relativity, 308–311
    and analytic/synthetic (language/
        theory) distinction, 310–311
Frege, G., i, vii, 1, 2, 3, 6, 12, 22, 23,
        24, 27, 37, 41, 48, 55, 66, 71, 86,
        87, 89, 102, 109, 115, 116, 124,
        125, 143, 144, 156, 160, 176, 178,
        205, 206, 207, 219, 235, 238, 239,
        240, 254, 286, 293
    intensionalism of, 325n 10

"Game," 109–113
Goedel, xi, 198
Goldfarb, W., 164, 165, 168
Goodman, N., x, 10, 250, 280, 300, 304,
        305, 306, 318
    on induction, 304–307
Grice, H. P., 40, 44, 45, 147

Hardy, G. H., 159
Heyting, A., 270
Hobbes, T., 250
Hornstein, N., 348n 48
Hume, D., 10, 198, 280, 291
Husserl, E., 6, 10, 254, 294

Ideal logical language, relation to
        natural language, 55–56
Idealization
    in linguistics, 122–126
    in science, 264–265
Intuition, 159–161
    ethical, 284–290
    vs. introspection, 160–161
Intuitionism, 270–272
    ultra-intuitionism, 270–271

Jackson, F., 349n 59
Johnston, M., 337n 10

Kant, 1, 70, 155, 177, 284, 291, 292, 295,
        315, 320
Kripke, S., vii, 70, 125, 128, 143, 163,
        164, 165, 167, 171, 172, 173, 175,
        301, 302, 317

inversion of the conditional, 301–303
    on rule following, 163–174
Kripke's dilemma, vii–ix, 317–320
Kuhn, T., 308

Language
    creativity of, 98
    expressive completeness of, 99–100,
        330n 79
        vs. notational completeness of, 47–
            50
    type notion of, 46, 50
    vs. speech, 97–98
Leibniz, G. W., 1
Lipps, T., 253, 254
Lewis, C. I., 217
Lewis, D., 211, 212, 213
Linguistic Realism, 125–126, 254
Linguistics
    foundations of, 268
    limits of, 319

Mates, B., 205
McDowell, J., 213, 214, 215
McGinn, C., 125, 159, 160, 161, 164,
        165, 168
Meaning (see also Sense)
    common-sense notion of, 30
    postulates (semantic rules), 190
    and use, 36–44
Meaninglessness, 329–330n 73
Megasentences, 42, 269
Meinong, A., 238
Mill, J. S., 12, 176, 177, 238
Moore, G. E., 6, 37, 102, 107, 115, 238,
        239, 240, 241, 242, 244, 260, 267,
        285, 293
    criticisms of, 241–242, 344–345n 11
Multiply self-embedded sentences, 43

Nagel, E., 10
Nagel, T., 288
Nativism, and empiricism, 318–319
Naturalism, ix, 235–239, 280–281
    and empiricism, 319
    epistemological problem for, 255–256
    ethical, 281–290
    and justification, 300
    and necessary truth, 155–157
    philosophical, 236–239
    Quinean and Aristotelian, 237–239

scientific, 237–239
  Strawson on, 344n 1
  type-token argument against, 216
Naturalistic fallacy, 239–281
  new notion defined, 245
Nominalism, 250
Non-naturalism, 291–320
Normativity, linguistic, 122–125

Occam, 250
Ontological commitment, 345–346n 18

Peirce, C. S., 39, 45, 141, 276, 304
Perry, J., 342n 23
Philosophical progress, vs. scientific
  progress, 314–317
Platonism, extensionalist vs.
  intensionalist, 172–174
"Plus," 172–173
Port Royal Grammar, 53
Possible-worlds semantics, 210–216
Postal, P., 17
Pragmatics, 90–93
Prichard, H. A., 284
Problem of delimitation, 248–249, 257–
  260
Problem of open-endedness, 247–249,
  257–260
Proto-theory, 66, 67, 71–72, 81–82, 87,
  96, 102–103, 129–130
  and analysis, 104–107
  autonomy of, 81–82
  and limits of language, 57–58
  and meaningfulness, 116–117
  on names, 121–122
  and scepticism, 166–174
  and senselessness, 117
  simplicity and complexity in, 102
Putnam, H., x, 10, 19, 143, 144, 216,
  217, 218, 219, 220, 221, 222, 223,
  224, 225, 226, 241, 243, 244, 255,
  296, 309, 310, 343n 36
  mathematical realism, 255–256

Quine, W. V., x, 10, 11, 12, 13, 14, 15,
  56, 67, 70, 155, 172, 176, 177, 179,
  180, 181, 182, 183, 184, 185, 186,
  188, 189, 190, 191, 192, 193, 195,
  196, 197, 198, 199, 200, 201, 202,
  203, 207, 209, 216, 219, 223, 232,
  237, 238, 245, 248, 249, 252, 261,
  271, 285, 295, 296, 299, 300, 301,
  303, 305, 306, 308, 309, 310, 315,
  316, 318, 340n 39, 337n 11, 338n
  17

Ramanujan, 159
Ramsey, F. P., viii, 122
Realism, 250–251
Reference, literal/nonliteral, 145–146,
  334n 7
Reichenbach, H., 304
(RLR), 146
(RLS), 145
Ross, D., 285
Russell, B., vii, 2, 6, 22, 24, 27, 33, 55,
  66, 102, 176, 238, 294

Salmon, W., 304
Santayana, G., 10
Schlick, M., 10, 294, 295, 316
Searle, J., 40, 41, 212, 213, 349n 59
  and decompositional representation,
  212–213
Semantic description, 60
  vs. semantic explanation, 60–61
Semantic essentialism, 135–137, 150
  and proto-theory, 141
  realist version of, 142–143
  and "top-down" approach, 142–143
Semantic facts, 28–31, 39
Semantic representation, 61
  Fregean view, 61–65, 329n 68
  proto-theory, 118–119
Semantic restrictions, 120
Semantic rules, 157–158
Semantic structure, and syntactic
  structure, 60–61
Semantics
  decompositional theory of, 64–66
  and logic, 71–73
  linguistic/extralinguistic distinction
    for, 44–46
  theoretical inference in, 56–66
  theoretical definition in, 191–192
Sense (see also Meaning)
  common-sense notion of, 30
  and indexicality, 91
  literal/non-literal, 145, 334n 7
  properties and relations, 62
  analyticity, 192

Sense (cont.)
   antonymy, 65
   expressional vs. nonexpressional,
      61–62
   superordination and
      subordination, 65, 118–119
   synonymy, 65
   synonymy vs. informational
      equivalence, 95–96
   and reference, 33, 89–93, 325n 10
   mediation vs. determination, 90–93
   weak principle, 33
   and use, 36–44
   pragmatic principles, 90–93
Sentences, kinds of, 96–100
Sigwart, C., 253, 254
Situation semantics, 342n 23
Socrates, 6, 135, 136, 314
Strawson, P. F., 40, 41, 304
Stroud, B., 125, 156, 303, 351n 23
Substitution criteria, 187–190
Synthetic a priori knowledge, 312–317

Tarski, A., 48
Theories, philosophical/meta-/object,
      245–247
"Theory," 52–53, 58
"Top-down" approach, 39, 50, 82, 86,
      88–90, 110–111
   vs. "bottom-up" approach, 39
   pragmatic correlation, 150
Translation
   actual (radical), 180–184
   and bilingualism, 195–196
   indeterminacy of, 184–202
   "pressing from below," 340n 39
   Quinean (radical), 180–184
   and Quinean physicalism, 338n 17
   and semantic evidence, 194
Type/token distinction, 39, 276–280

Use, 36–44, 47, 142–143
   and connotation, 40–41
   Humpty-Dumptyan, 146–147, 154
   literal, 144–145, 148–149
   and mention, 46
   non-literal, 147, 154

Vagueness, situational, 329n73
"Veil of ignorance" argument, 262

Whitehead, A. N., 2
Williams, B., 285–290
Wittgenstein, L., vii, viii, 1, 2, 3, 4, 6,
      7, 8, 9, 10, 11, 12, 13, 14, 15, 24,
      26, 27, 31, 34, 36, 37, 38, 39, 40,
      41, 44, 45, 48, 49, 50, 52, 57, 62,
      66, 67, 68, 69, 71, 72, 74, 76, 81,
      82, 83, 86, 87, 93, 94, 97, 99, 100,
      101, 102, 107, 108, 109, 110, 111,
      112, 113, 114, 115, 116, 124, 125,
      126, 127, 128, 130, 131, 135, 136,
      137, 138, 139, 140, 141, 142, 143,
      144, 149, 150, 151, 152, 153, 154,
      155, 156, 158, 159, 160, 163, 164,
      165, 169, 172, 175, 176, 198, 232,
      238, 239, 271, 285, 295, 296, 299,
      308, 309, 315, 316
Woodbridge, F. J., 10
Wundt, W., 253, 254

Yessenin-Volpin, A. S., 270, 271